AMBIVALENT ENGAGEMENT

GEOPOLITICS IN THE 21ST CENTURY

For a quarter century since the fall of the Berlin Wall, the world has enjoyed an era of deepening global interdependence, characterized by the absence of the threat of great power war, spreading democracy, and declining levels of conflict and poverty. Now, much of that is at risk as the regional order in the Middle East unravels, the security architecture in Europe is again under threat, and great power tensions loom in Asia.

The Geopolitics in the 21st Century series, published under the auspices of the Order from Chaos project at Brookings, will analyze the major dynamics at play and offer ideas and strategies to guide critical countries and key leaders on how they should act to preserve and renovate the established international order to secure peace and prosperity for another generation.

AMBIVALENT ENGAGEMENT

THE UNITED STATES AND REGIONAL SECURITY IN SOUTHEAST ASIA AFTER THE COLD WAR

JOSEPH CHINYONG LIOW

Brookings Institution Press
Washington, D.C.

Library of Congress Cataloging-in-Publication data

Names: Liow, Joseph Chinyong, 1972– author.
Title: Ambivalent engagement : the United States and regional
  security in Southeast Asia after the Cold War / Joseph Chinyong
  Liow.
Description: Washington, D.C. : Brookings Institution Press, [2017] |
  Includes bibliographical references.
Identifiers: LCCN 2017010288 (print) | LCCN 2017012103 (ebook) |
  ISBN 9780815729686 | ISBN 9780815729679 |
  ISBN 9780815729679 (hardcover : alk. paper) |
  ISBN 9780815729686 (ebook)
Subjects: LCSH: United States—Foreign relations—Southeast Asia.
  | Southeast Asia—Foreign relations—United States. | National
  security—United States. | National security—Southeast Asia. |
  United States—Foreign Relations—2001–2009. | United States—
  Foreign relations—2009–
Classification: LCC DS525.9.U6 (ebook) | LCC DS525.9.U6 L56
  2017 (print) | DDC 355/.0330959—dc23
LC record available at https://lccn.loc.gov/2017010288

9 8 7 6 5 4 3 2 1

Typeset in Sabon and Scala Sans

Composition by Westchester Publishing Services

Dedicated to the memory of
S. R. Nathan
July 3, 1924–August 22, 2016

Contents

Preface

BY THE END OF the Second World War, Southeast Asia had emerged as a region of growing strategic import to the United States. Wartime circumstances had compelled Washington to reassess its role in the wider Asia Pacific region. Although the United States had been hitherto reluctant to enter the war, the surprise attack on Pearl Harbor provoked an American response that by August 1945 transformed the country into a global superpower with global strategic interests. As the Second World War gave way to the Cold War, Southeast Asia became a major geopolitical shatterbelt, defined as "strategically oriented regions that are both deeply divided internally and caught up in the competition between great powers of the geostrategic realms."[1] For the United States, Southeast Asia assumed crucial importance to the grand strategy of containment designed to curb the growth of communism, which proved a particularly appealing ideology to elements within the anticolonial movements of the region. This grand strategy, predicated on the domino theory (namely, the belief that the falling of any regime in Southeast Asia into communist hands would trigger a domino effect), eventually culminated in the United States' doomed involvement in Vietnam. Etched deep into the American psyche, the Vietnam War eventually created a distaste for the deployment of American troops in military expeditions overseas and prompted a reassessment of the place of Southeast Asia in the wider strategic interests of the United States. For the rest of the Cold War, Southeast Asia fell off the American foreign policy radar.

Although the noncommunist Southeast Asian states did not expect American involvement in Vietnam to continue indefinitely, they were alarmed at the manner of the final disengagement and the immediate implications that followed. In the event, the fall of Saigon galvanized Southeast Asian states into action. In 1976, the Association of Southeast Asian Nations (ASEAN) convened at the level of a summit for the very first time. The summit was an offspring of Cold War politics. At the same time, to prevent the self-fulfilling prophecy of the domino theory, regional states adjusted their postures accordingly: Malaysia, Thailand, and the Philippines swiftly normalized ties with China, while other states worked diplomatically to improve relations with Beijing (short of formal normalization).[2] In the meantime, American ambivalence toward the region ushered in an era of policy neglect in U.S.–Southeast Asian relations, which exercised the noncommunist regional states throughout the 1980s.

Regional concerns were hardly placated by the uncertainties that confronted Southeast Asia at the end of the Cold War, especially when a major strategic reassessment of American global interests and priorities undertaken by the Clinton administration prompted speculative murmurs of American withdrawal from the Asia Pacific region. Although what eventually transpired was more a reordering of American foreign policy priorities rather than outright withdrawal, it nevertheless was interpreted in Southeast Asian capitals as a major downgrading of the region's importance in Washington's larger post–Cold War grand strategy, to the extent that one could be discerned. Attempts by American officials to explain this retrenchment using a congenial syllogism—that Southeast Asia was more peaceful compared with other regions in the world and hence there was no urgency for a strong U.S. presence—did little to assuage these fears. Conventional wisdom further holds that the lapse of American leases to Philippine military bases in the early 1990s and the subsequent withdrawal of U.S. military forces served to register a manifestation of this retrenchment, even though Philippine domestic political circumstances also doubtless played a part in hastening the U.S. departure.

If the Clinton administration's Southeast Asia policy can be described as "neglect," or even "estrangement" in the words shared to me by a senior Singaporean diplomat, the administrations of George W. Bush and Barack Obama saw something of a reinvigoration of American interest in the region, albeit for different reasons and with different outcomes. Most would agree that the foreign and security policy of the Bush presidency was defined by the signal issue of the war on terrorism. In that respect, Southeast Asia was no different. Indeed, with neoconservative hands firmly on the levers of national power, the Bush administration's fixation with the war on terrorism focused American energy and resources on maritime Southeast Asia, home to a number of extremist groups (even though many were at the time in fact opportunistic ragtag bandits), especially after the Bali bombings of 2002 and revelations that al Qaeda had attempted to gain a foothold in the region through unholy alliances with these groups. This prioritization of maritime Southeast Asia and tendency toward an issue-focus outlook meant that the region's mainland states commanded significantly less U.S. attention. In hindsight, the growing influence that China has come to command in regional affairs can arguably be traced to this period, when American inattentiveness to mainland Southeast Asian states like Cambodia and Laos inadvertently offered China greater leverage.

The Obama administration attempted to rectify the narrow focus of the Bush administration with the introduction of the Pivot to Asia. In her important November 2011 article in *Foreign Policy* magazine, then secretary of state Hillary Clinton heralded the coming of a "Pacific Century." This was hardly a hyperbolic declaration. Secretary Clinton's widely read article, which she carefully titled "*America's* Pacific Century," and President Obama's speech before the Australian Parliament in Canberra that same month together introduced the administration's Pivot to Asia policy. The Pivot, which has since been rechristened the "Rebalance," was meant to be a comprehensive strategy encompassing distinct diplomatic, economic, and military elements, which are collectively aimed at reorienting U.S. grand strategy toward this increasingly vital part of the world. By the advent of the second Obama term, discussions in policy circles both in Washington and in Southeast Asian capitals were talking about a "pivot within the Pivot," with Southeast Asia coming to command an even larger share of American resource, focus, and attention.

Yet by the twilight of the Obama administration, assessments of the Pivot found little consensus on its impact and effectiveness. The strategy has been attacked from opposing sides. Some critics say it was too weak: U.S. military deployments were marginal in scale; the legislative fate of the Trans-Pacific Partnership looked grim, and indeed was eventually sealed with Donald Trump's election victory and the Trump presidency's first executive order that withdrew the U.S. from the trade agreement; and America's friends and allies in the region wring their hands about the future of Washington's commitment to their security in the face of growing Chinese expansionism. Conversely, a number of critics claim the Pivot was too strong: the military pillar of the policy overshadowed the diplomatic and economic ones; it promoted recklessness and free riding by U.S. allies; and it unnecessarily exacerbated Sino–American security competition. Needless to say, the Obama administration and its friends in the think tank community insisted that, like Goldilocks's proverbial porridge, the Pivot was "just right": its military and nonmilitary dimensions were in rough balance; the policy successfully walked the fine line of reassuring without emboldening reckless behavior by U.S. allies; and most important, it sent a strong signal of America's resolve to maintain regional peace and stability while at the same time carefully refraining from ostracizing and antagonizing a rising China. All eyes now are on the Trump administration, which has been bequeathed the levers of national power, and there are questions over where and how it will locate Southeast Asia in terms of American strategic priorities and policy challenges and, correspondingly, how regional states will respond.

Throughout the post–Cold War years of three presidencies covered in this book (circa 1992–2016), a recurring theme in discussions and debates across Southeast Asian capitals on American foreign policy has been that of the need to keep the United States deeply engaged in the region. This theme is often accompanied by the perception that despite frequent expressions of interest and commitment through which different presidential administrations have over the years constantly stressed the importance of Southeast Asia to their wider engagement in the Asia Pacific, regional states continue to harbor apprehensions as to the credibility and sustainability of Washington's engagement efforts.

Those working on this topic or with professional interest in it would doubtless have noted how the theme of U.S. policy toward Southeast Asia has formed the focus of not a few policy reports produced by U.S. and regional think tanks, especially during the Obama administration. Informed (and, sometimes, ill-informed) commentaries and opinion pieces on U.S.–Southeast Asian relations have also frequently appeared in popular broadsheets and social media in recent years. Additionally, there have been several book chapters focused on Southeast Asia in broader compendiums of essays on the theme of the United States and Asia or the Asia Pacific. Despite all the ink expended on the topic at hand—or perhaps because of it—it is puzzling that, aside from Natasha Hamilton-Hart's fine study, *Hard Interests, Soft Illusions: Southeast Asia and American*

Power, published in 2012, there has been a dearth of recent serious book-length studies of the topic that cast analytical light on abiding themes as well as longer patterns and trends. Informed observers would point out that interest in producing (and supporting) serious scholarship on the United States and Southeast Asia has cooled considerably following the end of the Vietnam War. Clearly, this interest has not picked up as far as book publication is concerned.

It is in the hope of making a small contribution to attempts at redressing this imbalance (not to mention to fulfill my professional obligations as the Lee Kuan Yew Chair in Southeast Asia Studies at the Brookings Institution) that I wrote this book. Needless to say, I do not claim that this book is the definitive or final statement on the issue. Indeed, my objectives are far more limited. The book is but an attempt to explore some basic, intuitive questions, often asked by policymakers, especially from the region, but seldom satisfactorily answered, regarding the scope and extent of American engagement. In so doing, I hope to prompt further thinking about the importance of robust commitment to strong U.S.–Southeast Asia ties on the part of all parties concerned, why this has been challenging during the post–Cold War years, and how both parties might meet that challenge to advance their respective interests in a more consistent and strategic fashion not only in form but, more important, in substance, the uncertainties surrounding the foreign policy of the recently inaugurated Trump administration notwithstanding.

There is one final caveat. When this book was completed, the Obama presidency had just come to an end, and Donald Trump was inaugurated as the forty-fifth president of the United States. After a month in office, it remains a challenge to divine elements of a Trump administration grand strategy, let alone of possible policy toward Southeast Asia. Yet, although it may be too early to tell if the Trump administration will buck the trend of engagement with Southeast Asia set by his predecessors (whose administrations and policies form the substance of this book), there are indications that relations between the United States and Southeast Asia for the next few years are likely to be difficult and challenging if President Trump's statements and tweets are any indication. Even so, rather than be seized by the moment, the purpose of this book is to consider larger themes, patterns, and contexts that shape U.S.–Southeast Asia relations and that will outlast the Trump administration. It is in that spirit that I hope this book will be read.

The Brookings Institution acknowledges Ray and Barbara Dalio, Chevron, Hotel Properties Limited, Keppel Group, Robert Ng and Philip Ng, Sembcorp Industries Ltd., Edwin Soeryadjaya, STEngineering, and The Starr Foundation for their generous contributions to an endowment that established the Lee Kuan Yew Chair in Southeast Asia Studies in October 2013 at Brookings. We also thank Blackstone, Merrill Lynch, Morgan Stanley, and State Street for providing critical initial operating support for the Chair.

Acknowledgments

THIS BOOK WAS MOSTLY RESEARCHED and authored during my two-year tenure as the Lee Kuan Yew Chair in Southeast Asia Studies at the Brookings Institution in Washington, D.C., from August 2014 to July 2016, although my interest in U.S.–Southeast Asia relations extends much further back in time. Needless to say, the two years spent in Washington, D.C., were immensely enriching and rewarding professionally, for they afforded me the opportunity to observe foreign policy decisionmaking in the Beltway at fairly close quarters. The timing was also fortuitous, for, in hindsight, these were very much the halcyon days of the Obama administration's "Pivot to Asia" policy, when conscious efforts were made to focus more attention on Southeast Asia. These two years also provided numerous occasions where I could interact with Washington-based policymakers, think tankers, and scholars with abiding interests in Southeast Asian affairs. In addition to that, as the Brookings "go-to person" on Southeast Asia, I had frequent opportunities to meet with and discuss U.S.–Southeast Asia relations with a regular stream of scholars and officials from the region who would make their way to Washington for conferences, meetings, and bilateral think tank exchanges. It was the many discussions I had the privilege to partake in throughout the course of these interactions that both prompted and sharpened the thoughts and ideas that frame this book.

I have many people to thank for the honor of serving as the inaugural Lee Kuan Yew Chair in Southeast Asia Studies at Brookings. Foremost among them is Ambassador Chan Heng Chee, who first alerted me to the creation of the chair, encouraged me to throw my hat in the ring, and made the case to the leadership and governing board of the S. Rajaratnam School of International Studies (RSIS) to reduce my duties as associate dean and later dean of the school so that I could take up this position. At RSIS, I am indebted to the chair and deputy chair of the governing board, Eddie Teo and Ong Keng Yong, the members of the governing board, as well as my predecessor, Barry Desker, for their strong support. Although understandably reticent at the prospect of having the dean based abroad for two years, they nevertheless managed to look beyond the short-term inconvenience and see the longer term benefits that could be accrued for both the school and for Singapore of having one of their own in this position at Brookings.

At Brookings, I am grateful for the confidence shown in me by Strobe Talbott, Martin Indyk, Ted Piccone, Bruce Jones, and Richard Bush. Richard Bush in particular welcomed me into his team of fine Asia scholars at the Center for East Asia Policy Studies, which he very ably led. I would also like to record my gratitude to my colleagues at the Center—my home away from home—for their friendship, help, and collegiality. These include Jonathan Pollack, Kathy Moon, Mireya Solis, Hunter Marston, Paul Park, Jennifer Mason, Maeve Whelan-Wuest, Kevin Scott, and Aileen Chang. Kevin and Aileen in particular were immensely helpful in assisting me and my family as we settled in the United States.

Given the number of meetings, discussions, and chats over coffee, beers, lunches, and dinners involved in the course of researching this book, it would be difficult to single out any among the large number of serving and former officials, whether from the United States or from Southeast Asia, who candidly shared their personal as well as official perspectives on issues related to U.S. policy in Southeast Asia. I would nevertheless like to express special thanks to several in the United States who were especially generous with their time and views: John McCain, Kurt Campbell, Amy Searight, Collin Willett, Vikram Singh, and Stapleton Roy. My old friends Donald Emmerson, Don Horowitz, and Sumit Ganguly were, as usual, always ready and willing to help with ideas on how to approach the topic. Michael Brown, Mike O'Hanlon, Richard Bush, and Hunter Marston read many of the draft chapters and provided useful suggestions on how to sharpen my arguments. A word of thanks is also due the anonymous reviewers who provided helpful comments and suggestions that have contributed to what is hopefully a stronger book than the one they initially read. At RSIS, numerous discussions with my good colleagues Ang Cheng Guan, Tan See Seng, Ralf Emmers, Bhubhindar Singh, Evan Resnick, and Pascal Vennesson helped refine my ideas and introduce new angles from which to approach my research questions. Wen Yi, Shuo Yan, and Hunter helped considerably with research assistance in Washington, tracking down sources and information, sometimes on obscure events, while Joel Ng compiled the excellent record of congressional bills on Southeast Asia listed in the appendix. Colleagues at Brookings Institution Press, especially Bill Finan and Janet Walker, were immensely professional and helpful in shepherding the publication process through to conclusion.

Time spent apart from family is never easy. Although I was blessed to have my family with me for most of my two years in Washington, because I had to make numerous trips back to Singapore and Southeast Asia both to undertake research and to discharge my duties at RSIS, there were also far too many periods of separation. In light of this, I must place on record my great debt to my lovely wife, Ai Vee, for holding the fort during these absences, and my children, Euan and Megan, for tolerating them. Completing this book no doubt brought an immense sense of satisfaction. But as the Old Book instructs: "Whatsoever thy hand findeth to do, do it with thy might" (Ecclesiastes 9:10). Whatever has been accomplished in this book may have been by my hands, but it is Christ who has guided the effort, and it is to his glory alone.

CHAPTER ONE

Ambivalent Engagement?

SOUTHEAST ASIA IS A REGION of considerable economic growth potential. Collectively, the ten states of Southeast Asia possess the third largest workforce behind China and India, command a greater share of global capital flows, are home to a growing middle class and consumer base, and form the world's fourth largest exporting region. In many respects, this economic potential has been captured in the creation of the ASEAN Economic Community (AEC), announced in December 2015, envisaged to further enhance the economic connectivity of the region.

But the essence of Southeast Asia as a region is characterized by more than its economic dynamism. Since the signing of the Paris Peace Agreement in October 1991, which brought about Vietnamese withdrawal from Cambodia and ended the Cold War in Southeast Asia, the region has enjoyed a quarter of a century of relative peace and stability. Although periodic social unrest continues to afflict almost every state in the region—with Thailand arguably the most notable and disconcerting—these have not reached the scale of political violence witnessed over the same period in the Middle East, Central Asia, and many parts of South Asia. Moreover, with the exception of a brief border conflagration between Thailand and Cambodia in 2008, interstate peace has prevailed in Southeast Asia since the end of the Cold War. To be sure, mutual mistrust and border disputes between many neighboring regional states still exist, but most important is that they have not given rise to conflicts that can imperil overall regional stability. This fact should not be belittled given that the region was once known in popular parlance as a

1

"region in revolt" and home to the bloodier of the two "hot wars" that broke out during the Cold War. If anything, it is a mark of how far the region has come in terms of regional security and stability.

On balance then, the political stability and economic growth that has obtained in Southeast Asia since the end of the Cold War ought to render the region of some strategic import to the United States, for Washington would have an interest in preserving this regional stability and partaking in its growth, rather than conceive of its role in the narrow sense of merely a "trouble shooter" that appears only when a crisis materializes. Indeed, if public speeches offer any indication, the economic dynamism and presumed vast economic potential of Southeast Asia is already frequently acknowledged by the American political leadership and foreign policy decisionmaking community. Added to that are several further reasons why the region should command American policy attention. Southeast Asia encompasses waterways that are crucial to international trade, such as the Malacca Straits and the South China Sea; this, too, is a point that has been recognized by consecutive U.S. administrations, although it has only been more recently that this recognition has found expression in concrete policy action with Washington's more proactive position on the South China Sea.

For the U.S. foreign policy establishment, Southeast Asia should possess further strategic and policy appeal. The region is home to large Muslim communities—especially in Indonesia and Malaysia—whose theological and political climes offer potential alternative religio-cultural narratives to those that have seized the Middle East, South Asia, and Central Asia. Southeast Asia, too, can claim a legacy of successful democratization processes that stand in stark contrast to the outcome of the Arab Spring. Setting aside the present regression of democracy in Thailand, few would deny that the outcomes of the "People's Revolution" in the Philippines, *Reformasi* in Indonesia, and, now, the self-initiated withdrawal of the military from politics that is taking place in Myanmar compare favorably to the failed revolutions in Egypt and Libya. These trends speak to the twin themes of democratization and U.S. relations with Muslim societies, which remain signal foreign policy priorities for the United States. There is another less sanguine but no less important strategic character to the region that punctuates consideration of its significance to the United States: it has become increasingly evident in recent years that there is a picture gradually unfolding of Southeast Asia becoming a key arena for Sino–U.S. strategic rivalry and economic competition. Indeed, the point can plausibly be argued that in Southeast Asia today we are witnessing the first signs of a brewing strategic rivalry that will shape global politics in the twenty-first century.

Although the above observations may provide some compelling reasons why Southeast Asia should command considerable attention in American strategic thinking and foreign policymaking, the question that this begs is: does it?

On the face of it, several observations can be offered in response to this question. First, "Southeast Asia," as those more reticent toward an American role in the region frequently remind us, is in Washington policy discourse usually wrapped up in conversations on broader concepts of "the Pacific," "the Asia Pacific," "East Asia," or even "East Asian littoral running from the Sea of Japan to the Bay of Bengal," as described in the 2001 *Quadrennial Defense Review.* The portents of this nomenclature should be self-evident—priority tends to still be rendered to American allies in Japan and South Korea, security commitments to Taiwan, and growing interest in India, as compared with Southeast Asia. Indeed, even South Asia appears to command comparatively more attention with its long history of animosity between India and Pakistan, not to mention the threat of terrorism, nuclear proliferation, and chronic instability in Pakistan. In short, American strategic thinking tends to treat Southeast Asia as an extension of a wider geostrategic footprint rather than as a region with its own inherent strategic significance and logic. As one official who served in the Bush and Obama administrations admitted: "It is difficult to focus exclusively on Southeast Asia as an area of strategic priority, although the situation has improved over the last eight years (namely, during the Obama administration)."[1]

Second, if Southeast Asia has featured at all in post–Cold War policy discussions and debate swirling in Washington, D.C., circles, it has for the most part been dominated by specific policy themes: either human rights and democratization (during the Clinton administration), counterterrorism (during the Bush administration), or, increasingly, the South China Sea (during the Obama administration). In other words, the United States has largely been either neglectful or narrow—or both—in its thinking about Southeast Asia.

Finally, this state of affairs belies the fact that there is much at stake for the United States, as suggested above, in terms of what Southeast Asia has to offer, how regional affairs in Southeast Asia unfold, and where the region fits in broader U.S. grand strategy in the coming years.

To the extent that Asia and the Pacific will feature more prominently for American strategic interests, the inescapable reality is that the relationship between the United States and Southeast Asia must be a key element of future policy: for the United States, for Southeast Asia, for U.S.–Asia relations in general, and for the stability of the Asia Pacific region.

THE GEOSTRATEGIC SETTING

Notwithstanding the fact that regional economies (sans Japan) have generally been trending upward at laudable growth rates in the past two decades since the end of the Cold War (discounting the period of the Asian financial crisis in the late 1990s, of course), and regional institutions have proliferated, drivers of instability, insecurity, and potential conflict remain. Several flashpoints can easily be identified, where unresolved issues of border demarcation, irredentism, and territorial disputes can easily spill over to conflict if not managed properly.

A major consideration that frames the investigation of U.S. engagement in Southeast Asia undertaken in this book is the fact that the geostrategic patterns and logics in East Asia have been in transition since the end of the Cold War. With the collapse of the Soviet Union, the United States remains the preeminent regional security actor, freed from the inhibitions of having to deal with a global rival with hostile intentions. Even so, few would suggest that regional stability today relies solely on the United States the way it arguably did during the Cold War (at least for noncommunist Southeast Asia until American withdrawal from Vietnam). Certainly, the financial crisis that beset the United States in 2008 not only significantly tempered talk of American power, it in fact prompted discomfiting murmurs of American decline.

For East Asia, the "unipolar moment" very quickly transmogrified into a more uncertain world as putative regional powers and competitors began asserting themselves, with China very much at the head of the pack. Concomitantly, regional order has come to bear some hallmarks of complex multipolarity where economic interdependence sits uncomfortably with strategic rivalry. Indeed, if the logic obtains that power transitions are inherently destabilizing, then it stands to reason that multiple vectors of power transitions taking place at the same time and within the same geopolitical footprint can only further sharpen anxieties. Needless to say, of paramount consequence to this shifting geostrategic logic is the advent of a new regional power (with global potential, it should be added) in the form of a China that is exuding hegemonic tendencies. Indeed, a recurring theme through much of this book will be the matter of growing Chinese influence assiduously taking place during periods when American engagement of the region is distracted by other considerations or myopically focused on specific issues. More on this will follow in the ensuing chapters. Suffice to say for now that it is already received wisdom that China's economic growth over the last two decades has translated to political and strategic influence—which it has brought to bear on its relations with Southeast Asian states—and it is poised to fundamentally transform the distribution of power and balance of influence in the region.

Turning to the small and medium-sized states of Southeast Asia, beneficiaries of the economic rise of the greater East Asian region but also inherently vulnerable to its geopolitical shifts, this state of affairs poses interesting, and potentially grave, security challenges and implications. All the more so as Southeast Asia is situated geographically at the intersection of these competing forces. In retrospect, these circumstances are, at least to some extent, not entirely new. Alert to the pitfalls of centrifugal pulls as well as the danger of external power intervention as early as the late 1960s in the wake of decolonization and at the height of the Cold War, efforts were made to grasp the nettle by stressing the neutrality of the region. These efforts culminated in the futile declaration of Southeast Asia's aspiration to be recognized as a Zone of Peace, Freedom, and Neutrality (ZOPFAN), freed from external power interference, in 1971. Somewhat similar great power dynamics obtain today, although, as this discussion will later demonstrate, the response of regional states has been to enmesh, rather than exclude, major powers in a regional order centered on ASEAN.[2]

In the face of the element of unpredictability and strategic uncertainty occasioned by competitive and potentially adversarial relationships among otherwise interdependent major powers, the Southeast Asian gaze remains transfixed on the United States to contribute to stability as an active and committed actor in regional affairs, perforce, on grounds that it has historically been a "benign, stabilizing force" in the region.[3] The late Lee Kuan Yew, one of the staunchest Southeast Asian supporters of the U.S. presence in the region, offered the following insight to accent the import of American engagement:

Why should the United States stay engaged to help East Asia's combined gross national product to exceed that of North America? Why not disengage and abort this process? Because this process is not easily aborted. No alternative balance can be as comfortable as the present one, with the United States as a major player. The geopolitical balance without the United States as a principal force will be very different from that which it now is or can be if the United States remains a central player. My generation of Asians, which experienced the last war, its horrors and miseries, and which remembers the U.S. role in the phoenix-like rise from the ashes of that war to prosperity of Japan, the newly industrializing economies, and ASEAN will feel a keen sense of regret that the world will become so vastly different because the United States becomes a less central player in the new balance.[4]

Reinforcing sentiments toward the role that Southeast Asian states have ascribed to the United States in regional affairs, especially on security issues, Truong Tan Sang, the conservative Vietnamese president, opined on the occasion of his visit to Washington that the United States had "an important role and responsibility in dealing with hotspots in the region such as the South China Sea and such global issues as energy security, food security, transnational crime, climate change, and so on. This has become ever more imperative."[5] Needless to say, coming from Vietnam, such a view is all the more significant for obvious reasons.

Notwithstanding the generally positive reception that the United States receives in the region today, an element of ambiguity and ambivalence nevertheless obtains in regard to how the U.S. role is perceived by and received in Southeast Asia. Indeed, it is hardly axiomatic that expectations for the United States to express commitment to regional order betray any intent on the part of Southeast Asia to align strategically with Washington or to offer blanket support for any and all displays of American presence and interest in the region. On the contrary, even as Southeast Asian states articulate a desire for the United States to enhance its engagement, not a few have also made clear, in subtle but sometimes also not-so-subtle ways, their intention to retain more than a modicum of national and regional autonomy. This is evident, for instance, in the constant refrain across the region of decisionmakers not wanting to be in a position where they are forced to "choose sides" in relation to the United States and China. At the same time, given the role that Southeast Asia is prepared to accord to the United States, this also begs the question of whether, and how, regional expectations dovetail with American strategic interests and objectives, and the degree to which Southeast

Asia demonstrates a collective will in their reception of American intent in the region. This question will be pursued in greater detail in the next chapter.

A word must be said about the factor of geography. An evident feature of enduring significance that informs the strategy of any given power must surely be political geography. Geographical forces influence human and state behavior in predictable ways and, as some have argued, provide a compelling explanation for the economic and political power that some states wield.[6] Geography, as the historical record attests, has also been one of the most rampant causes of wars between states. For its part, the factor of geography plays a crucial role in influencing strategic thinking and strategic culture as well. As Colin Gray noted, "national strategic culture is very much the product of geographical conditioning."[7]

For the United States, the factor of geography has historically had a significant impact on the shaping of grand strategy and application of national power. Its role was evident in the imperative to prevent the emergence of powers from either its Pacific or Atlantic flanks that could undermine the security of the mainland. Geography also featured as the fundamental premise to the Monroe Doctrine, articulated in 1823, that was predicated on the idea that the Western Hemisphere was the immediate geographic sphere of influence for the United States. According to this logic, the response to Japan's surprise attack on Pearl Harbor in 1941 and Soviet attempts to locate medium- and intermediate-range ballistic missiles in Cuba in 1962 demonstrated the imperative of meeting the threat posed by other powers seeking to assert a presence in the U.S. sphere of influence.

Geography also informs American commitments to friends and allies. In keeping with this premise, it is inherently more difficult for the United States to make credible grand strategic commitments to allies and friends in Southeast Asia because of geography, where the arid reality remains that the United States is far away from the region and therefore less proximate to the threats that either emanate from or confront it. Further to that, since the United States is congenitally more secure than its partners and allies in Southeast Asia, it has to send more costly signals of its commitment to their security, especially given constraints of finite resources and the need for accountability to its population.[8] More important, the question of how much of this cost the United States is prepared to bear in order to maintain the confidence of regional partners and friends in American resolve continues to be asked, and remains unanswered, or at least not satisfactorily answered, even among Americans themselves. This is especially so given the U.S. domestic climate, which has witnessed stalemates over defense spending, entitlements, the civilian budget, and taxation policy, as well as heated debates over burden sharing on the part of regional allies. On the other side of the coin, the partners and allies in question will be more acutely sensitive to perceived fluctuations in American commitment because of their close proximity—ergo, vulnerability—to more localized threats.[9]

This ambivalence was captured in what appeared a rhetorical question posed by an American politician during a discussion on how the United States should respond to Chinese assertiveness in the South China Sea: "Why would it be detrimental to our [U.S.] interests if we ceded influence in the South China Sea to China? Why should the United States risk entanglement and possibly war with China over a few rocks situated far away and of minimal strategic consequence?"[10] The fact is that this view echoes those of naysayers who, though not proponents of isolationism per se, nevertheless caution against American overstretch into areas geographically too distant to pose any remote existential threat to the survival of the United States and its people. Indeed, such statements are to Southeast Asian decisionmakers the cause of as much anxiety as hawkish demands for the United States to do more militarily to push back against China or to engage in a trade war with Beijing.

A further point to register is the fact that a strategic logic of fundamental power asymmetry obtains between the United States and Southeast Asia. According to this line of reasoning, American power far outweighs the collective capabilities of all Southeast Asian states, let alone any individual state. Given this discrepancy in the distribution of power, it is perhaps understandable that Southeast Asia is likely to be overly sensitive to the United States whereas the United States would tend to be negligent toward the region.[11] In other words, it is an unequal relationship, and this inequality is reflected in expectations and perceptions of obligations.

A corollary to this is the matter of the weight of Southeast Asia compared with other regions of the world in terms of American priorities writ large. Received wisdom dictates that, relative to other regions, Southeast Asia may pale in comparison in terms of its importance to the United States. On the surface of it, this appears to be the picture if we consider that Latin America is at the doorstep of the United States and hence in its immediate and incontrovertible sphere of influence, Europe shares deep historical and cultural ties to the United States (ties that have also been cemented with the North Atlantic Treaty Organization), the Middle East has long been of great strategic value because of energy security and the relationship with Israel but also of potential threat with the presence of the Islamic State terrorist group, and Central Asia has in the last decade and a half emerged as a direct threat to the United States owing to the presence of al Qaeda in that region and the fact that it remains the only foreign enemy to have successfully launched an attack on the American mainland for a long time. Yet, although this logic may have held for a large part of the post–World War II era, the policy discourse and practice of the administration of President Barack Obama appeared to indicate that at least some measure of strategic reprioritization has been taking place.

UNPACKING SOUTHEAST ASIA FOR U.S. POLICY

In considering American regional engagement, there is, of course, the obvious fundamental question of whether U.S. policymakers should consider Southeast Asia as a single unit, which may imply the existence of a common or even coherent outlook and attitude among regional states. Indeed, the use of the term "Southeast Asia" here is not intended to suggest existence of such a common or even coherent outlook and attitude toward the role of the United States at any given time, let alone across the decades since the end of the Cold War. In point of fact, this will be a recurrent theme through the course of this book. Southeast Asia is a collection of ten countries (eleven, if one wishes to include Timor-Leste, which obtained its independence from Indonesia in 2002). Southeast Asian states have embarked on different trajectories of political evolution and are at different stages of political and economic development. They range from open political systems and liberal democracies to single-party communist and socialist regimes, not to mention an absolute monarchy as well. Some have openly embraced free market principles, while others have centrally planned (albeit gradually liberalizing) economies. Still others are given to periodic tendencies toward protectionism and economic nationalism. From a cultural and anthropological vantage, Southeast Asia is also home to diverse religions, languages, and cultural practices and worldviews.

In geopolitical terms, this diversity and plurality that defines Southeast Asia as a region suggests the difficulty of identifying a singular perspective, a uniform, collective position on foreign policy, or even a shared outlook toward, and perception of, security threats and challenges. In fact, these perspectives, positions, outlooks, and perceptions among regional states more often than not stand at odds with each other. Equally salient, this innate diversity of the region does not lend itself easily to the creation of an integrated sense of regional identity and community, even though this has been articulated by ASEAN, the regional organization that purportedly binds Southeast Asian states together, to be its signal objective. By the same token, it is difficult—in fact, impossible—to speak or think of an ASEAN or Southeast Asian foreign policy, the absence of which continues to be cause for lament on the part of those who insist on understanding the organization's prospects through a path-dependent lens informed by the European Union experience, a view that is as misguided as it is orientalist. A further regrettable downside of this diversity has been the persistence of strains in the relationships between Southeast Asian states that continues to find expression in bilateral rivalries, competition, and, on occasion, open, if controlled, hostilities, and the challenges ASEAN faces in fulfilling its self-assumed obligation of regional order management.

Pertinent for present purposes is the fact that the diversity of Southeast Asian viewpoints on regional security has historically found expression in divergent outlooks and attitudes toward the role and involvement of the United States in the region. During the Cold War, regional perceptions coincided with ideological blocs and patterns of contending alignments. Corresponding to the ideological imperatives of the Indochina communist states of Vietnam and Laos, a list to which Myanmar (Burma) can be added as well, the United States was clearly an existential threat, whereas for the noncommunist founding members of ASEAN, Washington provided a crucial security umbrella under which stability and the necessary conditions for economic development were created even if, in some cases, the United States played a less than constructive role in internal affairs of certain states. After the end of the Cold War, some Southeast Asian states nursed fears for how a potential American withdrawal could create an unhealthy strategic vacuum. Others continued to harbor deep-seated suspicions born of their own encounters with the United States during the Cold War years (for instance, U.S. complicity in political turmoil in Indonesia, Thailand, and the Philippines, or the American carpet bombing of Cambodia) but also Washington's eagerness to criticize their political systems after the end of the Cold War. Concomitantly, their respective governments frequently fulminated against Washington in the state-controlled media, not least because of American foreign policy imperatives of democratization and human rights, which gathered swift momentum after the end of the Cold War and which were construed in these states as unwarranted interference and a threat to regime survival and legitimacy. All this is to say that, as subsequent chapters will show, even though broad agreement obtains among Southeast Asian states that the United States should remain an engaged actor in the regional security architecture, different perspectives in response to how America has played, and should play, this role are still discernible.

By the onset of the Bush administration, the impact of regional dissimilarities in strategic outlook on relations between the United States and Southeast Asia would come to be manifested on a new plane. Following the September 11 terrorist attacks, Southeast Asia reemerged on the strategic radar of the United States, only to be cast as yet another arena for the Bush administration's ill-conceived "Global War on Terror." Controversially designated the "Second Front" in this "war," American attention descended on maritime Southeast Asia, home to large Muslim populations and a number of militant and terrorist groups. While mainland Southeast Asia suffered a season of comparative neglect, maritime Southeast Asia bemoaned what it saw for the most part to be the "one issue agenda"—namely, counterterrorism—which Washington repeatedly tabled in interactions with the region.

It was against the background of the war on terror that relations between the United States and the Muslim-majority countries of Indonesia and Malaysia became acutely strained. The tension was most apparent in the anti-Bush sentiments, which quite seamlessly (if inaccurately and unfairly, in light of other more constructive aspects of American engagement in the region) transformed to anti-American sentiments, expressed by Muslim civil society groups and domestic constituencies in these two countries. These groups mobilized to condemn the war on terror as a surreptitious war against their religion, and in the process prevented the governments of both Indonesia and Malaysia from public expressions of support for U.S. policy. Conversely, the governments in Singapore and the Philippines moved to align themselves with the war on terror, despite private misgivings harbored by many of their decisionmakers about how the "war" was actually being conducted. For its part, Washington prioritized the war on terror for understandable domestic and ideological reasons. Although the context and circumstances were less than auspicious, the fact was that by dint of the Bush administration's prioritization of counterterrorism, Southeast Asia was returning to a more central place in American grand strategy (a shift that was sustained during the Obama administration but over different priorities). Indeed, so overwhelming was the influence of the imperative of counterterrorism as a guiding principle in American foreign and security policies, it overshadowed efforts gradually taking place in economic policy and security planning circles to reconsider U.S. strategy in the Asia Pacific and the place of Southeast Asia in this strategy, particularly during the second term of the Bush administration.[12] In short, American ambivalence toward Southeast Asia and the elusiveness of a coherent Southeast Asian outlook toward the United States are two sides of the same analytical coin.

This was also the perceptual challenge inherited by the presidency of Barack Obama, the first American president to have lived for an extended period in Southeast Asia (he spent many formative years in Indonesia). To its credit, the Obama administration professed, and for the most part carried through, its intent to broaden and deepen its engagement with the region under the rubric of the administration's much discussed "Pivot" or "Rebalance" strategy (to be referred to subsequently as the Pivot as this was the original term used). Under President Obama, the United States signed the Trans-Pacific Partnership Agreement (TPPA), a major trade agreement that included several Southeast Asian states and prompted interest on the part of several others, and which was an important demonstration not just of American intent to be a factor in regional economic growth but also of Washington's long-term commitment to the region.[13] Washington joined the East Asia Summit (EAS) in 2011 on ASEAN's terms. This involved the signing of the ASEAN Treaty of Amity and Cooperation (TAC), a move that surprised many, including officials from ASEAN member states at the time. Notwithstanding reservations toward the Pivot nomenclature, the region collectively embraced this newfound energy, ambition, and purpose behind American engagement in Southeast Asia. Beneath the surface, however, differences still existed with regards to states' individual assessments of the details of the Pivot in terms of the policies that flowed (or should have but did not flow) from it, although regional states have taken care not to allow these differences to bedevil the broader issue of the virtue of an American presence and renewed commitment.

To allay regional fears and convey clarity of intent, the Obama administration responded robustly in both word and deed to Chinese assertiveness in the South China Sea, a matter that has caused considerable consternation to Southeast Asia, more so in some states than others, it should be added. Even then, the support from Southeast Asia has been less than categoric, with some regional states taking the United States to task for escalating tensions even as they question Washington's ability and commitment to stay the course. Indeed, the surfeit of enthusiasm in response to the Pivot could not conceal an abiding sense of uncertainty in the capitals of Southeast Asia. Since the withdrawal from Vietnam, the reliability and sustainability of American commitment has been a constant theme in relations between Southeast Asia—both as individual states as well as collectively as ASEAN—and the United States.[14] Of paramount concern for regional leaders are the prospects that the United States could be distracted from strategic engagement with Southeast Asia. This has become an all-too-frequent refrain. Numerous political leaders, officials, and diplomats from the region—too many to detail here—have voiced this concern in various settings, both public and private. In so doing, they are questioning not so much the fact that the United States has a desire to be engaged with Southeast Asia at any given point as they are the reliability and sustainability of this desire.

Also underlying this uncertainty is a perception of disconnect between pronouncement and practice, intent and implementation. Mindful of the vicissitudes of U.S. electoral cycles and the propensity of the political leadership and foreign policy establishment to shift attention to other regions depending on the crisis of the day, Southeast Asian decisionmakers predictably develop anxieties toward the fidelity and sustainability of American professions of interest and engagement in the region, defined as Washington's ability to play an active and constructive role in fostering regional security by leading and shaping strategic interaction among the region's powers and stakeholders.

MAIN ARGUMENTS

Although much has been written and debated about U.S. engagement in Southeast Asia in both the scholarly as well as the policy analysis communities, there remains a lacuna in the literature and policy discussions on several counts. First, the numerous policy reports and monographs that are currently available on the topic have for the most part been written from a U.S. perspective, with American interests serving as a point of entry. There is nothing inherently wrong with this approach, but this literature tends to elide, downplay, misunderstand, misrepresent, or altogether ignore regional views and perspectives on what should be the issues of interest to the United States and how these interests can be pursued, as viewed from the vantage of the region (as opposed to Washington, D.C., or Pacific Command). Second, some of this literature at times betrays a quite fundamental misunderstanding of what is realistic in the context of the region's history, the nature of its regional diplomacy, dissimilarities in outlook and perspectives, and character of its regional institutions. As but one example, criticisms of the incapacities of ASEAN, especially its shortcomings in terms of the organization's decisionmaking process and inability to foster much-needed coherence, are certainly warranted. But at the same time, some of the expectations of the organization, couched as "policy recommendations"—for example, that ASEAN should somehow morph into a collective security institution or that it should devise a common foreign policy not unlike that of the European Union—may simply lie beyond the pale at this point. Third, there is not nearly enough attention given to the role of domestic politics in influencing U.S.–Southeast Asia relations. For these reasons, it behooves scholars, analysts, policymakers, and political leaders to consider some of the fundamental drivers and obstacles to relations between the United States and Southeast Asia. It is toward these ends that this book is written.

By dint of the above observations as a point of entry, this book advances the argument that U.S. policy toward Southeast Asia in the post–Cold War era has gone through several phases that coincide with American presidential administrations and, more important, with priority issue areas around which policy agendas were fashioned. During the Clinton administration, immediately after the end of the Cold War, the region was effectively relegated to the backburner as American policy was drawn to focus on the Middle East, the Balkans, and Russia. Thematically, the Clinton administration's emphasis on human rights and democracy set it at odds with several key Southeast Asian states, thereby creating obstacles to deeper engagement. The Bush administration witnessed a shift in the tone of relations with Southeast Asia, where the weighty emphasis on counterterrorism cast a long shadow over American engagement in the region to the detriment of broader, more holistic interests. Finally, the purported attempt by the Obama administration to broaden and deepen U.S. engagement in Southeast Asia by way of the Pivot was gradually drawn into the familiar pattern of selective issue attentiveness, with the South China Sea this time emerging as the keystone matter at hand. Because of these shifting agendas, American policy attention has fluctuated, with the implications being the existence of gaps in U.S. understanding of Southeast Asia, which in turn spawn deep and abiding concern in the region that the United States will be distracted—by problems either in other parts of the world or within its own borders—and, if not choosing to disengage as a consequence, will downgrade Southeast Asia's importance and attendant demands on American attention. Needless to say, this anxiety is prominent and persistent in the region. In short, irrespective of the momentum gained over the last two decades or so, prospects for deeper and more sustained U.S. engagement with Southeast Asia are still afflicted by obstacles, which give pause and account for residual regional anxieties.

This book further contends that, on closer scrutiny, a combination of three factors serves to register the basis of these anxieties. First, despite American interests in the region, it is not clear both at an intellectual and at a policy level how and where Southeast Asia fits into U.S. grand strategy. At times, Southeast Asia appears to come into its own as an area of strategic import while on other occasions it is subsumed into a wider strategic context. There have even been periods when the region has been victim of "benign neglect" and treated as something of an afterthought. Even when American interest and intent is evident, at certain points in time the United States has prioritized bilateralism over multilateralism, while other episodes have witnessed an emphasis on ASEAN. The point to stress here is that against the backdrop of increasingly complex evolving structural realities, the maintenance of American primacy on which U.S. strategy is predicated and the application of American power and influence toward that end have given rise to uncertainties because of the challenge of locating Southeast Asia within these contours of U.S. grand strategy and striking a balance between strategic intent and policy implementation. Second, domestic politics generates additional uncertainties. Domestic exigencies—whether ideological, political, economic, or even idiosyncratic—in both the United States as well as Southeast Asia periodically contrive to obstruct foreign policy decisionmaking; and while domestic factors may not prove decisive ultimately, they have on occasion frustrated attempts at deepening mutual engagement in the post–Cold War era. Third, the region is itself often ambivalent about the United States. Regional states have different views on the role the United States should play in the region, even as the future of regional cooperation among these states themselves toward the end of regional order management is clouded with uncertainty. This is a crucial point, for the region's diversity contributes to the challenges in formulating a consistent, overarching, systematic strategy on grounds of the inherent strategic significance of the region. Here, a primary concern is that the limits of Southeast Asian regionalism in terms of regional unity and cohesion toward the objective of playing a managerial role in the sustenance of regional order suggest a conspicuous paradox—namely, a continued reliance on the United States playing an active role despite it being an external power and despite the prevalence of different views within the region as to what precisely is the sort of role the United States should play.

STRUCTURE OF THE BOOK

The chapters that follow will attempt to elaborate on the arguments outlined above by investigating, illuminating, and understanding the factors of strategic circumstance, policy implementation, domestic politics, and regional disconnects that shape and influence U.S. engagement with Southeast Asia. Following this introductory chapter, chapter 2 elaborates on the three key elements of the argument: the place of Southeast Asia in the conceptualization and implementation of U.S. grand strategy, domestic influences on engagement policy, and the challenges of regional order management. Chapters 3 to 7 will form the empirical bulk of the book. The chapters are divided according to U.S. presidential administrations, but in a way that also coincides with policy themes and preoccupations in U.S.–Southeast Asia relations. Chapter 3 covers the Clinton administration, a period widely known for the relative neglect of Southeast Asia but also its prioritization of issues of human rights and democracy in a manner that obstructed the deepening of relations with key regional states. Chapter 4 explores the "Global War on Terror," which cast a long shadow over much of U.S. engagement during the administration of George W. Bush, while chapter 5 analyzes issues of free trade, regionalism, and the rise of China in the context of Bush administration strategy and foreign policy in Southeast Asia, emphasizing how piecemeal progress was made—but also stymied—in broadening engagement beyond counterterrorism cooperation. Chapter 6 introduces the Pivot strategy of the Obama administration and how the South China

Sea eventually emerged as its signal focal point, while chapter 7 discusses economic and diplomatic elements to the Pivot in terms of advances and obstacles rooted in the respective domestic realms, with specific attention paid to the TPPA and the evolution of U.S. relations with Vietnam and Myanmar, two key Southeast Asian states where American interest and engagement has lagged until recently. The final two chapters will provide concluding observations, discuss policy implications, and suggest ways in which present policies can be continued, recast, or, in the case of arguably more counterproductive policies, scaled back.

CHAPTER TWO

Sources of Anxiety

ONE ISSUE LOOMS large in any conversation with members of the foreign policymaking fraternity in Southeast Asia—the role of the United States in the region. At issue is persistent disquiet over the nature and extent of the U.S. commitment to play an active role in regional affairs. These concerns have come to be expressed in inconvenient but valid questions that register a sense of uncertainty about where Southeast Asia stands in American strategic thinking and policy priorities: What is the strategic value of Southeast Asia to the United States? Is the Pivot/Rebalance effective and can the United States sustain it? Will the U.S. engagement strategy be able to resist the temptation of distraction by other global issues and crises?[1]

What is the source of these regional anxieties, and how should one understand their implications for relations between Southeast Asia—both collectively and as individual states—and the United States? To get at this question, it is imperative first to appreciate that for Southeast Asian states, particularly the founding members of ASEAN, there is something of a historical hangover that informs this apprehension. The American withdrawal from Vietnam in 1973 and the accompanying years of "benign neglect," where the United States was more a spectator than actor in the theater of regional affairs, cast a long shadow that lingered after the end of the Cold War. More to the point, that period in relations between the United States and Southeast Asia continues to serve as a reminder—however implausible according to protests from American officials and analysts—of the possibility that American domestic politics

could perforce compel another round of truncation, neglect, and retrenchment of interest, perhaps even withdrawal, under any given circumstance.
To suggest that on these grounds certain developments that have taken
place in the years following the end of the Cold War, such as the occasional absence of high-level U.S. representatives at major regional meetings that discombobulated their Southeast Asian partners and hosts, give
reason for pause may not be too far-fetched. In addition to this, regional
policymakers have also been quick to note that the analogous American
withdrawal from Iraq and drawdown from Afghanistan, both undertaken, yet again, in response at least in part to domestic political duress,
serve as yet another reminder of the vulnerability of strategic commitments that can and have become obstructed by, if not made subservient
to, domestic forces.[2]

The consequence of all this has been a tinge of regret over how American engagement with Southeast Asia has somehow failed to maximize
its potential (whatever that potential is). Even worse, this sense of regret
has periodically taken the form of jeremiads that question the validity of
American assurances and the sustainability of American attention.[3] The
following remarks—hardly unique, one should hasten to add—articulated
by the former Malaysian prime minister Abdullah Badawi, on the occasion of a 2005 visit to the United States, offer insight into this sense of
unfulfilled potential:

> Although the ASEAN–U.S. dialogue relations is 28 years old this
> year, I feel this partnership still suffers a considerable problem with
> expectations which do not match. ASEAN expects the United States
> to be an important strategic economic and development partner as
> much as it is an important strategic partner. The United States, on
> the other hand, gives higher priority to ASEAN as a strategic part-
> ner for political and regional security purposes. The only strong
> meeting point is a recognition by both sides of the relevance and
> relative importance of the relationship in the context of the dynam-
> ics of Southeast Asian regional security, regional diplomacy, and re-
> gional prosperity.[4]

Conversely, it should be recognized that misgivings that emanate from
Southeast Asia have also run athwart at least some quarters in the policy
community in the United States, particularly officials from the Departments of State, Defense, and Commerce, as well as the Office of the U.S.

Trade Representative, who have been intimately involved and professionally invested in the formulation and implementation of policy related to
Southeast Asia. A White House official made explicit this frustration
when he expressed dismay at how a major policy speech on Southeast
Asia by a senior colleague was received equivocally by ASEAN diplomats who clamored for even more assurances: "What more do they
want from us?" A different but no less significant manifestation of this
enthusiasm for Southeast Asia is evident from the large number of influential Washington think tank policy reports that have argued for the
United States to do more and be more assertive in regional affairs, chief
of which being the South China Sea disputes, and that swiftly register
protests when the United States is accused of not doing enough in and
for the region.

The ubiquity of misgivings surrounding the attentiveness of the
United States notwithstanding, it can be argued that the United States
has readily and willingly embraced its role as a global superpower since
the end of the Second World War—indeed, the sole global superpower
since the end of the Cold War—as its "manifest destiny," and this fact
obliges it to possess the necessary strategic bandwidth to fulfill that role.
In this sense, the logic of those who contend that the asymmetry of
power between both parties means that it is understandable if Southeast
Asia is relegated to the margins of American strategy and policy may to
some extent be misplaced. After all, the logic of asymmetry holds true
with respect to virtually every relationship that the United States has
today, be it bilateral, multilateral, or regional. And yet, this has not prevented Washington from identifying and articulating key strategic interests at each level.

More compelling, this logic did not prevent the Obama administration
from publicly declaring its intent to specifically deepen U.S. engagement
with Southeast Asia, just as it did not prevent the Bush administration
from making notable advances in relations with Southeast Asia, albeit
advances that were eventually either distracted by or limited to the imperative of counterterrorism. In this respect, it is important to acknowledge that the Pivot strategy of the Obama administration was for the most
part as much a continuation and deepening of preexisting U.S. policies
toward Southeast Asia—policies that, as the chapters that follow will
demonstrate, have themselves waxed and waned, evolving unevenly along
with American strategic thinking about Southeast Asia and structural
shifts that impinge on American interests. In retrospect, however, there

was one important distinction between the Bush and Obama administrations when it came to Southeast Asia. Whereas the Bush administration essentially continued the United States' practice of prioritizing bilateral relationships in Asia strategy, it can be argued that the Obama administration pursued a multilateral engagement strategy predicated on Southeast Asia as a collectivity possessed of inherent strategic logic, even as it retained existing bilateral relationships. All this is to say that if President Obama's successors intend to make good on his assurances that the Asia Pacific, and, within it, Southeast Asia, is and will remain a matter of priority for American strategic planning, then it follows that American policy toward, and presence in, Southeast Asia warrants more careful analytical scrutiny in terms of where and how it fits into the broader contours of American grand strategy. This investigation begins with a closer exploration of conceptions of American strategy and interests as they relate to Southeast Asia.

THE EVOLUTION OF GRAND STRATEGY
AND U.S. INTERESTS IN SOUTHEAST ASIA

Most scholars of strategic studies will maintain that all great powers must have a grand strategy to govern their policies. Whether they do, in fact, possess one, and what form this takes, is of course a separate matter. Grand strategy entails possession of a clear strategic objective along with a coherent agenda and implementable measures that would allow a state to marshal resources at its disposal to pursue that objective. The crafting of grand strategy further entails the ability to think expansively across a range of interrelated issues to plan for, and deal as much as possible with, the inevitable reactions and response to the pursuit of this strategy in any given domain so as to not be inadvertently found in a position of unpreparedness, ergo vulnerability. Toward these ends, grand strategy must not be dogmatic and should involve an element of adaptability and adjustability as well. To suggest a degree of flexibility in grand strategy is not to dilute its essence. Rather, it is to stress that the implementation of policies derived from and aligned to grand strategic imperatives must also be able to adapt to changing circumstances and internal and external constraints that might emerge. In a sense, therefore, grand strategy speaks of a relationship between means and ends, repercussions and recalibrations. Pulled together, grand strategy involves developing clear objectives and harnessing a state's wherewithal in a comprehensive sense to achieve them, but also putting resources against tasks in an iterative fashion and further, adjusting objectives, approaches, and resource allocation as appropriate to changing circumstances.[5]

Although the study of grand strategy has its origins in the field of military studies and strategic studies, where the focus was primarily on military matters, given the changing nature of security actors and threats today it is necessary to adopt a more holistic understanding of the tenets of grand strategy to reflect the full suite of capabilities available to the state to pursue strategic objectives.[6] With respect to the present study, a more holistic appreciation of grand strategy is necessary for proper analysis of how Southeast Asian states assess and respond to American engagement: for instance, where there has been an abiding concern that an evident feature of the policies of the Bush and Obama administrations was apparently an excessive emphasis on the sharp edge of engagement—in Bush's case, the war on terror, while in Obama's case, enhancing American military presence in the region particularly in the South China Sea—at the expense of other less provocative, "softer" means and avenues. For Southeast Asia then, the preference is clearly for American grand strategy to be built on the full suite of military, economic, and diplomatic capabilities and "soft power." At the same time, holistic and all-encompassing grand strategy has to be balanced by the equally pertinent reality that even a global power like the United States will have to prioritize issues and regions when it comes to deploying these in pursuit of American interests, particularly when resources are finite.

Since the subprime crisis of 2007–08 that crippled the American economy, a debate among scholars and commentators on U.S. strategy over the question of American decline has gathered pace. The debate itself is far too meandering and complex to rehearse here. Suffice to say that it turns on two essential questions: Is the United States in decline and, if so, what are the implications for America's place in the world? Notwithstanding the sometimes heated nature of this debate between those who support and those who oppose the proposition that the United States is in decline, both in fact share three assumptions: the United States enjoys (enjoyed) a position of primacy, that primacy was good for America and the world, and that primacy is worth restoring or reinforcing (whether it can be, or not, is necessarily a different matter). By extension then, it can be argued that the overarching core strategic interest of the United States during the post–Cold War era has always been reasonably clear;[7] having seen the only real competition of the Cold War era vanquished when the Soviet Union collapsed, the strategic objective of the United States has been the preservation of American primacy and influence globally through the maintenance of its military preponderance and economic might and the perpetuation of its values through a liberal international order that it created, nourished, protected, and advanced after the conflagration of the Second World War. To that end, the imperative of security, prosperity, and democracy pursued globally under American leadership and harnessed toward the end of maintaining and leveraging American primacy to shape global affairs has been a consistent theme across all the administrations that have served since the end of the Cold War.

In terms of the time frame covered in this book, the pronouncements of successive presidents are illustrative. The intent and objectives of American post–Cold War strategy of primacy and leadership were made clear in the 1996 National Security Strategy of President Bill Clinton:

> Our military might is unparalleled. We now have a truly global economy linked by an instantaneous communications network, which offers increasing opportunities for American jobs and American investment. The community of democratic nations is growing, enhancing the prospects for political stability, peaceful conflict resolution and greater dignity and hope for the people of the world. The international community is beginning to act together to address pressing global environmental needs. Never has American leadership been more essential—to navigate the shoals of the world's new dangers and to capitalize on its opportunities. American assets are unique: our military strength, our dynamic economy, our powerful ideals and, above all, our people. We can and must make the difference through our engagement.[8]

Similar strategic perspectives were advanced in the 2002 National Security Strategy articulated by the administration of President George W. Bush:

> The United States possesses unprecedented—and unequaled— strength and influence in the world. Sustained by faith in the principles of liberty, and the value of a free society, this position comes with unparalleled responsibilities, obligations, and opportunity. The great strength of this nation must be used to promote a balance of

power that favors freedom. . . . This is also a time of opportunity
for America. We will work to translate this moment of influence
into decades of peace, prosperity, and liberty.[9]

Finally, cognate themes were repeated in the 2010 National Security
Strategy of the Obama administration:

> Our country possesses the attributes that have supported our lead-
> ership for decades—sturdy alliances, an unmatched military, the
> world's largest economy, a strong and evolving democracy, and
> a dynamic citizenry. Going forward, there should be no doubt:
> the United States of America will continue to underwrite global
> security—through our commitments to allies, partners, and insti-
> tutions; our focus on defeating al-Qa'ida and its affiliates in Af-
> ghanistan, Pakistan, and around the globe; and our determination
> to deter aggression and prevent the proliferation of the world's
> most dangerous weapons. . . . Our national security strategy is,
> therefore, focused on renewing American leadership so that we can
> more effectively advance our interests in the 21st century. We will
> do so by building upon the sources of our strength at home, while
> shaping an international order that can meet the challenges of our
> time.[10]

President Obama further sought to put to rest talk of an erosion of
American power and primacy as a consequence of economic travails:
"anyone who tells you that America is in decline or that our influence
has waned, doesn't know what they're talking about."[11]

Assessments from the National Intelligence Council (NIC) were, in
comparison, perhaps slightly more withheld but nonetheless arrived at
similar conclusions. Forecasting ahead—a fraught but necessary task
for policymakers—the latest NIC report predicted that

> whether the U.S. will be able to work with new partners to rein-
> vent the international system will be among the most important
> variables in the future shape of the global order. Although the
> United States' (and the West's) relative decline vis-à-vis the rising
> states is inevitable . . . the U.S. most likely will remain "first among
> equals" among the other great powers in 2030 because of its pre-

eminence across a range of power dimensions and legacies of its leadership role.[12]

Additionally, the report maintained that "the replacement of the United States by another global power and erection of a new international order seems the least likely outcome in this period. No other power would be likely to achieve the same panoply of power in this time frame under any plausible scenario."[13] The main point here is that even a more reticent assessment essentially echoes prevailing wisdom that American primacy and leadership is crucial for the world.

It is not difficult to infer from these remarks that what stands out in the articulation of American strategic objectives is the matter of American leadership and primacy in setting and shaping global and regional agendas, as opposed to merely responding to developments, and the relative power (of the soft, hard, and smart varieties) the United States can bring to bear to influence the thinking and behavior of other states, including contenders for regional leadership and primacy. It is about seizing the strategic initiative as opposed to ceding influence to other powers; to steer events rather than respond reflexively, in order to advance its objectives of security, prosperity, and democracy. In other words, it is about the preservation of American primacy in regional, if not global, affairs, an objective that, it should be added, enjoys bipartisan support. Apropos these observations, where does Southeast Asia fit in the elaboration of core American strategic interests, and how does the United States conceive of its role in the region in terms of advancing these interests, especially given the stark picture once painted by members of the House Committee on International Relations, who conceded in the wake of the September 11 terrorist attacks that Southeast Asia "lack[s] the intrinsic strategic significance of Northeast Asia"?[14]

If grand strategy refers to the mapping of a comprehensive approach to frame engagement as suggested earlier, it follows that statecraft concerns the matter of policy implementation. Scholars have argued how an important aspect of grand strategy is the ability of the state to possess a sense of a complete picture in terms of how constituent parts fit together as a coherent whole. Steve Yetiv conceives of grand strategy as a "conceptual road map, describing how to match identified resources to the promotion of identified interests, and a set of policy prescriptions" to achieve national goals.[15] In this respect, grand strategy requires the coordination and harnessing of military, diplomatic, and economic tools of statecraft toward the end of furthering a state's defined interests in the international system. According to David Baldwin, "among students of foreign policy and international politics the term [statecraft] is sometimes used to encompass the whole foreign policy-making process, but more often it refers to the selection of means for the pursuit of foreign policy goals."[16] Put differently, statecraft is concerned with the implementation of foreign policy goals and objectives to create or maintain an environment in which the state's grand strategy can be pursued and interests protected or advanced. Conversely, the inability to follow through on implementation poses considerable challenges for states, possibly even compounding preexisting difficulties that, ironically, these policies were designed to ameliorate in the first place.[17]

The need to analyze not just the place of Southeast Asia in the evolution of U.S. post–Cold War grand strategy but also the implementation of American strategy in the region is warranted given a remark by a former American ambassador to several Southeast Asian countries, who was of the view that "it is not in strategy but implementation that we may have got it wrong." The preceding point is crucial for how it suggests periodic disconnect between policy pronouncement and policy practice. This disconnect, it can be further added, commonly arises in the course of moving grand strategy from conceptualization to implementation.[18]

Southeast Asia sets great store by American follow-through of strategy in the region. Consequently, it cannot be denied that the inconsistencies that derive from this disconnect between intent and implementation, and the doubts they sow over where and how the region fits in American grand strategy, have accented attendant anxiety. For some scholars, these inconsistencies and contradictions may in fact reflect a deeper malaise in American strategic culture:

Americans, in foreign policy, are torn to the point of schizophrenia. They are reluctant, then aggressive; asleep at the switch, then quick on the trigger; indifferent, then obsessed, then indifferent again. They act out of a sense of responsibility and then resent and fear the burden of responsibility they have taken on themselves. Their effect on the world, not surprisingly, is often the opposite of what they intend. Americans say they want stability in the international system, but they are often the greatest disrupters of stability. They extol the virtues of international laws and institutions but then violate and ignore them with barely a second thought. They are a revolutionary power but think they are a status quo power. They want to be left alone but can't seem to leave anyone else alone. They are continually surprising the world with their behavior, but not nearly as much as they are continually surprising themselves.[19]

DEBATING U.S. INTERESTS IN SOUTHEAST ASIA

Why is there any reason to think that the United States should have a single strategy for the region? After all, as the previous chapter conceded, the difficulty in formulating an overarching, systematic policy seems a "natural" consequence of the region's diversity. To address this question, several points should be borne in mind. First, although scholars may not have done so in a very systematic or theoretical manner, the literature on U.S. grand strategy has in fact addressed the question of regional engagement and the role of regional groupings.[20] Second, although certainly a potential obstacle in terms of coherence of outlooks with which the United States can engage, diversity within a region itself need not ipso facto preclude any possibility or prospect of crafting a regional strategy on the part of the United States, especially if there is strategic imperative toward that end. Such an imperative was arguably in evidence during the Cold War, when the domino theory lent something of strategic coherence to Thailand and archipelagic Southeast Asia (as well as South Vietnam), and also in the Middle East, which consecutive American administrations have approached with a single strategy (flawed or otherwise). Third, from an institutional perspective the Obama administration itself declared belief in and support for ASEAN, its diplomatic centrality, and its norms, which it deemed to coincide with what the United States was trying to do in the region. Fourth, a united, coherent Southeast Asia cannot but be an important element of the balance of power for the United States as it casts its eye on emerging regional powers. The point here is not so much to make a normative argument about why Southeast Asia is (or should be) approached strategically as a region premised on a philosophical disposition that this is the "right" approach, but rather to note that there is ample evidence that the United States at least tries to *think* about the region strategically in regional terms. This can be distilled not only from policy statements but from actual engagement, for instance, with ASEAN. This is not to say that regional policy is pursued at the expense of bilateral relations, or even that the United

States has been successful or consistent in its efforts at engagement on a regional level—far from it, for these efforts have often waxed and waned and fallen short, indeed, at times compromised by the prioritization of bilateralism. Nevertheless, it is precisely for this reason that we should interrogate how the United States has attempted to approach Southeast Asia as a region even as it seeks to build on bilateral relationships with key regional partners.

Collectively as ASEAN, Southeast Asia has since 2000 been the second fastest growing economy in Asia after China.[21] Its ten constituent countries have a combined gross domestic product of $2.4 trillion, a consumer base of approximately 626 million, and a growing middle class. Alert to this economic potential, the United States has strengthened its economic ties with the region through a range of initiatives, such as the Trade and Investment Framework Agreement (TIFA), signed in 2006. Until President Donald Trump withdrew the United States from the agreement, the TPPA offered yet another means through which American economic engagement with the region could be enhanced.[22] The United States is presently ASEAN's third largest trading partner and the fourth largest destination for American exports. As the largest and most sophisticated economy in the world, the United States has been, and remains, a key source of investments as well and is an important market for Southeast Asian goods. Since 2001, the total value of U.S.–ASEAN trade has risen from $137 billion to $234 billion.

Critics can nonetheless parse these economic data under something of a more ambiguous light. For instance, the point can be made that the economic picture is impressive but distorted by the fact that Singapore has been the largest Southeast Asian trading partner for the United States by some distance and is also the destination for the lion's share of American foreign investments into the region, while U.S. trade and investment links to Laos, Cambodia, and Myanmar pale in comparison to China.[23] Moreover, U.S.–ASEAN economic relations have always had to deal with protectionist tendencies in the United States in reaction to trade deficits. Indeed, it was precisely such sentiments that proved injurious to American commitment to the TPPA.[24] The bias against American exports is also reflected in the fact that according to the economic report cited above, ASEAN's surplus of goods with the United States totaled $48 billion in 2012. Of course, if one subscribes to a theory of absolute gains, it follows then that all this should not detract from the point that given Asia's expanding share of the global economy, the growth potential in Southeast Asia, and the anticipated strengthening of the region's institutional capacity with the ASEAN Economic Community, Southeast Asia will continue to provide opportunities for the United States from the vantage of economics and trade. But it is also a reminder of the prudence of disaggregating "Southeast Asia" in order to get a different sense of American interests in the region.

Comparing American and Chinese economic relations with Southeast Asia, however, throws up a more disconcerting picture. Although the United States has enjoyed long-standing economic relations with the region, the post–Asian financial crisis era has seen the exponential expansion of Chinese economic influence, an expansion that according to most indicators is only going to accelerate in the coming years. This influence, as later chapters will discuss, has found both political and strategic expression in ways that have enthused but also worried the United States and Southeast Asia. What this means is that efforts to counterbalance the growing economic clout that China is amassing in the region will for all intents and purposes be critical to American interests.

Southeast Asia is not only an important economic partner for the United States. The region is also located astride crucial sea lanes linking the Persian Gulf to major American allies in Asia: Japan and South Korea. A corollary to this is freedom of navigation and the openness of sea lanes for international commerce. For their part, American leaders have removed any element of equivocation with repeated assertions that freedom of navigation is a matter of national interest to the United States.[25] To serve this end, the U.S. navy has been intentionally conducting operations in the South China Sea for the explicit purpose of responding to irredentist and expansionist activities by claimant states and to push back amid perceptions that increased Chinese activity in the waters may be intended to limit or police freedom of navigation. The question remains, though, just how far and how hard the United States is prepared to push back.[26]

Southeast Asia also provides important military facilities for the United States. The United States is committed to an alliance relationship with two Southeast Asian states—Thailand and the Philippines, both of which were designated "Major Non-NATO Ally" during the Bush administration in recognition of their deployment of forces in support of U.S. military operations in Iraq.[27] Over the years, the United States has also developed close defense relations with Malaysia and Singapore. In fact, the defense relationship with the latter is one of the closest that the

United States enjoys with any non-ally. Washington has also deepened defense relations with Vietnam in recent years.

One might argue that the evident utility of access to Southeast Asian bases is derived from the fact that their role is limited to the provision of storage and repair facilities designed to support American military operations elsewhere, such as in Afghanistan and Iraq in recent years, thereby implying a less consequential defense relationship compared with that which exists with Japan or South Korea. This contrasts with a scenario where American offensive capabilities may enjoy a more permanent presence, signifying greater strategic value and significance (or lack thereof).[28] Although this comparison is well noted, it should still be contextualized. The absence of a significant permanent American military presence accords with Southeast Asian desires to ensure that the region will eventually be free of permanent foreign military bases. This aspiration was expressed in the 1971 ZOPFAN declaration alluded to earlier and reiterated in the 1976 Declaration of ASEAN Concord, both of which contained references to the qualified proscription of foreign military bases in Southeast Asia. Although more an expression of hope rather than a declaration of a state of being, it does highlight a fundamental premise on the part of Southeast Asian states with regards to the hosting of an American military presence.

More can be said of this matter. American basing policy in Southeast Asia also reflects the evolution of strategic thinking in the United States with regards to its power projection platforms and capabilities. This change was registered in how defense priorities have been determined and revised in consonance with changing strategic circumstances at the end of the Cold War and consequently found expression in the shift away from permanent military bases toward dexterity achieved through ready access to indigenous facilities and rotational deployments. This thinking was captured in the remarks of former commander of U.S. Pacific Command Robert Willard, who maintained with reference to reports of Australian and Singaporean offers of military facilities: "Initiatives such as Australia offered, or such as Singapore offered, to allow us to rotate forces from locations that are closer and more adjacent to Southeast Asia affords Pacific Command the opportunity to more conveniently have its presence there and felt, and not rely so terribly much on sustainment at great cost in the region . . . but there's no aspiration for bases in Southeast Asia."[29]

A further manifestation of this evolutionary shift in strategic thinking was evident from the intensification of multilateral engagement alongside the traditional emphasis on bilateral relations with individual Southeast Asian states, conceptualized in the form of the hubs-and-spokes configuration of American defense policy in the region. Granted, there were occasions when this shift sat uneasily with other strategic imperatives—such as the emphasis on unilateralism and pre-emption that shaped foreign policy under the neoconservative presidency of George W. Bush—implying, thereby, the problem of inconsistent and imperfect implementation. Yet even so, the move from an instinctive preference to act as a hegemon with its military allies to a readiness to operate within a climate of multilateral interaction and consultation with regional partners should not be simply dismissed as an empty gesture, particularly as it laid the ground for Southeast Asian engagement that followed during the Obama administration.

Thus far, it is intuitive that the United States has evident interests in Southeast Asia on the basis of some strategic value. But how do these speak to "core" or "vital" American interests, defined as interests that affect the sovereignty, safety, territorial integrity, and power position of the United States? On the face of it, one might be hard-pressed to make the case. Although greater trade and commercial interaction with the economies of Southeast Asia may generate opportunities for the United States, one can contend that they are hardly imperative to core American national interests. Few would argue that the U.S. economy would suffer in any existential way should trade, market access, and investment opportunities in Southeast Asia diminish. Likewise, the vast global network of friends and allies the United States has established affords it invaluable access to any number of military facilities. That and the fact that the United States also enjoys long-standing alliance relationships with three states in geographical proximity to Southeast Asia—South Korea, Japan, and Australia—mean it is difficult to make a categorical case that military access to Southeast Asian facilities is, again, vital to core American security interests.

Does this mean, then, that Southeast Asia stands, at best, at the margins of the American strategic imagination? Not necessarily so, if one recalls the initial assumption that the strategic objective of preserving primacy is core to the national interests of the United States. If the preservation of American primacy and influence globally through the maintenance of its military and economic power and the perpetuation of its values through a liberal international order that it created remains of signal strategic interest to the United States, it stands to reason that this global power and influence is in danger of being undermined by the rise of a presumptive challenger—China.

In a sense, the preceding statement is quite unexceptional, if not patently obvious, since for any great power, sustaining, if not augmenting, power is a matter of priority for the state. But this assumption is nevertheless integral to the present study in a specific sense. China's emergence over the last two decades has altered the regional strategic environment in which the United States seeks to entrench its primacy. More to the point, it is in Southeast Asia that the growing competition between the United States and China has begun to play out most acutely. This rivalry, it should be added, has both provided opportunities and posed challenges for Southeast Asia: opportunities in terms of how the major powers have sought to deepen their economic engagement and court the region through the "charm offensive" in the case of China and the "economic prong" of the American Pivot, but also challenges in the form of strategic rivalry that generates destabilizing cadences and threatens to overwhelm Southeast Asia. The National Intelligence Council's *Global Trends 2030 Report* sounds the following words of caution: "An increasingly multipolar Asia lacking a well-anchored regional security framework able to arbitrate and mitigate rising tensions would constitute one of the largest global threats. Fear of Chinese power, the likelihood of growing Chinese nationalism, and possible questions about the U.S. remaining involved in the region will increase insecurities. An unstable Asia would cause large-scale damage to the global economy."[30] For Southeast Asian states, maintaining equidistance from both powers is as challenging as it is crucial.

However precarious, there is a further, controversial point that can be registered regarding where Southeast Asia might fit in American perceptions of its core interests, at least during the period of the Bush administration. Following the tragic events of September 11, 2001, the Bush administration made clear that it considered the nexus of terrorism, weapons of mass destruction, and rogue states to pose an existential threat to the United States. Donald Rumsfeld, the secretary of defense under George W. Bush, talked of how a "nexus between terrorist networks, terrorist states, and weapons of mass destruction . . . can make mighty adversaries of small or impoverished states and even relatively small groups of individuals."[31]

This view was reinforced in President Bush's remarks at West Point, re-produced in the 2002 *National Security Strategy* document: "The gravest danger to freedom lies at the crossroads of radicalism and technology. When the spread of chemical and biological and nuclear weapons, along with ballistic missile technology—when that occurs, even weak states and small groups could attain a catastrophic power to strike great nations. Our enemies have declared this very intention, and have been caught seeking these terrible weapons."[32]

Notwithstanding the fact that the alarm that terrorism provoked (and still provokes) was in truth incommensurate with the actual magnitude of the threat, the Bush administration's articulation of the above perspective led it to view Southeast Asia through the optics of terrorism and religiously inspired militancy. On that score, even though the center of gravity for the existential threat this unholy trinity posed to the United States was ultimately in the Middle East and Central Asia, Southeast Asia also garnered some attention by virtue of being home both to large progressive Muslim societies (conceived of as a potential bulwark to the ideological appeal of more militant interpretations of the faith) as well as fringe extremist Muslim groups who have sympathized with, claimed allegiance to, and drawn support from transnational terrorist organizations that have identified the United States as a primary target for their nefarious activities. Needless to say, in some quarters of the American decisionmaking establishment, this threat is still pertinent today. Indeed, as a Defense Department senior official suggested: "terrorism has returned as a major strategic challenge for the United States, including in Southeast Asia."[33]

What essentially follows from this discussion is the point that, whether by design, propitious circumstance, or persuasion through the efforts of regional diplomats, Southeast Asia does find itself possessing some measure of strategic significance for the United States, although there is a limit as to how far this idea can be pushed.

DOMESTIC INFLUENCES

There is a tendency in certain schools of thought in the fields of strategic studies and international relations theory to downplay the influence that domestic politics exerts on foreign and security policies.[34] For them, states are best considered metaphorically as billiard balls and black boxes, as the late Kenneth Waltz famously described, and their internal complications and contradictions best left untampered lest they get in the way of elegant structuralist theories that purport to explain with analytical parsimony how the world works.[35] The problem, however, is that neither the world of decisionmaking nor the world *in* decisionmaking lend themselves to gross simplification in the name of "scientific" theorizing of social phenomena. Ultimately, foreign policy decisions are navigated and made by humans who are social creatures given to perceptions and misperceptions and emotional responses to the environment around them. To the extent that decisionmaking can be "scientific" and rational, it works best with full and perfect information, which seldom, if ever, is available in reality. In other words, knowing what (in theory) must be done and being willing and able to do it are two fundamentally different prospects altogether. It is against this backdrop that domestic politics assumes crucial importance in foreign policymaking.

The role of domestic politics can be discerned in the process through which American grand strategy has been conceptualized. In brief, the notion of American global primacy and leadership premised on the preponderance of power rests ultimately on the conception of American exceptionalism, the sense of unique identity and destiny that cuts across the political spectrum in the United States.[36] Likewise, the insistence on the part of American diplomats and policymakers that the United States practices "values-based diplomacy" and a "moral foreign policy" is predicated on the paradoxical belief in the *universalism* of the very values that underpin American *exceptionalism*. That is to say, the celebrated American values of liberal democracy, individual freedom, and the triumph of the free market of goods, services, and ideas upon which self-conceptions of exceptionalism rest are also believed to be universal values, and American foreign policy must be pursued as a validation of these values.[37] Hence, there is no gainsaying the fundamental and foundational influence that domestic factors have as key determinants of strategy and policy. But to dwell on the conceptual and philosophical implications of this would take the current study too far afield. For present purposes, domestic politics is considered not for its role in informing the conceptualization of strategy and policy but, following on from the previous section, as posing possible obstacles to its implementation. In other words, the intent in this book is to specifically consider the vitiating effect of domestic politics on foreign policy.

To take this line of analysis further, if grand strategy is about coordinating the variety of tools of statecraft as well as the actors and agencies involved toward a strategic objective (in this case, preservation of primacy), and the road from strategy conceptualization to policy implementation is invariably paved with all sorts of challenges, then it stands to reason that some of these challenges are surely rooted in the realm of domestic politics. In essence, the constituent parts involved in strategy conceptualization and implementation can (and do) work in ways that undermine each other, such as when strategy making and implementation are bedeviled by narrow, parochial domestic interests, partisan politics, ideological baggage, or bureaucratic rivalry.[38] A cautionary analytical word to that effect was sounded by the sociologist Joel Migdal, whose pioneering work on "State-in-Society" warns against assuming coherence and unity of the state, especially in the context of bureaucratic hierarchical culture where the institutional identity of the state is often given to challenge and negotiation by competing interests at the levels of both policy formulation and implementation.[39]

It is not only bureaucratic politics that impedes policymaking but also the polarization of political interests that impinge on foreign policy. Arguably the most glaring recent illustration of this is evident in the impact that political polarization has had on American foreign policy, especially during the second term of the Obama administration. As President Obama himself protested in the face of congressional gridlock over the federal budget:

> Oftentimes I hear from folks up on Capitol Hill, the need for American leadership. The need for America to be number one. Well, you know what, around the globe, part of what makes us a leader is when we govern effectively and we keep our own house in order, and we pass budgets, and we can engage in long-term planning, and we can invest in the things that are important for the future. That's U.S. leadership. When we fail to do it, we diminish U.S. leadership.[40]

The reality of such constraints is not lost on Southeast Asians and continues to vex regional policymakers tasked with factoring a U.S. role and presence into their strategic calculations. The case of the South China Sea is instructive of this, where diplomats from several ASEAN member states have hinted that the source of their reticence toward taking a stronger position against China derives from their uncertainty over whether the United States can be relied on to provide diplomatic and strategic heft in support, particularly if American public opinion cannot be persuaded that such efforts would advance their interests.

The most striking historical example of how domestic interests and politics can fundamentally cripple strategy implementation was evident in the debacle of Vietnam, where mounting domestic pressure compelled the ignominious U.S. withdrawal, which ushered in more than a decade of neglect and led to Southeast Asia's rapid slide down the list of American strategic priorities. At the time, this effect was captured profoundly in the following remarks by Congressman Peter McCloskey with regards to requests from the White House to provide financial aid to the armed forces of the Republic of South Vietnam in order to stave off the marauding North Vietnamese army: "There was no way in 1975 that the Congress was going to vote any money to go to the aid of South Vietnam. We had pulled out our troops in 1973 and public opinion at that point shifted. The people of the United States, having seen Watergate, having seen the deception of the generals, weren't about to give any help in Southeast Asia."[41] Apropos of Vietnam, because the U.S. Congress has also come to represent growing Southeast Asian immigrant communities residing in the United States, it has been subject to intense lobbying by these communities that are intent on obstructing Washington's dealings especially with authoritarian and communist regimes of the region.

For Southeast Asia, historical analogies became all too disconcertingly familiar when congressional gridlock arising from partisan competition over budgetary issues precipitated a government shutdown in Washington, D.C., in 2013, which in turn resulted in the cancellation of President Obama's scheduled trip to Asia to attend several crucial regional summits and bilateral meetings. Regional reactions were captured in illustrative remarks articulated by an Indonesian official, who lamented that "the fallout from the government shutdown is reviving doubts about the U.S.'s standing in Asia."[42] The immediate fallout was indeed significant. The oblique yet signal effect the gridlock had on America's regional standing was amplified by how, in the absence of the American president, Chinese diplomacy gained even greater purchase when Chinese president Xi Jinping held court at the Asia Pacific Economic Cooperation meeting and seized the opportunity to announce a slew of regional initiatives that were embraced by regional states, even as they cast a worrying eye toward Washington and registered disappointment at the perceived ambivalence of the United States expressed in the absence of the president. Another official made explicit the incipient misgivings of Indonesia and the region: "Like many other East Asian countries, Indonesia has been in doubt regarding America's ability to sustain the pivot strategy, with the huge cuts in the defense budget over the next five years."[43]

Presaging the discussion to be picked up in greater analytical and empirical detail in the following chapters, domestic opposition in the United States has also cast a long shadow over trade engagement with Southeast Asia. Losing presidential contender Hillary Clinton's opposition to the TPPA, an initiative that she had previously actively championed while serving as secretary of state as she sought to appeal to the interests of lobby groups and trade unions, provided compelling commentary on how domestic imperatives potentially obstruct engagement policy even in the case of the well intentioned. Alluding to the risks that domestic obstacles pose for the United States to play a central role in regional affairs, the late Lee Kuan Yew offered the perspective that while the American military presence

> is very necessary . . . unless the U.S. economy becomes more dynamic and less debt laden, this presence will be much reduced by the end of this decade. The longer-term outlook then becomes problematic. Even if U.S. deficits are reduced, industrial productivity improves, and exports increase, the United States nevertheless cannot afford and will not be willing to bear the whole cost of the global security burden. The great danger is that the U.S. economy does not recover quickly enough and trade frictions and Japan bashing increase as America becomes protectionist. The worst case is where trade and economic relations become so bad that mutual security ties are weakened and ruptured. That would be a dreadful and dangerous development. The world has developed because of the stability America established. If that stability is rocked, we are going to have a different situation.[44]

At this point, it should be said that the factor of domestic politics is evident not only on the American side of the equation. The logic cuts both ways. If the vicissitudes of American domestic politics pose obstacles that feed regional anxieties, so too, it can be argued, do the domestic constraints in at least some Southeast Asian states. The phenomenon of anti-Americanism is illustrative in this regard, particularly in how it encouraged a disposition toward the United States that prevents regional states from deepening their own engagement with Washington or from closer strategic alignment with the United States, even in the face of clear strategic interests to do so. What is striking in this respect is the tension that has come to exist between traditional reliance on the United States for the security umbrella it provides, on the one hand, and the occasional chorus of anti-American attitudes and behavior that spawn from an ongoing albeit uneven process of political transformation and democratic transition, on the other. This, in turn, speaks to the curious paradoxical correlation between democratization, a hallmark of American values-based foreign policy, and anti-Americanism that derives precisely from a climate of greater political liberalization, as evident in the case of the Philippines, where the United States was viewed suspiciously for propping the authoritarian regime of Ferdinand Marcos, and Indonesia, where Muslim social and political activism found expression in anti-Americanism especially after the U.S. military actions in Afghanistan and Iraq.

During the Cold War, the image of the United States then held by many in noncommunist Southeast Asia, though by no means a pristine one, was still relatively generous. However, the same certainly could not be said of Southeast Asia in the post–Cold War era, especially in the immediate aftermath of September 11. Then, regional appeals for demonstrations of American commitment held alongside growing concerns for the turn in American foreign policy toward pre-emption and unilateralism, although these tendencies were in truth already apparent in the preceding Clinton administration.[45] The effect of this was felt in respect to negative perceptions of the United States held in various quarters across the region. Traditionally regarded as the region's stabilizer and "honest broker"—a view still held by a not insignificant number of policymakers— the United States nevertheless had to make do with unflattering characterizations of its identity and behavior. As the late Samuel Huntington observed, perhaps somewhat exaggeratedly: "While the U.S. regularly denounces various countries as 'rogue states,' in the eyes of many countries it is becoming the rogue superpower . . . the single greatest external threat to their societies."[46]

The most obvious recent illustration of the potentially deleterious effect of anti-Americanism can be found in response to the rise in religious militancy within Southeast Asia, particularly the view held in many quarters in Indonesia and Malaysia that the Bush administration's unilateralist war on terror was in fact a contrived war against Islam. But it has also been registered in the residual impact that the colonial experience has had on contemporary relations with the Philippines, where Manila has had to balance the imperative of security, which it depends on its American ally to provide, and popular resentment against "American imperialism," a recurring theme that one official admitted remains "a considerable force" in bilateral relations.[47] At more muted but no less consequential levels, it is also evident in terms of the ideologically informed suspicions that the hitherto foe Vietnam and the military in Myanmar continue to harbor even as they gradually gravitate toward the United States. In the latter case, even Aung San Suu Kyi, Myanmar's state councilor and democracy icon, has had to distance herself from the United States over pressure from Washington to take action against the persecution of the Rohingya minority by members of the security forces of Myanmar.

At the same time, although domestic factors should not be ignored and certainly warrant careful attention, their influence should also not be exaggerated. As the compilation of congressional bills related to Southeast Asia between 1993 and 2016 provided in the appendix illustrates, for instance, congressional attention given to Southeast Asia has predominantly concentrated on human rights, mostly centered on Vietnam and Myanmar, and it is on this issue that it has been most influential. This also means that the influence Congress wields on other issues has been considerably weaker, save perhaps for some issues related to trade.[48] A similar case can be made in relation to anti-Americanism at the height of the war on terror, where despite being confronted with a groundswell of popular opposition, regional states persisted in close cooperation with the United States, albeit in very low-key fashion in order to elide popular scrutiny, and as a consequence managed in most instances to improve their counterterrorism capabilities even as anti-American sentiments persisted within their Muslim populations.

In essence then, although domestic factors may on their own perhaps be insufficient to stop policy initiatives, they may be—and indeed have proven—sufficient to inconvenience implementation, dampen the diplomatic mood, and sow doubts between leaders and foreign policy establishments.

THE CHALLENGES OF REGIONAL ORDER

Several scholars of international security have argued that after the Cold War, the underinstitutionalized nature of diplomacy in East Asia, where the necessary formal mechanisms through which the more debilitating effects of power balancing among rising regional states could be managed and mitigated were lacking (as opposed to the more informal and non-binding tenets of Asian regionalism), lent to instability.[49] At the heart of the matter is the management of shifts in distribution of power and relative power positions, and the consequences of these shifts, that were already under way in East Asia. The strategic uncertainty these shifts precipitated served to fuel pessimistic predictions about the future of regional stability, notwithstanding protestations from those who contend that the deep economic interdependence that now characterizes the interactions between regional states makes conflict unlikely. Concomitantly, this gave rise to a cottage industry that hypothesized how the region was "ripe for rivalry," a "cockpit" for great power conflict, exposed to the "Thucydides's trap," and that its future would resemble Europe's past. Underlying these assumptions is a structuralist logic that suggests great powers like the United States and China take certain actions because they can by virtue of their status and wherewithal as great powers, which in turn leaves smaller states like those in the Southeast Asian region to suffer what they must. To this, several responses can be mustered.

First, it would be a mistake to simply dismiss the regional states of Southeast Asia as passive victims of great power dynamics, presented with a fait accompli. To be sure, small states have limited room to maneuver in relation to great powers. But limited room is not no room, and with creativity, diplomacy, and unity small states can, and have, been able to exercise some leverage and extract concessions from larger powers to further their own interests and elaborate a regional order ostensibly on their own terms at least in form, if not in substance. At the same time, however, the amount of strategic latitude should not be overstated, particularly when, as the later discussion on ASEAN Centrality will show, the aspiration and ability of the indigenous organization to manage regional affairs relies heavily, and paradoxically, on the acknowledgment and accommodation of major powers.

Second, unlike the security climate of the Cold War, where the pressures of great power rivalry and alignment were so strong that it was difficult for smaller states to stay neutral (attempts at nonalignment notwithstanding), attendant regional circumstances in the post–Cold War era in East Asia have been far more complex and fluid, and although the logic of "choosing sides" between the United States and China may be conceptually luculent, it fails to capture the ambiguity of the reality confronting Southeast Asian policymakers. Whether Southeast Asia can seize on this strategic ambiguity to advance its own interests, however, depends in large part on the ability of regional states to share a common agenda and outlook. It is for these reasons that indigenous attempts to manage regional order, and how the role of the United States either reinforces or undermines this, warrant closer scrutiny.

Indigenous attempts at regional order management toward the ends of mitigating the adverse effects of the present state of strategic flux, all while maintaining a degree of regional autonomy, are registered in the concept of ASEAN Centrality. In brief, the concept of ASEAN Centrality captures the self-assumed obligation of the organization to play a leading role—to be the "primary driving force" or, as is often said in the context of the ASEAN Regional Forum (ARF), in the "driver's seat"—in influencing (not so much dictating) events and policy outcomes in the region, albeit in a multilateral framework that includes external powers.[50] ASEAN Centrality thence is the region's attempt to manage the changing distribution of power and regional balance so as to create strategic latitude and autonomy while minimizing the prospects of the region being overwhelmed by great power politics. Centrality has come to be expressed in ASEAN's convening capacity evident in its creation and hosting of a raft of regional processes, such as ARF, EAS, and the ASEAN Defense Ministers' Meeting (ADMM) Plus. Significant in these respects is ASEAN's ability to extend its institutional and diplomatic model to encompass issues and actors from the wider Asia Pacific region. Centrality also takes the form of agenda setting and chairing (or cochairing) of these processes and the acceptance of the organization's Treaty of Amity and Cooperation, where current signatories include all the major regional powers, as the foundational premise for the regional security architecture.

It is significant that this role that ASEAN assumes has been acknowledged in Washington. This was evident from comments then secretary of state Hillary Clinton made in Hawaii in October 2010, endorsing ASEAN's centrality and describing the organization as "the fulcrum of an evolving regional architecture."[51] This view was later reiterated during the landmark Sunnylands Summit in February 2016, where Article 5 of the Sunnylands Declaration specified the signatories' "respect and support for ASEAN Centrality and ASEAN-led mechanisms in the evolving regional architecture of the Asia-Pacific."

CONCEIVING WEAKNESS AS STRENGTH

As a prescription for regional order, ASEAN Centrality rests on what is in essence a conceptual anomaly, where the locus of initiative centers on weak states rather than regional powers. In other words, centrality is counterintuitively articulated on the basis of a recognition of weakness rather than strength. Why would major powers agree to play by ASEAN's rules since it defies a fundamental logic of international politics? To major powers, the appeal of the notion of centrality has been tolerated because it articulates the premise for the provision of a neutral platform for them to engage each other on regional issues. In this sense, Southeast Asia's diplomatic centrality reflects the imperative of "reactionary activism," an attempt to manage rather than transcend exogenous great power dynamics.[52] A former senior Singaporean diplomat offers the following insight into the crux of the matter: "it is precisely because ASEAN is, more often than not, unable to influence events that major powers have for their own purposes found it useful to work with rather than against ASEAN-established platforms. ASEAN is 'central' because it can occasionally be useful to major powers but has been essentially powerless when their most vital interests are engaged and so cannot foil their most important designs."[53] Put differently, in contradistinction to ZOPFAN, the acknowledgment of the role of major powers is a prerequisite—in fact, an essential condition—for ASEAN to make good its "centrality."

The resolution of the Cambodian conflict is instructive in what it demonstrated of the possibilities and limitations of ASEAN's role in managing regional affairs. The Vietnamese invasion of Cambodia in 1978 created a defining challenge for the then nascent organization and its evolving practice of regional diplomacy. By dint of regional resolve and a collective fear of communism spreading south via the domino effect, ASEAN managed to overcome the challenges confronting intraorganizational diplomacy and served to play a consequential role throughout the course of the 1980s by challenging the legitimacy of the Vietnamese invasion of Cambodia and subsequent installation in Phnom Penh of a compliant government that genuflected in the direction of Hanoi. The Cambodian conflict was eventually resolved following the end of the Cold War through the intervention of the permanent members of the United Nations Security Council. Although the resolution process quickly passed into ASEAN lore as an example par excellence of its diplomatic success, it also exposed the limitations of presumptive regional efforts to manage affairs in their backyard as ASEAN was shunted aside by the proclivities of major power politics in the process of final resolution of the conflict.

The above observations are crucial to understanding the relationship between ASEAN-centered regionalism and Southeast Asian anxieties regarding the role of the United States in the region. If ASEAN aspirations to shape regional order extend to managing major power activity, then its relevance hinges precisely on major power assent. Therein lies the rub: for even as the states of Southeast Asia entertain such aspirations, they are exposed—individually and collectively—to coercion, fragmentation, and, possibly, marginalization by the major powers.[54] More to the point, if a major power behaves in a manner or pursues a course of action in contradiction to ASEAN's interests, there is little recourse for the organization. In fact, it is precisely given these limitations to Southeast Asian regionalism that the constructive presence and participation of the United States are viewed as imperative even as regional states continue to stress ASEAN's "centrality" in the management of regional order. By this logic, because regional order is at stake, any indication of disinterest or distraction on the part of the United States cannot but cause anxiety to the region.

An additional point needs to be registered with regards to the practice of ASEAN's diplomatic centrality. The effort to accent centrality ultimately turns on the ability of members of the organization to at least speak with one voice even if they cannot think with one mind. Concomitantly, ASEAN is often at risk of being frustrated by the challenges of forging and maintaining unity of purpose and perspectives within the organization itself. Notwithstanding laudable advances in community building, relations between regional states continue to suffer from a residual climate of suspicion and, periodically, also visible differences and hostility between neighbors, all of which call into question the efficacy of ASEAN diplomacy. At issue is the ability of diverse Southeast Asian states to maintain a united approach to the promotion of regional stability. This unity is dependent on the strength of shared interests as well as the normative "glue" that holds the grouping together. Conversely, perverse norms and competing interests could imperil ASEAN by setting member states at odds with each other and pulling them in separate directions, thereby disabling the organization from playing its role in the "driver's seat" of regionalism. More to the point, this illustrates the risk that ASEAN states could "turn inward" or "strategically disengage" from each other during times of crisis. During the Asian financial crisis, for example, it was observed with some accuracy that ASEAN states' "first instincts were to turn inward and away from regional responses."[55] Not only did ASEAN states fail to coordinate a coherent joint response, they allowed the crisis to exacerbate underlying bilateral tensions between them. Indeed, some have begun to discern familiar dynamics that have beset ASEAN in recent days, as it is confronted by growing Chinese assertiveness.

A further indicator is the tendency toward divergent outlooks and threat perceptions during crisis moments. This had been one of the problems that ASEAN had to surmount following Vietnam's invasion of Cambodia in December 1978. Indonesia and Malaysia saw China, which launched a punitive action against Vietnam in early 1979, as a greater threat to regional security while Thailand and Singapore perceived Vietnamese aggression to be the more urgent threat. Although these differences were eventually reconciled, the example serves as a reminder that the notion of a monolithic ASEAN with shared security outlooks and threat perceptions is a chimera. If anything, this challenge of forging and maintaining coherence of purpose and outlook has intensified with the expansion of the organization in the 1990s.

Indeed, to focus on regional anxieties is hardly to suggest a uniformity of thought or outlook irrespective of the state in question or the given circumstances. While Southeast Asian states share a general belief in the virtues of American involvement in the region, there remain discernible differences among them in terms of views as to how the United States is and should be playing this role. Whereas states such as the Philippines (domestic politics notwithstanding) and Singapore have been supporters of a strong U.S. presence, others, such as Indonesia, which has preferred a more diversified approach that hews closer to its stress on autonomy and a "free and active" foreign policy, have been more ambivalent, mindful to be construed as acting not in America's interest but in their own. Another case in point is Thailand, at least under the current junta government, which seeks a deeper engagement with China even as the ostracized coup government casts a longing eye toward "old friends" in Washington; or Cambodia, which was subjected to an intense bombing campaign during the height of the Vietnam War yet, as Washington reminds them, remains indebted to the United States today to the tune of more than $400 million for credit extended to the government of Lon Nol in the 1970s.[56] In short, regional anxieties about American commitment can also be educed from deeper introspective anxieties of Southeast Asian states toward each other, toward the United States, and toward the realistic prospects of managing regional order under circumstances of strategic uncertainty.

The chapters that follow aim to develop these themes in the course of analysis of the U.S. role in the region and Southeast Asian responses since the end of the Cold War.

CHAPTER THREE

Engagement and Estrangement

THE COLLAPSE OF THE SOVIET Union in 1991 under the weight of decades of strategic competition with the United States marked the end of the Cold War. It also ushered in a season of exuberance, perhaps even triumphalism, for the Western world and the principles of liberal democracy and capitalism it championed. In academia, this outlook was arguably most profoundly epitomized in the concept of "the end of history" popularized by the neoconservative scholar Francis Fukuyama and, ironically, drawn from Marx and also Hegel. The central premise of Fukuyama's "the end of history" thesis was not only that the defeat of communism was inevitable but that Western principles of democracy, liberalism, and individual rights and freedoms were the pinnacle of political evolution. In many ways, this outlook began also to inform American foreign policy following the denouement of the Cold War strategic rivalry and the beginning of the U.S. consolidation of global power and its capitalist model that served as the template for the international order.

Although the advent of the so-called post–Cold War era coincided with the twilight of the Republican administration of George H. W. Bush, it was during the Democratic administration of Bill Clinton, sworn into office in early 1993, that the crafting of foreign policies predicated on the use of American preponderance of power to build a global order compatible with, if not shaped by, the values enumerated above began in earnest. To be sure, this agenda was hardly novel or unique. All previous administrations sought similarly to use American power in some way, shape, or form to lead the world and shape its institutions. What made the Clinton administration stand out was the fact that it would be doing so from a position of unparalleled strength. American predominance at the end of the Cold War was described vividly by Stephen Walt in the following manner:

> The end of the Cold War has left the United States in a position of unprecedented preponderance. America's economy is 40 percent larger than that of its nearest rival, and its defense spending equals that of the next six countries combined. Four of these six countries are close U.S. allies, so America's advantage is even larger than these figures suggest. The United States leads the world in higher education, scientific research, and advanced technology (especially information technologies), which will make it hard for other states to catch up quickly. This extraordinary position of power will endure well into this century.[1]

Significantly, this "unipolar moment" also afforded the United States the luxury of stepping back from a strategic perspective that guided foreign and security policy during the Cold War, into a frame of mind that was more tactical and opportunistic even as the United States sought to rationalize its position as the sole, albeit somewhat reluctant, global power.

During the first Clinton term, one of the administration's early foreign policy objectives found expression in a global "strategy of enlargement" that involved enlarging the number of democracies, expanding the number of market economies, supporting liberalization in states hostile to democracy, and pursuing a humanitarian agenda of providing aid precisely in order to nurture this spread of democracies and market economies. Of note is the fact that these foreign policy objectives dovetailed with the president's domestic agenda of economic revival, on which platform he campaigned and won election. Indeed, although a litany of international challenges—the explosion of conflict in Rwanda and the former Yugoslavia; crisis in the Middle East—soon conspired to compel a jolt of political realism, for the most part this values-based agenda continued to influence the thinking and conduct of American foreign policy for much of Bill Clinton's presidency.[2]

In the course of his presidential election campaign, Bill Clinton sought to distance himself from his predecessor by emphasizing the need to pay greater attention to the domestic economy and cooperative security in its effort to petition various domestic and international constituencies. What eventually materialized was an "uneasy amalgam of selective engagement, cooperative security, and primacy" as captured in the Clinton administration's blueprint for the post–Cold War world, *A National Security Strategy for Engagement and Enlargement*. The concept of engagement, alluded to above and as envisaged in the *National Security Strategy*, was seen as vital to the shaping of a domestic consensus on the international role of the United States. As the national strategy document observed: "clear distinctions between threats to our nation's security from beyond our borders and the challenges to our security from within our borders are being blurred; . . . the separation between international problems and domestic ones is evaporating; and . . . the line between domestic and foreign policy is eroding." Guaranteeing domestic prosperity and national security was thus considered inseparable from a strategy of ongoing international engagement. Moreover, given growing acceptance of the adage that democracies do not fight each other, it followed that the enlargement of the number of democracies was an important—and natural—objective for the strengthening of U.S. as well as international security. In sum, engagement and enlargement served as the twin pillars of the Clinton doctrine, which was to be accomplished through "(1) our efforts to enhance our security by maintaining a strong defense capability and employing effective diplomacy to promote cooperative security measures; (2) our work to open foreign markets and spur global economic growth; and (3) our promotion of democracy abroad."[3]

Because democracy promotion obtained as a means to a strategic end, it followed that the Clinton administration sought to incorporate it into foreign policy formulation, framing it as a means through which national security and economic objectives could be achieved.[4] The aims of democracy promotion and democratic enlargement, as described by National Security Advisor Anthony Lake, were "strengthening the community of major market democracies, fostering and consolidating new democracies and market economies, countering backlash states and helping market democracy take root in regions of humanitarian concern."[5] At the heart of this outlook and approach was the unwavering belief, held in the White House, that it was in the national interest of the United States to promote its liberal internationalist values abroad. Their goal to enlarge the domain of free markets and liberal democracy for the furtherance of American security and wealth echoed their faith in the "unity of goodness" and the "utilitarian value of democracy" and what mind-sets in the Clinton administration believed to be the inexorable link between international economic policy and the spread of market democracies. As President Clinton himself put it categorically, "our overriding purpose must be to expand and strengthen the world's community of market-based democracies."[6]

Hewing closely to the agenda of democracy promotion was the issue of human rights, where the enthusiasm of the White House was not only matched but surpassed by Congress. As a former Defense Department official conceded when she lamented the difficulties of dealing with a Congress fixated on human rights issues in Southeast Asia: "There are a lot of people on the Hill who have spent their entire careers looking at human rights issues in Southeast Asia and they know how to jam language into legislation. More importantly, there is no countervailing lobby to check them."[7] For the Clinton administration, the virtues of a values-based foreign policy were underscored by Warren Christopher: "Securing and expanding the community of democratic nations and respect for human rights are consistent with American ideals and advance our interests. Democratic nations are far less likely to go to war with each other and far more likely to respect international law. They are more likely to promote open markets and free trade, and to pursue policies that lead to sustained economic development."[8] Of course, the reality was discernibly different from the tagline. Although these lofty principles of American values-based democracy were undoubtedly declared with even greater purpose especially during President Clinton's first term, their implementation was, at best, inconsistent, with the most glaring anomaly being Washington's continued support of dictatorships in the Middle East even as it doubled down on criticism of and restrictions on Suharto's Indonesia.

The Clinton administration's demonstrative penchant to emphasize American political values of human rights and democracy, elevating them to the status of universal values for global governance, brought its relations with Southeast Asia into sharper focus. In essence, it became an impediment to efforts to engage with and reassure Southeast Asian states not given to sharing these values, at least not in the manner that was articulated and expressed in American policy. This concern was encapsulated in the following remarks by Goh Chok Tong, former prime minister of Singapore:

> With the end of the Cold War, however, the national priorities of the U.S. and its allies have changed. It seems that greater attention is now accorded to domestic interests. Demands and pressures of

domestic lobbies and specific interest groups are growing. Human rights, the environment and humanitarian interests are now active players in the U.S. foreign policy process. These have complicated U.S. relations with some countries in Asia, and distracted the U.S. from its longer-term strategic interests in engaging Asia. Politics in an election year will confound and obscure these interests even more.[9]

How the values-based stress on democracy bedeviled relations with Thailand, America's oldest ally in the region, was instructive in this regard.

Thailand is a long-standing U.S. treaty ally. Throughout the Cold War, it was an unwavering supporter of a U.S. presence in the region and, on that score, readily offered access to logistical port and airfield facilities during the Vietnam War. Since 1982, Thailand has been hosting Cobra Gold, a large-scale U.S.–Thailand military exercise that over the years has expanded to include several other regional states as well. In return for this staunch support, Thailand had been a recipient of U.S. military technology, essential supplies, training, and assistance for the construction and improvement of facilities and installations. The relationship, however, came under some strain after the end of the Vietnam War, when Thailand took the decision to limit American access to military facilities following the unilateral U.S. move to respond to the seizing of the American merchant vessel SS *Mayaguez* by the navy of the Khmer Rouge by using the Utapao airbase to launch operations without consulting Bangkok.[10]

Although it should be acknowledged that the Clinton administration did work to reinforce and expand the bilateral relationship by cooperating with Thailand on military exercises and in combating other transnational nontraditional security threats, bilateral differences emerged over several additional issues that threatened to imperil relations. Two stood out in this regard. First, the bilateral defense relationship was tested by legislatively mandated reactions to military coups against elected governments—an all-too-frequent development in Thai politics. Yet for Thailand, this was perceived to be a failure of the U.S. to honor their historical alliance relationship.[11] In 1992, in the face of the Thai military's violent reaction to peaceful protests, the United States suspended Cobra Gold exercises. Thereafter, U.S. law proceeded to legislate the cessation of economic and security assistance in response to extraconstitutional acts against duly elected governments. This was followed by a series of congressional challenges to Thailand's record regarding human trafficking, human rights abuses, and support for democracy, which further dampened Thai enthusiasm for the bilateral relationship. Another provision, this time on the U.S. International Military Education and Training (IMET) program under which about 100 Thai soldiers go to the United States for training each year, required the State Department to report on "the extent of Thai Government efforts to impede support for Burmese democracy advocates, exiles, and refugees." Although the amount received by Thailand under IMET was small, onerous congressional requirements nevertheless hurt Thai pride. Correspondingly, Thai politicians reacted angrily and the parliamentary budget committee talked of retaliation against "American imperialism" by stopping financial contributions to the joint panel on Thai–U.S. military cooperation, although the threat was never carried out.[12]

The second obstacle took the form of the Kampuchean issue. Although the issue itself was moving to a definitive solution by 1992–93, Thailand still found itself accused in the corridors of power in Washington for its alleged covert support for the swiftly diminishing Khmer Rouge in Cambodia. Indeed, despite the fact that by the 1993 elections in Cambodia the Khmer Rouge had essentially atrophied into irrelevance, these allegations were nonetheless followed by congressional threats to cut off military assistance to Thailand if the latter persisted in black market trading with the Khmer Rouge at a rate and volume that, according to U.S. legislation, provided the money the latter required to buy arms on the open market, thereby setting them at odds with United Nations efforts to disarm competing Cambodian factions.[13] In September 1994, Congress passed a Foreign Operations Bill, which legislated for the secretary of state to report to Congress (by February 1, 1995) on the state of Thai military support for the Khmer Rouge and also the degree of the Bangkok government's support (or lack thereof) for Burmese democracy advocates, exiles, and refugees.[14] This legislation, calling for a freeze on military assistance to Thailand if it was proven that the Thai military had persisted in its support for the Khmer Rouge, was signed into law by President Clinton on August 21 that year.[15]

SHIPS PASSING IN THE NIGHT

On the question of human rights advocacy in U.S. foreign policy, it should be noted that its salience to relations with Southeast Asia was not due to it being a new item on the engagement agenda, which in any event was never the case. At issue, rather, was the zealous, vocal, and persistent manner in which the Clinton administration pressed its cause. Indeed, it was this, more so than the issue itself, that became an irritant in relations between the United States and several Southeast Asian counterparts and fed a growing perception that Washington was prepared to compromise the imperative of long-term strategic engagement for a values-based, normative agenda that set it at odds with many regional partners.

The administration's formulaic approach to the issue found expression in the persistent linking of human rights to foreign aid, belaboring cases of human rights abuse and openly criticizing governments for such acts, spreading the message of human rights through radio broadcasts across Asia, and supporting nongovernmental organizations that advocated for political change through the provision of funding and public platforms. Not surprisingly, this led the United States and several Southeast Asian governments, including long-standing strategic partners, to cross swords on a range of issues, from labor rights in Malaysia and Indonesia to the issue of East Timor (whose annexation in 1976 by Indonesia the United States had tacitly supported) to the caning of an American youth convicted in the court of law for vandalism in Singapore.

Not only were American and (some) Southeast Asian views and positions on human rights athwart each other, they also took on a sharp ideological edge. A highly publicized debate emerged over the matter of "Asian values" as being distinct from "Western values." The chief advocates of "Asian values" were members of the Singapore political and policy elite, who promulgated the notion in response to the U.S. stance on the universality of human rights. They found a curious ally in the imperious Malaysian prime minister Mahathir Mohamad, who on just about everything else was at odds with his Singaporean counterparts. In response to regional calls for deeper American appreciation of and, where necessary, adjustment to the worldviews of their regional counterparts, Assistant Secretary of State for East Asia Winston Lord gave no quarter, retorting that "each country must find its own way, given its history and economic situation, and its culture; but we believe that there are some universal principles, and we believe . . . open societies are in countries' self-interest for development as well as for security."[16]

At this point, it is important to stress that the zeal with which the Clinton administration pursued its human rights and democratization agenda contrasted somewhat sharply with its cautionary approach on security matters. Indeed, at the same time that the United States was espousing a more deliberately values-based foreign policy (in word, if not always in deed), it was wary of making extensive security commitments in Southeast Asia. It is noteworthy to consider how much this reticence was informed by the experience of the Vietnam War, which at the time continued to weigh on discussions regarding the deployment of U.S. forces in far-flung regions. Clinton himself referred to the "Vietnam syndrome" periodically during his campaign. Madeleine Albright, UN ambassador during the first Clinton term and secretary of state during the second, described Vietnam as "a searing experience for that generation of decision makers."[17] Samuel "Sandy" Berger, national security adviser in the second Clinton administration, conceded that Vietnam—the "quagmire vision"—was "very much in all our minds." Berger further stressed: "Every time the president deployed force, it was a very difficult decision for him. I think this is probably a legacy of Vietnam. I mean I think he had an acute sense that he was sending young American men and women to die."[18]

In the case of Southeast Asia, however, there was at least one exception to this general aversion. During the first Clinton term, the United States had expressed a desire to station a U.S. navy depot flotilla in the Gulf of Thailand, which "would have augmented the pre-positioned equipment aboard ship at Diego Garcia and Guam. The proposed new offshore logistics basing in SEA [Southeast Asia] would have the capacity to sustain a heavy brigade for 15 days, contributing to flexibility of U.S. force deployment in crises."[19] However, political leaders in the region did not welcome the prospect of a permanent U.S. security presence in the region, especially one that would take the form of a military base, as it went against the region's declarative aversion to such arrangements. In September 1994, Clinton made a personal request to the Thai prime minister, Chuan Leekpai, but was rebuffed on grounds that such an arrangement would strain both Thai and American relations with the rest of the region.

Because of this reluctance to make excessive commitments on the security front, the United States was especially careful not to be drawn into potential regional entanglements as well. Something of this logic could be discerned in how the United States approached an issue that at the time had barely begun to hint at its potential to undermine regional stability and security—territorial disputes in the South China Sea against the backdrop of a strengthening China, at which other regional claimants were casting a wary eye.

The South China Sea comprises some 648,000 square miles and is bounded by China, Vietnam, the Philippines, Indonesia, Malaysia, and Brunei. The South China Sea provides important maritime communication routes between the Indian and Pacific oceans, most notably for energy supply from the Gulf of Arabia to Japan's home islands. It also provides rich fishing grounds crucial to the dietary needs of many coastal communities in all the claimant states and many nonclaimant states as well that are in close proximity to the area. Within the South China Sea, there are several main island groups, none of which is the natural geographic extension of any coastal state's continental shelf. These groups have in different ways become the object of serious contention between coastal states. China is in control of the northerly Paracel Islands, which are contested by Vietnam and Taiwan. (At issue between China and Taiwan is the question of governmental legitimacy, not sovereignty over specific territories. Control of the northerly Pratas Islands by Taiwan is challenged only by China as part of its general challenge to the government in Taipei.) The Macclesfield Bank is permanently submerged and the issue of control has not yet arisen. Greatest contention arises over the Spratly Islands comprising many reefs, shoals, and sandbanks, which spread out from the very center of the sea. Jurisdiction is contested between China, Taiwan, Vietnam, Malaysia, and the Philippines, with Brunei concerned only with maritime space arising from its continental shelf. The main attraction is the prospect of discovering and exploiting extensive reserves of oil and natural gas and fishing waters, although strategic considerations also influence the claimant governments, especially China, which is mindful of American surveillance being conducted under the rubric of freedom of navigation and, more generally, of the imperative of power projection in what Beijing considers its own backyard.

The disputes have fairly long antecedents in the contemporary era. In 1973, the government of South Vietnam awarded eight exploration contracts to areas of the South China Sea to major multinationals. This move was followed by the stationing of troops in five of the Paracel Islands in order to reinforce South Vietnam's declaration of the area to be within its administrative purview. Already in control of the Amphitrite Group of islands known as the Eastern Paracels, China responded to South Vietnam's unitary assertion of control over the Western Paracels with a limited military action over a period of three days, beginning with clashes over Duncan Island on January 17, 1974, which resulted in China wresting control of the Crescent Group from South Vietnam.[20] Notwithstanding the fact that the People's Liberation Army (PLA) navy was hardly a major military force at the time, with the help of assets from the PLA air force stationed in Hainan Island the victory over the South Vietnamese still proved effortless. For South Vietnam, one navy ship was sunk and another three forced to retreat. The decisive manner of the defeat was in part also a result of the absence of any American support for its South Vietnamese allies save for assistance toward the evacuation of Vietnamese civilians and military personnel from the islands.[21] Subsequent attempts by the Vietnamese military to retake the islands, in 1979 as well as in 1982, failed. In March 1988, Vietnam and China clashed again in the South China Sea, this time in the Spratly Islands. The result of these clashes was the establishment of Chinese control in six islands in that area. In 1995, Chinese forces occupied Mischief Reef, some 135 miles to the west of the Philippine island of Palawan.

In July 1992, the foreign ministers of ASEAN issued a Declaration on the South China Sea, which called on contending claimants to resolve issues of sovereignty without resort to the use of force. In hindsight, however, the declaration did little to arrest rising tensions and in fact was emblematic of the struggles that ASEAN faced—and would continue to face—in dealing with the assertion of competing claims in what is the geographical heart of Southeast Asia. It is under such infelicitous circumstances that the role of the United States warrants scrutiny.

The United States first articulated a formal position on the South China Sea dispute in a policy statement released in May 1995, in the aftermath of the Mischief Reef incident. Issued by the state department, this position was encapsulated in the following five points:

1. Peaceful Resolution of Disputes: "The United States strongly opposes the use or threat of force to resolve competing claims and urges all claimants to exercise restraint to avoid destabilizing actions."
2. Peace and Stability: "The United States has an abiding interest in the maintenance of peace and stability in the South China Sea."
3. Freedom of Navigation: "Maintaining freedom of navigation is a fundamental interest of the United States. Unhindered navigation by all ships and aircraft in the South China Sea is essential for the

peace and prosperity of the entire Asia-Pacific region, including the United States."

4. Neutrality in Disputes: "The United States takes no position on the legal merits of the competing claims to sovereignty over the various islands, reefs, atolls, and cays in the South China Sea."

5. Respect for International Principles: "The United States would, however, view with serious concern any maritime claim or restriction on maritime activity in the South China Sea that was not consistent with international law, including the 1982 United Nations Convention on the Law of the Sea."[22]

Beneath the details contained in the statement was a clear message that the United States was reluctant to be drawn into the South China Sea imbroglio. Rather, its interest lay primarily in "preventing a degeneration of events into any general, sustained conflict which would disrupt regional stability, trade, and access."[23] Even under those circumstances, the act of "preventing a degeneration of events" would not assume the form of intervention of any sort. It bears noting that the noncommittal tone of American policy on the South China Sea would eventually take on different shades with the more muscular expression of American interests in the area under the presidency of Barack Obama. But in the 1990s, American disinclination toward any involvement was the order of the day. And indeed, it was this disinclination that at least in part prompted Southeast Asian states to develop regional multilateral mechanisms as a means not only to attempt management of potential security challenges, such as the South China Sea, but also to ensure that the United States did not disengage entirely. Over time, these multilateral mechanisms would come to express the strategic alignments among the United States, China, and Southeast Asia.[24]

EMBRACING MULTILATERALISM: CAUTIOUS STEPS

The U.S. security umbrella in East Asia during the Cold War was predicated on a series of bilateral alliances, all of which remain in place today (with Japan, South Korea, the Philippines, and Thailand). These alliance agreements provided bases in the region in exchange for American deterrence and, where necessary, commitment of forces, as well as access to U.S. markets. With the possible exception of the Southeast Asia Treaty Organization (SEATO), which in any case was never invoked for reasons of the elusiveness of consensus, what was absent from the Cold War regional security architecture was any semblance of a multilateral framework that linked the United States to its allies in a collective fashion, or indeed the allies with each other.

The end of the Cold War prompted a reassessment of the American force posture in East Asia. This reassessment found expression as the East Asian Strategy Initiative (EASI), conceived by the Department of Defense. EASI envisaged a gradual reduction of forward-deployed support personnel commensurate with reductions in the Defense Department budget, but without compromising the necessary ground, air, and naval capabilities required to reassure regional friends and partners.[25] Aside from budgetary pressures, reduction was also guided by two other imperatives: burden sharing, where regional partners were expected to contribute to the provision of the public good of security, which hitherto had been provided by the United States for their benefit; and the absence of a plausible and immediate threat, which rendered more difficult the task of the executive branch and foreign policy establishment of convincing Congress to maintain a substantial defense budget especially following the demise of the Soviet Union.[26]

Given the circumstances, as the Clinton administration sought to recalibrate U.S. alliances and conceptualize a broader security strategy in the region accordingly, an opportunity presented itself for the United States to supplement its forward military presence anchored on the existing alliance structure with an exploration of multilateral approaches to regional security. This view was registered by Assistant Secretary of State for East Asia and Pacific Affairs Winston Lord in 1993, when he identified "a commitment to enhanced multilateral security dialogue" as one of the incoming Clinton administration's priority policy goals for Asia.[27] Beneath this was a realization that the establishment of East Asian regional groups being explored at the time would progress with or without American involvement and also that American participation in such initiatives would serve the purpose of legitimizing American interests in the region in a low cost fashion and signaling the Pacific identity of the United States.[28]

Significantly, American reception to the idea of multilateralism also dovetailed with a new narrative on regional security that was emerging within the diplomatic circles of an ASEAN increasingly anxious that major powers were beginning to lose interest in the region. It bears noting that the inclusion of the United States in any new multilateral initiative was considered a priority among the ASEAN states. Given uncertainties surrounding China's growing assertiveness and the prospects that Japan would rearm in reaction, the United States was viewed in ASEAN as the crucial stabilizer in the Asia Pacific distribution of power. In January 1992, the heads of government of ASEAN, convening in Singapore for the ASEAN Summit, agreed that it was time to place security dialogue formally on the ASEAN agenda; such dialogue could be undertaken through the vehicle of the Association's Post-Ministerial Conference. This conference, which convened immediately after the annual meeting of foreign ministers, involved ASEAN's major dialogue partners, which at that time were Australia, Canada, the European Union, Japan, New Zealand, South Korea, and the United States.

At Singapore's initiative and with backing from its neighbors, an unprecedented meeting of senior officials from ASEAN states and their dialogue partners was convened in May 1993. They agreed to invite the foreign ministers of China, Russia, Vietnam, Laos, and Papua New Guinea to a special meeting in Singapore in July 1993 concurrent with the scheduled meetings that involved ASEAN foreign ministers and their dialogue partners. The declared purpose was "for ASEAN and its dialogue partners to work with other regional states to evolve a predictable and constructive pattern of relationships in Asia-Pacific." Thus was birthed the idea of a bespoke platform to explicitly discuss security matters, a practice hitherto anathema to the ASEAN process. This platform would find institutional expression as the ASEAN Regional Forum, which formally convened for the first time in Bangkok in July 1994. A primary, if unspoken, objective of ARF was to encourage and facilitate the continuation of an American commitment to regional order and security in the post–Cold War era and the international good citizenship of a rising China, whose behavior by then was already beginning to hint at some elements of irredentist ambition in the South China Sea. At issue, too, for Southeast Asia were misgivings that the region risked being marginalized on regional security issues, given that the geostrategic center of gravity was located in Northeast Asia, where the two major regional powers, China and Japan, were located and where the United States had concentrated its forward-deployed forces. Likewise, ASEAN was wary not to allow the emergence of a concert of powers where major regional players would come to dictate regional affairs and make decisions on regional issues at the expense of the interests of Southeast Asian states. To address these concerns, ARF would serve as a multilateral platform to ensure the centrality of ASEAN in the regional security architecture. This centrality would be expressed as ASEAN's self-assumed obligation of regional order management in setting and shaping the agenda for ARF.

For its part, the promotion of institution building and multilateral cooperation in the Asia Pacific region was a central element of Clinton's neo-Wilsonian "Engagement and Enlargement" strategy alluded to earlier, especially during his first term. Crucially though, this was not intended to be pursued at the expense of American primacy and leadership.[29] On the contrary, the case can be made that the Clinton administration in fact viewed endorsement of ASEAN-type cooperation as a means of reinforcing American primacy, albeit within the less clear-cut structure of post–Cold War international affairs in the Asia Pacific, as well as a strategy of diversifying and delegating financial and political responsibilities. In this respect, American support for ARF was considered in Washington circles to be a low-cost, low-stakes policy that supplemented— not supplanted—the existing "hubs and spokes" bilateral security arrangements on which the U.S. presence was predicated.[30] To accent this point, even as it embraced ARF and multilateralism in general, the United States consistently reiterated its determination to maintain a significant military presence in the region, albeit concentrated in Northeast Asia, to play the role of regional stabilizer. This was made clear by Secretary of Defense William Cohen during a high-profile trip to East Asia, including Southeast Asia, in April 1997.[31]

Washington's commitment to multilateralism in the security sphere through active participation in ARF was balanced by its endorsement of multilateralism in the economic sphere predicated on its leadership of and participation in the Asia-Pacific Economic Cooperation (APEC). Unlike ARF, however, American interests in APEC had their roots in domestic politics. Running a presidential election campaign that stressed economic rebound, the Clinton presidency sought to advance globalization and trade liberalization, convinced that economic growth and interdependence would help reduce chances of military conflict abroad and reverse economic slowdown at home. East Asia, with its rapid economic growth rates enhancing its strategic importance, loomed large in this picture. The Clinton administration's interests in East Asia's economic strength led the United States to give considerable emphasis to boosting the APEC forum as a mechanism that would tie the United States to Asia as Washington sought to advance the goal of trade liberalization.[32]

President Clinton's desire to emphasize geoeconomics prompted his move to change the character of APEC in July 1993, when he hosted a meeting of APEC's political leaders following a scheduled ministerial meeting in Seattle in November of the previous year. His grandiose scheme to use APEC as the prime vehicle for creating a so-called New Pacific Community was greeted with caution by some ASEAN governments, with Malaysian prime minister Mahathir Mohamad taking particular offense and boycotting the meeting.[33] In the event, the summit transpired without incident but failed to rise above declaratory commitments on trade liberalization. Be that as it may, it did mark a qualitative change in the structure and intended role of APEC by dint of the White House's initiation of an annual pattern of summits. In other words, at a stroke, Clinton's upgrading of APEC transformed it into the most important regional diplomatic platform of the day as far as the matter of the level of representation was concerned, although the inclusion of Taiwan necessitated the casting of the organization as a gathering of economies rather than of governments.

The Clinton administration's resounding demonstration of support for APEC in July 1993 set in motion a series of events that resulted in the Bogor Declaration in 1994 to achieve free and open trade by 2010 for developed members and 2020 for developing member economies. By 1995, the roadmap for APEC, including more detailed principles and technical areas for cooperation known as Individual Action Plans and Collective Action Plans, was outlined in the Osaka Action Agenda, a blueprint for achieving the Bogor targets. However, a major dent in its credibility as the Asia Pacific's premier economic institution was made during the Asian financial crisis when APEC was found wanting. Today APEC operates in a completely new global climate with different sociopolitical and economic conditions and the expectations remain high even though outcomes have, in hindsight, been underwhelming. The emergence of newer institutions like the ASEAN Plus Three (a process of which the United States is not a member) and the East Asia Summit, with their own multilateral economic agenda, and a proliferation of free trade agreements have contrived to dilute the role of APEC even further. Regardless, with its interest and participation in APEC and ARF, it was evident that the United States was beginning to see how regional multilateral organizations served as useful vehicles for promoting greater political and economic cooperation, enhancing regional security, and supporting U.S. interests.

In supporting APEC and ARF, the Clinton administration had departed from its predecessor's suspicions of multilateralism, which it feared would weaken the bilateral alliance structure on which American presence and primacy in the region was established. Instead, the Clinton administration embraced a form of "assertive multilateralism" by encouraging Asia to adopt the Helsinki model of consultation and confidence building.[34] Needless to say, this was a step too far for regional states that did not quite share American enthusiasm to set the pace for multilateralism and that instead took the position that multilateralism in Asia would evolve not in a path-dependent manner drawing from the European experience but in a manner consonant with the region's own histories and dynamics.

Not surprisingly, the lukewarm response from the region toward Washington's brand of "assertive multilateralism" eventually redounded to dampen American enthusiasm. After the initial burst of multilateral activity spearheaded by Assistant Secretary of State Winston Lord during the first Clinton term, the second Clinton term saw the United States pay decidedly less attention to multilateral engagement. A former official, Susan Shirk, offers the following view into the de-prioritization of multilateralism in the minds of American decisionmakers:

> As I saw for myself when I served in government, the State Department treated participation in multilateral meetings as a lower priority than bilateral meetings. The Secretary of State was sometimes absent from the ARF annual meeting, which is an important ritual of regional ML [multilaterals]. High level inter-agency meetings by principals or deputies almost never discuss regional multilateral forums, and government funding of multilateral activities is minimal. East Asians have been very actively engaged in developing the multilateral architecture of the region but the U.S. largely marginalised itself from the process.[35]

At issue was Washington's frustration at the region's tendency to prioritize form over substance in regionalism, resulting in slow and cumbersome collective decisionmaking and meetings from which American delegations emerged without, to their mind, any significant achievements to speak of. Indeed, this would be a constant, if at times muted, theme in U.S. perspectives on multilateral initiatives originating from within the region for many years to come.

Given the circumstances, American strategy remained anchored on bilateral alliances and other U.S.-led security arrangements, whose operations Washington could control at closer quarters to ensure they were complemented and not impeded by its experimentation with multilateralism in the region. Although multilateral initiatives did manage to secure some concrete policy outcomes—the freezing of North Korea's Yongbyon plutonium facility in 1994 being a case in point—for the most part it was bilateral channels through which the United States preferred to tackle regional problems that arose.[36] For the Clinton administration, it was the case that the range of issues it confronted in the wider East Asian region, from the emergence of a North Korean nuclear threat and the growth of China's strategic capabilities to uncertainties over the region's emerging balance of power, lent themselves to the logic of existing U.S. bilateral security alliances.

Having said that, it is also noteworthy that this structure of alliances itself gradually shifted away from traditional "hubs-and-spokes" hierarchical arrangements based on asymmetrical U.S. power to "web networks," where the underlying logic was grounded on a strategy of "places not bases," which focused on the pre-positioning of supplies and equipment and access to military facilities, rather than maintaining a large, embedded military presence in the region, and, significantly, on burden sharing by regional partners.[37] This final point, however, has introduced a further element of uncertainty and ambiguity to Southeast Asia's relations with the United States. The ability of regional states to share the burden, as it were, relies on their possession of defense capabilities that are sufficiently modernized and professional. Therein lies the paradox that circles the question back again to the United States and what it desires of its regional partners. Given that American training, aid, and equipment has been crucial, if not indispensable, to the modernization and professionalization of regional armed forces, the objective of burden sharing ultimately hinges on the continued support that regional militaries can obtain from the United States. Yet, as the case of Thailand discussed above has illustrated—and a later discussion on Indonesia will reinforce—the ability of regional states to take on a greater share of the burden for the public good of regional security, as desired by the United States, has at the same time frequently been placed in jeopardy whenever the improvement of their armed forces was held hostage to American demands for congressional accountability, especially in relation to human rights.

RECALIBRATING STRATEGIC RELATIONSHIPS

Apropos the retention of strong impulses to prioritize bilateral relationships in overall U.S. engagement strategy in the region, it would perhaps be useful to turn attention to how several sets of these bilateral relationships evolved in terms of how the Clinton administration's pursuit of its strategic, political, and economic objectives unfolded and was received in Southeast Asia.

Philippines

Because of popular sentiments in opposition to the presence of foreign forces, relations between the United States and the Philippines encountered complications at the end of the Cold War. Nowhere was this more evident than in the politics surrounding the renewal of American leases to military bases in the Philippines in the early 1990s.

Subic Bay Naval Base and Clark Air Field were integral to U.S. strategy in the Pacific at the height of the Cold War, which saw the Soviet Union eventually gain a foothold in the region through the establishment of a presence in Vietnam at Cam Ranh Bay, and China gradually extend its reach into the heart of Southeast Asia. Subic Bay served as the logistics hub of the U.S. Seventh Fleet and with a strength of 8,000 American soldiers could support several aircraft carrier battle groups at a time. Meanwhile, Clark Air Base was the only U.S. tactical air base in Southeast Asia with almost 10,000 personnel. Together with four other smaller bases, the United States paid a compensation of $481 million annually for the use of these facilities.[38] When the leases to the bases expired in 1991, popular pressure in the Philippines contrived to block their renewal. As a former U.S. diplomat reportedly intimated, "The bases are an affront to Philippines national pride and a symbol of imperfect independence, and continuing dependence. In Third World circles, Filipinos are condemned and ostracised because of the bases. As a consequence, the Philippines is a country that is difficult to take seriously. Thus, with the bases closure, the Philippines can move forward."[39]

Nor were American politicians in a mood to accommodate Philippine demands, especially after the June 1991 eruption of Mount Pinatubo created additional disincentives to maintain the bases. Congress rejected suggestions for increased assistance or payment for use of the bases, further rendering negotiations more difficult. In the Philippines, the popular view quickly took hold that the United States was biased against Manila given that the amounts it received for the use of these military facilities were apparently lower than what was offered to Israel and Egypt. Indeed, this was allegedly the reason put forward by President Corazon Aquino to justify the cold shoulder that was given American defense secretary Dick Cheney during his visit to Manila, calling the U.S.–Philippines mutual defense treaty "a lingering vestige of our colonial past," even though it was patently clear that she was also keen to demonstrate her independence from the United States at a time when rumors were circulating that she required American support to ward off an attempted coup in December 1989.[40]

Though the source of heated discussion, the controversy over U.S. bases in the Philippines was, in fact, not new. As early as 1947, Philippine nationalism, burdened by the baggage of American colonialism, had been mobilized in opposition to the Military Bases Agreement, which aimed to establish a permanent U.S. military presence in the country. The Philippine president at the time, Manuel Roxas, defended the idea by arguing that in allowing the bases, the Philippines was in fact contributing to regional security and stability. This view was rejected by many in the Philippine Senate, many of whom questioned whether the United States would still come to the aid of the Philippines should a conflict break out.[41] This doubt continues to linger within many quarters of the Filipino establishment to this day.

Similar reservations were expressed toward the Mutual Defense Treaty, signed on August 30, 1951. Senator Claro M. Recto captured the sentiments of a significant segment of those opposed to the treaty: "In ratifying it for lack of something better, let us not believe we are getting a good bargain. It is bad enough to be outwitted. Let us not fool ourselves, and let us not build a fool's paradise for our trusting people."[42] Correspondingly, the views of American policymakers were divided between those who took an altruistic view on matters and others who manifested a more pragmatic strategic outlook.[43] Even so, these differences obtained over reasons why American bases needed to be retained and not the decision over whether to retain them, for which the response was almost unanimous.

The Damocles sword of Philippine dependence on the U.S. security umbrella cast an inconvenient shadow and presented obstacles for Manila's aspirations to draw closer to its Southeast Asian neighbors in the context of ASEAN, at the time a new initiative for which the matter of foreign military bases located permanently in the region was a point of contention. Pressured to overcome the stigma of being pro-American, the Philippines sought to play an active role conceptualizing regional organizations such as the Association of Southeast Asia and MAPHILINDO (an acronym for a Malaysia–Philippines–Indonesia confederation), although it was eventually drawn into the Vietnam conflict in support of U.S. operations.

In October 1986, the Philippines Constitution was amended to require the renewal of the U.S. bases to be ratified by Congress. During the ratification hearings for the Treaty of Friendship, Cooperation, and Security, proposed and signed on August 27, 1991, for purposes of a ten-year extension on the lease to the bases, several reasons were put forward in support of the treaty. The first rationale was economic: the point was that the withdrawal of the bases would take a considerable toll on the Philippine economy. Not only that, it would also deny the country the opportunity to benefit technologically from an American presence the way the Asian "tiger economies" evidently already had.[44] Second, the prevailing logic still held that the bases were an important, if not integral, element to regional stability. Opponents, which included former defense minister Juan Ponce Enrile, who called the treaty a "constitutional abomination," took the view that the bases were evidence of foreign occupation and that American nonchalance toward the human rights abuses being perpetrated by the government of Ferdinand Marcos in fact posed a threat to Philippine security.[45] These views were summarized in the following remarks expressed by Senator Salonga: "It does not strike me as a treaty of friendship, it is a treaty of surrender; it is not a treaty of co-operation, it is a treaty of capitulation; it is not a treaty of security, it is a treaty of greater insecurity."[46] In the face of popular opposition, the treaty was eventually narrowly defeated by a Senate vote of 12–11 on September 16, 1991, in favor of "Non-Concurrence to the Treaty of Friendship, Co-operation and Security," which effectively denied the government the two-thirds Senate majority required to ratify the treaty.[47] This was followed by Manila's announcement that "The Government of the Philippines hereby notifies the Government of the United States of America that the 1947 Philippines-United States Military Bases Agreement ends on 16 September 1991 and cannot be extended."[48] The defeat of the motion to ratify the treaty was described by Senator Agapito Aquino as such: "It is a vote for a truly sovereign and independent Philippine nation. . . . It is a vote to end a political adolescence tied to the purse strings of America—a crippling dependence."[49]

In contrast to the triumphant sense of satisfaction expressed by Filipino nationalist elements, regional states responded to the withdrawal of American military forces with a heavy dose of trepidation. At issue was the fact that with the termination of the leases, American withdrawal from Southeast Asia was no longer hypothetical but a reality confronting the region. Mindful of the power vacuum that American withdrawal from the Philippines as well as defense budget cuts in Washington might portend, leaders of several ASEAN founding member states, all of whom were staunch supporters of the American presence during the Cold War, sought reassurance and called for the United States to clarify its position on its military presence in the region and role as the guarantor of security in Southeast Asia.[50] Singapore moved swiftly to offer facilities to support a continued presence of American military forces in the region through the signing of the Quayle-Lee Agreement (signed by U.S. vice president Dan Quayle and Singapore prime minister Lee Kuan Yew), which provided the U.S. military access to facilities in Singapore, including a newly constructed naval base. For its part, Indonesia cautioned that a total withdrawal could be a harbinger of regional instability.[51]

Nationalist euphoria notwithstanding, the closure of the bases did not bring down the curtain on Philippine security reliance on the United States. Though initial attempts to extend the Status of Forces Agreements were impeded by the lack of congressional support in the Philippines, this later morphed into the Visiting Forces Agreement (VFA), which was eventually signed on February 10, 1998. With a concerned eye cast toward Chinese assertiveness and the challenge of intractable armed insurgencies in the southern Philippine islands, the VFA provided for joint training and exercises, interoperability of forces from both countries, and the supply of American military equipment to the Philippine armed forces. Of note was the fact that two senators who were ardent opponents of the Treaty of Friendship and instrumental in the defeat of the treaty in 1991, Joseph Estrada and Orlando Mercado, played the part of advocates of the VFA. Filipino civil society groups, however, mobilized to condemn the VFA on grounds that included concerns for the risks of nuclear proliferation, threats to the health of locals, and the growth of a sex trade that might accompany the presence of U.S. soldiers.[52]

Notwithstanding opposition from a wide spectrum of Filipino society, the agreement was eventually ratified with a vote of 18–5 in favor on May 27, 1999. A major consideration in the successful ratification of the VFA was without doubt the changing geostrategic circumstances of the day. In 1995, Philippine reconnaissance aircraft discovered what proved to be Chinese-built structures on Mischief Reef in the Spratly Islands, 150 miles from Philippine territory. This was followed soon after by the discovery of Chinese naval activity in the vicinity. Together with the realization that the Philippine military was ill equipped to deter any aggressive posturing in the vicinity of its territorial waters, the creeping presence of China hastened a reality check in Manila and added impetus to the reconsideration of defense ties with the United States.

Even so, questions remained as to the extent of American commitment to the security of the Philippines despite the signing and ratification of the VFA, particularly in relation to the Spratly Islands. Ambiguity surrounds the extent of coverage the Mutual Defense Agreement of 1951 provides, namely, whether it covers Philippine claims in the Spratlys given that it predated Manila's assertion of those claims. This, in turn, led Philippine lawmakers to cast doubt on American support of the Philippine cause. As Senator Maceda opined: "The Americans have made it clear that the bases cannot be called on to support us in the event of an open dispute in the Spratly Islands. Yet this is the only imminent external security problem that we foresee over the next few years."[53] This uncertainty and concern for the ambiguity of American commitments in response to the most likely emerging threat to Philippine security underscores the tension between nationalist sentiments expressed in the aversion to dependence on the United States, on the one hand, and the arid reality of the indispensability of the United States to Philippine security, on the other. As later chapters will demonstrate, this tension still plagues Manila today.

Indonesia

U.S. strategic interests in Indonesia at the dawn of the post–Cold War era were twofold: maintaining U.S. naval access to the Indonesian Straits connecting the Pacific and Indian oceans; and the ability to tacitly influence Indonesia's political evolution through close contact with the Indonesian military, which at the time was perceived as the chief arbiter in the Indonesian political system dictated by Suharto's New Order regime.[54] With its expulsion from military bases in the Philippines, the U.S. navy negotiated with the Indonesian government in 1992 to gain access to ship repair facilities at Surabaya. Yet the strategic imperative of retaining a presence in the region via cooperation with the largest state in

Southeast Asia often collided with congressional pressure hostile toward
the authoritarian rule of Suharto. This led to frequent calls from Congress for the United States to deal with the Indonesian military in transactional fashion on the basis of day-to-day actions, including the imposition of punitive measures where necessary in response to known
human rights abuses perpetrated by ABRI (Angkatan Bersenjata Indonesia, or Armed Forces of the Republic of Indonesia, as the Indonesian
military under the Suharto New Order was called) or when U.S. interests
were compromised in any manner. Concomitantly, congressional pressure
over the East Timor issue became a matter of resistance between Congress
and the executive branch, bearing in mind again the latter's policy of
burden sharing.

A turning point in this regard was the 1991 Dili Incident, where Indonesian soldiers killed fifty pro-independence East Timorese protestors, to
which Congress responded in 1992 with the cancellation of the $2.3
million IMET program for Indonesia, restrictions on Indonesian access
to foreign military financing, and the cutting of ABRI's eligibility for
U.S. military equipment under the Foreign Military Sales program.[55] In
Washington, the Dili Incident introduced an element of tension between
progressive antiwar Democrats in Congress and successive presidential
administrations, including that of the Democratic president Bill Clinton,
over U.S. engagement with the Suharto regime and ABRI.[56] Even so,
mindful of the larger strategic picture of American interests, others in
Congress sought a meeting point between the hitherto contradictory imperatives of human rights accountability and strategic engagement and
took the view that a more calibrated approach to the 1992 sanctions was
required and that U.S. assistance should be made "contingent on the Government of Indonesia conducting a thorough and impartial investigation
of these killings and prosecuting those responsible for them."[57] Yet it was
precisely this treading of a fine line that resulted in constant fluctuations
in policy toward Indonesia that hardly inspired regional confidence.

In 1993, the United States reversed its previous stance in the United
Nations Human Rights Commission and supported a resolution in
March 1993 that noted the continuing human rights violations in East
Timor, criticized light sentences given to soldiers involved in the Dili
shooting, and called for increased access to the region for United Na-
tions and other monitors.[58] In July 1993, a veto of a Jordanian sale of
U.S.-made F-5 fighters to Indonesia and a prohibition of U.S. sales of
lethal crowd control equipment to Indonesia were passed.[59] In September

1993, the Senate Foreign Relations Committee unanimously adopted the Feingold Amendment, requiring the president to determine "whether there have been improvements in the human rights situation in East Timor" before authorizing arms sales to Indonesia.[60] The original version of this amendment had called for the "withdrawal of Indonesian armed forces from East Timor" and the "right for self-determination," but the language was eventually softened in response to pressures from the administration. Although the amendment was not adopted by the Senate, it nonetheless expressed growing unfavorable congressional sentiment toward Indonesian political developments.[61] This mood further contrived to prompt the Senate to revisit the 1958 U.S.–Indonesia Treaty restricting the use of U.S.-supplied weapons to "legitimate self-defense" and strictly forbidding their use for "an act of aggression." Meanwhile, the Appropriations Bill continued the IMET ban and prohibited the supply of light arms and riot-control equipment to Indonesia. Significantly, the ban was the first across-the-board prohibition on any type of weapons sale to Indonesia.[62] In 1995 and 1996, the list of prohibited items was expanded to include helicopter-mounted equipment and armored personnel carriers.[63]

In the summer of 1996, an agreement for Indonesia to buy nine F-16 fighters from the United States was placed in jeopardy by the Suharto government's move to respond to antigovernment protests in Jakarta by arresting members of the opposition PDI (Partai Demokrat Indonesia, or Democratic Party of Indonesia) and dissident organizations. The Clinton administration protested the arrests and initiated a review of the F-16 sale. In September 1996, citing congressional objections to Jakarta's crackdown on protestors, it was announced that the sale would be postponed.[64] In March 1997, the House Foreign Operations Appropriations Subcommittee heard administration testimony that the Pentagon had provided military training to Indonesian counterparts without congressional notification or consent throughout 1996.[65] This led the House of Representatives to unanimously approve an amendment to the Foreign Relations Authorization Act in June 1997 criticizing human rights abuses in East Timor.[66] In November 1997, Congress passed the Foreign Operations Appropriations Act for 1998, which specifically required military contracts involving Indonesia to specify that the United States "expects" that any lethal weapons or helicopters would not be used in East Timor. This act also renewed the ban on IMET training, called for the dispatch of an envoy to East Timor, and encouraged the administration to support international efforts to resolve the

East Timor crisis.[67] Even though the IMET program was suspended, the Department of Defense still continued to discreetly fund training for Indonesian special forces under the Joint Combined Exchange and Training (JCET) program—an effort that though not in violation of the law skirted the spirit of congressional efforts to restrict training, especially for the elite Indonesian special forces unit deployed in East Timor, Kopassus. But the JCET program was not beyond the reach of congressional oversight either. Indeed, it was eventually suspended in 1998 under the weight of heavy political scrutiny within Congress in reaction to Kopassus abuses in East Timor and increased media scrutiny of the JCET program.[68]

On several occasions, the executive branch had to push back in order to sustain engagement with Indonesia at a minimum level. In 1993, the Clinton administration successfully lobbied against a proposed amendment in the Senate to the Foreign Operations Appropriations Bill that would have made all U.S. arms sales to Indonesia contingent on a reduction of Indonesian military presence in East Timor. In 1994, the administration also opposed attempts in the Senate to bar U.S. military equipment purchased by Indonesia from being used in East Timor. A concerted push was also made by the Clinton administration and the U.S. military annually to restore funding for Indonesian participation in IMET. Deputy Assistant Secretary Aurelia Brazeal highlighted the normative value of engagement with the Indonesian military by pointing out that U.S.-trained Indonesian officers for the most part are "strong advocates for human rights and accountability for the armed forces. We can think of no better means of encouraging better human rights performance by Indonesian military officers than giving them extensive exposure to U.S. military forces with our doctrines of respect for civilian authority and the rights of civilian populations."[69] Partly as a result of this lobbying, Congress authorized conditional funding for a revised version of the IMET program, known as the Expanded-IMET (E-IMET) for 1996 and 1997, which required all parties to recognize the principle of civilian control of the military. The approval for E-IMET afforded Washington the latitude that precipitated a steady but limited flow of arms deliveries from the United States to Indonesia through the rest of the decade.

For its part, Jakarta was predictably incensed by the postponement of the F-16 sales, the release of State Department reports criticizing Indonesia's human rights record, and overall the congressional criticism it constantly found itself at the receiving end of.[70] In a demonstration of Indonesian frustration in reaction to the proposed Feingold Amendment, then Indonesian minister of defense and security General Edi Sudrajat opined that "if the American government is unwilling to sell weapons to Indonesia, we will buy defence equipment from Britain, Germany, France and Russia."[71] In fact, Indonesia eventually withdrew from the IMET program in June 1997 and cancelled the F-16 fighters purchase order.[72] Suharto was of the opinion that such issues of aid, the Indonesian military's role in domestic affairs, and allegations of human rights violations were preventing progress on more important and broader aspects of bilateral relations. In a letter to President Clinton, Suharto explained that these actions were taken due to "wholly unjustified criticisms in the United States Congress against Indonesia," criticisms that doubtless prevented progress on more important and broader political and strategic issues that could have benefited from stronger bilateral cooperation.[73] Privately, Suharto also expressed concern for overreliance on the United States for military equipment, which left Indonesia exposed and vulnerable to pressure from an external power, a position the Suharto administration was not prepared to accept. The Indonesian ambassador to the United States Arifin Siregar disclosed that the decision to diversify arms purchases was also intended to give "shock therapy" to Washington in order to "open their eyes to the fact that Indonesia cannot be continuously insulted without retaliating."[74] Indonesia subsequently announced plans for the acquisition of twelve Russian SU-30MK and eight Mi-17 helicopters but suspended this following the onset of the 1997–1998 Asian financial crisis.

The pressure from the United States continued after the resignation of Suharto under duress from domestic uprisings at the height of the Asian financial crisis. On July 10, 1998, the Senate unanimously adopted Resolution No. 237, which called on President Clinton "to encourage the new leadership in Indonesia to institute genuine democratic reforms. The Resolution also urged the president to work actively to carry out the U.N. resolutions on East Timor and to support an internationally-supervised referendum on self-determination."[75] Displeased with developments in East Timor, Clinton suspended all military transfers and training and, in a move that incensed Jakarta and elicited expressions of regret from other Southeast Asian states, further announced the coordinated suspension of pending World Bank and International Monetary Fund (IMF) monies to Indonesia in September 1999. Yet its frustrations belied its position of weakness, and Jakarta could do little more than grant permission for the Australian-led peacekeeping force (INTERFET) and withdraw its military troops on September 15, 1999. On October 20, Indonesia's national assembly ratified the August 30 vote in East Timor, renounced any claim over the territory, and formally handed over the administration of the territory to the United Nations. A year earlier, in 1998, the House of Representatives introduced House Congressional Resolution 258, which supported a referendum and called for direct Timorese participation in United Nations–brokered negotiations. Congress further adopted the Foreign Operations Manager's Statement accompanying the 1999 Omnibus Appropriations Act, which incorporated language from this resolution supporting a "referendum to determine a comprehensive settlement of the political status of East Timor."[76] Advisors to Suharto's successor as president, B. J. Habibie, cited such congressional actions as influencing his eventual decision to allow the United Nations vote and later to create a task force to investigate human rights allegations.

It should be pointed out that in terms of responding to American and international pressure against human rights violations and "taking effective measures to bring to justice members of the armed forces and militia groups against whom there is credible evidence of human rights abuses," the Indonesian government had in fact made, at best, glacial progress. Although several investigations were eventually initiated and charges pressed against a number of field officers of lower rank, there had been only a few convictions, none of which involved senior officers. At issue was a general culture of impunity within the armed forces as well as among the militia leaders that prevailed at the time, not to mention a deep-seated reluctance on the part of the Indonesian leadership to convey the impression that it had capitulated under external pressure. For instance, many officers who held command positions in East Timor in 1999 were not tried. Several, in fact, were promoted. The militia leader Eurico Guterreshad was sentenced to a mere six months' imprisonment for "disturbing a ceremony to surrender arms" to Indonesian authorities in 2000 but was not tried for his central role in 1999 East Timor violence.[77] Even the parliamentary decision to establish a special human rights court for purposes of trying offenses in East Timor was empowered to investigate only the period following the 1999 referendum—it had no remit to look into any violations that occurred in the preceding months.[78]

Vietnam

Making progress with Vietnam proved a necessary but challenging and politically delicate issue for the United States in the 1990s. Not only was there the backdrop of historical baggage in the form of the Vietnam War, which was still fresh in the minds of many Americans at the time, the fact that President Clinton had himself dodged the draft during the war and had held antiwar convictions introduced extra complications to these efforts. In keeping with the somber mood toward Vietnam, influential lobby groups pressed for administration officials to prioritize the matter of MIA American soldiers in their discussions with Vietnamese counterparts. Conversely, U.S. businesses called for attention to focus on market access for American goods. These competing interests required of the Clinton administration a delicate balancing act.

In October 1991, the United States put bilateral relations with Vietnam on a road map to normalization, which comprised the establishment of ambassadorial-level diplomatic relations and the granting of most favored nation trading status to Vietnam. Trade restrictions were eventually removed in February 1994. This paved the way for the normalization of ties on July 11, 1995, ending twenty years of frosty relations that included a trade embargo that crippled the Vietnamese economy. Formal exchange of ambassadors took place in May 1997. The first American ambassador after normalization, Douglas "Pete" Peterson, was himself a former prisoner of war interned in Hanoi for six years. The month prior to that saw the two sides sign a bilateral agreement to settle debts owed by the former regime in Saigon.[79] Both parties also expressed readiness to assist each other with the healing of old wounds as personified in American POWs and MIA and Vietnamese victims of Agent Orange, all of which served to remind of the acrimony that marked the Cold War years and especially the Vietnam War.[80] In point of fact, the Senate Select Committee on POWs and MIAs comprising senators Bob Smith, John Kerry, and John McCain that was established in 1991 played an instrumental role in this effort, providing a further rationale for the gradual move toward resumption of bilateral relations between the United States and Vietnam.

Significant though this turning of a page in U.S.–Vietnam relations was, it remained clear that the outlooks and perspectives of the former adversaries would take longer to reconcile and perhaps even longer for mutual distrust to subside. Vietnamese leaders remained guarded for fear that normalization of relations would be treated by Washington as an opportunity to undermine the Vietnamese Communist Party and effect domestic change with the familiar refrain of democratization and human rights. That these fears were not necessarily ungrounded was evident when the statements of respective leaders on the future of bilateral ties after normalization are considered. Whereas Vietnamese leaders expressed the hope that "normalization has brought the relations between the two countries into a new era of equality, mutual benefit, respect for each other's independence, sovereignty and territorial integrity, as well as non-interference in each other's internal affairs," President Clinton opined in response: "normalization and increased contact between Americans and Vietnamese will advance the cause of freedom in Vietnam, just as it did in Eastern Europe and the former Soviet Union."[81] Indeed, from the standpoint of Washington, progress in economic relations, such as through a bilateral trade agreement (BTA), was seen precisely as a means through which political change and liberalization in Vietnam could be set in motion. As a *Wall Street Journal* report surmised, with the BTA: "Vietnam's powerful military will have to give up its monopoly on several state-owned industries to meet the terms of the BTA."[82] The article also argued the point that "economic openness might lead the Communist Party to lose control over key industrial sectors or invite political instability." In hindsight, this had the makings of a fortuitous forecast. At the party congress in October 2012, storm clouds gathered as the prime minister, Nguyen Tan Dung, came under heavy pressure for purportedly mismanaging the Vietnamese economy on grounds of the weak performance of State-Owned Enterprises, bastions of the party's control over certain sectors of the economy.[83]

Nevertheless, apropos of the matter of relations with the United States, the concern was that the BTA would oblige Vietnam to implement significant legislative and structural reforms, such as the application of most favored nation principles on custom duties, levies, and charges for U.S. goods. In addition, Vietnam would have to accede to "national treatment to U.S. nationals or companies with respect to competent courts and administrative bodies (in accordance to international law)" and to permit U.S. companies to "comment on formulation of laws, regulations, and administrative procedures."[84] Negotiations hit a roadblock over American access to several sectors of the Vietnamese economy, such as telecommunications, via the lifting of nontariff barriers and tariff reduction schedules. Vietnam's reluctance to proceed was further compounded by the approach of U.S. Secretary of State Madeleine Albright to the issue, where, on the occasion of a visit to Hanoi, "she sidestepped . . . the trade agreement and asked about Vietnam's plans to implement true democracy and multiparty politics." In response, the secretary-general of the Vietnamese Communist Party Le Kha Phieu "was surprised and peeved to be receiving more advice from another American about how to run Vietnam."[85]

Doubts and reservations about Vietnam's human rights record also prolonged the deliberation on the U.S.–Vietnam BTA in the U.S. Congress, whereas in Vietnam finalization of the BTA met staunch resistance in the Politburo of the Vietnamese Communist Party. Such were domestic pressures exerted on the government of Prime Minister Phan Van Khai, the anticipated signing of the BTA at the September 1999 APEC meeting in Auckland failed to materialize despite American preference that the signing take place prior to President Clinton's scheduled visit to Vietnam the following year, the first by an American president since the visit of President Richard Nixon in 1969. Instead, Prime Minister Phan's decision to agree to a September 1999 signing was overturned by conservative elements within the Politburo who remained deeply suspicious of U.S. intentions. This was attributable, at least up to a point, to the fact that conservative Vietnamese leaders "still demonstrate a tendency to view foreign relations mainly in terms of likely foreign threats to national independence and political stability."[86]

Notwithstanding the aforementioned concerns, the BTA was eventually signed on July 13, 2000, and ratified by both the U.S. Congress and the Vietnamese National Assembly so as to enter into force on December 10, 2001. Predictably, the signing of the BTA triggered a sharp rise in bilateral trade. Yet while the economic leg of the relationship made fairly rapid progress, political and security relations moved at a considerably slower pace, only gathering speed when the Obama administration came to power in 2008 amid heightened tensions in the South China Sea.

THE ASIAN FINANCIAL CRISIS

Originating in Thailand but spreading to regional countries such as Indonesia, Malaysia, South Korea, and the Philippines through the contagion effect, the Asian financial crisis of 1997–98 was likely the most severe economic crisis to afflict the developing world since the 1982 debt crisis.[87] To discuss the origins and causes of the crisis would take this study too far afield. Suffice for current purposes to note that the crisis can be attributed to a number of causes, including the mismanagement of banks and financial institutions in the region, corruption and crony capitalism, policy missteps by respective governments at the onset of the crisis, financial panic and political uncertainty, and poorly designed international rescue programs.

Prior to the onset of the Asian financial crisis, East and Southeast Asian economies had been experiencing a decade of unprecedented economic growth, which led pundits to proclaim that an "Asian economic miracle" was shaping the post–Cold War order in the region. This growth was undergirded by a boom in international lending and large-scale foreign capital inflows into regional financial systems seeking to capitalize on high interest rates, itself rising on the back of upbeat sentiments. Underlying this economic growth, however, were structural deficiencies that were compounded by corruption and nepotism and which resulted in capital inflows mostly being short-term (and short-sighted) in nature. As a consequence, once the Thai economy started to buckle under pressure from currency speculators, foreign funds were quickly withdrawn first from Thailand and then, increasingly, from several other key Southeast Asian markets as well. Although the crisis exposed existing underlying problems in the Asian economies at the macroeconomic and microeconomic levels in the financial sector, the severity of the crisis can be attributed to cascading speculative pressures and panic, which led to large capital outflows. The swift outflow of capital in turn caused a massive reduction in productivity and slowdown of economic activity. Before long, local stock and currency markets plummeted, while state debt in the affected countries increased almost overnight. In fact, it was estimated at the time that several regional stock markets lost over 70 percent of their value as their currency depreciated against the U.S. dollar at alarming rates.

In response to the rapid devaluation of their currencies, Thailand, Malaysia, and Indonesia each floated their respective currencies on the international market and imposed some form of capital controls to reduce the outflow of speculative money. Yet this initial implementation of monetary policy reform was still tepid. Indeed, it was only after further devaluation that regional states ventured to implement more serious monetary tightening measures. Thailand tried to discourage capital outflows with the introduction of tighter capital controls while also requesting

IMF financial assistance. In deference to conditions set by the international lender in order to secure urgent loans, Thailand hastened major restructuring of several sectors of its economy. In hindsight, however, the conditions imposed by the IMF arguably had a further deleterious effect on the struggling economy. The IMF's contractionary measures—such as demands for the imposition of fiscal restraint through higher taxes, lower public spending, and privatization—all but signaled to creditors an impending crisis and had the inadvertent effect of accelerating the outflow of foreign funds. Conversely, Malaysia refused help from the IMF and responded to the crisis by adopting a strong capital control policy and a fixed exchange rate regime in order to stabilize the exchange rate and boost the financial sector. This allowed Malaysia to eventually weather the storm but not before suffering an economic downturn that claimed as victims several high-profile government-linked corporations, and a political crisis that threatened to debilitate the ruling regime.

In the early months of crisis, with Thai markets beset by economic woe, the United States remained on the sidelines. When the IMF planned a $17.2 billion bailout package for Thailand, the United States was involved in crafting the terms but did not provide any of the finances based on its assessment that it seemed unlikely at the time that Thai financial difficulties would be dire enough to spread to other markets.[88] Indeed, American assistance was forthcoming only when the contagion effect looked to be spreading the Asian crisis beyond the region, to Russia and Brazil. This point was acknowledged when U.S. Treasury Secretary Robert Rubin elaborated Washington's position on the crisis in a Georgetown University speech on January 21, 1998, during which he conceded that markets in Asia could not be stabilized independently and that intervention from the IMF, international institutions, and governments was required to prevent the crisis from spreading to other markets in Latin America and Eastern Europe.[89] In taking action, however, Washington prioritized backing of the IMF and its unilateral arrangements with afflicted countries.

U.S. support for IMF bailouts notwithstanding, at issue for regional states was the perception that American assistance was not only slow in coming but also that when it arrived, it came with onerous political demands and expectations that invariably contributed to the further destabilization of Southeast Asia. This was demonstrated, for instance, in Washington's move to obstruct development of financial mechanisms indigenous to the region, such as the Asian Monetary Fund proposed by

Japan at a September 1997 IMF conference in Hong Kong, on the presumption that such an institution would not demand the needful economic reforms and hence would be a risky proposition by American standards.

Apart from severe economic and financial dislocation, the crisis also had severe social and political consequences in affected countries. Thailand suffered a change in government, while in Malaysia, Prime Minister Mahathir Mohamad faced the sternest test to his legitimacy when the crisis catalyzed an opposition movement that rallied around his charismatic deputy, Anwar Ibrahim, who was removed from office for mounting a challenge against Mahathir and whose challenge was tacitly, if not openly, supported in several influential quarters in the Washington establishment. In point of fact, it was over the dismissal and incarceration of Anwar, who over the years had cultivated strong personal ties with many senior American officials, that U.S.–Malaysia relations hit a low. In 1998, U.S. vice president Al Gore famously breached diplomatic etiquette at the APEC meeting in Kuala Lumpur when he publicly snubbed his host, Mahathir, criticized the Malaysian government for its treatment of political dissent, and spoke out for the opposition movement. The Asian financial crisis also exposed institutional weaknesses of ASEAN. In the early months of the crisis, ASEAN dismissed the initial signs as simply domestic difficulties and played no role in devising a regional response to provide assistance to the affected member states. In not doing so, it all but failed to demonstrate capacity for effective regional leadership.

Yet the political consequences were by far most profound in Indonesia, where the financial crisis triggered a political crisis that precipitated a series of bloody riots in May 1998 that ultimately culminated in the resignation of Suharto after more than three decades of authoritarian rule. Indeed, it was the danger of political turmoil in Indonesia, and all the implications that portended, that quickened U.S. concerns and sparked Washington to action.

The Clinton administration waded carefully into Indonesia's murky economic-political crisis in 1998, concerned primarily with how the Indonesian military would deal with growing antigovernment protest that was mobilizing in response to increasing economic hardships. Initially mindful of the need to tread cautiously, U.S. missions to Indonesia in early 1998 deliberately avoided raising issues of political reform and focused discussions on economic reforms. Secretary of Defense William Cohen visited Indonesia in January 1998 and reportedly emphasized the need to strengthen security cooperation with the Indonesian government and expand U.S. military ties with ABRI, including the (by then) customary call for resumption of Indonesian participation in the IMET program. No mention was made during the visit of political reform or ABRI's role in dealing with brewing social discontent.[90] However, by April 1998, the treatment meted out to civilian dissenters by the Indonesian military prompted the administration to reconsider its practice of side-stepping inconvenient political questions. Reports of disappearances of protestors and allegations targeted at Kopassus drew U.S. attention and calls for restraint in the handling of growing student protests. Even as U.S. officials claimed that such overtures had resulted in the release in late April of some disappeared persons, key members in Congress intensified their criticism of the Clinton administration for not severing ties with ABRI.

On January 8, 1998, Clinton personally called Suharto, and in mid-January, Deputy Treasury Secretary Lawrence Summers, Secretary of Defense William Cohen, and IMF managing director Michael Camdessus visited Suharto on separate occasions and successfully persuaded him to agree to the implementation of urgent reforms. These reforms included halting infrastructure projects connected to associates and members of his family, eliminating tax breaks for a failing national car project managed by his youngest son, and terminating government assistance for an aircraft manufacturing project, and ending food and fuel subsidies. In return, Clinton lobbied Congress to back his administration's request to the IMF for a bailout package. In the event, the Indonesian government failed to enforce the requisite IMF programs as the regime dug in its heels and overlooked most of its commitments until the severe deterioration of economic conditions led to a full-fledged collapse of the Indonesian rupiah.[91] Four tranches of funds were eventually promised Jakarta by the IMF, but actual disbursement was subjected to reviews, which in turn resulted in several occasions where funds were deferred or delayed as a consequence of the unsatisfactory pace of reforms.

Further complicating American policy in Southeast Asia during the financial crisis was the fact that the Clinton administration also found itself caught between domestic trade unions on one hand and free market advocates on the other, both of which criticized the administration for using American tax dollars to bail out poorly governed Asian economies. Testifying to such domestic obstacles, a March 1998 congressional vote to endorse American contributions to IMF bailouts for Asian economies barely passed, and only after a compromise was reached with American steel, shipbuilding, and semiconductor businesses. The compromise included amendments that committed the administration to enforce punitive measures on Asian countries that dumped products in the U.S. market by trading them at below-market prices and that disallowed IMF monies from being utilized to strengthen sectors that might threaten American industry.[92]

In the meantime, on May 12, 1998, Indonesian security forces fired into a student protest at Trisakti University, killing six. This marked the first occasion of ABRI using open violence against student demonstrations during the Asian financial crisis. In response, a scheduled joint training exercise with Indonesian military units was cancelled, and the U.S. administration assembled a high-level military delegation to Jakarta to register Washington's disapproval of the use of violence against civilians. In the event, the mission was cancelled following massive rioting in Jakarta on May 14. Notwithstanding mounting evidence incriminating ABRI of violence against protestors, Defense Department officials continued to stress the need for open channels to and contact with ABRI, even following the resignation of Suharto on May 21.

Nevertheless, in response to a new spate of violence by the Indonesian military in East Timor, virtually all military-to-military contact was terminated, including all exports of military articles and services, which Congress subsequently codified into legislation. Washington suspended all joint military exercises and commercial arms sales to, and exchanges with, Indonesia by an executive order of President Clinton that supplemented congressional restrictions already in place.[93] The Leahy Amendment to the Foreign Operations Appropriations Bill, mentioned earlier, was passed in November 1999, banning military training and weapons transfers and foreign military financing until significant progress on the protection of human rights could be demonstrated, and the Indonesian military, by now renamed TNI (Tentera Nasional Indonesia, or the Indonesian National Armed Forces), was made to account for its actions in East Timor. Specifically, the legislation called for Indonesia to end support for pro-Indonesia militia groups in West Timor and furthermore that such militia groups be prevented from making incursions into East Timor and from terrorizing refugee camps in West Timor; that Indonesia repatriate refugees wishing to return to East Timor; and that Indonesian military personnel and militia members responsible for specific acts of violence in East Timor be identified and brought to justice.[94]

As noted previously, the Clinton administration exerted considerable pressure on the Indonesian government to accept a multinational peace-keeping force (INTERFET) under Australia's leadership to enforce peace in East Timor. In 1999, however, in an attempt to strike a balance and show measured support for an Indonesia still reeling from the impact of political and economic crises, Clinton vetoed a bill containing broad East Timor–related sanctions against Indonesia. Congress, however, succeeded in retaining the IMET ban despite the spirited argument presented by Deputy Assistant Secretary for East Asia and Pacific Affairs Ralph Boyce, that the reinstatement of IMET could facilitate the transformation of the TNI into a force for modernization and democratization in a manner analogous to what had happened in Turkey.[95] Following Undersecretary of State Thomas R. Pickering's visit to Jakarta in March 2000, the Clinton administration began inching toward the resumption of military cooperation, albeit within the scope allowed by existing legislative prohibitions. Among other things, this facilitated a gradual resumption of Indonesian participation in combined exercises, including the annual Cobra Gold exercise in Thailand. In addition, the United States granted a waiver for commercial sales of C-130 spare parts in September 2000.[96] The administration also approved the sale of spare parts for CN-235 aircraft being assembled in Indonesia for sale to South Korea.[97]

However, this limited progress in engagement with the Indonesian military was in danger of being set back again when three United Nations workers in West Timor were killed by militia in September 2000. Concerned that Congress would resume pressure for relations with the Indonesian military to be cut, administration officials spoke out to emphasize the need for continued engagement: Paul Wolfowitz, former ambassador to Indonesia and deputy secretary of defense, spoke in favor of lifting the ban in a testimony to Congress, saying that cancelling military training programs "did nothing to improve the human rights situation in East Timor. But it did diminish U.S. influence with the Indonesian military and deprived us of the opportunity . . . to teach them important things about how our democratic system works." Admiral Dennis Blair, commander of Pacific Command, expressed a similar sentiment in congressional hearings in 2000, opining, "I believe that the [Indonesian] police also require a lot of assistance and training. . . . I support that and think that should be increased."[98] By the end of the year, Congress was prepared to entertain a budget that included a modest $200,000 for IMET funding for Indonesia.

All said, American policy toward Southeast Asia during the Asian financial crisis registered in regional minds the view that Washington was unsympathetic—perhaps even opportunist considering how it used the crisis to push its democratization and human rights agenda even further—because it allowed relations with major partners such as Indonesia and Thailand to be debilitated to such an extent over questions of economic and political reform. In addition, there was grave concern for the danger of the United States losing sight of the larger picture of strategic engagement. The manner in which the Clinton administration dealt with Indonesia was instructive, as was its conduct of the diplomacy of arms sales with its ally, Thailand, during the crisis. In April 1996, the United States had sent a letter of offer and acceptance (LOA) for eight F/A-18 aircraft to Thailand. However, by September–October 1997, the Thai government was forced to trim the military budget by considerable margins in the face of enervating currency devaluation. On these grounds, the Royal Thai Armed Forces proceeded to submit a revised payment schedule for the LOA and requested from the Defense Security Assistance Agency special dispensation for a restructuring of the payment plan so as not to impact the delivery schedule. On December 19, 1997, the Thai prime minister, Chuan Leekpai, wrote to Clinton "asking for U.S. Government agreement to a rollover of payments for the arms procurement program of the Thai armed forces until the economy stabilized. Within months, the sale would fail, the United States would buy back the eight aircraft, and the issue of sunk costs invested in the production line would become a major sticking point in the bilateral relationship."[99]

LESSONS LEARNED

Needless to say, Washington's response led not only to a souring of bilateral relations; it fed anxieties about the reliability of the United States as a treaty ally and long-standing friend of the region and raised doubts in the minds of regional policymakers over certain elements of the relationship with the United States. Concomitantly, these doubts found expression in public pushback and criticism of the United States in Southeast Asia, a new emphasis on regionalism, and renewed emphasis on strategic autonomy and avoidance of alignment with any single major power. But there was to be an important—indeed consequential—caveat to this evidently more reticent view of the United States. China's seizure of Mischief Reef in 1995 ensured that a traditional security item remained on the agenda of a region otherwise preoccupied with economics. Viewed in this light, an American presence continued to be deemed necessary, if not crucial, to a regional security architecture whose form still remained unclear at the end of the first decade of the post–Cold War era. By 1998, Singapore, Thailand, Indonesia, and Malaysia had signed military access arrangements with the United States to ensure this presence and commitment remained as robust as possible under the circumstances.

The Asian financial crisis laid bare the deficiencies in the capabilities and resources of most regional states. The crisis spoke further to how transnational security challenges would soon come to assume even greater salience in U.S.–Southeast Asia relations as the Clinton administration made way for the presidency of George W. Bush. The Asian financial crisis was illustrative of how the problem in U.S.–Southeast Asia relations during the Clinton years was very much one of perception. American engagement in Southeast Asia during the Clinton years has often been described as years of "benign neglect." Technically, this was not entirely accurate, but the impression was what mattered. Although domestic policy remained the priority during the Clinton years, it was hardly the case that the United States was entirely disengaged from Southeast Asia. Rather, it was a case whereby, in pursuing American interests and objectives in the region, the Clinton administration conveyed the impression of disinterest in and lack of appreciation of regional perspectives, especially in the event they gave rise to differing conclusions that might have contradicted American viewpoints.

Perhaps the most profound example of this was the zealous and persistent pursuit of a human rights agenda and a seeming reluctance to "agree to disagree." The consequence of this, as Donald Emmerson describes, was the inability of the United States to "take advantage of something it had to offer that Southeast Asian governments clearly wanted—a security role in the region—to bring about other goals."[100] Indeed, the frustrations of Southeast Asian states to that effect were made plain by a senior Singaporean diplomat who, in reflecting on a trip to Washington during the Clinton years, remarked, "I went seeking engagement, but all I got was estrangement."[101]

CHAPTER FOUR

Global Terrorism's "Second Front"

DURING A GOP DEBATE at the height of the 2000 presidential election campaign, candidate and eventual victor, George W. Bush, was asked which area of U.S. foreign policy he would change if he came into office. He responded without hesitation: "Our relationship with China. The president [Bill Clinton] has called the relationship with China a strategic partnership. I believe our relationship needs to be redefined as competitor. Competitors can find areas of agreement, but we must make it clear to the Chinese that we don't appreciate any attempt to spread weapons of mass destruction around the world, that we don't appreciate any threats to our friends and allies in the Far East."[1] Bearing in mind the tendency of candidates to play to the audience by way of deliberately provocative remarks on campaign trails, the statement nevertheless offered insight into what President Bush might signal as a foreign policy priority for his administration.

Needless to say, this objective of meeting the China challenge was informed by the imperative of preserving American primacy in the Asia Pacific region against presumptive challengers from the region, an objective outlined in the 2001 Quadrennial Defense Review: "Although the United States will not face a peer competitor in the near future, the potential exists for regional powers to develop sufficient capabilities to threaten stability in regions critical to U.S. interests. . . . Maintaining a stable balance in Asia will be a complex task. The possibility exists that a military competitor with a formidable resource base will emerge in the region."[2] Yet, soon after the GOP debate, and after Bush won the party

84

nomination and subsequently the presidential election, unforeseen events contrived to eventuate a fundamental shift in America's strategic and security priorities.

On September 11, 2001, terrorists linked to the international terrorist organization al Qaeda launched suicide attacks on New York's Twin Towers, into which two commercial airliners crashed, and the Pentagon in Washington, D.C., which was hit by one airplane. A fourth attack, apparently aimed for either Congress or the White House, was averted when passengers aboard the flight managed to force the plane to crash into an open field in Pennsylvania. The tragic events of September 11, 2001, which quickly entered the security lexicon and American popular consciousness as "9/11" or "September 11," prompted a sudden change of outlook and priorities that triggered a fundamental shift in both the focus and conduct of American foreign policy. Overnight, the defeat of terrorism and extremism perpetrated by groups claiming legitimacy in the name of the Islamic religion became the signal priority and provided the optics through which American foreign policy objectives and commitments worldwide were (re)assessed and pursued, after which political, economic, and military attention and resources were diverted accordingly.[3]

Significantly, in the immediate aftermath of September 11, this new agenda of counterterrorism, which soon took on the notorious policy nomenclature of "Global War on Terror" (used interchangeably with the more generic phrase "war on terror"), won overwhelming and animated bipartisan support as it was catapulted to the top of the Bush administration's list of national and international policy priorities. To that effect, Congress swiftly passed legislation that authorized President Bush "to use all necessary and appropriate force against those nations, organizations, or persons he determines planned, authorized, committed, or aided the terrorist attacks that occurred on September 11, 2001, or harbored such organizations or persons, in order to prevent any future acts of international terrorism against the United States by such nations, organizations, or persons."[4] The Senate passed the motion unanimously, while the House of Representatives passed it 420–1. The "Global War on Terror" would now begin in earnest.

The prosecution of the war on terror was predicated on a set of controversial strategic principles that introduced an entirely new vocabulary to U.S. foreign policy and collectively constituted what has come to be known as the "Bush doctrine." In a joint session of Congress soon after the September 11 attacks, President Bush introduced the first of these principles—a high-handed Manichean worldview that compelled all states to choose sides. In his address, he articulated his administration's intention to "pursue nations that provide aid or safe haven to terrorism. Every nation, in every region, now has a decision to make. Either you are with us, or you are with the terrorists. From this day forward, any nation that continues to harbor or support terrorism will be regarded by the United States as a hostile regime."[5] To this he would later add, in a 2002 speech delivered at West Point, a second principle, pre-emption:

> Our security will require the best intelligence to reveal threats hidden in caves and growing in laboratories. . . . Our security will require transforming the military you will lead. A military that must be ready to strike at a moment's notice in any dark corner of the world. And our security will require all Americans to be forward looking and resolute, to be ready for preemptive action when necessary to defend our liberty and to defend our lives.[6]

Finally, in defiance of international norms—and, in some instances, international law—the Bush administration pursued a third principle in the form of a unilateralist foreign policy on several fronts, such as its withdrawal from the Anti-Ballistic Missile Treaty and its refusal to ratify the Rome Statute of the International Criminal Court (despite the fact that the preceding Clinton administration played an instrumental role in the conceptualization of the court), although it is important to point out that in truth, elements of unilateralism were already becoming evident in the early, pre–September 11 months of the Bush presidency, when the United States unilaterally withdrew from the Kyoto Protocol to reduce greenhouse gas emissions worldwide. On this score, then, the signs were clear that the war on terror was heralding a significant shift in American strategic outlooks and objectives.

The element of resolve in countering the terrorist threat posed by nonstate actors was displayed in the emergence of a corresponding strategic outlook into which segued the identification and circumscription of "rogue states" as well as action against the proliferation of nuclear capabilities, both laid out in the 2006 *U.S. National Strategy for Combating Terrorism*. This 2006 national strategy outlined action to (1) prevent attacks by terrorist networks before they occur, (2) deny Weapons of Mass Destruction to rogue states and terrorist allies who would use them without hesitation, (3) deny terrorist groups the support and sanctuary of rogue states, and (4) deny the terrorists control of any nation that they would use as a base and launching pad for terror.[7] This was a notable departure from its 2002 iteration, most of which was authored before the September 11 attacks took place, in which the Bush administration sought to emphasize its intention to "develop a mix of regional and bilateral strategies to manage change in the Asia-Pacific region."[8]

In keeping with this shift in strategic outlook, relations between the United States and the states of Southeast Asia quickly fell in line as the region preoccupied the attention of Washington policymakers to extents never seen since American withdrawal from Vietnam during the Cold War.[9] Be that as it may, for many states in Southeast Asia, this newfound focus and sense of purpose in American foreign policy, derived from the contingencies of circumstance, had a mixed feel to it. On the one hand, talk of isolationism, an ever-present if oftentimes fringe feature of American policy debates and the perennial "worst-case scenario" for the region, all but receded into the background as a muscular U.S. foreign policy gathered pace. On the other hand, all portents were that United States strategy and policy would now be governed by the single-minded purpose of prosecuting the Global War on Terror. At any rate, after decades of "benign neglect," the era of the Global War on Terror saw Southeast Asia return to the fore of the U.S. policy agenda when it was dubiously designated the "Second Front" by influential quarters of the Washington policy establishment following the discovery that activity related to the planning of the September 11 attacks had taken place in Southeast Asia. This view was further reinforced with the October 2002 Bali attacks in Indonesia that unequivocally returned Southeast Asia back onto the U.S. security radar.[10] In fact, Admiral William Fallon went so far as to testify that Southeast Asia was the "front line in the war on terror in PACOM [Pacific Command]."[11]

TERRORISM IN SOUTHEAST ASIA

As suggested above, the Bush administration's orientation toward Southeast Asia stemmed in part from revelations that the region had served as a base from which terrorist attacks against the United States and its allies were planned and orchestrated. It was this that prompted Washington to turn its attention to Southeast Asia even as it took to labeling the region the "Second Front" on the terrorism war. Although

the attention was to some extent welcome, the nomenclature was received with misgivings in the region for its lack of a sense of proportion
or recognition that terrorism was not a new challenge to Southeast
Asia, given how the region had long been struggling with homegrown
violent radicalism and extremism.[12] Indeed, the maritime states of
Southeast Asia had a problem of their own with regards to local terrorist and militant groups, some of which had already developed relations
with al Qaeda (or were infiltrated by al Qaeda) when these groups
crossed paths during the Afghan jihad against Soviet occupation. These
Southeast Asian groups posed varying degrees of threat to the governments of the region, with the situation in the Philippines, where a host
of armed insurgent and terrorist groups have operated with relative
freedom of movement in the southern islands of the archipelago, arguably the most acute. Attendant to this, American security planners were
confronted by a further inconvenient fact: Southeast Asia was also home
to sizable Muslim populations, particularly in Indonesia and Malaysia, and this led to controversial and discomfiting assessments that by
that measure, the region was deemed more vulnerable to penetration by
Muslim terrorist and militant groups.

Although terrorism in Southeast Asia predated September 11, it nevertheless emerged as a policy priority and major security threat to regional
states following the attacks in the United States, when investigations
revealed that the al Qaeda transnational network had established a
presence in Southeast Asia some years earlier. In December 2001, Singapore authorities arrested members of Jemaah Islamiyah (JI), an extremist group with roots in the Indonesia-based Darul Islam movement
and which harbored self-aggrandizing ambitions to create, by means of
the use of force, a regional caliphate by overthrowing governments in
Malaysia, Indonesia, Singapore, Brunei, Philippines, and Thailand.[13]
The transnational character of international terrorism was demonstrated in the relationship between JI and al Qaeda that found expression in ideological and operational form. Further complicating matters
was the fact that JI also forged relationships of varying degrees of inti-
macy with other armed groups operating in Southeast Asia, such as the
Moro Islamic Liberation Front (MILF) and the Abu Sayyaf Group
(ASG). Communications between JI and these groups were established,
and relationships forged, in Afghanistan, where Southeast Asian Muslims descended to participate in the jihad against Soviet occupation in

the 1980s with an eye to developing capabilities which could later be used to wage armed struggle back home. As one indicator of the operational outcome of these ties, members of JI were also known to have trained in Camp Abu Bakar As-Shiddiq, headquarters of MILF until it was overrun in 2000.

On Christmas Eve of 2000, coordinated bomb attacks were launched in Jakarta and eight other Indonesian cities, causing eighteen deaths. The attacks drew attention to the threat that al Qaeda–inspired JI terrorist operations posed to the country. Indeed, its portents were alarming for, as we shall see later, Indonesia would encounter a series of high-profile terrorist incidents in the ensuing years. A document detailing plans to target Singapore, Malaysia, and Indonesia was later discovered in December 2001 by Indonesian police, sparking concerns over the extent of the regional footprint of the terrorist threat emanating from Indonesia. It was, however, the devastating attacks in the Indonesian resort island of Bali in October 2002 that brought home the gravity of the terrorist threat to the region. Following the Bali operation, an audio recording, purportedly of Osama bin Laden, surfaced on various al Qaeda–linked websites lauding the Bali bombing as retaliation for the American Global War on Terror and Australia's support for the secession of East Timor, the latter an intriguingly myopic "nationalist" cause for the seemingly "transnationalist" agenda of the terrorist group. The Bali bombing signaled a major escalation of the terrorist threat in Southeast Asia.

The 2002 Bali bombings were followed by a sobering sequence of terrorist attacks: a suicide bombing at the J. W. Marriott Hotel in the business district of Jakarta in August 2003, the bombing of the Australian embassy in Indonesia in September 2004, and a further attack in Bali in October 2005. Subsequent investigations proved these attacks in Indonesia to be the work of JI. These attacks presaged heavy criticism of the Indonesian government for its initial state of denial and lackluster approach to counterterrorism. In 2009, a faction within JI perpetrated a further round of coordinated attacks at the J. W. Marriott Hotel (again) and the adjacent Ritz-Carlton Hotel.

Terrorist activity has been equally rife in the Philippines, if not nearly so dramatic since this was for the most part contained in the islands of the south, as compared with the attacks in Indonesia, which took place in the capital Jakarta. Although the communist New People's Army has long adopted terrorism as a weapon in its struggle, it has been Islamist-inspired

terrorist acts that have preoccupied policymakers in the United States as
the Bush administration cast an eye at the security travails of its Southeast
Asian ally and former colony. The southern islands of the Philippines
archipelago, poorly governed and home to armed groups such as the
Moro National Liberation Front (MNLF), MILF, and ASG, provided a
safe haven for JI members escaping authorities in Singapore, Malaysia,
and Indonesia. Since 2000, the southern Philippines region also witnessed
an upsurge in terrorist attacks of varying scales, including grenade attacks
in markets, bombing of public transport facilities, and the taking of hos-
tages by ASG from the Malaysian resort island of Sipadan in 2000 and
from Palawan in 2001. The bombing of Super Ferry 14 in February 2004,
leading to more than 100 deaths, was the most lethal. Smarting from the
magnitude of the problem, the Philippines government had little choice
but to seek out American military assistance, which they did without
hesitation.

COUNTERTERRORISM COOPERATION

In partnership with regional governments, the United States sought to
premise its counterterrorism outreach to Southeast Asia on the following
grounds: "Placing emphasis on attacking the institutions that support terrorism; building up regional governments' institutional capacities for
combating terrorist groups, and reducing the sense of alienation among
Muslim citizens."[14] In response to the new strategic circumstances, the
Bush administration sought to strengthen U.S. cooperation with key
regional partners in order to counter the threat of terrorism especially in
the realms of defense operations and intelligence gathering and sharing.
Of note is the fact that what stood out from counterterrorism cooperation with regional states was the bilateral nature of this cooperation,
which was consonant with what prevailed as the preferred mode of security cooperation for the United States in Asia. As President Bush himself
observed, "Unlike Europe, where our security cooperation takes place
through the NATO alliance, America's security cooperation in Asia
takes place largely though bilateral defense relations. America places the
highest value on these partnerships. We're committed to strengthening our existing partnerships and building new ones."[15] To that effect,
the greatest attention was paid to the Philippines, an American ally
that was also arguably the least equipped of the Southeast Asian states
to deal with the upsurge in terrorist activities with transnational links.

Philippines

Washington's prioritization of counterterrorism provided a point of convergence with Manila's imperative of tackling a long-standing and intransigent insurgency originating from the southern islands of the archipelago. In point of fact, terrorist activity in the southern Philippines registered a tangible threat to U.S. citizens, if not interests, thereby giving new momentum to bilateral cooperation. An American, Jeffrey Schilling, was kidnapped by a faction of the ASG in August 2000. Later in May 2001, three Americans were among twenty kidnapped from the resort island of Palawan. In response, the United States began paying greater attention to Exercise Balikatan, a bilateral military exercise which began in 2000, and for which the kidnappings provided greater impetus. According to the United States, operations embarked upon under the rubric of the exercise were "part of a concerted effort to neutralize a geographic area where terrorist groups interact with drug kingpins, smugglers, pirates, money launderers, and other organized criminals."[16]

Underscoring the strengthening of defense cooperation was the deepening of political and diplomatic ties forged in the wake of the tragedy of September 11. In response to events of that day, President Gloria Macapagal-Arroyo immediately invoked the 1951 Mutual Defense Treaty with the United States and offered Washington access to Subic Naval Base and Clarke Air Base for any impending military operations. Manila also provided access to terrorist detainees and witnesses for Federal Bureau of Investigation interviews and access to criminal, immigration, financial, and biographic records via the mechanisms established in the U.S.–Philippine Mutual Legal Assistance Treaty.[17] In a public show of alignment, President Macapagal-Arroyo seized on American preoccupations and declared that the Philippines was prepared to "pay any price" to support the United States' antiterrorism operations.[18] Needless to say, the robust assurance from Manila met with resounding approval in Washington. It was also met with something of a commensurate response. The Bush administration reciprocated by multiplying military assistance to the Philippines tenfold over the course of a single year, from $1.9 million in 2001 to $19 million in 2002.[19] Beginning in October 2001, the United States sent groups of military observers to Mindanao to assess the Armed Forces of the Philippines (AFP) operations against ASG, render advice, and examine AFP equipment needs. The initial group of American personnel arrived from Special Operations Command—Pacific in

2001 and were tasked to advise and assist the AFP in operations against the ASG in Basilan. This initial team was a mobile-training team of special forces operators responsible for instructing a Philippine Light Reaction Company drawn from the ranks of the Philippine army's special forces and ranger units.

During President Macapagal-Arroyo's visit to Washington in November 2001, President Bush offered American forces to play a combat role against the ASG. Mindful of nationalist apprehensions back home, Macapagal-Arroyo demurred and kept American enthusiasm at a prudent remove by insisting that it was best the American military role remain advisory in nature while the AFP retained full operational responsibility.[20] Although enhanced American military support possessed undoubted appeal for a Philippine military that had long struggled to cope with homegrown insurgencies and the urgent need for security sector reform, given lingering sensitivity surrounding the presence of American troops on Philippine soil, the American role in these operations had to be confined to noncombat activity and the provision of intelligence and communications support. These activities included the deployment of P-3 surveillance aircraft, deployment of Navy Seals and Special Operations advisors alongside AFP ground units, joint training exercises (Exercise Balikatan), assistance to the AFP in planning operations, and the formulation and implementation of civic action projects (medical treatment, water purification installations, renovation of schools) with the AFP that aimed at improving living conditions for local populations.

In the event, a deployment of 660 American troops soon followed under the auspices of the 1999 Visiting Forces Agreement for a "training mission" to the southern Philippines to advise the Philippine military in their fight against ASG and MILF in Mindanao.[21] By 2002, American troop commitment to operations in the southern Philippines had built up to almost 2,000 advisors under the auspices of Operation Enduring Freedom-Philippines launched in January that year. This was accompanied by massive injections of aid. From January to July 2002 alone, Washington committed a total of $93 million in military aid to assist operations against ASG in the southwest of Mindanao. In 2003, the Philippines became the largest recipient of IMET funding in Asia and the second largest globally. It also became the top recipient in Asia of Excess Defense Articles from the United States military.[22]

In a reaffirmation of alignment with the United States, Manila adopted a position of unequivocal support for the American-led war in Iraq and to that effect approved the deployment of about a hundred peacekeepers in support of operations.[23] In return, the Philippines was designated a "major non-NATO ally" on the occasion of Macapagal-Arroyo's visit to Washington in May 2003, a status that created favorable circumstances for the Philippines to receive more—and more sophisticated—arms and military training. Concomitantly, officials from both sides began negotiations for new and improved schemes for military cooperation against the ASG. What resulted from these negotiations was the conduct of two joint operations in 2005 in western Mindanao and Sulu, which involved a further 450 American troops. During this period, American arms sales to the Philippines also increased considerably. According to the Center for Defense Information, arms sales to the Philippines were 63 percent higher in the five years after September 11 than during the five years prior.[24] Conversely, the Pentagon's plan to announce the deployment of 3,000 "combat troops" to the Philippines in February 2003 had to be withdrawn in the face of widespread Philippine nationalist opposition. At risk was no less than the political survival of Gloria Macapagal-Arroyo, as "some Philippine congressional opponents had warned that they would impeach their president if U.S. combat troops landed in violation of the country's constitution."[25]

Even though support for Philippine operations was already ramping up in considerable ways, the Bush administration continued to hasten requests for Congress to legislate more substantial aid for the Philippines. This resulted in the provision of more than $400 million worth of military equipment in 2004 earmarked to enhance the counterterrorism capability of AFP.[26] The Philippines was also a beneficiary of the Regional Defense Counter Terrorism Fellowship Program (CTFP) and received several hundreds of thousands in funding annually under its auspices. Since 2003, the Philippines has also been receiving counterterrorism funding from the Foreign Operatives Budget's Anti-Terrorism Assistance Program, which is part of the Non-Proliferation, Anti-Terrorism, Demining, and Related Activities account, receiving over $4 million in 2006 alone.[27]

Indonesia

By sheer coincidence, Megawati Sukarnoputri, president of Indonesia, found herself the first foreign dignitary to visit Washington after the tragic events of September 11. Yet although the trip was pre-planned, the timing and optics of a visit by the president of the largest Muslim-majority democracy in the world was, in the event, hugely significant. Speaking in Washington, President Megawati openly condemned the attacks and offered Indonesian support to the American objective of destroying terrorist networks. In return, President Bush assured his counterpart of his administration's support to secure a considerable amount of aid for Indonesia, a task that in practice required finessing of U.S. security ties with Indonesian agencies given standing congressional legislation against the Indonesian military for human rights violations (already discussed in detail in the preceding chapter). Significantly, though, Megawati stopped short of offering any endorsement of military actions. Her words of sympathy in Washington notwithstanding, back home the Indonesian president proved characteristically lethargic and indecisive in dealing with a mounting cacophonous opposition to American operations in Afghanistan. Such was the extent of her inability or reluctance to contain or confront the rising tide of anti-Americanism, it resulted in the repatriation of U.S. diplomats from Jakarta in late September 2001 for reasons of safety, ironically, not from terrorist attacks but from the threats made on them by several Indonesian activist groups that opposed American actions in Afghanistan.[28]

Cognizant of the fact that Indonesia was a society plagued by terrorism but also riven by internal conflicts at the same time, most notably in Maluku, Sulawesi, Aceh, and Irian Jaya (West Papua), the Bush administration pledged a sizable sum of aid for infrastructure construction, the building of schools, and assistance for internally displaced persons.[29] The reestablishment of relations with the Indonesian military proved a trickier, more delicate matter. As the previous chapter showed, since 1999 military aid to Indonesia had been suspended on account of human rights violations perpetrated during the occasion of East Timor's referendum on independence. In February 2005, the United States eventually allowed Indonesia to participate in IMET, followed by a decision in May that year to resume nonlethal foreign military sales (FMS) to Indonesia after the election of Susilo Bambang Yudhoyono into high office a year earlier in the first open contest for the Indonesian presidency.[30] In November, the Bush administration exercised a National Security Waiver provision in the Foreign Operations Appropriation Act, passed in the House and Senate in June and July, respectively, that year, which permitted aid, arms sales, and training to be provided to the Indonesian military while discounting consideration of its record on the matter of human rights abuses.[31]

Resumption of cooperation with the Indonesian special forces, Kopassus, however, had to be pursued in more creative fashion because of its track record of human rights abuses.[32] Legal obstacles, such as the 1997 Leahy Law discussed previously—which blocked the United States from training with foreign military units with known records of human rights abuses and called for investigation and legal action to bring those responsible to justice—had to be navigated, for instance, through implementation of training programs with younger members of Kopassus for whom the case could be made that by virtue of their age, they could not have been involved with the unit during the periods when abuses were believed to have taken place.[33] Significantly, the United States also played a crucial role, together with Australia, in the establishment of Densus-88, the elite police counterterrorism unit that has since its formation been the vanguard of the Indonesian state's counterterrorism operations throughout the archipelago in the wake of the Bali bombings of 2002.

Despite the making of some degree of common cause between leaders of the United States and Indonesia, the reality, as it soon dawned, was that the Indonesian government found it difficult to rein in the activities of extremist and radical Muslim groups who were allowed to speak and act with impunity across the country. Indeed, it was only after the Bali attacks of October 2002 that the Indonesian government, hitherto reluctant to acknowledge the presence of terrorist elements on its shores, stirred to recognize the reality, if not the magnitude, of the threat. Even then, concerted action against groups like JI—responsible for the Bali attacks and several other terrorist incidents thereafter—faced considerable difficulty because of the popularity of radical Islamic preachers such as Abu Bakar Ba'asyir, the emir of JI, and the following they commanded across the country, as well as weaknesses and loopholes in the Indonesian legal process. Nevertheless, after the election of President Yudhoyono, who proceeded to develop much better personal rapport with Bush than his predecessor and who was more prepared to recognize the urgency of the challenge posed by terrorist activity in Indonesia, incremental progress was made in Indonesian counterterrorism efforts with assistance from the United States. Of note was the strengthening of Densus-88 into a highly professional and competent counterterrorism force, as well as the interdiction of terrorist finance and the strengthening of the legal and judicial system.

Thailand

The imperative of counterterrorism provided a boost to security relations between the United States and Thailand, which since the heights of the 1954 Manila Pact (upon which an alliance relationship was established), the 1962 Rusk-Thanat Joint Statement, and Thailand's active support for American military operations during the Vietnam War had experienced something of a gradual deceleration over time. On the back of this long-standing albeit (today) somewhat dormant defense relationship, Thailand provided increased support for American counterterrorism efforts, including the alleged provision of venues—the controversial "black sites"—for the Central Intelligence Agency (CIA) to hold and interrogate suspected al Qaeda operatives. Facilities used by the United States military in Thailand fell under the Pentagon's "cooperative security location" concept, in which countries provide access to facilities in exchange for upgrades and aid.[34] Meanwhile, Thailand continued to participate in the U.S. Department of State's Antiterrorism Assistance program. In recognition for its support of operations in Iraq, Thailand was accorded "major non-NATO ally status"—the second Southeast Asian state after the Philippines, in 2003, which allowed it even greater access to U.S. aid and military assistance, including credit guarantees for major weapons purchases and arms transfers in the form of loan guarantee arrangements for private banks to finance American arms exports to Thailand.[35] As a major non-NATO ally, Thailand also qualified for the Excess Defense Articles program, which allowed for the transfer of used American naval ships and aircraft to defense partners.

As with the case of the Philippines and Indonesia, a crucial aspect of the U.S.–Thailand security relationship during this period involved the IMET program, the Foreign Military Financing (FMF) program, and the FMS program. Figures for 2006 alone showed that Thailand received $2.4 million in IMET and $1.5 million in FMF support. In May 2006, Thailand also received $11 million from a Department of Defense fund authorized by President Bush to "build the capacity of foreign military forces" under section 1206 of the National Defense Authorization Act.[36] The September 2006 coup in Thailand, which saw the overthrow of the democratically elected government of Prime Minister Thaksin Shinnawatra by royalists and their political allies among the traditional elite, set back counterterrorism cooperation to some extent. Unspecified counterterrorism funds appropriated under the National Defense Authorization

Act were suspended in 2006, but other programs "deemed to be in the U.S. interest" continued, and Thailand, like the Philippines, remained a beneficiary of the CTFP, receiving substantial amounts over the years.[37] By 2008, after a democratically elected government was restored in Thailand, legal restrictions imposed (or activated) to prevent the provision of assistance to Thailand following the coup were removed.[38]

Intelligence cooperation was a particularly strong feature of bilateral relations during this period. With American assistance, the Counter-Terrorism Intelligence Center (CTIC) was established in Thailand. Comprising personnel from Thailand's intelligence community as well as specialized branches of the armed forces, the CTIC provided a platform for collaboration between the CIA and its Thai counterparts. Activities of the CTIC revolved around the sharing of information and facilities, coordinating work among Thailand's security agencies on counterterrorism matters, disrupting and interdicting terrorist finance networks, and providing access to military bases in Thailand. The CIA reportedly assigned some twenty agents to the CTIC in 2002 and also provided initial funding to the tune of $10 to $15 million.[39] The payoff was almost immediate as a major operational success of CIA–CTIC cooperation came in the form of the capture of several JI operatives, the most notorious being JI operations commander Hambali, who was apprehended in a joint operation in Ayutthaya.

Malaysia

In its pursuit of the objectives of its Global War on Terror, Washington found a somewhat more ambivalent partner in Malaysia. The spotlight fell on Malaysia following revelations that the country served as a venue for the planning of several terrorist attacks abroad. In 1995, Wali Khan Amin Shah, an international terrorist and a known accomplice of Ramzi Ahmed Youssef, the man responsible for the 1993 World Trade Center bombings in New York, was arrested in Malaysia. Another known terrorist linked to Ramzi Youssef, Khalid Shaikh Mohammad, who was later identified to be a chief plotter of the September 11 attacks, was also believed to have visited Malaysia on a number of occasions throughout the 1990s. One of the suspects involved in the planning and implementation of the September 11 attacks, Zacarias Massaoui, who had been accused of conspiring with Osama bin Laden and the al Qaeda network to launch the attack on civilians in the United States, was known to have entered Malaysia as well. During his stay, he was tracked by the Malaysian Special Branch and is believed to have received assistance in the country from a former Malaysian military officer, Yazid Sufaat. Yazid was himself accused of providing shelter to two Yemeni hijackers who participated in the September 11 attacks, Khalid Al-Midhar and Nawaf Al-Azmi, as well as Tawfiq bin Atash, who would later be identified as one of the masterminds behind the October 2000 bombing of the U.S.S. *Cole* in Yemen.

The fact that Malaysia had been identified as a base from which militant Muslim groups and individuals operated led Washington to label Malaysia a "Terrorist-Risk State" in 2002. In certain respects, there was some basis to Washington's concern. Although Malaysian leaders publicly expressed their annoyance at being linked in any way to terrorist activity, Malaysian security officials admitted in private that Kuala Lumpur did face such problems. Many were of the view that these problems were rooted in the government's "visa-free" policy toward most Middle Eastern states, which might have enabled international terrorists and sympathizers to enter the country without detection in the guise of financiers, businessmen, and tourists.[40]

Keen to burnish their religious credentials, Malaysian leaders positioned themselves as vocal opponents of American counterterrorism policies. The outspoken prime minister Mahathir Mohamad, who already had a difficult relationship with Bush's predecessors, was characteristically excoriating in his attacks on U.S. foreign policy and its support for Israel, which he argued fanned the flames of grievance that terrorists tapped into. Mahathir's criticism of the United States fed into domestic awareness of Malaysia's presumed identity as a leading Muslim nation and sensitivities toward U.S. policies, particularly those pertaining to Muslim societies. In fact, Malaysia waged its own rhetorical confrontation with terrorism—"state terrorism" to be precise—whereby Israel, according to the Malaysian government, was the chief culprit backed by the United States. Despite sharing American concerns for the threat of terrorism, for reasons alluded to above Malaysian leaders and security officials were mindful of risks to their credibility as Muslim leaders in the eyes of domestic audiences if they were seen to share a similar strategic outlook on terrorism with the United States or, worse, to be doing America's bidding. Consequently, Malaysian authorities were deliberately measured and selective in their public support of U.S. counterterrorism programs and initiatives in Southeast Asia. Privately, however, they readily expanded intelligence sharing and military exercises and granted overflights in connection with U.S. operations in Afghanistan on condition that Washington not draw public attention to these arrangements.

Of particular interest was the establishment of a regional antiterrorism center in Malaysia, ostensibly in collaboration with the United States, in November 2002. Given Mahathir's vehement opposition to Washington's prosecution of its Global War on Terror policies and the potentially heavy political cost of being seen as an apologist for American interests, the establishment of the antiterrorism center posed a problem for the Malaysian government insofar as matters of public opinion and domestic political legitimacy were concerned. A quandary was quickly averted, however, when Malaysian leaders swiftly declared that Washington would have neither influence over nor representation in the antiterrorism center, and that as far as Malaysia was concerned, the initiative was undertaken independently as part of its own counterterrorism strategy.

Singapore

The September 11 attacks prompted the United States to further enhance an already long-standing strategic partnership with Singapore, as Singaporean authorities launched their own punitive operations to counter terrorist activities, arresting dozens of suspected militants and extremists under internal security legislation. Since September 11, Singapore has increased intelligence sharing with the United States by deepening its military and security cooperation with Washington by way of offering itself as a "forward positioning" and servicing location. Singaporean authorities shared information gathered from suspected militants held under the Internal Security Act with U.S. officials, reportedly providing detailed insights into JI and al Qaeda's structure, methods, and recruiting strategies in Southeast Asia. The 2005 U.S.–Singapore Strategic Framework Agreement formalized the bilateral security and defense relationship, allowing the United States to operate resupply vessels from Singapore and to use a naval base, a ship repair facility, and an airfield on the island state. Under its auspices, the U.S. navy also maintains a logistical command unit—Logistics Group, Western Pacific—in Singapore, that serves to coordinate warship deployment and logistics in the region, while naval vessels make regular port calls. In addition to military cooperation, Singapore was a founding member of the Proliferation

Security Initiative, a program that aimed to interdict shipments of weapons of mass destruction–related materials, and was the first Asian country to join the Container Security Initiative, a series of bilateral, reciprocal agreements that allowed U.S. Customs and Border Patrol officials to prescreen U.S.-bound containers.[41]

MUSLIM SOUTHEAST ASIA: FOR OR AGAINST THE UNITED STATES?

As described in the preceding section, immediately after the September 11 attacks, Southeast Asian governments rallied to express sympathy and solidarity with the American government and people. Concomitantly, the prioritization of counterterrorism catalyzed a swift upturn in security relations between the United States and Southeast Asian states deemed key to this new strategic objective. Foremost among this category of states stood Indonesia and Malaysia, for whom strategic alignment with the United States had never come naturally.

Nevertheless, when America's post–September 11 outlook took shape and found expression in a turn away from multilateralism to focus on unilateralism, pre-emption, and the pursuit, by intervention and use of force if necessary, of democratization as an antidote to the threat of terrorism, sympathy soon gave way to something more vexed and ambivalent. Matters were made all the more disconcerting when the Bush administration set out to corral allies toward the prosecution of its Global War on Terror on the basis of a notorious and unfortunate ultimatum:

A coalition partner must do more than just express sympathy; a coalition partner must perform. That means different things for different nations. Some nations don't want to contribute troops and we understand that. Other nations can contribute intelligence sharing. . . . But all nations, if they want to fight terror, must do something. Over time it's going to be important for nations to know they will be held accountable for inactivity. You're either with us or against us in the fight against terror.[42]

With the Bush doctrine firmly in place and the reticence it elicited from the region, it was only a matter of time before Washington's reorientation to Southeast Asia paradoxically created new fault lines and widened old ones within the region, fueling domestic debates over the intemperate activism associated with it. Because of the administration's binary reading of the war on terror, where the international community had basically to choose to be "with us or against us," states in Southeast Asia perceived that they were being presented with a fait accompli as the policy appeared to give little choice to smaller and weaker states that were expected to either comply or risk some sort of retribution.[43]

Foremost among the complexities of the problems this posed for Southeast Asia was the perception of the war on terror in the eyes of the region's vast Muslim community. These complexities were highlighted in the following stark comments articulated by the foreign minister of Singapore, S. Jayakumar, to his own Parliament:

> America's pre-eminence means that there is no real alternative for any Southeast Asian government than to try to forge good relations with the U.S. Good relations with the U.S. are not possible unless governments cooperate in the anti-terrorism campaign. But many Southeast Asian governments will also have to find ways of assuaging the anxieties of their Muslim ground which may be uneasy or unhappy about U.S. policies while at the same time taking firm action to neutralise extremist Islamic elements in their societies. But how governments deal with this matter is a political conundrum. How they deal with this will have a profound influence on Southeast Asia now.[44]

In the event, the public relations full-court press of American diplomats and politicians did little to convince the vast majority of the global Muslim population that the U.S.-led war on terror was not a war against Islam. Indeed, as Richard Betts bluntly warned, despite strident efforts of several American leaders to divorce the two, "U.S. leaders can say they are not waging a war against Islam until they are blue in the face, but this will not convince Muslims who already distrust the United States."[45] These perceptions precipitated suspicion across the Muslim populations in Southeast Asia and could not but inform much of Southeast Asia's response to the American counterterrorism policies in ways that proved inimical to U.S. efforts to advance its interests. In Thailand and the Philippines, where ethnic separatist movements were active in mobilizing Islamic motifs and metaphors to legitimize their resistance, governments found themselves hard-pressed to downplay their security relations with the United States. Even Singaporean leaders went through great pains to engage their Muslim minority in dialogues that were geared toward disabusing them of their suspicions and explaining the logic of alignment with the United States on counterterrorism.

Misgivings toward U.S. counterterrorism strategies were most pronounced in Indonesia, home to the largest Muslim population in the world, and Malaysia, which had served as chair of the Organization of Islamic Cooperation (OIC, formerly Organization of the Islamic Conference) from October 2003 to March 2008, even though both states were, paradoxically, also potentially instrumental partners for the discursive and public relations dimension of the war on terror. The point has already been made that leaders of Indonesia and Malaysia were quick to offer their sympathy, both private and public, to the United States after the September 11 attacks. Even as Indonesian president Megawati Sukarnoputri was among the first foreign heads of state to visit the White House after the terrorist attacks, the Malaysian prime minister at the time, Mahathir Mohamad, also turned his characteristically caustic verbal attacks, often reserved for American leaders in particular but also more generally for the "West," on Islamic militants as well as Muslim governments that had created the domestic political, economic, and social conditions that gave rise to them. Given the numerous diplomatic tussles between his administration and Washington over the years, some of which were documented in the previous chapter, the red-carpet treatment accorded Mahathir on the occasion of his visit to the United States in May 2002 certainly looked to indicate that U.S.–Malaysia relations had perhaps turned a corner. In the event, Muslim Southeast Asia's sympathy for the United States proved short-lived, and support soon gave way to frustration and anger in the wake of Washington's hasty and ill-conceived reprisals under the banner of the "Bush doctrine."

Statistics painted a stark picture. According to results of surveys conducted by the Pew Foundation, the image of the United States in the eyes of Southeast Asians had deteriorated considerably over the years immediately following September 11, a time frame that coincided with the waging of war in Afghanistan and Iraq. The Foundation documented the percentage of favorable Indonesian views of the United States and threw up the following figures: 75 percent in 1999–2000, 61 percent in 2002, 15 percent in 2003, and 38 percent in 2005.[46] Predictably, these statistics prompted further political posturing. President Megawati's initial expression of sympathy and support was soon overshadowed by the launch of American military operations in Afghanistan, which occasioned a swift turn in Indonesian sentiment. In veiled reference to the United States, Megawati publicly condemned the use of force to deal with the challenge of terrorism. Meanwhile, Muslim civil society groups and political leaders inveighed against the invasion of Afghanistan. Massive student and civil society demonstrations against the war took place in Palau, Makassar, East Java, and Jakarta, with demonstrators carrying pictures of Osama bin Laden even as they torched the American flag along with effigies of George W. Bush. Radical Muslim groups such as Laskar Jihad (Jihad Army) and Front Pembela Islam (Islamic Defender's Front) threatened retaliation against U.S. citizens if Washington persisted with a policy of aggression against their Muslim co-religionists.[47] The mood in Indonesia at the time was captured in the comments of a legislator: "I am deeply concerned over the U.S. attack against Afghanistan. It is a terrorist act. Terror should not be confronted with terror. The U.S. should make efforts to end terrorist acts without creating new terror."[48] Adding insult to injury, a steady stream of Indonesian political leaders including the vice president Hamzah Haz, speaker of the House of Representatives Akbar Tandjung, and defense minister Matori Abdul Jalil, spoke out publicly against the American invasion of Afghanistan.

The Indonesian government was further incensed when barely a few weeks after September 11 President Bush described the "Global War on Terror" as a "crusade"—an unfortunate choice of words given the images it conjured—and stated that the United States was prepared to intervene anywhere in order to fight terror.[49] Relations deteriorated further in the wake of Washington's reluctance to hand over Hambali (Ridzuan Hishammudin), a major terror suspect believed to have been the mastermind behind the Bali attack of October 2002, to Indonesian security forces for interrogation after he was captured in a joint CIA–Thai intelligence operation in the Thai city of Ayutthaya on August 11, 2003[50]—this, despite the fact that Indonesian authorities had handed al Qaeda terrorist Omar al Farouq over to the United States when he was arrested in Indonesia in June 2002. In April 2004, Admiral Thomas Fargo, chief of U.S. Pacific Command, alluded to the possibility that as part of the Bush administration's plan to implement a Regional Maritime Security Initiative, U.S. marines and special forces could be deployed to patrol the waters of the Malacca Straits for purposes of countering maritime terrorism and piracy operations and intercepting ships suspected of carrying weapons of mass destruction. The comments sparked shrill protests in Indonesia and Malaysia. Admiral Bernard Kent Sondakh, chief of staff of the Indonesian navy, reportedly cast the discussion in conspiratorial terms, suggesting that the threat of piracy was overblown as a deliberate plot by "external parties" to gain control of the Straits and provide a pretext for interference.[51] At issue was not so much the presence of U.S. forces in the region but the fact that such proposals were made without prior consultation with regional states.

Indonesia's handling of its own terrorism problem gave cause for reservation, in particular the Jakarta government's initial reluctance to even acknowledge the existence of JI. The arrest and trial of the spiritual leader of JI, Abu Bakar Ba'asyir, was greeted with allegations that the Indonesian government was doing the bidding of the United States, and provoked protests in several quarters within Indonesia's kaleidoscopic Muslim community.[52] Stoking controversy, Hamzah Haz, leader of the United Development Party and later vice president of Indonesia, paid high-profile visits in 2002 to Abu Bakar Ba'asyir at his *pesantren* (Islamic boarding school) in Ngruki and to Ja'afar Umar Thalib, the leader of Laskar Jihad, after his arrest in May. In the face of criticism, and despite Indonesia's frustrating foot dragging on counterterrorism, the Bush administration, to its credit, exercised restraint in waiting for Jakarta to publicly label JI a terrorist organization (after much discrete lobbying by the United States among others, it should be said) before it proceeded to do likewise. Washington did so despite having already arrived at that conclusion soon after the October 12, 2002, Bali bombings. The public restraint shown by American security officials belied private frustrations at the lack of support from Jakarta for the war on terror despite Indonesia itself being confronted by the problem, as well as the blatantly provocative actions of Indonesian leaders such as Hamzah Haz.

Malaysian reactions to the Afghanistan campaign closely approximated those that unfolded in Indonesia. The Malaysian government condemned the attack and fanned the embers of growing anti-Americanism by sanctioning public protests staged by rancorous civil society groups against the United States.[53] Relations between Malaysia and the United States took a further turn for the worse following the invasion of Iraq. Both Kuala Lumpur and Jakarta challenged the legality of Washington's twin objectives of the destruction of weapons of mass destruction and regime change, which they saw to be strictly a matter of Iraqi internal politics. The profound irony that democratization was being, perforce, compelled upon Muslim lands by a foreign government—and a Western one at that—at gunpoint, and which in any case was never intent on ascertaining the will of denizens it claimed it was "liberating," was certainly not lost to either political leadership or popular opinion across Muslim Southeast Asia.

The Malaysian government was especially vocal (and visceral) in its condemnation of the U.S. war on Iraq. Prior to the outbreak of hostilities, Malaysia was already actively involved in marshaling international diplomatic opinion in opposition to U.S. policy. The outspoken Malaysian leadership further took advantage of Malaysia's chairmanship of the Non-Aligned Movement to formulate a resolution rejecting a U.S.-led attack on Iraq that would proceed without the sanction of the United Nations. The Malaysian government also led the OIC in protest against military action. In response, the American ambassador to Malaysia saw fit to sound out a telling caution to the Malaysian leadership that its visceral attacks on the United States risked triggering a deterioration of bilateral relations.

At home, the Malaysian Parliament unanimously adopted a motion condemning the unilateral military action against Iraq by the United States and its allies, and leaders of both government and opposition parties orchestrated a rare bipartisan demonstration outside the premises of the U.S. embassy on March 25, 2003. The protest followed a massive state-organized, antiwar demonstration at the Merdeka Stadium that was attended by 50,000 people, including the entire Malaysian cabinet. Elements within government, the opposition, and vocal Muslim civil society further mobilized by way of a national peace movement (Aman Malaysia) that sought to lobby the United Nations to investigate the "war crimes" purportedly perpetrated by America and its allies during the course of the Iraq invasion and to bring the "perpetrators" to justice.

Official positions of regional governments aside, at the heart of popular discontent in Southeast Asia toward the United States also lay the evident display of American hypocrisy manifested in a major policy disconnect between the Bush administration's purported pursuit of democracy and freedom and its support of undemocratic practices and human rights violations in some Southeast Asian countries. For example, persistent criticisms of the Internal Security Act and other forms of legislation deemed authoritarian violations of human rights that had regularly been leveled at several Southeast Asian regimes from the corridors of power in both the White House and Capitol Hill fell conspicuously silent when the "Global War on Terror" was at its apogee. Instead, the fledgling Indonesian democratic system was taken to task for not putting in place terrorism laws that in effect amounted to a recrudescence to the Suharto-era culture of surveillance and heavy-handedness that Congress and human rights lobbies had previously railed against. Likewise, the use of the Internal Security Act in Malaysia and Singapore, hitherto also frequently a point of contention with the United States, was tolerated, if not tacitly encouraged, by an ascendant neoconservative Washington establishment as a critical element of their respective counterterrorism campaigns.[54] This disconnect was not lost to large segments of civil society and popular opinion in the region, with many regional civil society groups viewing it as illustrative of American duplicity, and further deepened the skepticism of public opinion that was already questioning how Washington's refrain of liberty and democratization was being pursued in illiberal and undemocratic fashion with the unilateral use of force toward the ends of regime change.

A further issue of contention was registered by Indonesian leaders who readily leveled accusations of hypocrisy and double standards on the Bush administration when the latter willy-nilly sidestepped international law in its conduct of the war on terror even as members of Congress maintained that Indonesian army personnel linked to bloodshed in East Timor should be tried by the International Court of Justice for war crimes.[55] When the State Department released its 2004 Human Rights Report containing criticisms of the actions of Indonesian security forces in the restive provinces of Papua and Aceh, it elicited a caustic response from Jakarta. This was conveyed in the remarks of Indonesian Foreign Ministry senior official Marty Natalegawa (who would later become foreign minister), who responded that "the U.S., as Indonesia has consistently stated, and especially since the horrific disclosures on Abu Ghraib, does not have the moral authority to assume the role of judge and jury on matters of human rights."[56]

UNPACKING THE TERRORISM MILIEU

In order to understand Muslim Southeast Asia's responses to the war on terror and U.S. policy during the Bush administration, one would need to understand the complex domestic political forces at play that informed the framing and conduct of foreign policy, particularly in Jakarta and Kuala Lumpur. Since the fall of President Suharto in 1998, the advent of democracy has facilitated the reemergence of political Islam in Indonesia. This has taken the form of not only a plethora of Muslim political organizations and parties that have emerged and have become part of the mainstream political process but also the flourishing of a number of popular radical Islamist groups that stand at the fringes but yet have been at the forefront orchestrating anti-U.S. demonstrations throughout the country.

Because of the increasing salience of Islam in Indonesian politics, populist leaders often sought to court the Muslim vote by making common cause in the public eye with vocal radical groups.[57] At the minimum, they were cautious not to have their religious credentials called into question, which would almost certainly have been the case in some quarters if they took action against purveyors of the view that American intent was precisely to undermine Islam and Muslim interests by way of a contrived war on terror. By this same token, the Jakarta government was also restrained in its own handling of radical Muslim activism on grounds that any punitive action taken "could radicalize the moderate Muslim majority, if it were perceived as unjust and taken at American behest."[58] In other words, with respect to counterterrorism, the growing social and political clout of more radical Muslim organizations, though incommensurate with the actual size of these organizations, meant that Jakarta was in effect constrained in terms of policy options and responses to calls from the United States and others to take more resolute action against radical and extremist groups and voices.

Cognate logics obtained in the case of Malaysia, where the politicization of Islam can be traced further back to the early 1980s with the emergence of the Islamist opposition party PAS (Parti Islam Se-Malaysia, or Pan-Malaysian Islamic Party) and the consequent "Islamization race" between it and the incumbent United Malays National Organization–led regime.[59] As part of this contest, politicians from both parties have regularly burnished their Islamic credentials to enhance their popularity and support base, while at the same time working to undermine those of their opponents by alleging how they have departed from the tenets of faith. Part of this brinkmanship came to be expressed in distorted discourses on American and broader "Western" proclivities to neocolonialism, cultural hegemony, and anti-Muslim antagonism.

It bears noting, however, that away from the public eye, post–September 11 relations between the United States, Indonesia, and Malaysia in reality were considerably more ambivalent, and conducted in more pragmatic fashion, than the strident anti-American rhetorical broadsides suggest. As evident from the exploration of its cooperation with Southeast

Asia above, the United States played a critical role in the counterterrorism calculus of regional states—a role that was accepted by these states, it should be added. Although Jakarta and Kuala Lumpur constantly engaged in megaphone diplomacy toward the United States, this had little actual bearing on prevailing cooperation in defense and security matters. In some respects, such as in intelligence sharing and collaboration against terrorist financing, cooperation even gathered pace. At Washington's tacit behest, Malaysia even created a regional center for counterterrorism to conduct training for various state security forces from Southeast Asian countries, even though, as was pointed out earlier, both parties took care to manage the optics. Similarly, defense ties enjoyed by both Malaysia and Indonesia with the United States also remained steady, and in the latter case actually gradually intensified to some degree.

For its part, Washington also made efforts to tread carefully in the implementation of counterterrorism policy in Southeast Asia. Although adamant that its own national security justified unilateralism and preemption at any cost—a position that proved a bugbear for the foreign policy of the Bush administration in general—the United States did try to demonstrate more sensitivity and sophistication in its dealing with Muslim regimes and constituencies throughout the region. Consequently, as the war on terror ensued, the United States navigated potential diplomatic and political minefields adroitly for the most part by assuming what has largely been an auxiliary role in counterterrorism operations in Southeast Asia, offering support only upon request (such as the case in the Philippines); it has also limited tangible cooperation chiefly to bilateral arrangements, where it was easier for the United States to assume a lower, more manageable profile. In the main, notwithstanding the imperative for the war on terror of the Bush administration and the controversial doctrines that guided its conduct, discretion was the better part of valor in counterterrorism cooperation between the United States and both Indonesia and Malaysia. Concomitantly, while sensitivities may have prevented this cooperation from achieving its full potential, there was in the final analysis still sufficient convergence of interests between the United States and its Muslim-majority Southeast Asian partners to allow collaboration.

At a broader strategic level, the almost single-minded focus of the Bush administration on the Global War on Terror also created anxieties in regional states whose preference was doubtless for a strategy of engagement premised on a wider raft of issues over a longer term horizon. Even so, although Southeast Asia was drawn into the strategic orbit of the Global War on Terror by virtue of the presence of terrorist groups in the region and its own travails of terrorism, it remained nevertheless marginal compared with the Middle East and Central Asia as far as American priorities were concerned. The war on terror lens moreover posed further conundrums for the region. For some states—those that had to deal with their own problems of terrorism at home—the leadership of the United States on this front was welcomed. As the prime minister of Singapore Lee Hsien Loong articulated during the course of a 2007 visit to Washington,

> I thanked the President for the steadfastness and resolve with which he's tackling the very complicated problems in the Middle East and Iraq as well as the Israel-Palestinian issue. It's critical for us in Southeast Asia that America does that and that the President continues to give strong leadership on that because it affects America's standing in Asia and the world and also the security environment in Asia, because extremists, the jihadists, watch carefully what's happening in the Middle East and take heart or lose heart depending on what's happening there.[60]

At the same time, however, there was a concern that the war on terror had become the dominant lens through which the Bush administration was approaching engagement with Southeast Asia, which necessitated some form of prioritization of relations with certain regional states (those in archipelagic Southeast Asia with large Muslim populations) over others (mainland Southeast Asia). It is likely for that reason that the prime minister of Singapore went on to add in his remarks that "within Southeast Asia, I encouraged the President to deepen and strengthen the already good ties . . . between the Southeast Asian countries, ASEAN and America."[61] For its part, the overarching challenge for U.S. relations with Southeast Asia during the presidency of George W. Bush was to demonstrate that Washington's regional engagement policy was not solely informed and dictated by the singular imperative of counterterrorism. In hindsight, this would prove a tall order.

CHAPTER FIVE

Missed Opportunities

AS THE PREVIOUS CHAPTER DEMONSTRATED, the evolution of the war on terror in Southeast Asia showcased how the theme of domestic influences on foreign policy had cast a shadow over the matter (and manner) of U.S. engagement in the region for a large part of the George W. Bush presidency, particularly in its first term, when it had serious ramifications in light of the Bush administration's strategies of unilateralism, preemption, and regime change. If, in the president's own words, the "survival of [America's] liberty" is increasingly dependent on "the success of liberty in other lands," then this begged the question: how might a program of democratic expansion to "other lands" ensure America's liberty, particularly since opposition to such a policy (and, by extension, to the United States itself) became increasingly virulent in societies where political liberalization and democratization has transpired, not least in Southeast Asia?[1]

To be sure, the spread of democracy, certainly in word if not always in deed, was already a major feature of American foreign policy when Bill Clinton was in office, although some have argued that it had antecedents even before that.[2] The point, however, is that the imperative gathered further pace and purpose during the Bush administration when it dovetailed with counterterrorism. Indeed, during the Global War on Terror milieu, this was given substantive policy expression in America's military campaigns in Afghanistan and Iraq, both of which had regime change and the introduction of "free and fair elections" as their primary declaratory objective. For the Bush administration, then, the advancement of democracy was both a virtuous end in itself and also a means—a crucial one at that—to the end of victory over terrorism. As the *U.S. National Strategy for Countering Terrorism* released by the National Security Council stated unequivocally, advancing "effective democracies" would be the "long-term antidote to the ideology of terrorism."[3]

Though the United States was careful to reassure its Southeast Asian counterparts that the means of regime change it had exercised thus far, namely, the use of force, need not be a matter of concern for them, it remained adamant that the ends of democracy promotion justified the means, and such ends would continue to inform much of its policy toward the region.[4] Then deputy assistant secretary of state Eric John indicated as much when he testified before the House International Relations Committee in 2005 that insofar as Southeast Asia was concerned, "the most important and encouraging trend in recent years has been the strengthening of democracy."[5] Given the primacy of this objective, it is telling, too, that later in the same testimony John intimated that "ASEAN has not done all it could or should to promote democracy."[6] These seemingly contradictory statements reflected the long-standing frustration that Washington policy quarters have felt toward Southeast Asian states that continue to resist American encouragement to democratize even as they reaped the fruits of the U.S. "security umbrella" that was afforded the region. At least one reason for this complicated picture is the fact that the democratic transition process is taking place in what are essentially weak states in the region but which are also home to the most virulent public expressions of anti-Americanism in Southeast Asia.

The Southeast Asian region underwent a prolonged yet incomplete period of democratic transition whose origins dated back to the so-called Third Wave of Democratization[7]—"people power" in the Philippines in 1986 and the bloody street demonstrations in Thailand in May 1992. This process, arguably lasting more than a decade in Southeast Asia, climaxed most emphatically in the downfall of Indonesia's authoritarian president, Suharto, after thirty-two years in power. The rise of participatory democracy in these Southeast Asian societies should not be underestimated, not least the growing involvement (or "intrusion") of civil society actors and social movements in domains that were traditionally the exclusive preserves of Southeast Asian governments.[8] It was this historical experience of political transition that informed how several Southeast Asian societies interpreted the counterterrorism and foreign policies of the Bush administration.

During the Bush era, regional perceptions of the United States appeared to be marked by an underlying antithesis rooted, on the one hand, in a traditional reliance and investment on the part of arguably all Southeast Asian governments on a sustained U.S. security presence in the region that, on the other hand, was increasingly being met by a growing anti-Americanism in many segments of their civil societies that has been a product of democratization.[9] Indeed, this point bears repeating. Although a surfeit of antagonism against the United States has been linked to the rise in religious militancy within Southeast Asia, one should also be mindful of the backdrop against which the growth of visible anti-American attitudes and behavior burgeoned, to wit, anti-Americanism during the era of the Global War on Terror can conceivably be considered at least in part to be an outcome of the unfolding, albeit uneven, process of democratic transition and political liberalization that the United States has persistently championed in the region and beyond. The fact that misgivings toward American policies arose amid democratic transitions compelled regional states to rearticulate, if not recalibrate, the traditional terms of their relations with the United States under the leadership of George W. Bush. The implications of this were significant. To be sure, this paradox did not imply that regional states would seek to balance against U.S. power or revise the international status quo, no matter how self-righteous, duplicitous, and heavy-handed they, or more appropriately their respective domestic constituencies, perceived the United States to be.[10] What it did mean, however, was that the state of U.S.–Southeast Asian relations was becoming a shade more unpredictable and given much more to the vicissitudes of domestic politics than before.

The purpose of identifying this paradox here is neither to revisit the debate on the correlation between democratization and conflict nor to hold the democratization process as primarily accountable for the rise of anti-Americanism in Southeast Asia.[11] At most, one should allow that democratic transitions, especially in weak states reacting against an illiberal past, tend to be somewhat unstable according to certain measures so long as democratic consolidation has not been achieved.[12] What does seem apparent, however, is that the tension stemming from the traditional dependence on a robust U.S. presence on the one hand and mounting domestic pressure against strategic alignment with Washington on the other was already fast becoming palpable by the turn of the century, particularly in Southeast Asian countries that were experiencing democratic transition but not necessarily consolidation (certainly not at that time), notably Indonesia, the Philippines, and Thailand. But such tensions were not restricted to weak developing democracies; they were also discernible in more developed semi-democratic countries with fairly substantial Muslim populations, such as Malaysia.

Several specific examples bear this out. In the Philippines, the return of American troops under the auspices of the Visiting Forces Agreement (VFA), signed in 1998 ostensibly to strengthen the capacity of the AFP in its fight against communist and separatist rebels, was overshadowed by allegations of the involvement of American servicemen in the gang rape of a local woman in November 2005. The groundswell of discontent as a result of these allegations erupted into street protests in Manila as well as several cities in Mindanao.[13] American reluctance to hand over the suspects to Philippine authorities further hardened resentment and pressured the Macapagal-Arroyo administration into taking a tougher stand against Washington. Similarly, the Thaksin administration in Thailand was besieged by large anti-U.S. demonstrations in Chiang Mai and Bangkok in January 2005 in opposition to free trade negotiations between America and Thailand. Rumors that Thailand played host to CIA covert interrogation centers only served to further fan the flames of popular anger. Indeed, these anti-American protests in Thailand reached a level never before seen since nationwide student protests in the mid-1970s against the presence of American military bases.

At issue, too, is the fact that insofar as the nexus between democratization and anti-Americanism is concerned, it is telling that Southeast Asian societies in which these trends registered most prominently often were also where relatively weak governance and poor state capacity obtained. For instance, Indonesia and the Philippines stood out as weak states in terms of incomplete administrative coverage over their extensive territories—in comparison to the strong, well-resourced states of Singapore and Malaysia[14]—and, where law and order were concerned, were hampered by an excessive legalism created to prevent the possibility of authoritarian reversals. Sharing this view, Sheldon Simon made the observation that "The two Southeast Asian states where terrorist movements are strongest, Indonesia and the Philippines, are weak states unable to enforce basic law and order, with the political and economic marginalization of large portions of their populations despite the fact that both are functioning democracies."[15] The lack of central governmental coverage over its remote southern part suggests that Thailand might in some respects demonstrate elements of state weakness as well.[16]

That said, a final caveat is in order. One should also bear in mind that states with significant Muslim constituencies themselves might not be above using the unpopular Global War on Terror as an opportunity for their politically repressed populations to vent—so long as their vitriol is reserved for targets other than their own incumbent governments. In this regard, the proclivity of not a few ruling governments in the Southeast Asian region to engage in the politics of scapegoating unfairly rendered the United States a convenient target of distrust and hostility.[17] In this respect, although some analysts were quite right to be concerned with the detrimental effects of excessive state controls, potential repression, and abuse of power in the course of their own operations against extremism, the opposite extreme might be equally inimical, namely, the rise of vitriolic anti-American attitudes and behaviors facilitated by freedom of speech, which, left unchecked, could have had equally deleterious effects on the stability of the region in terms of how such a climate lent to the growth of extremism.

ECONOMIC ENGAGEMENT

If democratization was one side of a "softer" approach to strategic counterterrorism (even if, according to the logic of the Bush administration, it sometimes had to be brought about through the hard application of force), economic development was the other. The reorientation of U.S. attention to Southeast Asia after September 11 also provided crucial impetus to economic engagement. This was rationalized on grounds that economic development was an essential ingredient to broader American counterterrorism strategy. This assumption was predicated on the underlying logic, held in many Washington decisionmaking and think tank circles, that the radicalism and extremism from which terrorism spawned were the outcome of lack of economic development and opportunity, which in turn exacerbated the condition of state weakness. This approach on the part of the Bush administration to consider economic development alongside terrorism was captured in the following statement articulated by then assistant secretary of state for East Asian and Pacific Affairs James A. Kelly, in testimony before Congress:

> The focus you have put on Southeast Asia is well placed, for this region is important to the United States, politically and economically. The region is home to some of the world's fastest-growing

economies and a number of significant trading partners of the United States. Last year, the U.S. sold to this market of a half-billion people $57 billion in goods and services, almost twice as much as to China and Hong Kong combined. Large U.S. investment, totaling $53 billion in the ASEAN countries, has both strengthened our economic ties with the region and expanded opportunities for American business. These economic ties are part of deep and longstanding alliances and friendships in the region that are as critical to our security as they are to our prosperity. Virtually every country in the region has stood beside us in the war on terrorism. The Bali bombing last October drove home to all of Asia that combating terrorism is a global challenge for local, regional, and worldwide security. Steadfast friends such as Singapore, Indonesia, and the Philippines are helping in the fight against terrorism in many ways.[18]

This perspective was reinforced by the National Security Strategy propounded in 2002, which declared:

A strong world economy enhances our national security by advancing prosperity and freedom in the rest of the world. Economic growth supported by free trade and free markets creates new jobs and higher incomes. . . . We will promote economic growth and economic freedom beyond America's shores. . . . The lessons of history are clear: market economies, not command-and-control economies with the heavy hand of government, are the best way to promote prosperity and reduce poverty.[19]

For the Bush administration, then, if terrorism was intimately tied to economic underdevelopment, it stood to reason that economic development and education opportunities were critical not only for prosperity but for internal stability through democratization that was a crucial antidote to the ill-conceived attraction of radical and extremist ideologies. As the American deputy trade representative and former presidential candidate Jon M. Huntsman Jr., maintained,

With regard to trade, the [Bush] Administration's policy on Asia reflects President Bush's goals of pursuing trade liberalization globally, regionally, and with individual countries. Not only does such a policy promise rewards for America's manufacturers, farmers and service providers, but open markets mean stable societies. As President Bush has said, "Trade creates jobs for the unemployed. When we negotiate for open markets, we are providing hope for the world's poor. And when we promote open trade, we are promoting political freedom. Societies that open to commerce across their borders will open to democracy within their borders."[20]

The increase in financial and military aid to Southeast Asian states critical to the counterterrorism effort has already been detailed in the previous chapter. These bilateral efforts were further bolstered by multilateral economic engagement with the region that centered on the Enterprise for ASEAN Initiative (EAI). Announced at the summit of the APEC forum in October 2002 by President Bush, EAI aimed to create a network of bilateral free trade agreements (FTAs) in Southeast Asia between the United States and regional states who were members of the World Trade Organization (WTO) and with whom the United States had a preexisting bilateral Trade and Investment Framework Agreement (TIFA). At the point of its announcement, the eligible states were Singapore, Malaysia, Indonesia, Thailand, Brunei, and the Philippines, all coincidentally also states that had vested interests in the American-led Global War on Terror. In order to conceptualize a broader engagement strategy, the agreement was also envisaged to provide American support to the efforts of Cambodia, Laos, and Vietnam to seek membership in the WTO.

The significance of FTAs should not be overlooked, particularly given how these emerged as the United States' preferred vehicle of economic engagement. As one scholar observed in the context of the Bush administration's trade policies:

> Especially in a world in which U.S. popularity is low, U.S. foreign aid has dwindled to a very low level as a percentage of gross domestic product (GDP), and U.S. influence derived from its military power has declined from cold war levels, the rise of the FTA as a foreign policy tool is perhaps inevitable. It is the most widely desired carrots the United States has to offer. As a result of the large and attractive U.S. market, access is a significant inducement to other countries. The FTA is the most significant and credible (and widely used) carrot in the U.S. foreign policy arsenal. FTAs do allow the United States to harness the strength of the U.S. econ-

omy directly to move other countries on foreign policy issues. . . . it is worthy of note that FTAs have gone from a little-used economic device to being a principal tool of U.S. foreign policy.[21]

Further to that, others have noted an additional motivation for Southeast Asian states that met the requirements to leverage on EAI: "the need for a defensive strategy in the current international economic environment."[22] The point here is that it has been an "irrefutable reality" that FTAs and other forms of economic integration have driven international economic and commercial policy, as opposed to multilateral initiatives.[23] The United States, Japan, and European Union—all crucial markets for ASEAN member states—had already signed FTAs with ASEAN's competitors, and in this sense, regional states ran the risk of losing ground in these markets.

EAI made specific mention of the FTA with Singapore, signed in May 2003, as the benchmark for other FTAs the United States intended to pursue with Southeast Asian partners. This was notwithstanding the fact that economic relations with Singapore were already established on firm ground prior to the FTA. Despite its size, Singapore was at the time the twelfth largest trading partner and export market for the United States, while total trade between the two countries amounted to almost $31 billion in 2002. As an earlier chapter pointed out, Singapore was by considerable lengths the largest recipient of American investments in Southeast Asia as well. With the FTA, this bilateral economic relationship was primed to be catapulted to greater heights. As the chairperson of the American Chamber of Commerce in Singapore observed, the U.S.–Singapore FTA meant "increased access to the Singapore market, landmark intellectual property protection, removal of barriers in the financial services sector, and reduced restrictions on professional services."[24]

But the significance of the U.S.–Singapore FTA transcended the reaping of mere economic dividends. As the Singaporean political and foreign policy leadership were quick to remind, the FTA was of considerable strategic significance as well in how it expressed wider American interests in the region beyond counterterrorism, even though commentators have speculated that the signing of the FTA with Singapore might also have had something to do with Singapore's sturdy support for the war on terrorism. From the perspective of Washington, the signing of this FTA was also conceived as a trigger and incentive for other Southeast

Asian states to enter into FTA discussions with the United States. On that score, it is noteworthy that following the signing of the U.S.–Singapore FTA, negotiations began with Thailand in 2004 and Malaysia in 2005 for respective FTAs under the auspices of EAI. Mirroring the FTA with Singapore, in both instances it was also clear that if successfully concluded, the respective FTAs were tools to advance not only economic cooperation but equally salient political and strategic cooperation as well. The possibilities of an FTA with Thailand had potential to further enhance a long-standing bilateral strategic relationship. In elaborating on the virtues of a potential U.S.–Malaysia FTA, the office of the U.S. trade representative enumerated the following: creating new opportunities for American manufacturers, farmers, and service providers; strengthening American competitiveness; creating jobs; strengthening U.S. economic relations with the region; and advancing broader U.S. strategic goals both in Southeast Asia and, specifically with reference to Malaysia, in the Muslim world.[25]

Although the theoretical benefits of FTAs were clear to all relevant parties concerned, actually shepherding negotiations to a satisfactory conclusion proved a decidedly more complicated and difficult prospect. To that effect, progress toward completion of the bilateral FTAs was, at best, glacial, not least owing to domestic pressures in both Malaysia and Thailand. In fact, in the Thai case, it stalled altogether because of the military coup in 2006, and was resumed after the democratic election of a government, only to stall again as a consequence of another coup in 2014. In the case of Malaysia, despite attempts by the Bush administration to hasten conclusion of the FTA before the expiration of the Trade Promotion Authority then in place (which was scheduled to expire on July 1, 2007, although it was eventually renewed), the Malaysian government did not share this sense of urgency.[26] In Malaysia, words of caution were sounded in many quarters, with many making the point that the structure of the Malaysian economy did not lend itself easily to an FTA.[27] Meanwhile, out in the streets, popular protests broke out, spearheaded by environmental groups and medical and health sector lobbies concerned that an FTA with the United States would limit access to critical medicines and accelerate environmental degradation. Yet the biggest obstacle was identified to be Malaysian government procurement practices, which granted privileged access based on discriminatory principles of affirmative action for the ethnic Malay majority. This script would rehearse itself in the lead up to the TPPA discussions that would take place a decade later (discussed in chapter 7). Obstacles in Thailand, although expressed in different forms, proved equally intractable. As mentioned earlier, negotiations with Thailand were suspended following the military coup of September 19, 2006, which took place as the prime minister at that time, Thaksin Shinnawatra, was visiting the United States. The United States promptly halted negotiations, which Washington indicated would only resume upon the restoration of full democracy. Be that as it may, it was notable that opposition to an FTA from a wide spectrum of Thai society was already evident prior to the coup, for instance, when several thousand protestors protested during negotiations that took place in Chiang Mai in January 2006.[28]

Obstacles to free trade were not only evident in Southeast Asia. Apropos of the subject, some commentators have noted that congressional politics in the United States have made it difficult for American leadership to concretize trade deals that are popular in East Asia, and as a result, Asian leaders were cautious about the amount of political capital they needed to invest in FTA negotiations while knowing that these FTAs might not, and may never, be approved by Congress.[29] Elsewhere, others have put things in harsher light, suggesting that "trade policy is the Achilles heel of U.S. Asia policy."[30] Indeed, the point has been stressed that at a time when East Asian states were focusing on trade and economic integration as part of regional community-building efforts, acrimonious domestic politics swirling around the issue of trade and speculation of job losses have made it difficult for Washington to embark on an active trade policy.[31] Reflecting on these domestic constraints, Amy Searight averred that

> The American public has grown much more skeptical about the benefits of free trade and free trade agreements. In Congress, the bipartisan coalition for free trade that sustained a liberal U.S. trade policy for most of the postwar period began to fray in the 1990s, in the wake of negotiating NAFTA. Although traditional protectionism remains relatively low, new resistance to FTAs has emerged out of concerns over the social costs of trade. In particular, many Democrats are concerned about labor rights and environmental protection in partner countries. More broadly, the American public is much more skeptical about the benefits of free trade deals for American workers and the domestic economy, viewing FTAs as primarily benefiting multinational corporations and foreign trade

partners. At the same time, American politics has grown far more partisan and divided, which has affected trade policy as well. The bipartisan cooperation that used to characterize trade policymaking in Congress has completely broken down.[32]

Yet while the Bush administration was frustrated by domestic obstacles in its attempt to extend the web of FTAs beyond Singapore, it managed to make incremental progress in broader, albeit more modest, economic engagement with the conclusion in August 2006 of a U.S.–ASEAN TIFA, which further provided the rubric for a formal ministerial dialogue between the United States and ASEAN aimed at deepening commercial and trading initiatives. The United States also supported the Southeast Asian region's own economic strategies. In 2007, the United States launched the ASEAN Development Vision to Advance National Cooperation and Economic Integration project, which worked on trade liberalization issues and facilitated cooperation with the ASEAN Secretariat. A bilateral market access agreement was also signed with Vietnam to facilitate Vietnam's membership in the WTO. Nevertheless, formal economic engagement with ASEAN remained hampered by the fact that Laos was then not yet a member of the WTO and, more consequentially, by the imperative of upholding the policies of isolation and sanctions against the reclusive regime in Myanmar.

At this juncture, it bears highlighting that such was the congressional aversion to the military junta in Yangon, by the end of the Bush administration, the U.S. sanctions language on Myanmar had become arguably the most precise of all sanctions regimes, ranging from broad sanctions involving visa bans, restrictions on financial services, prohibition on imports of goods, bans on investment, and restrictions on U.S. assistance, to more targeted sanctions that addressed functional issues, such as drug trafficking, child soldiers, money laundering, and religious freedoms. Even American states and cities such as Massachusetts, New York, and Berkeley passed their own sanctions specifically targeted at Myanmar.[33] An extensive sanctions regime was put in place when the Burma Freedom and Democracy Act was signed into effect by President Bush on July 28, 2003, containing wide-ranging restrictions on interactions with the military junta in response to the continued incarceration of political prisoners including Aung San Suu Kyi.

It is noteworthy that pressure on the American government to retain sanctions on the Myanmar junta came not only from within Congress but also from a wide array of civil society groups, including groups and ethnic organizations based in Myanmar.[34] Yet it remains debatable if sanctions actually yielded the results that the United States and its European partners had hoped. Although the Myanmar population undoubtedly suffered under the weight of sanctions on top of the depredations of the junta, the economy was still able to lurch along through economic and trading relations established with other regional states, including China and members of ASEAN. From the standpoint of diplomatic engagement with the region, not only did sanctions impose tremendous costs on the welfare of the population of Myanmar, it also denied the United States an opportunity to cooperate with ASEAN in engaging Myanmar.[35] To borrow a metaphor popular in ASEAN circles in the early 1980s, the Myanmar sanctions tail was wagging the dog of economic engagement with ASEAN.

Despite the diverse efforts at economic engagement outlined above, many in the region still felt that U.S.–ASEAN relations were on the decline, especially in light of deepening relations between the Southeast Asian organization and other dialogue partners, which were proceeding along a much broader scope. This view was buttressed by the fact that unlike many other major economic actors, the United States had not sought to negotiate an FTA with ASEAN as a group. The constraints that the United States faced on that score were duly acknowledged by the State Department itself, which noted the following: First, the United States would require that a trade agreement with ASEAN collectively comply with the U.S. FTA model, a condition that ASEAN would not find acceptable. Second, the United States maintained a comprehensive ban on direct trade with Myanmar, a member of ASEAN. Third, the ASEAN economies are diverse in terms of their level of economic and legal development, and this diversity would pose structural obstacles to the pursuit of an FTA, such as a detailed specification of compliance requirements upon which such an agreement could be established.[36]

Nor did the Bush administration fare too well in using existing regional initiatives to enhance trade engagement with the region. Under the long shadow cast by the war on terrorism, APEC trade liberalization initiatives were all but sidelined. Rather than focus on its core business of trade, American officials chose to give greater attention to counterterrorism and regional security, compelling the matter onto the APEC agenda in the form of agreements on information sharing, baggage screening, and the use of technology to interdict potential terrorists. President Bush sought to use the organization to marshal support in order to further his Global War on Terror agenda, as evident in the priority he gave to interactions with Russian president Vladimir Putin on the sidelines of APEC especially after the latter's own terrorism crisis materialized with the events in Moscow in October 2002, when Chechen rebels temporarily seized control of the Dubrovka Theater. Describing the presumed "natural" extension of the APEC agenda as a vehicle for counterterrorism cooperation, White House press secretary Scott McClellan maintained, "The big priorities [at APEC] will focus on the security and economic side because they really go hand in hand. You need to make sure you have security so that you can move forward on the economic side."[37] In 2002, the United States secured the support of member economies for this agenda in the form of an APEC leaders' "Statement on Fighting Terrorism and Promoting Growth." This was followed by the creation of an APEC Counter-Terrorism Task Force and formulation of a Counter-Terrorism Action Plan in February 2003. With all these initiatives, APEC, a trade body by nature, was fast morphing into a vehicle for regional counterterrorism cooperation under the weight of American pressure.

In point of fact, by approaching APEC in this manner, Washington found the organization a more amenable institutional platform for counterterrorism cooperation, in part because attendant initiatives could be couched in nonpolitical, functional terms as efforts to facilitate commerce and the safe transit of people and material. To that end, it was hardly a surprise when Bush administration officials described APEC as "by far the most robust multilateral grouping in Asia."[38] Verisimilitude aside, the Bush administration's attempt to fixate APEC on a more overt security agenda nevertheless also encountered resistance, as regional states such as Indonesia and Malaysia began to look askance at the securitized agenda of APEC under American leadership and expressed desire for the organization to return to its original mandate of trade liberalization. Moreover, domestic considerations of the sort discussed in the previous chapter posed significant impediments to positive regional reception of the Bush administration's attempt to steer APEC toward a more deliberate security agenda as well. As Elizabeth Economy and Adam Segal observed on the eve of the 2004 APEC meeting in Bangkok,

> From their [regional states'] perspective, the war on terror is in
> danger of being derailed by growing anti-U.S. sentiment. These lead-
> ers also have their own domestic economic concerns, and believe

the United States is misguided in its focus on others' economic policies as the source of its woes. In addition, several leaders in Asia will be engaged in election campaigns in 2004, and are unlikely to be interested in American proposals that don't meet their immediate political needs.[39]

In 2006, Malaysian prime minister Abdullah Badawi urged the APEC forum to return to its original purpose of promoting economic growth and to leave security concerns to ARF.[40] To this can be added the fact that any real or perceived ASEAN reticence to support APEC may be founded more on concerns about the pace of achieving specific trade liberalization targets, or the specific commodities targeted, rather than the inherent value of APEC objectives themselves, be they trade, economic, or security related.

At any rate, Washington's attempts to mobilize the organization for security purposes ultimately proved counterproductive as regional attention shifted from APEC to other emerging regional initiatives, which effectively saw the importance of the "most robust multilateral grouping in Asia" incontrovertibly subverted. In December 2005, the first EAS meeting was held in Kuala Lumpur. Significantly, the meeting did not include the United States, which was not invited since membership had the precondition that applicants have to be signatories of the ASEAN Treaty of Amity and Cooperation, which directly contravened at least one of the main pillars of the Bush doctrine: pre-emptive use of force.[41] More to the point, whereas the Bush administration insisted on viewing just about everything through the lens of counterterrorism, Southeast Asia was intent on focusing on broader strategic issues that lay over the horizon. In other words, even as the United States and key Southeast Asian states shared similar security concerns for the problem of terrorism, in terms of the larger strategic picture outlooks and priorities between Washington and the region in general were in fact more divergent than they seemed, with the possible exception of Singapore, for whom concern for the threat of terrorism loomed large.

THE CHINESE "CHARM OFFENSIVE" IN SOUTHEAST ASIA

Notwithstanding debates about the controversies surrounding the Bush doctrine, the Global War on Terror, and the attendant post–September 11 reorientation of strategic priorities, regional policymakers continued to

stress the broader point that American commitment to the region was
vital to regional security, for fear that Iraq and Afghanistan were driving the United States to distraction. This reluctance to distance themselves too far from Washington despite domestic pressures and ethical
dilemmas was illustrative of the magnitude of longer term geostrategic
concerns that weighed on Southeast Asian leaders. To that end, one
question seized regional policymakers—how to deal with China. The
fact that the rise of China was a geostrategic reality that had major strategic and economic implications for Southeast Asia was by the end of
the 1990s very much already a given. Of immediate concern for the region was how to read China's policies and intentions as the development
of its economic and military capabilities expanded rapidly in the first
decade of the new century.

The fact that China's relations with Southeast Asia had by the end of
the Bush presidency undergone a fundamental transformation compared
with the state of affairs at the end of the Cold War is undeniable. Although previously suspicious of ASEAN and concerned that the regional
organization was little more than an artifact of the Cold War that would
throw its weight behind a United States intent on containing China, for
most of the first decade of the new century Beijing had embarked on what
commentators had salubriously termed a "charm offensive" toward
Southeast Asia. This charm offensive found concrete expression in conciliatory gestures such as restraint (at least to some extent) on its claims to
South China Sea territories, enhanced economic and trade relations with
Southeast Asian economies, active diplomatic and political support for
ASEAN initiatives such as ARF and the newly minted EAS, an important
decision not to devalue the renminbi during the height of the Asian financial crisis, and accession to ASEAN's TAC. Already impressive in comparison to earlier years of mutual suspicion between China and Southeast
Asia, the positive net effect of these initiatives was further amplified when
juxtaposed, as they surely were in regional circles in private if not in
public, to the state of Washington's engagement with the region.

With the United States strategic outlook obscured by the Global War
on Terror and seized by intractable crises of its own making in Afghanistan and Iraq, Chinese economic development accelerated, and with this
its diplomatic influence invariably grew as well, acquiring new meaning
and impetus along the way. It is a matter of record that during the Asian
financial crisis, China won the goodwill of regional states by not devalu-
ating its currency. In a matter of years, the Chinese economy had under-

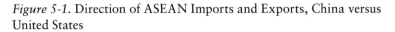

Figure 5-1. Direction of ASEAN Imports and Exports, China versus United States

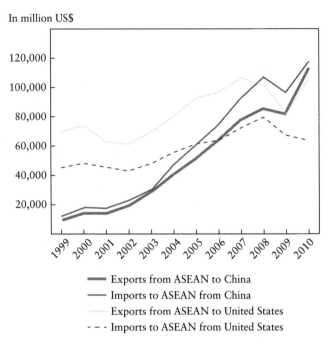

In million US$

- Exports from ASEAN to China
- Imports to ASEAN from China
- Exports from ASEAN to United States
- – – Imports to ASEAN from United States

Source: ASEAN Statistics Yearbook, *China Daily*, Office of the U.S. Trade Representative (from Munir Majid, "Southeast Asia between China and the United States," http://www.lse.ac.uk/IDEAS/publications/reports/pdf/SR015/SR015Majid-China-vs -US.pdf).

gone transformation of such speed and magnitude that by the turn of the century, it was primarily China's phenomenal economic growth that underpinned predictions that the new century would be an Asian century, implying an anticipated Asian dominance of the global economy (predicated foremost on Chinese dominance of the Asian economy).

For Southeast Asia, the math was inescapable. ASEAN's exports to China increased by a hefty 34 percent between 2001 and 2002 alone and a further 39.9 percent in 2003.[42] From 2003 to 2008, Chinese trade with Southeast Asia effectively tripled from $59.6 billion to $192.5 billion and, as figure 5-1 illustrates, catapulted it past the United States as ASEAN's third largest trading partner after the European Union and Japan.[43]

As trade figures grew so did a slew of initiatives, many at China's behest and initiation. China surfaced the idea of a China–ASEAN FTA at the ASEAN Plus Three meeting in Brunei in 2001. In November 2002, China and ASEAN signed an ambitious Framework Agreement on China–ASEAN Comprehensive Economic Cooperation at the Sixth China–ASEAN Summit in Phnom Penh. China further signed an agreement on Trading in Goods under the rubric of the Framework Agreement on Comprehensive Economic Cooperation with ASEAN on November 29, 2004. The agreement aimed to reduce and eventually eliminate tariffs on trade in goods between the parties and establish a mechanism to adjudicate ASEAN–China trade disputes. More significant, it served to set the stage for the subsequent China–ASEAN FTA by laying out an incremental, staggered approach to liberalization of trade in goods with the ASEAN-6 (referring to the founding ASEAN members and Brunei) by 2010 and the rest of the organization by 2015. As a further gesture, China unilaterally reduced tariffs on agricultural imports before reciprocal reductions by regional states were introduced. In terms of foreign direct investments (FDI), as figure 5-2 illustrates, although Chinese figures were still adrift of the United States in real terms in the first decade of the new century, in relative terms the gap had begun to close, with China in the process of becoming a source of increasing investments in the region. Perhaps more instructive from figure 5-2 is the steady climb in Chinese FDI compared with the more erratic swings that have defined American investments since 1999.

The Greater Mekong Subregion

China's presence in the Mekong region and on the Mekong River itself, the lifeline of mainland Southeast Asian communities since time immemorial, is in many ways emblematic of its growing weight in Southeast Asia, for it is there that arguably the most significant increase in the Chinese stake in, and influence over, regional economic development was registered during this period. Multilateral cooperation in the Mekong region dates as far back as 1957, when Cambodia, South Vietnam, Thailand, and Laos reached agreement on a Mekong Development Project that was created under the auspices of the Committee on the Coordination of Investigations of the Lower Mekong Basin. However, for reasons of the many decades of war and the lack of wherewithal in most signatory states to capitalize on the resource potential of the Mekong, this institution effectively lay dormant. It was only at the turn of the century that the outlook on the Mekong on the part of riparian states began to

Figure 5-2. China versus U.S. Foreign Direct Investment in ASEAN

In million US$

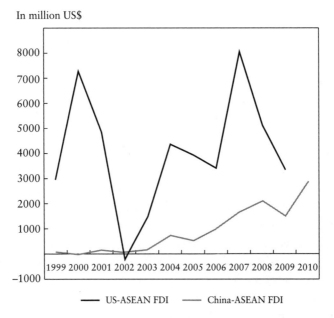

——— US-ASEAN FDI   ——— China-ASEAN FDI

Source: ASEAN Statistics Yearbook, *China Daily*, Office of the U.S. Trade Representative (from Munir Majid, "Southeast Asia between China and the United States," http://www.lse.ac.uk/IDEAS/publications/reports/pdf/SR015/SR015Majid-China-vs-US.pdf).

change in a substantive way from (quite literally) backwater to dynamic development. Chinese interest in the region accounted significantly for this change.

Since 2000, the Mekong region has witnessed China gradually expand economic cooperation with the riparian mainland states of Thailand, Cambodia, Laos, Vietnam, and Myanmar, which together with China collectively form the Greater Mekong Subregion. Initiatives included the building of hydroelectric dams along the Mekong, which proliferated in the 2000s, creation of economic corridors, building of infrastructure, advancements in hydro-agriculture cooperation, and tourism. China, Thailand, Myanmar, and Laos also signed an agreement in 2002 to expand strategic stretches of the Mekong River so as to facilitate the movement of large cargo ships through the region to foster even greater subregional economic integration. On the back of these initiatives, the Greater Mekong Subregion appeared primed to be an engine of economic growth and integration between China and mainland Southeast Asia, with China making a great play of its leadership in binding the two into a shared economic space. But there was more to it than that. The development of the Mekong region did not proceed devoid of controversy. On the contrary, some regional states harbored concern for the overwhelming (some would argue overbearing) presence of China in the region over a relatively short period of time that resulted in a grossly asymmetrical relationship. These states shared a deep discomfort toward the implications of China's dam building upstream in particular, especially for the downstream environmental effect on a river that had long proven crucial to the Southeast Asian riparian states for reasons of irrigation, flood control, and food security.

Something of the vulnerability of these riparian states to the preponderance of Chinese power and influence over the Mekong region became evident in March 2016, when a severe drought in the region of the Lower Mekong (the Southeast Asian region) was alleviated only by the release of water by China at the upstream Jinghong Dam. Beneath the kindly offer to provide immediate and welcome relief lay the harsh reality that China was in a position to dictate water management norms for the Mekong region. More pertinent, the combination of its geostrategic position as the uppermost riparian state and the availability of resources and wherewithal casts China as the unequivocal preponderant power in the Mekong region, in the process neutralizing to some extent the Lower Mekong Initiative of the United States as well, a considerably smaller effort initiated by Washington in 2009 to enhance cooperation between the Southeast Asian Mekong states.[44] Indeed, the following assessment holds out the prospect of this geopolitical reality confronting the riparian states: "China is essentially the giant neighbor ensconced at the river mouth. It can block the Mekong waterways at will. To date, it has completed six of 15 planned dams along the Mekong. The governments of the countries in the lower basin, particularly those of Cambodia and Vietnam, are either too beholden to or dependent on Beijing's generosity and policy decisions to cry foul too vocally."[45]

Expanding Economic Engagement

Chinese economic policies were governed by the notion that to advance the economic interests and well-being of its population, outward-looking foreign trade and economic policies were required, and in order for such to bear fruit, they had to be underpinned by a stable and secure regional environment. Describing how these issues were interlinked, Chinese premier Wen Jiabao, tasked with the responsibility of overseeing relations with Southeast Asia, promptly noted in celebratory fashion:

> China–ASEAN friendship and cooperation have contributed to economic and social progress in our respective countries and made life better for our peoples. Moreover, our cooperation has facilitated regional integration, raised the competitiveness and international profile of our region and promoted peace and stability in Asia. China–ASEAN relations are a fine example of friendly exchanges between countries in the region. They have brought real benefits to the peoples of China and ASEAN countries and made important contributions to peace, stability, and prosperity in Asia and the world at large.[46]

A major diplomatic effort was designed to persuade Southeast Asian states to China's thinking. Mindful of the need to go beyond rhetoric, active Chinese participation in ASEAN-led regional initiatives intensified, including signing the TAC in 2003 and joining EAS in 2005, both mentioned earlier. Multiple familiarization visits were made by high-ranking People's Liberation Army officers to Southeast Asia, and these were always accompanied by invitations for reciprocal visits. Cooperation expanded to nontraditional security issues as well. What was significant was that in deliberate contrast to the United States, Chinese leaders frequently reiterated the point that China was willing and ready to cooperate with regional states irrespective of political leanings or proclivities. A case in point was Myanmar under junta rule, where trade with China provided a crucial lifeline for an economy that was otherwise subject to severe sanctions from the U.S. and European countries.

Southeast Asia required little persuasion to the logic that economic growth and regional stability went hand in hand. Indeed, Southeast Asian states shared the objective of the creation of a stable regional environment that would permit them individually and collectively as ASEAN to maximize opportunities for trade and investments, while minimizing the possibility of the pursuit of regional hegemony by any major external power intent on asserting dominance. To achieve this, the states of Southeast Asia set great store by the principle of regional autonomy, expressed as an ASEAN-driven regional order, and a distribution of power that would prevent the rise of a hegemon. It was through this lens that the rise of China as an economic and military power was viewed. Concomitantly, Southeast Asian states prioritized multilateral settings for their collective engagement of China on security and economic issues, the principle mechanisms of which were EAS, ARF, and ASEAN Plus Three.

From the vantage of geopolitics, the fact that China shares maritime and land borders with a number of Southeast Asian states accents the paramount importance of relations with the region, an importance that is only further animated by the fact that the region holds vast natural resources crucial to Chinese economic development. Geography has afforded China a distinct advantage over the United States in its engagement with Southeast Asia, which, as the discussion thus far has indicated, Beijing leveraged successfully with the imprimatur of its "charm offensive." As Catharin Dalpino noted, "Beyond its markets for exports, China has location on its side. Its proximity to Southeast Asia enables Beijing to dispatch an 'A team' of leaders to the region on short notice. Premier Wen Jiabao holds the ASEAN portfolio."[47] Geography is not the only advantage, for

> ethnic Chinese in Southeast Asia, whose numbers are vaguely estimated at 20 to 40 million, have helped open economic and political doors with China for their adopted countries. China also has cultural roots in common with many Southeast Asian societies, which extends to popular culture in the present day. In many younger generation Southeast Asians, kung fu easily tops hip hop. These factors combine in Chinese policy to stress the "family" aspects of China's relations with Southeast Asia, which the United States cannot as easily claim.[48]

That being said, the ethnic Chinese dimension can also be a double-edged sword, complicating relations by way of posing the challenge to Beijing to exercise restraint in the event that ethnic Chinese communities in Southeast Asian states found themselves subject to any form of perceived discrimination. In fact, this was exactly what happened in Malaysia in 2016, when the Chinese ambassador's visit to Chinatown during the height of a heavily politicized debate over affirmative action in favor of the ethnic Malay community (presumably at the expense of Malaysia's large ethnic Chinese community) sparked a round of criticisms of

Chinese "interference" in Malaysian domestic affairs. If we cast our minds further back, we recall, too, how Beijing was vexed by the anti-Chinese violence that consumed Jakarta during the dark days of the Asian financial crisis. A related portent obtains in Beijing's conduct of relations with Singapore, where the island-state's large ethnic Chinese majority has prompted Chinese leaders to take the view that Singapore should be especially sensitive to China's interests.

To be sure, the challenge that China was beginning to pose to American primacy in regional affairs was not lost on the Bush administration. Cognizant of this, then assistant secretary of state for East Asian and Pacific Affairs James Kelly testified that

> China's rising economic power in particular has made it a new presence in Southeast Asia. . . . We cannot ignore the fact that China's growing economic power has created a competition for influence in the region, which makes it all the more important for the United States to remain actively engaged with our Asian allies. While China has not moved aggressively to garner political capital from its growing economic strength, there is no denying its prominence on the Asian political stage. We need only to look as far as Taiwan . . . to see how quickly economics can change a political dynamic.[49]

Yet the hard truth was that the Chinese charm offensive effectively stole a march on the United States. The contrast had become disconcertingly stark. Adroit Chinese foreign policy messaging in Southeast Asia and attention to atmospherics struck a powerful chord in Southeast Asia and amplified the perceived insensitivity of the United States under the Bush administration, casting an even harsher light on the disconcerting premises of unilateralism and pre-emption upon which Washington's strategy on global security was predicated. This was rendered all the more acute in a region where diplomatic culture is anchored on consultation and consensus in a multilateral institutional context, irrespective of the outlooks of individual states. In contrast, China was lauded in Southeast Asian circles for its multilateral approach, as well as "its ability to understand the needs of regional actors, and its desire to address the region's concerns."[50] Needless to say, this went some distance in allaying regional apprehensions about China's rise and the intentions behind it— allaying but not removing them. Indeed, so significant was the upturn in

China–Southeast Asia relations during the Bush years that some analysts even suggested that Southeast Asian states were beginning to consider China a "benign power," although even at the height of cordiality
(let alone in hindsight) this was probably an excessively optimistic read
on the situation.[51]

By and large, Southeast Asian states welcomed China's rise. Of significance, this welcome was extended not only on the back of the opportunities that China's newfound prosperity and economic power proffered
for the region but also out of concern for the opposite effect of a China
weakened by frustration and domestic disenfranchisement and the instability that such a state of affairs might spawn. Singapore's former
prime minister Goh Chok Tong sketched out the stark outlines of this
contrast: "A prosperous and globally integrated China is in all our interests. The alternative of a poor and isolated China will be like having
sixty North Koreas at our doorstep. It will pose challenges without the
opportunities."[52] Ensuring China's peaceful rise to prosperity was also
deemed imperative by regional states on at least two further counts.
First, Chinese prosperity would doubtless have a positive spillover effect
on the rest of the region. Though embracing Chinese economic inducements in a climate of uncertain longer term Chinese intentions risked
putting some regional states in a vulnerable position of dependence, as
former Malaysian prime minister Abdullah Badawi saw it there was still
a clear and practical enough logic to commend such an effort: "China is
today a creator of prosperity of the highest order. Political and social
linkages are bound to eventually follow suit. It is therefore important to
use every opportunity and establish ties."[53] Second, growing Chinese
influence in Southeast Asia is an inescapable reality, and hence a cardi-
nal objective for regional diplomacy would be to nudge China to wield
this influence in ways that would advance the cause of regional stability
and economic progress. Although a strong supporter of the American
presence in the region and still harboring residual reservations toward
China's longer term strategic and political ambitions, even Singapore
was exercised by the hostile and obdurate language that segments within
the American political community tended to employ toward China,
which the leaders of the island state felt were unnecessarily provocative.
This apprehension was captured in the following remarks by the late
former prime minister Lee Kuan Yew: "We distanced ourselves from
[the United States'] hostile rhetoric against China. We feared that talking and acting as if China was an enemy would make it into one. We did

not want this to happen; no country in Southeast Asia wanted to go out of its way to make China an enemy."

While some Southeast Asian states focused on embracing the economic prospects of improved relations with China, others were prepared to explore possibilities for an even more substantive, strategic relationship. Recognizing China's rise and keen to project a position on foreign affairs that hewed closely to the tenets of "free and active" foreign policy principles articulated by the architects of Indonesian independence, the then newly elected Indonesian president Susilo Bambang Yudhoyono worked toward the expansion of bilateral political and security relations alongside the heady progress that was by then already taking place in the economic realm. Toward those ends, Indonesia and China issued a joint declaration, "Building a Strategic Partnership," in April 2005. A particularly telling aspect of this strategic partnership was the potential role China was envisaged to play in the development of Indonesia's indigenous defense industry, given Jakarta's experience with and presumed vulnerability in its overreliance on the United States. To that effect, as Ian Storey surmised, "During the 1990s Jakarta learned the painful reality of being overly dependent on one country for its defense needs when the United States, its primary military partner, imposed a series of weapons and training embargoes on Indonesia in response to human rights violations perpetrated by the TNI in East Timor and Papua. Cognizant of this fact, China was keen to position itself as an alternative arms vendor to Indonesia."[54] This view was reinforced by the Chinese ambassador in Jakarta, who claimed that China was prepared to supply weaponry to the Indonesian military "without political strings attached," although the anticipated collaboration between the two parties has yet to materialize in any substantive way.[55]

It is important to note that the positive climate of relations between China and Southeast Asia provided conditions for some progress on the South China Sea disputes. China's objective has always been to settle the South China Sea disputes without the involvement of nonclaimant states and, especially, external powers such as the United States. To that end, Beijing managed to make significant advances through a combination of deft diplomacy and economic incentives, capitalizing on America's policy of distance and not taking sides on the claims and the Bush administration's susceptibility to distraction by the war on terror. Part of Beijing's strategy was to position itself as the putative driver of the regional economy, a role that it gradually enhanced over the course of the first decade of the new century. In addition to that, diplomatic overtures were made to Southeast Asian states in an attempt to dull the edges of their South China Sea ambitions and neutralize, at least to some extent, latent regional suspicions. Mindful of their increased dependence—ergo vulnerability—to China's growing economic influence, Southeast Asian states were careful to avoid raising questions of territorial sovereignty in the course of discussions with China. After several years of discussions, China and ASEAN reached agreement on a nonbinding Declaration on the Conduct of Parties in the South China Sea (DOC) in November 2002. At the time, this looked to be (indeed, it was also made out to be) a monumental success of regional diplomacy.

The path to the DOC, however, was not without travail, but the point nevertheless was that claimant states were prepared to make concessions to bring it to fruition. It is notable that Vietnam had to stand down on its initial demand for the Paracel Islands to be specifically mentioned in the agreement, possibly even in reference to its return to Hanoi's presumed possession, whereas the Philippines agreed to moderate its original position calling for a halt to the erection of structures in areas in dispute. Manila also had to accept that the code could not take on the legally binding form that it preferred.[56] Chinese desires that mention be made of a prohibition on naval exercises involving foreign navies were also not fulfilled in the face of resistance from ASEAN. In the event, the signing of the DOC marked some measure of concession on the part of China, especially in view of how until the late 1990s it maintained a steadfast position that the disputes should only be discussed bilaterally among claimants and that ASEAN had no role to play either in its management or resolution. Following the signing of the DOC, ASEAN and China entered into a season of protracted negotiations for the Guidelines for the Implementation of the DOC, which was eventually signed only in July 2011. Meanwhile, claimant states flirted with periodic talk of joint exploration, but nothing ever materialized in any substantive fashion.

Although there was little doubt that as a result of its charm offensive over the first decade of the new century China had begun progressively to dispel some of the suspicion that regional states harbored about its hegemonic intentions in the wake of diplomatic altercations involving competing territorial claims in the South China Sea (primarily in 1992, 1995, and 1997), the region still continued to hedge against the possibility of future Chinese revisionism.[57] Indeed, for all China's efforts, Chinese engagement was still received with a degree of reticence. Three issues in particular stood out as matters of concern for the policy community in Southeast Asia. First, despite its support of "joint exploration" initiatives or the fact that it was a signatory to the DOC, China remained adamant in pressing vague but robust claims to the South China Sea. Second, the Chinese establishment continued to expressly maintain that although its objective is peaceful reunification with Taiwan, it is prepared to use force against any Taiwanese government that unilaterally declares independence. Although the outbreak of hostilities across the Taiwan Straits is not likely to spill over into Southeast Asia, it is the likelihood that heightened tensions would almost definitely have a dire impact on the regional, if not global, economy that provokes sharp alarm and accounts for yet another dimension to the deep reservations and anxieties that regional governments share regarding the potential negative complications arising from Chinese assertiveness. Moreover, given Taiwan's intimate relations with the United States, Southeast Asian leaders have often expressed candidly that they do not wish to find themselves caught between the two sides in the event of conflict. Finally, Sino–Japanese relations continued to vacillate between restraint and open hostility. Here again regional states are confronted with the same trepidation of the dire economic impact on the region on the one hand and, on the other, the potential political and diplomatic costs of being trapped in the middle of a conflict between major regional powers. In fact, in both instances the existence of close defense ties to the United States and Washington's expressed, if at times still vague, assurances of military support in the event of the outbreak of hostilities generates contradictory effects—a presumed stronger deterrence against such an occurrence but, in the event deterrence fails, the almost certain increase in the regional—and global—costs of conflict.

It is through these lenses that Southeast Asia's policymakers from Vietnam, which continued to harbor historical suspicions of Chinese hegemony, to Indonesia and Malaysia, who were wary of American unilateralism and foreign policy rhetoric, still viewed the United States as a strategically important countervailing force vis-à-vis an increasingly powerful China. That said, Southeast Asian states, including Washington's traditional allies, were reluctant to pursue overt balancing strategies against China, conscious of the danger that such an approach might inadvertently "will" a hostile China into being. This being the case, concerns were understandably aroused at the discourse of strategic competition that obtained at the inception of the Bush presidency. Yet the fact that the envisaged strategic competition failed eventually to materialize was hardly reassuring, for its absence owed much to the fact that the United States eventually found itself distracted by the war on terror and attendant foreign policy commitments elsewhere. And because it was consumed by the singular logic of the Global War on Terror, Washington in effect lost sight of the greater imperative, which was to stake a presence in a region whose geostrategic logic was changing rapidly.

Conversely, irrespective of the strengthening of economic and diplomatic ties, a careful parsing of regional responses to China on a raft of issues, ranging from Beijing's activities in the Mekong region to its ambitions in the South China Sea, betrayed the absence of a coherent Southeast Asian position on China. Not unlike their sometimes contrasting (and occasionally competing) outlooks toward the United States, a common perception of the extent of the challenge or threat posed by China was absent among regional states. Not only that, the absence of such a unity of perspective also created anxieties within Southeast Asia toward each other in terms of concern for the susceptibility of some states to Chinese inducements, persuasion, and/or pressure, which might then lend to the breaking of ranks in ASEAN. In hindsight, this concern would grow only more acute over time.

Because member states were mindful of the need to foster greater regional coherence, discussions within ASEAN began in earnest on an ASEAN Charter, which was eventually adopted in November 2007. The charter was notable for the bold claims it made on issues such as human rights and strengthening of democratic institutions, themes that hitherto seldom featured in the organization's discourse or proceedings. Nevertheless, a dark cloud hung over the adoption of the charter in the form of the Myanmar junta's crackdown on popular dissent several months earlier and the organization's inability to take any action other than despairing calls for the crackdown to stop and expressions of disappointment from the ASEAN chair, Singapore, and the democracies of the region. Indeed, given that the charter ambitiously attempted to speak to matters that were the internal prerogative of member states, such as human rights, rule of law, democracy, and fundamental freedoms, matters that ASEAN avoided in fidelity to its principle of noninterference, it was hardly a surprise when doubt was yet again cast by detractors at the credibility of the organization over its inability to take any concrete action against the Myanmar regime's flagrant undermining of these lofty principles.

However, even as ASEAN was grappling with matters of organizational unity and coherence in response to China's growing influence on regional matters, the policy challenges posed by the dynamism and complexities of a region in geostrategic and economic flux was perhaps most evident in Vietnam, for whom relations with both the United States and China were changing in very significant ways.

U.S. RELATIONS WITH VIETNAM

Since the signing of the Bilateral Trade Agreement in July 2000, economic ties between the old Cold War adversaries have improved gradually. The strengthening of economic ties also played an important role in opening up new channels of communication and creating conducive conditions for gradual engagement in the security and political sphere. In 2003, the Communist Party of Vietnam passed a resolution at its Eighth Plenum that justified the gradual establishment of closer relations with the United States on grounds that advancements in Sino–U.S. relations against the backdrop of shared interests against terrorism required Hanoi to reassess prevailing reservations toward the United States.[58] On November 19 of that year, the U.S.S. *Vandergrift* became the first U.S. warship to make a port call in Vietnam in almost thirty years. Of note, the visit took place just slightly over a week after Minister of Defense Pham Van Tra visited Washington, the first visit by a Vietnamese defense minister since the end of the Vietnam War. A few years later, in 2005, Prime Minister Phan Van Khai became the first Vietnamese head of government to visit the United States. During that visit, Phan managed to secure President Bush's commitment to visit Hanoi for the APEC meeting as well as his personal support for Vietnamese accession to the WTO.

The cautious upturn in relations with the United States was registered as part of a broader shift in Vietnamese strategic thinking away from a foreign policy based on revolution to one that embraced regional cooperation. This was signaled at the Communist Party of Vietnam Congress of 1991, when the party leadership declared a multidirectional foreign policy within a framework of "independence, self-reliance, multilateralism, and diversification." Two factors accounted for this turn of events:

concern for shifts in the balance of power with the demise of Vietnam's erstwhile patron, the Soviet Union, and alarm at the overthrow of communist parties in Europe. At the same time, in keeping with the legacy of ideological antagonism between communism and Western capitalism, party conservatives remained fixated on the need to defend Vietnam against Western imperialist influences and reticent toward too rapid a pace of reform and expansion of foreign relations, especially with the "hostile forces" of the West, although to be fair, this reticence had already begun to gradually give way to the logics of necessity and pragmatism.[59] In any event, state-controlled media still periodically castigated the United States as the eternal enemy, while official party documents made pointed references to attempts by "hostile forces"—doubtless a euphemism for the United States—to destabilize the country and threaten regime security through "peaceful evolution." In 2009, the secretariat of the Communist Party's Central Committee disseminated Directive 34-CT/TW on "stepping up the fight against the scheme of 'peaceful evolution' in the fields of culture and ideology."[60] A subsequent paper written by the party's Central Department of Propaganda and Education, charged with directing the execution of the aforementioned directive, carefully scrutinized what it described as the U.S. plan of "peaceful evolution," where, among other things, it identified the attempt to dispatch Peace Corp volunteers to Vietnam as a veiled move to foment a "color revolution" in Vietnam, and efforts of U.S. education aid agencies such as the Vietnam Education Fund and the Vietnam Fulbright Economic Teaching Program as covert instruments of political transformation through which a generation of subversive pro-American and pro-Western thinkers would be created.

Hanoi's move to gradually improve relations with the United States also stemmed in part from growing apprehension toward China, which in turn had much to do with a series of events in the South China Sea. In December 2006, China's move to plant markers in the Paracel Islands inflamed Vietnamese sentiments.[61] In April 2007, Chinese vessels detained four Vietnamese fishing boats near the Spratly Islands. In June of that same year, Chinese pressure led British Petroleum to announce it was halting seismic work off southern Vietnam. A month after that, Vietnamese fishing vessels were fired at by Chinese patrol boats in the Spratlys, leading to the sinking of one boat and the death of a crew member.

Reports that China had passed legislation to create Sansha City in order to administer Beijing's claims in the South China Sea provoked

further nationalist backlash in Vietnam when hundreds protested outside the Chinese embassy in December 2007, accusing China of "invad-
ing" Vietnamese territory.[62] The demonstrations were significant on
several counts. First, given the tightly controlled climate in Vietnam, it
is inconceivable that such demonstrations could have taken place without tacit, if not explicit, endorsement by the government in Hanoi and,
more significant, by the party. In fact, it may well have carried the imprimatur of high Vietnamese leadership. Second, the demonstrations
also took place at a time when an increased Vietnamese assertiveness
regarding their own claims in the South China Sea was palpable. In the
event, Vietnamese social media came alive to condemn China, while
commentaries critiquing Chinese belligerence proliferated in the mainstream newspapers. Even so, the reality of the need to balance between
the expression of nationalist sentiments and the danger of antagonizing
China led to a Politburo decision to eventually intervene to contain the
outpouring of nationalism and to halt all public displays of anti-China
sentiment. Concern for Chinese reprisals sat uncomfortably alongside
fears that dissident activists might take advantage of anti-Chinese mobilization to destabilize the political system.[63]

In May 2008, General Secretary Nong Duc Manh visited China with
an intent to improve relations and to implement hotline communications.
The timing, however, proved inauspicious. Just prior to Nong's visit, Beijing commercial satellite imagery was released that showed the building of
a naval base on Hainan Island that was large enough for good-sized military vessels to dock. In a clear signal to China, Prime Minister Nguyen
Tan Dung elected to visit the United States in June that year, where he
obtained President Bush's support for "Vietnam's national sovereignty,
security and territorial integrity."[64] Bush also agreed to an inaugural
security dialogue with Vietnam. In apparent reaction to the success of
Nguyen Tan Dung's U.S. visit, China pressured ExxonMobil to withdraw from joint exploration with Vietnam Oil and Gas Corporation in
July. Following this, Chinese-language websites started floating stories
on an alleged Chinese plan to invade Vietnam. One such report claimed,
"Vietnam is a major threat to the safety of Chinese territories, and the
biggest obstacle to the peaceful emergence of China. Vietnam has to be
conquered first if China wanted to exercise traditional influence in the
region."[65] In May 2009, China unilaterally announced a three-month
moratorium on fishing in the South China Sea at the height of Vietnam's
fishing season and backed this up with several fishery vessels sent to

enforce the ban.[66] Cautious not to be drawn into the brewing bilateral dispute between China and Vietnam, the U.S. embassy in Hanoi declined an invitation to send observers to the inaugural diplomatic conference on the South China Sea hosted by Vietnam in December 2009, arguably to distance itself from Vietnam's sovereignty claims.[67]

In a sense, brewing tension between China and Vietnam during the first decade of the twenty-first century went somewhat against the grain of Chinese engagement in Southeast Asia writ large over the same period. As a matter of fact, even as Chinese actions in the South China Sea became a source of provocation for Vietnam, its diplomatic efforts and economic inducements to disabuse the rest of Southeast Asia of lingering discomfort with its rise was gathering pace, and with significant implications for perceptions of the U.S. role and place in regional affairs.

CHAPTER SIX

The "Pivot" and Southeast Asia

WITH THE BUSH ADMINISTRATION consumed by its Global War on Terror, preoccupied with executing strategy predicated on unilateralism
and pre-emptive war, and coping with political and diplomatic fallout
from its unpopular invasion of Iraq, the reality for Southeast Asia was
that any confluence of interest with the United States was for the most
part limited to counterterrorism. As the previous chapter maintained,
despite some attempt especially during its second term to place Southeast
Asia policy on a more even keel, given the prevalence of the overarching
strategic imperative dictated by the war on terror, the interest and attention of the Bush presidency persistently gravitated back to the issue no
matter how far afield it ventured. This caused predictable apprehensions
about American credibility and leadership in the Asia Pacific region beyond the counterterrorism frame of reference.

In stark contrast, Barack Obama's presidential campaign promises of
a more finessed foreign policy posture across a broader range of issues
that would stress the need to strengthen relations with allies, make new
friends, and open dialogue with rivals and adversaries was met with
both relief and anticipation in a Southeast Asian region for whom the
issue of deficit in American policy attention, whether real or perceived,
has always been a delicate matter. With the United States on the cusp of
a major reassessment regarding its role in international affairs, the fact
that the new American president had his own personal encounters with
Southeast Asia—he grew up in Jakarta and spent four formative years in
an Indonesian public school—fueled romantic expectations in certain

quarters, particularly in Indonesia, that Southeast Asia might come to command a special place in Obama's foreign policy.

Much has already been said of how the international image of the United States was tarnished by Bush administration policies and missteps over the course of two terms but especially during the first term. There was a realization among a new foreign policy team in the corridors of American power that overstretch in Iraq and Afghanistan had distracted from core U.S. strategic and economic interests, which they surmised were increasingly to be found in Asia. The former national security advisor Tom Donilon offered insight into how this awareness laid the foundation for attempts to reorient American policy in the region:

> Renewing U.S. leadership has also meant focusing our efforts and resources not just on the challenges that make today's headlines, but on the regions that will shape the global order in the decades ahead. That's why, from the outset—even before the President took office—he directed those of us on his national security team to engage in a strategic assessment, a truly global examination of our presence and priorities. We asked what the U.S. footprint and face to the world was and what it ought to be. We set out to identify the key national security interests that we needed to pursue. We looked around the world and asked: where are we over-weighted? Where are we underweighted? That assessment resulted in a set of key determinations. It was clear that there was an imbalance in the projection and focus of U.S. power. It was the President's judgment that we were over-weighted in some areas and regions, including our military actions in the Middle East. At the same time, we were underweighted in other regions, such as the Asia-Pacific. Indeed, we believed this was our key geographic imbalance.[1]

With this the stage was set for a purported shift of American foreign policy priorities to the Asia Pacific, which quickly entered the lexicon as "the Pivot"—later rechristened "the Rebalance." Over time, the Pivot would become the defining foreign policy of the Obama administration.

This robust declaration of intent, captured by the Pivot metaphor, predictably prompted intense discussion and analysis of its portents. Arising from this was a curious debate over semantics: whether the use of the term "Pivot" (borrowed from basketball, where players would "pivot" side by side in order to retain flexibility of movement) implied a shift in direction and policy orientation or was in fact something of a misnomer given that the United States never "left" the region in the first place, ergo, there was no need to pivot "from" something "to" Asia. In truth, while the aspirational elements of the Pivot undoubtedly thrust U.S. engagement forward, Obama's Asia policy in fact also benefited from some tailwinds of continuity. As Obama administration officials have constantly reiterated, the premise of the Pivot was not that the United States ever withdrew from the region but rather that there was the need to further enhance a preexisting presence in a way consonant with ongoing reassessment of U.S. interests.

In keeping with Asia policy priorities of previous administrations, Northeast Asia remained a key imperative, and the Pivot saw American commitments to its allies in Japan and South Korea strengthened. Of interest for current purposes, though, is the enhanced engagement of Southeast Asia. Accordingly, as he elaborated on what he saw to be a necessary reframing of American strategic interests and objectives, President Obama, who frequently professed to care deeply about developments in Southeast Asia, seized the opportunity to pay explicit attention to the region:

> Perhaps no region on earth has changed so dramatically during the past several decades. With this change comes growing influence, and greater opportunities to engage on the world's stage. Asia's rise in global affairs is due in no small part to Southeast Asia's contributions. That's why the nations of Southeast Asia are and will remain a central focus of America's rebalance to Asia. We see the nations of Southeast Asia as equal partners in our mission to advance a vision that promotes growth and development, bolsters the security of nations, strengthens democratic governance, and advances human rights for all people.[2]

While adamant that the United States would enhance its presence in and commitment to the region, it was also clear that accompanying re-engagement was an expectation for Southeast Asian partners to make a more concerted contribution to their own security—burden sharing, as it were—and to move away from the tradition of heavy reliance on the American security umbrella. This view was expressed by then secretary of defense Robert Gates, who explained in June 2009 that "continuing to fulfil our commitments to the permanent presence of, and direct action by, U.S. forces in the region—places ever greater emphasis on building the capacity of partners to better defend themselves."[3]

Notwithstanding the cooperative atmosphere governing this reorientation, it remained the imperative of American regional leadership and primacy that anchored the Pivot. Asked in the course of interview about China's challenge to American primacy, President Obama responded: "I actually think that America can be number one for a very very long time but we think that there can be a whole host of countries that are prospering and doing well. Here's one way to think about it. The Chinese standard of living and industrial output per capita is about where the United States was back in 1910, I mean they've got a lot of catching up to do."[4] A similar perspective was implicitly registered in the Obama administration's reaction to the stillborn proposal of the Australian prime minister Kevin Rudd for an Asia-Pacific Community to manage regional affairs, to which U.S. assistant secretary of state for East Asian affairs Kurt Campbell responded: "I think the fact that there's a greater interest in finding appropriate forums, not just in Australia but in China, Japan, the United States, is a healthy thing and the key role of the United States is to harness that energy and to direct it in appropriate ways."[5] Elsewhere, Obama also proclaimed: "There must be no doubt, as America's first pacific president, I promise you this pacific nation will strengthen and sustain our leadership in this vitally important part of the world."[6]

Bestowed form and substance by dint of the efforts of Secretary of State Hillary Clinton, National Security Advisor Tom Donilon, and a strong team of Asia hands assembled across the administration, the Pivot possessed three attendant components: military, economic, and diplomatic. Spearheading the Pivot was the sharp edge of an enhanced military presence. This was to be demonstrated through a forecasted deployment of 60 percent of U.S. military assets to the Asia Pacific by 2020 along with the intensification of a range of bilateral and multilateral military exercises and defense interactions, such as Cobra Gold, Balikatan, and a newly minted Maritime Security Initiative introduced toward the end of the administration's second term. This military dimension would be accompanied by deeper economic engagement of a strategic nature, which eventually found foremost expression in the form of the Trans-Pacific Partnership Agreement, which the Obama administration, to its credit, invested a substantial amount of political capital to push domestically. Cognizant of the fact that Southeast Asia sets great store by the attendance of the president and cabinet officials at regional summits and meetings, concerted efforts were also made by leaders to personify the Pivot through presence and active participation at these events. Such efforts were a noteworthy departure from the tendency of preceding administrations to skip meetings or lament behind closed doors how regional meetings frequently sacrificed substance for form. It was also a welcome signal that the Obama administration understood and appreciated regional diplomatic culture.

As noted above, one of the most palpable expressions of the Pivot was the number of high-level visits to the region beyond summitry and multilaterals. In an unprecedented feat, Hillary Clinton became the first secretary of state to visit all ten capitals of Southeast Asia during her tenure. President Obama himself made it a point to visit regularly. In April 2014, he became the first U.S. president to visit Malaysia since Lyndon Baines Johnson in 1966. In November 2012, he made historic visits to Cambodia and Myanmar, two "firsts" by a sitting U.S. president. He was also the first U.S. president to visit Laos when he attended the ASEAN Summit in 2016. If not for the cancellation of his participation at the October 2013 East Asia Summit in Brunei, Obama would have been the first sitting U.S. president to visit all ten ASEAN countries.

A string of actions and initiatives lent further currency to the reality of the Pivot. It was during the Obama presidency that the ASEAN Treaty of Amity and Cooperation was signed by the United States and a U.S.–ASEAN strategic partnership launched. In February 2016, President Obama hosted ASEAN leaders at Sunnylands, California, for the first ever U.S.–ASEAN Summit to take place on American soil. The Sunnylands Summit was symbolic on two counts. First, the significance of the choice of venue did not escape the notice of the Southeast Asian guests, given it was where Obama had previously hosted Chinese president Xi Jinping. Second, the Sunnylands Summit was by all accounts a personal initiative of President Obama himself.[7] Earlier, in April 2014, Secretary of Defense Chuck Hagel had also hosted his ASEAN defense counterparts at the first U.S.–ASEAN Defense Forum, held in Honolulu, Hawaii. On the face of it, the Sunnylands Summit and the Honolulu Defense Forum can—and did—quite easily draw criticism from detractors for not producing any substantive achievement or agreement. But such criticisms miss the point and indeed are an indictment of one of the fundamental problems in U.S.–ASEAN relations that bedeviled previous administrations. Simply put, the significance of these meetings lay in the fact that they even took place given, among other things, the divergent strategic outlooks of Southeast Asian states and the persistent draw of other issues on the global agenda of the United States. It is also important to reiterate the fact that these meetings were initiated by the leadership of the United States and not ASEAN, and this was of immeasurable consequence to the region for how it demonstrated a rare American appreciation of the Southeast Asian diplomatic culture and decorum, where oftentimes form is unapologetically pursued at the expense of substance.

Because of the publicity surrounding it, the Pivot predictably created expectations. In turn, this meant that when (regional) expectations were not met, disappointment was amplified. In other words, if regular appearances at major regional meetings and summits were taken as a litmus test of commitment, it follows that absences would then register volatility in that commitment, which would correspondingly give rise to uncertainty and anxiety. It was by this token that the postponement of three trips during the Obama administration, all done for reasons of domestic crises, gave pause. In March 2010, a trip to Indonesia (and Australia) was shelved as priority was given to the need to shepherd the passage of the Healthcare Reform Bill in Washington. Rescheduled for June 2010, the trip was pushed back again, this time as a consequence of the emergency registered by the British Petroleum oil spill in the Gulf of Mexico. Finally, a visit to the region that was to include stops in Malaysia and the Philippines in 2013 was postponed for reasons of a budgetary crisis that precipitated a government shutdown, which in turn compromised the staffing of the trip. Granted, these visits were postponed and rescheduled rather than canceled outright, and the White House did eventually make good on all of them. Nevertheless, the postponements themselves highlighted the reality of how elements of the Pivot (or any other foreign policy initiative for that matter) could quite easily be rendered subservient to domestic contingencies. Concomitantly, it was not surprising that these absences occasioned doubt. Presidential trips aside, there have been other litmus tests that were picked up very earnestly by regional policy planners. For instance, contents of major presidential foreign policy speeches were regularly parsed for references to the region or mention of the Pivot, and in turn, any absence of references to these matters was often quickly picked up by the regional press and provided conversation topics in regional diplomatic and think tank circles.[8]

It should be noted that ultimately the Pivot still required domestic support in the United States. This being the case, to the domestic audience the Pivot was stressed in terms of the centrality of the region to U.S. national interests. Germaine to this was the economic potential of the region as well as the matter of freedom of navigation, articulated as a key U.S. interest. This was made clear in the remarks by Hillary Clinton in her "Pivot speech" delivered in Hawaii in 2011: "And there are challenges facing the Asia Pacific right now that demand America's leadership, from ensuring freedom of navigation in the South China Sea to countering North Korea's provocations and proliferation activities to promoting balanced and inclusive economic growth. The United States has unique capacities to bring to bear in these efforts and a strong national interest at stake."[9]

At the same time, as was pointed out earlier, the Pivot was also undergirded by the expectation that regional states would play a more active role in the management of regional affairs and carry their fair share, especially of the security burden, while the United States pursued its policy of "leading from behind." To that end, the engagement of regional organizations was registered as a key feature of the Pivot strategy. As President Obama declared in Tokyo on the occasion of his maiden visit to Asia as president in 2009:

> In addition to our bilateral relations, we also believe that the growth of multilateral organizations can advance the security and prosperity of this region. I know that the United States has been disengaged from these organizations in recent years. So let me be clear: those days have passed. As an Asia Pacific nation, the United States expects to be involved in the discussions that shape the future of this region, and to participate fully in appropriate organizations as they are established and evolve.[10]

As for ASEAN, the premier regional organization in Southeast Asia, the United States was prepared to cede some measure of leadership while providing robust support, in the hope that the region could be encouraged to demonstrate a unity of purpose and outlook. In the words of one senior State Department official, the United States was ready "to let ASEAN take the lead on regional affairs."[11]

REGIONAL RESPONSES

As suggested earlier, the Pivot extended an encouraging expectation. Many Southeast Asian leaders were quick to react positively to Washington's declaration of intent to reorient its foreign policy priorities to the region and articulated appropriate sound bites in response. During a speech at the Washington-based Council on Foreign Relations, Pham Binh Minh, foreign minister of Vietnam, extended Hanoi's positive reception of the Pivot when he asserted that "We welcome the policy of increasing [cooperation] with the countries in the region by all countries, including the United States. . . . anything [that] happens in South China Sea will affect the freedom of navigation, [and] so, of course, affect other countries, not only United States. . . . So we see that—the efforts by countries inside and outside to make that stable. We appreciate that effort."[12] In 2012, President Susilo Bambang Yudhoyono of Indonesia came out in support of American reengagement with the region, commenting that the Pivot "represented a deeper sociocultural, economic, and political engagement."[13] During a joint press conference on the occasion of President Obama's visit to the Philippines in April 2014, President Aquino expressed Philippine support for "active participation in regional mechanisms such as ASEAN Regional Forum and the East Asia Summit" by the United States.[14] Meanwhile, Thai prime minister Yingluck Shinawatra stated that Thailand shared with America "democratic values and respect for civil liberties" that underpinned the strength of their bilateral relationship, a relationship that would be "further strengthened" by the Pivot.[15] This was, of course, before the 2014 coup derailed bilateral relations between the United States and Thailand. After the coup, senior officials of the post-coup government took to expressing the view that the United States was "not serious about the Pivot because, unlike China, it has not been followed up with any major initiatives."[16] Although there might be some truth to the point that the Pivot could have been better served through greater effort and attentiveness on Washington's part, at the same time it cannot be divorced from the fact that the coup posed obstacles to the relationship, much to the frustration of Thai officialdom.

The underlying strategic objective of strengthening relations and partnerships with Southeast Asian states was to serve the purpose of defending a regional status quo premised on American leadership and primacy that was being challenged by the rise of China. Michael R. Auslin offered the following vignette that holds forth on this correlation in a testimony before Congress:

> If you talk to our friends in the region—I know, Mr. Chairman and members of the committee, you do that repeatedly through

visits—they themselves obviously are concerned about the rise of China. They are concerned that as China has become stronger, it has become more assertive. They are concerned about their particular sets of territorial disputes and other issues in which they feel that there is little chance for each of them alone to resolve these on terms that would be most favorable to them.

Therefore, what we see over the past several years is an increasing tendency on the part of friends and allies to look to the United States for backup and support. In part, they do this because the administration has stated that it is rebalancing, it is re-engaged, it is back in Asia. And yet when we come down to the specifics that concern them and interest them, the United States often takes a pass.

We can look at the frustration that the Philippines feels, the frustration that Japan feels over territorial issues in both the South and East China Seas. And they wonder, as actually a Philippines senator publicly questioned during last year's problems over the Scarborough Shoals, "What is the use of the alliance with the United States if it will not back us up when we need it?"[17]

Though associated with a conservative political outlook (in terms of the American political spectrum), the key elements to the above perspective are, in fact, bipartisan, as chapter 2 attests.

Behind this veneer of widespread regional embrace of the Pivot, residual reticence, rendered by discernible differences in strategic outlook regarding the American role and presence in the region, still existed. Support for the Pivot masked a degree of lingering discomfort among some regional states. For some, the prospect of a greater American military presence in the region was in and of itself disquieting. The position of Indonesia, for instance, was invariably shaped by its long-standing aversion in principle to any foreign military presence. In the words of a Jakarta official, "if the Pivot entails deeper engagement, yes Indonesia supports it. But if it means stationing of troops or a militarized presence, then that's a no-no."[18] Historical memory accounted for much of this reticence. Narratives of sovereignty continue to be informed by nationalist memory of how the waterways of the archipelago were used by external powers to undermine Indonesia's fragile unity in the 1950s. For similar historical reasons, the move by the United States to station troops in Darwin was evidently assessed in some quarters among the country's political elite through the lens of Indonesian control of the province of Papua.[19] Beneath this lay a possibly more fundamental issue, for a more entrenched American presence could potentially undermine Jakarta's standing as primus inter pares in Southeast Asia. As for the communist states of Indochina, not a few among its senior leadership who were of conservative orientation still harbored memories of being at the receiving end of the American military intervention or subversion four decades prior. Cambodia serves as a case in point, where the reluctance of successive U.S. administrations to cancel the debt accrued by the Lon Nol administration in Phnom Penh in the early 1970s continues to grate. As a Cambodian scholar from a government-linked think tank expressed, not without irony: "You bomb us and still want to collect money from us?"[20]

Additionally, there was the perennial reservation toward the sustainability of the strategy and consistency in policy implementation, particularly in the wake of increasingly polarized U.S. domestic political climes. As a senior Thai diplomat felt compelled to forecast during a public lecture: "Importantly, we hope to see the rebalance in action and sustained. And given the bipartisan support for increased engagement with Asia, there's hope that the policy will continue for the long term, no matter what party wins the White House in 2016 or beyond."[21] It is further noteworthy, at the same time, that the diplomat emphasized how efforts had to be made on the part of the United States to see that engagement was multidimensional—encompassing all spheres—including not just defense and security but also economic, social, and cultural engagement.[22]

There were also those who, though prepared to accept an enhanced American military presence in the region, nevertheless worried for the reactions that this might provoke from China, which they feared could precipitate the unwelcome militarization of regional affairs. For these states, the overriding concern was how, if not well managed or calibrated, the sharp military edge of the Pivot could catalyze a deterioration of Sino–U.S. relations to degrees that would place the region in an undesirable position. This deep discomfort was compounded by fears for the impact of economic duress on the sustainability of American commitment. A sobering scenario weighs heavily on the minds of regional decision-makers on this score: should the United States take a robust position against a pertinacious China and set in motion a spiraling militarization, only to be compelled to a sequestration-style scale-back, the region would be left to its own devices to deal with an antagonized China. For this reason, even as they expressed support for the Pivot, Southeast Asian leaders have also repeatedly declared that the region does not wish to be caught in a situation where it has to choose between the United States and China. Although it might be tempting to dismiss this as a tiresome refrain, it does reflect the arid reality that the region is confronted with. Economic relations with China have deepened to such extents in recent decades that festering diplomatic tension with China, to say nothing of open conflict, will undoubtedly herald unwelcome portents for the region.

A final point bears noting. From a regional perspective, leaving aside for the moment the range of bilateral relationships between individual Southeast Asian states and the United States, relations with the United States should still reflect, and certainly not undermine, the self-assumed obligation of ASEAN Centrality, which Southeast Asia has always maintained provides guiding principles and a language for collective engagement with major powers. Yet it is also apparent that even if the Obama administration voiced support for ASEAN Centrality, intensification of Sino–U.S. rivalry triggered by the Pivot ran the risk of creating both strategic and policy conundrums for Southeast Asia that threatened to lay bare the challenges of fostering and maintaining regional solidarity and cohesion in the face of major power politics. Nowhere is this more evident than on the matter of the South China Sea disputes.

THE SOUTH CHINA SEA GORDIAN KNOT

Long seen as a potential flashpoint in Southeast Asia, the dense tangle of territorial claims in the South China Sea continues to be a diplomatic irritant and test of conflict resolution resolve of regional states (and China). It is true that diplomatic initiatives since the turn of the century, both at the bilateral and multilateral level, have managed to foster something of a climate of dialogue and restraint. Crucially, in the few years immediately following the signing of the DOC in 2002, tensions in the South China Sea between China and Southeast Asian claimant states had de-escalated to a considerable extent, enabled in no small measure by the Chinese "charm offensive" that lasted for an approximate decade, since the Asian Financial Crisis of 1997–98. The conciliatory climate, however, would not last.

In May 2009, new claims were submitted by the Philippines, Malaysia, and Vietnam to the United Nations Commission on the Limits of the Continental Shelf (CLCS) in response to directives that states that joined the United Nations Convention on the Law of the Sea (UNCLOS) before 1999 had to submit their supplementary claims to economic rights when their continental shelf extends more than 200 nautical miles beyond a baseline. Predictably, China reacted negatively to the submissions by these claimant states and branded these actions a violation of its presumed jurisdiction and sovereign rights over the South China Sea.[23] In response, Beijing established a new Department of Boundary and Ocean Affairs and enhanced its patrolling capabilities in an attempt to assert its sovereignty in the South China Sea. In a move that threatened to unravel diplomatic progress made up to that point, Beijing returned to the familiar narrative—hitherto mostly dormant after the signing of the DOC—reminding ASEAN that the majority of its members had no claim in the area, that the South China Sea was not, and should not be seen as, an ASEAN issue, and hence, any notion of a collective ASEAN involvement in the South China Sea disputes was not only immaterial and irrelevant, it would be an act of bad faith. In cryptic remarks during a meeting at the Chinese National Defense University, a Chinese general warned that "ASEAN is not a claimant in the dispute and should not be involved unless it is prepared to bear the consequences."[24] Yet arguably the most disconcerting of the Chinese reactions was the release of a Chinese map in which the vast expanse of the South China Sea was cordoned off with a U-shaped nine-dash line marking out the expanse of presumed Chinese territory in the area.[25] In the context of official discussions, this was the first time that ASEAN states caught sight of the now-infamous "nine-dash line" map that had its genesis in the cartography of the Republic of China back in the late 1940s. Since it resurfaced in support of China's own UNCLOS submissions, the map has in all its ambiguity and controversy become the primary premise of the geographical expanse of China's claims and a major irritant in Sino–ASEAN relations.[26]

Since the release of the map, Chinese naval and merchant marine presence in the waters of the South China Sea have increased exponentially, as has their molestation of vessels from other claimant states. Of particular note amid the flurry of Chinese activities was the appearance of four ships from the PLA navy off James Shoal, which is also claimed by Malaysia and which is located barely fifty miles off the coast of the east Malaysian state of Sarawak, in March 2013. The appearance of the Chinese vessels in the area was significant on two counts. First, it was the furthest that Chinese vessels had ventured southward for purposes of staking Beijing's South China Sea claims. Second, unlike Vietnam or the Philippines, Malaysia had up to that point consciously adopted a much more conciliatory, some would even suggest deferential, policy toward China on the South China Sea in favor of good bilateral relations. In that respect, the incident at James Shoal was a rude awakening that the dalliance would have little ameliorating effect on Chinese intent to press its claims without fear or favor and, indeed, by way of a show of force if necessary. As if to punctuate the point, less than a year later, in January 2014, three Chinese navy warships returned to James Shoal and conducted military drills and a controversial oath-swearing ceremony. These actions compelled the Malaysian defense minister Hishamuddin Hussein to break with Malaysian diplomatic convention and issue a call for ASEAN states to stand in solidarity against Chinese expansionism. Under the circumstance, if this Chinese behavior toward a hitherto "friendly" claimant state was indicative of anything, it was that Chinese claims have all but ossified with grim portent. Barely two months later, in March 2014, China attempted to dislodge Philippine soldiers based on Second Thomas Shoal, a feature within the Philippines' exclusive economic zone (EEZ) but claimed by China.

Chinese actions outlined above conform to a wider pattern as Beijing has embarked on an incremental strategy of development of the features it has occupied. It is noteworthy that although China is hardly the first claimant state to build structures—except for Brunei, all other claimants had already done so by the time China started—its activities have nevertheless sparked consternation given the opaqueness of its intent, resoluteness to which it has pressed its claims, the pace at which it is building structures, and the sheer size and magnitude not only of its claims themselves but also the capabilities it is increasingly able to muster to back these claims (relative to the capabilities possessed by other claimant states). Further to that, financed by newfound (and growing) wealth, Chinese fishing, merchant, and coast guard vessels have increased in size in recent years, allowing them to venture further afield into the South China Sea for longer periods of time, all in the name of resource extraction but also the assertion of a visible physical and, to some extent, armed presence. These capabilities have also afforded Beijing the wherewithal to reinforce the imposition of a unilateral ban on fishing activities of citizens from other claimant states. To give edge to all of this, the PLA navy has also conducted military exercises in the South China Sea, as previously noted, as far south as James Shoal, just off the coast of eastern Malaysia. Needless to say, these developments marked a sharp turn from the restraint exercised by China during the halcyon days of the charm offensive.

In December 2013, Chinese activity took a further turn as work began on expanding the size of several features it occupied, via large-scale dredging. In doing so, China had likely seized on the Obama administration's preoccupation with the Iran nuclear deal, the implosion in Syria, and Russian involvement in the Crimea to make progress in Southeast Asia just as it did a decade earlier when the Bush administration's attention was diverted by the war on terror, with one important distinction: Whereas the previous decade saw China take advantage of a distracted America by building bridges and enhancing goodwill through trade and investments with a Southeast Asia concerned for its growing power yet receptive to economic inducements, this time Beijing put in jeopardy those very bridges by way of a physical expansion of its claims into the South China Sea. These "land reclamation" projects, as they have been inaccurately termed since they are not so much reclaiming land as building artificial islands, most notably at Fiery Cross Reef and Johnson South Reef in the Spratlys but also Duncan Island in the Paracels, pushed the envelope and triggered alarm across the region, particularly given that airstrips were part of the "reclamation" projects.[27] Soon after, Chinese surface-to-air missiles and fighter jets found their way to Woody Island in the Paracels.

That the Woody Island deployment was made while ASEAN and U.S. leaders parlayed in California in February 2016 was nothing short of a clear statement of Chinese resolve in the face of gathering diplomatic protest. True to form, further deployments of a high-frequency radar system on Cuarteron Reef in the Spratlys speak to Chinese intentions to enhance monitoring and operational capabilities in the area and lend credence to suspicions expressed by not a few analysts and observers that China intends to be in a position to eventually implement an Air Defense Identification Zone over parts of the South China Sea, in the same manner it did in the East China Sea. If successful, this would allow China to pressure smaller claimant states and restrict their movements in the region under circumstances where the extent to which the United States would enter the fray in support of the latter remains unclear, particularly if these actions fell short of instigating open conflict. This reality is only too obvious for American allies in the Philippines, while Vietnamese leaders are also mindful that by virtue of being the only other claimant to the Paracels aside from Taiwan, the United States may hesitate and ultimately refrain from taking concrete actions against Chinese provocations in that part of the South China Sea.

The Canary in the Coal Mine

Although the U.S. navy had regularly been conducting Freedom of Navigation operations (FONOPS) in the South China Sea, such operations were brought to a halt by the White House in 2012 for reasons of great power diplomacy between the United States and China. To the dismay of regional partners, although the Department of Defense and U.S. navy pressured the White House to challenge China's claims through the resumption of FONOPS, President Obama demurred in the hope of persuading Beijing to exercise self-restraint. After further prevarication and reluctance on its part, and prompted ultimately by the persistence of Chinese activities in the South China Sea despite President Xi's personal assurances of China's peaceful intentions at the Obama–Xi meeting at Sunnylands in September 2015, the White House and Department of State eventually caved in to pressure and sanctioned the resumption of FONOPS in the area. This paved the way for two symbolic, high-profile operations to be conducted, first by the U.S.S. *Lassen* around several reefs claimed by China, Vietnam, and the Philippines (including Subi Reef) in October 2015 and, later, by the U.S.S. *Curtis Wilbur* around Triton Island in the Paracels in late January 2016. The U.S.S. *Lassen* FONOPS ought to have been a straightforward matter given the number of such operations the U.S. navy has conducted just about everywhere in the world, but poor coordination and the fact that Defense Department officials had kept counsel on the operation despite congressional calls to clarify the nature and intent of the FONOP resulted in the operation coming under a cloud of ambiguity and controversy.[28] As a consequence, the operation by the U.S.S. *Lassen* had the immediate effect of generating further confusion and raising questions in the region precisely about U.S. intent.

Ambiguity in the language used by the United States to describe the operation complicated matters and caused confusion as to whether and why the U.S.S. *Lassen* in fact conducted "innocent passage" at Subi Reef, as some analysts suggest, or, as Pacific Command (PACOM) officials maintained, the ship "behaved like it was conducting innocent passage."[29] Information that trickled out several days after described an operation that evidently conformed to a conventional understanding of innocent passage:

> New details about the Lassen's transit became available Oct. 30 from a U.S. Navy source, who said the warship took steps to indicate it was making a lawful innocent passage with no warlike intent. The ship's fire control radars were turned off and it flew no helicopters, the source said. Although a U.S. Navy P-8 Poseidon maritime surveillance aircraft was in the area, it did not cross inside the 12 nautical mile limit.[30]

If indeed this was what transpired, the impression conveyed (regardless of intent) was that the reference to innocent passage—whether in word or deed—implied recognition that the waters around the reefs are in fact territorial waters, since according to UNCLOS the innocent passage regime applies only to a twelve nautical mile territorial sea. The legal confusion was only later clarified by Bonnie Glaser and Peter Dutton, who explained that the Subi Reef FONOP had to be "innocent passage" according to international law because while Subi Reef would itself be entitled only to a 500-meter safety zone as it is a low-tide elevation, Subi lies within the twelve nautical mile territorial water entitled to Sandy Cay, an unoccupied reef claimed by China, the Philippines, Vietnam, and Taiwan, under article 13 of UNCLOS.[31] In other words, Subi Reef lies within a legitimate territorial sea, even though ownership of Sandy Cay is still undetermined.

Southeast Asian responses to the FONOPS were instructive of the ambiguity with which the region reacts to escalating major power activity in the region. Needless to say, by dint of the fact that they had been targets of Chinese adventurism, the response from the Philippines and Vietnam was predictably positive. The following view was offered by Tran Cong Truc, former director of the Government Border Committee of Vietnam: "I think we should welcome and support the U.S. action. . . . This is good news. . . . What the U.S. did helps in part to make China's claims [in the region] invalid."[32] This view was further echoed by Rear-Admiral Le Ke Lam: "Now [China] know that the U.S. will not withdraw from Southeast Asia or the Asia-Pacific. Otherwise China would have assumed the U.S. is weak, and they would have become more aggressive."[33] Philippine support was even more categorical. In addition to suggesting that the FONOPS were a necessary act of "balance of power,"

President Benigno Aquino III further averred that "Freedom of navigation has been expounded and propounded by all parties to the issues of
the South China Sea/West Philippines Sea. Everybody seems to be guaranteeing freedom of navigation, so I see no issue as to this U.S. naval
ship traversing under international law in waters that should be free to
be travelled upon by any non-belligerent country."[34]

By contrast, Indonesia registered disagreement with the FONOPS
through the comments of the influential coordinating minister for political, legal, and security affairs, Luhut Pandjaitan, who in expressing objections intriguingly likened the FONOPS to American operations in
Iraq and Afghanistan: "We disagree [with the FONOPS], we don't like
any power projection. . . . Have you ever heard of power projection
solving problems? In Afghanistan? In Iraq? The United States has spent
trillions of dollars in Afghanistan and Iraq. What are the results? Hundreds of thousands of people killed. And now, violence continues to happen in Iraq."[35] Luhut's animated reaction to the FONOPS followed on
from President Joko Widodo's cautionary words articulated during a
working visit to the United States several days earlier even as he refused
to be drawn into an endorsement of the FONOPS: "Indonesia is not a
party to the dispute. But we have legitimate interests in peace and stability there. That is why we call on all parties to exercise restraint and refrain
from taking actions that could undermine trust and confidence and put
at risk the peace and stability of the region."[36] Prior to the FONOPS,
the Indonesian defense minister Ryamizard Ryucudu also reportedly
asserted a position on the South China Sea that seemed curiously at
odds with those of some ASEAN counterparts: "If countries who have
interests in the South China Sea can calm tensions and are able to manage the conflict, there's no need to involve other parties in resolving the
dispute."[37] Needless to say, this view echoed China's long-standing position that nonclaimants had no dog in the fight.

As previously suggested, these Indonesian views register a strategic
outlook toward major external powers that has existed since independence in form, if not in substance. Yet once unpacked, it also implied
that Jakarta was just as likely to treat China with caution. Hence, Jakarta's response to American FONOPS should not be taken to suggest
deference or support for Chinese activity. In fact, on separate occasions
Indonesian security planners have expressed concern that China has yet
to clarify its intentions in relation to the waters around Natuna Islands,
located at the fringes of the nine-dash line map. Jakarta is also exploring

the building of a naval base to guard its border areas near the South China Sea, although this is not so much in reaction to Chinese incursions as it is the result of the implementation of modernization plans already determined by the mid-2000s.[38] Tensions mounted in March 2016 when a diplomatic fracas was triggered after a Chinese coast guard vessel used force on an Indonesian maritime authority vessel in order to compel it to release a Chinese fishing boat that had been interned for operating in Indonesia's EEZ in the vicinity of the Natuna Islands. Yet despite registering vigorous protest at Chinese actions, Indonesia seemed eager to also downplay matters, and the foreign minister, Retno Marsudi, quickly clarified that the altercation with China had nothing to do with the South China Sea disputes.[39]

The ambivalence of the Indonesian response sums up the situation and illustrates a predicament shared to some degree or other by several other Southeast Asian states. Although American involvement and participation in collective efforts to coax China to restraint are welcome, reservations still exist toward any course of action that would escalate the militarization that has already taken place or that might provoke China. As a senior Jakarta Foreign Ministry official cryptically conceded, "If China wants to do something, there is nothing Southeast Asia or the U.S. can do to stop it."[40] Meanwhile, Malaysian prime minister Najib Razak has taken the position that the competing claims "cannot . . . be addressed through military might but instead through negotiations and solidarity among ASEAN countries and parties who support us."[41] At a separate level, the discrepancy in Indonesian reaction to FONOPS is also illustrative of a deeper issue that often eludes analysis—that policy agencies within any given state often entertain divergent and competing perspectives that might lead them to issue contradictory statements or, worse, work at cross-purposes. The differing views between various Malaysian agencies over whether Chinese vessels were making incursions into Malaysian waters, and how to respond to these incursions, or those in Jakarta circles over how to interpret and respond to Chinese activities around the Natunas are illustrative of the lack of coordination between policy agencies within a government, as well as how they have worked at odds with each other so as to obfuscate and dilute national positions on the South China Sea.[42] Indeed, such is the extent of the problem in Indonesia, it has prompted President Joko Widodo to call for better coordination across agencies on Indonesia's position on the South China Sea.[43]

Confusion and controversy notwithstanding, the fact that American operations were beginning to be accompanied by strong accusatory language directed at Beijing is also noteworthy. This was apparent from Admiral Harry Harris's remarks: "China is clearly militarising the South China Sea, and you would have to believe in the flat earth to think otherwise. . . . I believe China seeks hegemony in East Asia."[44] Even so, the Obama administration's dithering on FONOPS since 2012 meant that by the time FONOPS were conducted, a physical Chinese presence was already entrenched, thereby allowing Beijing to accuse the United States—not without some degree of objective validity given the circumstances—of militarization even as Beijing was itself guilty of the same. All this is to say that in a limited, legal sense the FONOPS mattered as it related to freedom of navigation in accordance to international law. But in the broader scheme of strategic posturing, it may not have mattered nearly as much because it does not appear ex post facto to have had any deterrent effect given that it has not arrested the singular momentum of Chinese expansion. This is not to say, however, that FONOPS—to challenge "excessive claims" without giving prior notification of intent—should be abandoned. Rather, it is important that they continue nonetheless, as a means to dial up pressure on claimant states that persist in pursuing artificial island building and fortification projects on features whose status and ownership have not been determined either by international law or by diplomatic compromise.

Despite the high-profile FONOPS, or perhaps because of it, the Chinese response has gone according to script: it has justified its militarization polemically as its sovereign right "in accordance with the principles of heaven and earth" in response to American provocations and "militarization" in the form of FONOPS and "fly-bys" by strategic bombers. Chinese objections also related to the interpretation of what exactly is legal under the Freedom of Navigation regime, to wit, it rejects the majoritarian view—which is also the view held by the United States—that Freedom of Navigation permits the conduct of military activities such as surveillance and reconnaissance. In any case, although a signatory to UNCLOS, unlike other claimant states, China's claims in the South China Sea are being asserted not on the basis of international law but history, whereby China contends that "the beginning of Chinese presence in Paracels may be traced back to the Western Han Dynasty (206BC–25AD)."[45] The same narrative also maintains that China had controlled the Spratly Islands since the thirteenth century.[46] In truth,

China's supposed "historic claims" to the South China Sea are not "centuries old"; they date from 1947, when Chiang Kai-shek's nationalist administration marked out the alleged nine-dash line on Chinese maps of the South China Sea.[47] Nevertheless, quite apart from issues of polemics and historical authenticity, this is a disquieting claim also in how it renders international law subordinate to politics in a way that is pregnant with insinuation.

Legal Considerations

Much about the South China Sea dispute evokes international law. Although ultimately a sovereignty dispute, claims and counterclaims over the South China Sea possess a definite legal dimension. ASEAN states have called for the resolution of the imbroglio by way of diplomacy and in accordance with international law, and the Philippines (with the support of Vietnam) took China to arbitration in the hope that international legal institutions could compel the latter to at least clarify the extent of its claims. Meanwhile, ASEAN and China continued glacial discussions over the formulation of a (hopeful but unlikely) legally binding Code of Conduct to govern the pursuit of claims as well as other activities and interactions in the South China Sea.

The UNCLOS regime is instructive in this regard, and also one that disadvantages China despite the fact that Beijing, along with all the Southeast Asian claimant states, is a signatory to it. The fact that UNCLOS grants littoral states the right to establish a twelve nautical mile territorial sea and a 200 nautical mile EEZ was welcomed by the Southeast Asian littoral states as it translated, for instance, to sovereign rights to marine resource exploitation within the EEZ, particularly of fish, a main source of dietary protein for local communities in much of Southeast Asia. For China's South China Sea claims, however, UNCLOS has posed a problem as Beijing would not be able to make a legal claim extending from the mainland and can do so only from the Spratly Islands. As a nonclaimant but an interested party, the position of the United States on the issue of international law has generated its own complications. The fact that the United States is still not party to UNCLOS (by virtue of the elusiveness of congressional ratification), despite maintaining the regime's central role in providing the legal term of reference for the South China Sea disputes, has doubtless diminished the legitimacy of its statements on the issue and its claims to be defending a rule-based order.

International lawyers have weighed in on the debate, and the broad consensus in this legal community maintains that China's claim of historical rights over the South China Sea has no standing in the eyes of international law. In brief, China has not exercised continuous and uncontested sovereignty over the South China Sea (despite Beijing's insistence to the contrary), nor does the sea itself constitute coastal waters that might be accommodated by a claim based on historical rights. Others have ventured to propose legal ways to get around the impasse of competing claims, such as a more specific definition of an EEZ. For instance, Robert Beckman and Clive Schofield have elaborated that

> China could limit its exclusive economic zone (EEZ) claims to just larger islands, such as the 12 largest islands in the Spratlys. The same logic can be applied to the largest features among the Paracel Islands group, together with the Pratas Islands. Claiming only the larger islands will not limit China's maritime reach significantly. But it would bring these claims more in line with international law. . . . Under our proposal, the total land area of the larger islands that China might claim is only about 2 sq km. But they all have vegetation and in some cases roads and structures have been built on them. Therefore, it can be argued in good faith that they are "islands" entitled in principle to EEZ and continental shelf rights of their own, as allowed under the 1982 UNCLOS. They are not "rocks which cannot sustain human habitation or economic life of their own" that are only entitled to a territorial sea of 12 nautical miles. As "islands" they would be entitled to the full 200 nautical miles of exclusive economic zone activity. Next, China can trigger a paradigm shift in the disputes in the South China Sea if it were to issue charts indicating the outer limit of its EEZ claims from the islands over which it claims sovereignty. The EEZ extends to a full 200 nautical miles over the open sea from the coastal fringes of the islands being claimed.[48]

Although there are legal ways to get around the impasse, it can be argued that the legal speak is at present all white noise compared with the real matters of significance, which are political and strategic, and not legal, in nature. Hence, although it is in the interest of the international community that international law governing its waters is upheld, the South China Sea dispute is arguably ultimately not about international law, at least not in any significant sense. The reality of political will, or in this case lack thereof, is the reality that lies at the heart of the matter. Regardless of all the legal contents being put forward by claimant states to substantiate their claims, it all boils down to this: if there is political will on the part of these claimants to seek resolution and compromise, then legal recourse may offer several viable ways out. Conversely, if claimant states insist on the "indisputable sovereignty" of their respective claims, then international law will fall by the wayside as strategies of self-help will be pursued.

There is a further corollary, albeit an also distinctly disconcerting angle, to this discussion. In premising its claim on history, it follows that Chinese words and behavior are illustrative not only of the nature and expanse of their claims but also tellingly indicative of Chinese aspirations to regional primacy and dominance given that this was precisely the nature of the "history" of the Middle Kingdom's relations with Southeast Asia, according to Chinese interpretations. This logic is disconcerting because of the historical connections that China has had with Southeast Asia over several centuries. Needless to say, this logic is also fundamentally at odds with the regional order that presently prevails in Southeast Asia.

If anything, the shortcomings of international law were all but laid bare in the aftermath of the Arbitral Tribunal ruling on Manila's claims against Beijing. The long awaited ruling by the Arbitral Tribunal on the Philippine case against China was delivered on July 12, 2016. The ruling was comprehensive in its rejection of China's vast and expansive claims in the South China Sea, at least on the terms contained in the Philippines' legal submission. The hardest blow to China was the Tribunal's conclusion that "there was no legal basis for China to claim historical rights to resources within the seas areas falling with the 'nine-dash line.'" On top of that, the Tribunal also ruled that Chinese actions in the South China Sea, such as its persistent interference in Philippine fishing and exploration activities, large-scale land reclamation and construction of artificial islands, failure to regulate its own fishing activities, and enforcement activities in the same area, were either in violation of the sovereign rights of the Philippines or had breached various obligations under UNCLOS.

As anticipated, China categorically rejected the ruling and expressed every intention to continue its current South China Sea policy trajectory. Significantly, its recalcitrance has come at little, if any, cost to its international standing. Conversely, Southeast Asian states were also muted in their response, even as ASEAN failed to reach the necessary consensus required for some semblance of an ASEAN statement on the ruling. Even the Philippines, which by then was led by the newly installed president Rodrigo Duterte, was deliberately restrained in its reaction to an outcome that was clearly in its favor. In point of fact, this was in line with President Duterte's desire to distance Philippine foreign and security policies from the United States even as he sought to improve relations strained by the South China Sea disputes and his predecessor's legal actions with China.

The U.S. (Non)-Position on the South China Sea

Not unlike the effect of the Global War on Terror on the Bush administration's engagement of Southeast Asia, for better or worse the South China Sea disputes have asserted something of a centripetal pull on U.S. policy in the region. Concomitantly, in the view of many American decisionmakers, the issue has also become the litmus test of American resolve and commitment, even as regional counterparts lament how it has begun to overshadow all else.

According to then deputy assistant secretary of state Scot Marciel, the United States has always had a "vital interest in maintaining stability, freedom of navigation, and the right to lawful commercial activity in East Asia's waterways."[49] Over half of the world's merchant fleet flows through the South China Sea alone, thus "serv[ing] as the prime arteries of trade that have fueled the tremendous economic growth of the region and brought prosperity to the U.S. economy as well."[50] During the same testimony, Marciel established American intent to observe the provisions of UNCLOS, even though the United States has not ratified the treaty and customary international law that is predominantly practiced. The United States has also consistently maintained its position that it "takes no position" on the South China Sea disputes and the attendant competing legal claims over territorial sovereignty. Its expressed concern is for claims that are not aligned to international law, such as the extension of territorial waters in ways inconsistent with international norms and which are not derived from a land territory.[51]

Most analysts agree that although the U.S. declaratory policy on the South China Sea had already been articulated in the mid-1990s, it nevertheless gathered strength with the Pivot, and this was accompanied by a deepening of diplomatic, military, and economic ties with key Southeast Asian claimant states, notably the Philippines and Vietnam. A key turning point to that effect was the 2010 ARF meeting at Hanoi. Alarmed by the portents of the nine-dash line map, Chinese assertiveness in the South China Sea, and Beijing's purported declaration of the region as a matter of "core interest," where it would brook no interference (not least from the United States), several Southeast Asian states including the ASEAN chair for the year, Vietnam, prodded the United States to table the South China Sea on the agenda of the formal ARF ministerial meeting.[52] According to a State Department official who was involved in the meeting, Southeast Asian officials desired that the United States raise the issue of the South China Sea "because [the Southeast Asian states] can't raise it, and because they needed assurance that the U.S. was not talking to China behind their backs."[53]

At the behest of Vietnam, the American secretary of state in attendance, Hillary Clinton, abandoned America's previous prevarication on the South China Sea disputes and proceeded to articulate how "peace and stability" and "respect for international law" in the South China Sea was a matter of "national interest to the U.S." Specifically, she said: "The United States has a national interest in freedom of navigation, open access to Asia's maritime commons and respect for international law in the South China Sea."[54] This marked the first time that a senior American cabinet official had unequivocally stated the point that the South China Sea was a matter of U.S. national interest.[55] Needless to say, Secretary Clinton's robust articulation of American interest sparked the ire of the Chinese. Concomitant Sino–U.S. contretemps at Hanoi culminated in Yang Jiechi's peremptory remarks that the secretary of state's comments were tantamount to "an attack on China."[56]

The Hanoi meeting marked a sharp turn from the days of the charm offensive and pushed matters further down the path of escalation. Slightly over a year later, during a visit to the Philippines, Clinton would refer to the South China Sea by its local nomenclature: "We are strongly of the opinion that disputes that exist primarily *in the West Philippine Sea between the Philippines and China* should be resolved peacefully. Any nation with a claim has a right to exert it, but they do not have a right to pursue it through intimidation or coercion."[57] Deliberate or otherwise, the significance of this gesture was not lost on the Philippines, whose officials expressed "pleasant surprise" at the endorsement they were receiving by means of reference to the South China Sea as the West

Philippine Sea.⁵⁸ Thus, for the Philippines, a weak claimant state but a
U.S. ally, this was a moment of serendipity, whereas for China, it provided further evidence that the United States was intent on undermining
its claims in the area as part of a broader strategy of containment.

Diplomatic brinkmanship and rhetorical saber rattling aside, it is invariably the issue of the likelihood of a U.S. military intervention in the
event of an outbreak of hostilities in the South China Sea that seizes
decisionmakers in Beijing, Washington, and the capitals of Southeast
Asia. Simply put, how far is the United States prepared to go to defend
its "national interests" in the South China Sea?

Notwithstanding the flurry of military and diplomatic activity in recent
years, it is prudent to bear in mind that the United States has consistently maintained that it does not take a position on claims in the South
China Sea and continues to do so. Indeed, Washington's current position
on the South China Sea hews closely to its original stance (introduced in
chapter 3) articulated in 1995 in the wake of China's occupation of Mischief Reef in the Spratly Islands. That being said, recent developments
have occasioned, if not a reconsideration, certainly a recalibration of
this position. Under the circumstances, several new elements have also
been introduced to frame U.S. policy on the South China Sea and bol-
ster the initial five points. These include, as articulated on different occasions, "resolving disputes without coercion"; Washington's support
for "collaborative diplomatic process by all claimants" to willingly "facilitate initiatives and confident building measures consistent with the
2002 Declaration on the Code of Conduct, support for drafting of a full
code of conduct"; and the position that legitimate claims to maritime
space in the South China Sea should be derived solely from legitimate
claims to land features.⁵⁹ Yet arguably the most controversial shift in
American position on the South China Sea as perceived from Beijing remains the possibility of active military intervention should a crisis materialize: specifically, would the United States hazard a military engagement, whether of a deliberate or accidental nature, in the South China
Sea, especially if the likely adversary is China, and if it involved an ally?

Several U.S. officials have on occasion suggested that Washington
would, in fact, come to the aid of its allies in times of crisis. Indeed, former U.S. secretary of defense Chuck Hagel apparently assured the Philippines of American protection in its dispute with China.⁶⁰ This may be
a comforting thought for claimant states who are U.S. allies and partners, and it certainly should not simply be dismissed as bloviation. But

for a clear-eyed assessment of the prospects of American military intervention, several factors come into play that cannot but be considered in all gravity.

First, although the United States and the Philippines are doubtless bound together by the Mutual Defense Treaty that dates back to 1951 and was reinforced with the Manila Declaration of 2011, it remains unclear whether Washington considers the remit of the agreement to cover Philippine claims in the South China Sea, particularly since their very status as part of the sovereign territory of the Philippines is being disputed, not only by China but in some cases by Vietnam and Malaysia as well. In other words, would the United States be departing from a position where it takes no position on the disputes if it actively intervened under the terms of the treaty, which specifies coverage for "an armed attack on the metropolitan territory of either of the Parties [the U.S. or the Philippines], or on the island territories under its jurisdiction in the Pacific" but also for "armed forces, public vessels or aircraft in the Pacific?"[61] Compounding this ambiguity is the fact that the Philippine claim to the Spratlys was made after the signing of the 1951 treaty and therefore was obviously not taken into account by Washington when it made that commitment. Nor have American officials offered clarification on what actions would trigger their "protection" of the Philippines, for instance, if Philippine forces came under attack in areas outside of Philippine territory.[62]

Second, while acknowledging that American statements on the South China Sea have grown clearer about U.S. interests at stake, it remains questionable if these have amounted to anything resembling a strategy. This is largely due to the fact that rather than "wise policy and solid strategy supported by judicious application of military force," U.S. policy appears to have put the cart before the horse with its emphasis on military capabilities and presence in the region over a more sophisticated approach to engagement that involves effort to encourage, and even facilitate, a diplomatic agreement among claimant states.[63] Indeed, in the absence of necessary guiding strategy, the willy-nilly application of military force would be reckless.

Third, it is unlikely that the United States would risk triggering a larger conflagration with China for the sake of an ally's contested claims over atolls and features in the South China Sea. Even measured military intervention by the United States on behalf of the Philippines would hazard an escalation that might cascade into a direct, if unintended, Sino–

U.S. conflict. In turn, such escalation would redound upon the United States to undermine its interests as this could compromise sea lines of communication, the interest of American energy companies, U.S. relations with some Southeast Asian states from whom unfettered support for the United States in such an event is far from a given, and indeed its own image as a benign power that contributes constructively to the management of tension and conflicts in the region. More to the point is the fact that Chinese officials and strategists have carefully watched the Obama administration's reactions to international crises, especially in relation to Iran, Libya, Syria, Georgia, and Crimea; they have undoubtedly noted the reluctant response of the United States in all these situations, where it has struggled to follow up on bold declaratory statements with actual punitive measures.[64] It is this lens that Beijing has used to interpret the statements of Obama administration officials on the South China Sea.

Finally, the administration of Rodrigo Duterte has taken a different tact from his predecessor and in so doing has introduced an element of uncertainty to the bilateral relationship with the United States. The approach of the new administration in Manila to relations with the United States stands decidedly at odds with that of Benigno Aquino, at least in terms of rhetoric. Since coming to power in May 2016, President Duterte has spoken openly about distancing Manila from Washington. He also placed at risk long-standing defense cooperation with the United States when he purportedly announced a "separation from the U.S." on the occasion of a state visit to China. No doubt, there is quite clearly an element of showmanship and posturing on the part of the maverick Philippine president, and on other occasions President Duterte has been more measured in his remarks about the United States. Nevertheless, the fact of the matter is that such statements have caused not a small amount of confusion within the foreign and security policy establishment in the United States, not to mention the Philippines as well, and other regional capitals.

Although the South China Sea is a matter of national interest for the United States, its explicit interest is freedom of navigation and unimpeded commerce, both of which China has guaranteed—despite both parties still needing to arrive at agreement over acceptable military activities under the rubric of freedom of navigation, especially in the South China Sea. Commerce, however, has little if anything to do with the concerns that both parties have. Underlying their differences on this matter is their competing interpretations of UNCLOS in relation to military activities within a state's EEZ. Whereas Washington has taken the position—despite not having ratified UNCLOS—that such activities are permitted under the Convention, Beijing has opposed this. From Beijing's perspective, this takes on urgency because of plans to use the naval base on Hainan Island, home to China's nuclear submarine fleet, as a major base from which to project forth naval power into the South China Sea, which Beijing views as its natural sphere of influence. These differences aside, it is unlikely that Washington will consistently raise this issue given that China is not the only regional state that has expressed reservations about military activities being pursued within a state's EEZ.[65]

A Glass Half-Empty . . . or Half-Full

Although not all Southeast Asian states are involved in the South China Sea disputes, it would be a mistake to dismiss the matter, as Chinese leaders consistently do, as merely one between claimant states. The bottom line is that without a proper means of managing, let alone resolving, the tensions that arise from competing claims, the disputes will pose a serious threat to regional stability. Attendant to this is the concern that the South China Sea has cast a harsh light on the singular fiction of ASEAN unity and threatens to undermine ASEAN's reputation as a diplomatic community given the divergent and sometimes competing interests of its members on the issue.

There is no gainsaying that the South China Sea disputes have emerged as one of the most urgent tests of ASEAN's unity, centrality, and resolve. The onus is for ASEAN to demonstrate that it has both the institutional mechanisms (or is prepared to build them in response to changing circumstances) and political will to meet the challenge posed not only by China's strident assertion of its claims in the very maritime heart of Southeast Asia but also by the competing claims that ASEAN member states are pressing against each other. The question is whether the norms of pendulous gradualism and the dilatory process of consensus through consultations that ASEAN would claim have served its members so well through previous turbulence are sufficient to underpin regional order in the face of these latest challenges, or whether something of a paradigm shift is required.[66]

In all its fifty years, ASEAN has proven reasonably effective in conflict management but ill equipped to promote conflict resolution. Indeed, the celebrated "ASEAN Way" has yet to prove a viable platform upon which long-term conflict resolution, not merely short-term conflict prevention and papering over of cracks in the edifice of regional order, can be achieved.[67] The DOC does not cover sovereignty resolution and cannot enforce restrictions on occasion of a breach. It is neither a treaty nor an official code of conduct. Likewise, the 2011 Guidelines to the DOC, the result of nine painstaking years of discussion and negotiation on the back of the DOC itself, does not guarantee the implementation of the DOC, nor does it guarantee implementation of any form of a compulsory code of conduct, to say nothing of attempting to solve sovereignty problems. More important, China is cognizant of the limits of the Guidelines and perceives its diluted form as evidence of American failure "to internationalize the issue, which is against the will of China."[68]

At the same time, widespread fixation with Chinese activity in the waters has tended to distract from the reality that the South China Sea dispute is in fact an atomized series of diplomatic tussles involving periodic saber rattling and demonstrations of strength, where China is by no means the only (other) actor in the script. Aside from China and Taiwan, four Southeast Asian states are also making claims to various parts of the South China Sea—Vietnam, the Philippines, Malaysia, and Brunei. With the exception of Brunei, the other three Southeast Asian claimants have physically occupied more features in the South China Sea than China, a statistical imbalance Chinese policymakers are quick to point out (and evidently in a hurry to remedy). More to the point, as the world's gaze remains transfixed on Chinese adventurism in the South China Sea, the Southeast Asian claimant states have struggled to find a common position among themselves on the matter of their respective claims and have prosecuted their claims against each other away from the glare of international media.

One of the first serious clashes between ASEAN countries in the South China Sea occurred in April 1988 in the Spratlys between the Philippines and Malaysia at Permatang Ubi (Ardasier Bank) when Malaysian authorities arrested forty-nine Filipino fishermen.[69] Intra-ASEAN disagreements over the South China Sea gathered pace in the early 1990s even as Chinese activities in the Spratly Islands resulted in clashes with Vietnam and the Philippines, and this led Indonesia to convene a series of informal workshops on the South China Sea. When they were launched, these workshops were envisaged to provide a confidence-building platform for claimant states and other ASEAN members to discuss ways to diffuse growing tension in the South China Sea. Nevertheless, by 1994 the workshops themselves became an issue of contention among ASEAN states, when some members expressed misgivings that Indonesia was attempting to transform the informal workshops into official conferences with the intent of "containing" China through multilateralism while others saw Malaysia as an impediment to progress.[70]

Tensions between Malaysia and the Philippines escalated with Manila's discovery of Malaysian features constructed on two Spratly reefs during the period between April and June 1999. Strains on the relationship between Manila and Kuala Lumpur peaked in July that year, when Malaysia's move to prevent the South China Sea issue from being tabled at the ARF meeting in Singapore elicited criticisms from the Philippines, which lamented the lack of support from one ASEAN member for another.[71] In all, that year alone witnessed at least six reported clashes between the Philippines and either Malaysia or Vietnam over respective South China Sea claims. Ownership of the continental shelf of the Natuna Islands in the South China Sea was also contested between Indonesia and Vietnam during this time, although both parties managed to avoid open confrontation over the issue. Since 2010, ASEAN's perceived unwillingness or reluctance to take a firmer stand against increased Chinese assertiveness has been a cause of frustration for the Philippines and Vietnam. Yet in spite of congruent interests, coordination and cooperation between the two claimant states has failed to obtain. For its part, Manila has expressed displeasure toward the Vietnam–China six-point agreement, which it interpreted as containing statements that demonstrated disregard for multilateral means of conflict resolution.[72]

Matters came to a head at the July 2012 ASEAN Ministerial Meeting in Cambodia, when ASEAN foreign ministers failed to find consensus in response to China's assertive behavior in the previous months, despite numerous attempts by senior officials of member states to propose different variations of an ASEAN statement and position on the issue. The result of this was something of an embarrassment, as the organization failed to conclude a joint communiqué for the first time in its history. In a despondent response, Indonesian foreign minister Marty Natalegawa lamented not only the incapacity of the ASEAN member states to deal with the South China Sea issue collectively and decisively but the toll this had taken on the organization:

Whenever there are incidents, that is . . . the moment that we should reinforce our efforts, not be grinding to a halt. This time last year we had a similar problem between Cambodia and Thailand—it was a more direct intra-ASEAN conflict, but it was not impossible to find a solution within ASEAN. And in this instance, I find it perplexing, and to be candid and honest, really, really disappointing.[73]

Subsequently, even though Natalegawa's shuttle diplomacy eventually paved the way for ASEAN states to agree to the "Six Point Principles" and an "early conclusion" to ongoing discussions for a Code of Conduct on the South China Sea, the damage to the organization's reputation had been done. For its part, Cambodia was indignant. Several years after the 2012 debacle, Prime Minister Hun Sen saw fit to assail his critics and ASEAN counterparts during a speech at a graduation ceremony, in which he recounted a discussion he had with John Kerry on the incident:

I told John Kerry I was disappointed when they said that Cambodia's closeness to China was the obstacle to realizing COC. I had John Kerry's attention that when, before Cambodia took its turn, Vietnam and Indonesia were rotating chairs of ASEAN, why could they realize it? After Cambodia's turn, Brunei, Myanmar, and Malaysia—did they do it? What could they say about it? Is now not the time that those who attacked Cambodia or me personally apologize to me and repay my justice and cleanness?[74]

As if to reinforce this recalcitrance, Cambodian officials responded to John Kerry's attempt to secure assurances of their commitment to ASEAN solidarity over the South China Sea issue with the patronizing response that they were "only a small country and a non-claimant state."[75]

Away from the glare of the media, the inability of ASEAN claimant states to manage their own differences has also been manifested in the legal sphere. The differing submissions to the CLCS by Vietnam, Malaysia, and the Philippines—alluded to earlier—were instructive in this regard.[76] On May 6, 2009, Vietnam and Malaysia made a joint submission to the CLCS concerning a "defined area" of the South China Sea. The

Philippines responded with a separate *Notes Verbale* in August 2009 contesting the Vietnamese and Malaysian joint submission. Vietnam replied by stressing that its submission to the CLCS concerning the outer limits of Vietnam's continental shelf beyond 200 nautical miles, including its joint submission with Malaysia, was in conformity with its rights and obligations as a party to UNCLOS as well as the Scientific and Technical Guidelines and the Rules of Procedures of the CLCS. Much in the same vein, Malaysia sent a note in August 2009 strongly rejecting Filipino claims over North Borneo, and in so doing perhaps betrayed an effort to link South China Sea disagreements between Malaysia and the Philippines with their long-standing territorial dispute over the east Malaysian state of Sabah.[77]

In the case of the Philippines, it delivered notes with respect to three submissions: the joint submission of Malaysia and Vietnam, Vietnam's partial submission, and a submission made by Palau. The Philippine note, concerning the joint submission by Malaysia and Vietnam, asserted that "[the] Joint Submission for the Extended Continental Shelf by Malaysia and Vietnam lays claim on areas that are disputed not only because they overlap with that of the Philippines, but also because of the controversy arising from the territorial claims on some of the islands in the area including North Borneo." The note did not name the exact area contested by the Philippines. Yet it is evident that the southern part of the Philippine claim in the Spratly Islands partly covers the area marked out under the joint submission completed by Malaysia and Vietnam.

As alluded to earlier, another subject of disputation was the territorial dispute between the Philippines and Malaysia over North Borneo (that is, the east Malaysian state of Sabah). The Philippines note concerning Vietnam's partial submission contended that the area enclosed by Vietnam's submission with regard to the northern part of the South China Sea was "disputed because they overlap with those of the Philippines." This seemed to point to a likely continental shelf claim by the Philippines originating from Scarborough Shoal. In these notes, the Philippines asked for the CLCS to abstain from taking into consideration the aforementioned submissions "unless and until after the parties have discussed and resolved their disputes." In reply to the Philippine objections, Malaysia reaffirmed its sovereignty over Sabah, and Vietnam did as previously described. During the twenty-fourth session of the CLCS in August 2009, Vietnam and Malaysia reiterated their respective positions, stressing that the joint submission was without discrimination to the query of delimitation between states.[78]

Although a nonclaimant in the South China Sea disputes, Indonesia objected to the addition of Palmas Island situated forty-seven nautical miles east–northeast of the Saranggani Islands off Mindanao in the Philippines. Meanwhile, the Philippine opposition to the Joint Submission of Malaysia and Vietnam and the partial submission by Vietnam appeared to have been a result of the country's consideration of the "regime of islands" and whether they were entitled to their own continental shelves or only territorial seas. This line of reasoning was made clearer in a note dated April 5, 2011, conveyed by the Philippines to the secretary-general of the United Nations in response to China's May 2009 notes with accompanying maps enclosed showing the nine-dash line. In this note, the Philippines expressed that "under the international law principle of 'la terre domaine la mer' . . . the extent of the waters that are adjacent to the relevant geographical features are definite and determinable under UNCLOS, specifically under Article 121 (Regime of Islands) of this said Convention."[79]

The point to stress is that the legal and diplomatic posturing between ASEAN claimant states (over their respective CLCS submissions and their relations with China), and within ASEAN more generally, clearly illustrates not only the gulf that remains between regional states over the South China Sea; it is also indicative of how difficult it is (and will continue to be) for them to present a common position on the disputes, which would in principle strengthen their negotiation position vis-à-vis China.

Frustrations at the inability of ASEAN to exhibit coherence on the South China Sea dispute as it bore the brunt of China's muscular policy in part led the Philippines to take its case to arbitration, mentioned earlier, in hopes of compelling China to clarify its claims. Though supportive in private, vocal unqualified endorsement of the Philippine submission from the majority of ASEAN members was not forthcoming. In fact, one senior official from an ASEAN member state opined that the Philippine Arbitral Tribunal submission was "inconvenient" in respect to ASEAN's efforts to conclude a Code of Conduct (COC) with China.[80] Yet despite the frustrations that prompted its legal submission, Philippine views of the glacial pace at which ASEAN and China were moving on the COC remained hopeful. Illustrative of this was the challenge thrown down by

Philippine foreign secretary Albert Del Rosario at the ASEAN Summit in Bali in November 2011 for ASEAN to "play a decisive role . . . if it desires to realise its aspirations for global leadership."[81] Even as it emphasized its determination to seek a diplomatic solution with ASEAN support, the Philippine leadership called on ASEAN to "assert its leadership, centrality, and solidarity. ASEAN must show the world that it has the resolve to act in the common interest" and, conversely, that any inaction in response to Chinese land reclamations "would undermine ASEAN's centrality, solidarity and credibility."[82]

Because of the notoriety of the Phnom Penh debacle in 2012, ASEAN has taken extra care to ensure at least the impression of unity and coherence in all subsequent discussions on the issue. At the conclusion of the ASEAN Ministerial Meeting in August 2014, the resulting joint communiqué expressed "serious concerns" on the part of ASEAN states in reaction to "recent developments which have increased tensions in the South China Sea."[83] No mention of China was made, although the allusion was thinly veiled given the circumstances at the time, when China had only just deployed an oil rig within Vietnam's EEZ and had begun artificial island building projects in the Spratlys some months earlier. The communiqué further "reaffirmed the importance of maintaining peace, stability, maritime security as well as freedom of navigation in and over-flight above the South China Sea." In addition, ASEAN urged "all parties concerned to exercise self-restraint and avoid actions which would complicate the situation and undermine peace, stability, and security in the South China Sea and to settle disputes through peaceful means, without resorting to the threat or use of force." This statement was noteworthy for its relatively more forceful character, implying not only collective concern in ASEAN but, arguably more important, a convergence of views.

Testifying to a growing sense of urgency around the problem of escalation, ASEAN leaders took pains to ensure that the South China Sea was mentioned not only in communiqués but also in stand-alone statements, such as those released in January 2014 after the ministerial retreat and in May 2014 after the Chinese deployment of an oil rig into Vietnam's EEZ. A September 2014 meeting in Bangkok to discuss the implementation of the DOC saw ASEAN ministers privately confront China about its artificial island construction activities that by then had gathered considerable pace. Although rebuffed by their Chinese counterpart, it was nevertheless still laudable that ASEAN managed to put forth a collective diplomatic stand in an attempt to hold China to account. By the same token, ASEAN succeeded in harnessing its collective weight to reject a Chinese attempt to release a press statement on China–Southeast Asia joint development projects in the South China Sea at the conclusion of the November 2014 East Asia Summit.

Similar collective action was expressed the following year. Shepherded by Malaysia (as the chair), the ASEAN Chairman's Statement following the April 2015 summit enumerated the following misgivings on behalf of the member states:

> We share the serious concerns expressed by some leaders on the land reclamation being undertaken in the South China Sea, which has eroded trust and confidence and may undermine peace, security and stability in the South China Sea.
>
> We re-affirmed the importance of maintaining peace, stability, security, and freedom of navigation and over-flight over the South China Sea. We emphasized the need for all parties to ensure the full and effective implementation of the Declaration on the Conduct of Parties in the South China Sea in its entirety: to build, maintain and enhance mutual trust and confidence; exercising self-restraint in the conduct of activities; not to resort to threat or use of force; and for the parties concerned to resolve their differences and disputes through peaceful means, in accordance with international law including the 1982 United Nations Convention on the Law of the Sea.
>
> While noting the progress made in the consultations on the Code of Conduct in the South China Sea (COC), we urged that consultations be intensified, to ensure the expeditious establishment of an effective COC.[84]

The statement at the ASEAN Summit in Kuala Lumpur in November 2015 reiterated these points and added an expression of concern for "the increased presence of military assets and the possibility of further militarization of outposts in the South China Sea."[85] That these expressions of concern were documented under Malaysian chairmanship was significant given the point registered earlier regarding how Malaysia had hitherto been known to take pains to avoid antagonizing China or drawing the organization into diplomatic confrontation with Beijing despite being a claimant state itself.

Often ASEAN statements are as noteworthy for what is not said as they are for what is. In keeping with diplomatic tradition not to cast too harsh a light on any particular member, statements expressing concern have not gone to the extent of fingering specific transgressors or transgressions, whether they involve an ASEAN claimant state or China, a nonmember but a claimant as well as dialogue partner. This has had the consequent effect of diminishing to some degree the diplomatic pressure that the organization can otherwise bring to bear on claimants whose actions threaten to undermine the stability of the region. The blunt reality is that ASEAN continues to struggle to arrest the slide toward greater tension as China continues to relentlessly and obdurately press its claims by changing the facts in the seas. In April 2016, this reality was made plain when China apparently secured the support of Brunei, Laos, and Cambodia for a four-point "consensus agreement," which, according to Chinese foreign minister Wang Yi, consisted of the following:[86]

1. The South China Sea disagreements are not disputes between China and ASEAN, and the matter should not affect China–ASEAN relations;
2. The rights of all countries to independently choose the way to resolve the dispute in accordance with international law should be affirmed. The imposition of a unilateral approach would be wrong;
3. In accordance with Article IV of the Declaration on Conduct of Parties in the South China Sea (DOC), China and the three states believe that the parties involved should resolve disputes over their territorial and maritime rights and issues through dialogue and consultation;
4. China and ASEAN states have the capacity to jointly safeguard peace and stability in the South China Sea, and external parties should play a constructive role, rather than the reverse.

How this four-point "consensus agreement" was arrived at was never clarified. In the meantime, Laos and Cambodia have distanced themselves from the Chinese claim, while Brunei has remained silent (at the time of writing). Similar controversy surfaced at the conclusion of an ASEAN–China ministerial held in Kunming in June 2016, when Malaysia released a purported consensus statement on the meeting, only to retract it on the advice of the ASEAN Secretariat for reasons of "urgent revisions" that were apparently required after China allegedly lobbied the Laotian chair of ASEAN (and, allegedly, Cambodia and Myanmar as well, although this could not be confirmed). At one level, the retraction can be interpreted as yet further evidence of a Chinese tactic of dividing ASEAN, as it surely was, as well as ASEAN's collective inability to deal decisively with Chinese pressure on any one of its members. Conversely, it was evident from individual statements made by member states that there was indeed an ASEAN consensus on the issue and, in particular, the absence of the Singaporean cochair from the concluding session of the meeting, which was interpreted by China as a calculated move to convey a categorical message.[87]

What was clear from China's actions was its intent to divide ASEAN, negate what at the time was an impending ruling of the Arbitral Tribunal on the Philippine submission, and cast American involvement in the South China Sea in a harsh light. More pertinent, it conforms to a pattern of Chinese diplomacy, which has seen it leverage ASEAN's diplomatic culture of consensus decisionmaking to devastating effect by way of persuasion and inducements of economically vulnerable regional states to Beijing's position on the South China Sea. Having said that, although China has rightly been called out for attempting to divide ASEAN in this manner, it also stands to reason that the periodic success of such an approach remains something of an indictment of ASEAN's own inability to collectively stand its ground and prevent the breaking of ranks. Indonesian foreign minister Marty Natalegawa paints a stark picture of the potential cost of disunity: "Absent a COC, absent the diplomatic process, we can be certain of more incidents and tension for our region. Absent an ASEAN unity, the question will become like a loose cannon in the way the issue is discussed."[88] Because of the ASEAN consensus model of decisionmaking and the fact that regional states have different interests and outlooks toward the external actors involved, the organization has often found itself incapacitated in terms of the diplomatic resources it can husband to stake a position on the South China Sea disputes. This, more than anything else, explains the elusiveness of any prospect that ASEAN would be able to push back Chinese assertiveness to any significant degree or to facilitate some manner of resolution between ASEAN claimant states themselves.

There is more at stake. If achieved and demonstrated resolutely, ASEAN unity and agreement on the South China Sea would, in fact, not only present an important diplomatic and political counterbalance to

China; it would also prevent overreliance on the United States.[89] Yet it is precisely under the weight of Chinese assertiveness that Southeast Asian states have chosen to emphasize the role of the United States in maintaining regional order and stability. This has been expressed most profoundly in the move by claimant states to enhance and embrace defense cooperation with the United States. Even so, as pointed out earlier, differences still exist among regional states. While some support a robust American military presence, others have been more reticent. Consider, for instance, Indonesian responses to the October 2015 American FONOPS discussed earlier. The further move by the United States to deploy an aircraft carrier group in the South China Sea in March 2016 has also caused consternation among some Southeast Asian states—concerned that this deployment would accomplish little more than further militarization and escalation of an already tense situation—even as it might reassure others.

At issue, too, is the prevailing anxiety over whether such intense U.S. engagement is tenable in the long run, even as Southeast Asian states recognize the severe limitations of their mode of indigenous regionalism, especially when it comes to mitigating potential conflicts and overcoming differences such as those that are already all too apparent over the South China Sea. Of deep concern for not a few Southeast Asian states is the possibility that the United States could raise the stakes in an attempt to enhance the deterrent effect of its actions, only to later retrench its presence for any number of reasons ranging from domestic constraints to economic distress to foreign policy distraction or a simple recalculation that getting entangled in the South China Sea against China is ultimately not in American interests. As suggested at the beginning of this book, there is precedent for such misgivings.

On the other side of the coin, the region considers itself confronted by an equally alarming prospect in the form of a Sino–U.S. condominium of sorts that may be arrived at without consultation or input from regional states and which could be at odds with regional interests. As Humphrey Hawksley intimated: "A deal struck between Washington and Beijing could trample on East Asia's more nuanced interests that might be forgotten amid horse-trading on a basket of global issues."[90] This was arguably the implicit subtext behind the notion of the G-2 popularized by Zbigniew Brzezinski in 2009 but eschewed by most states in the region.[91] Indeed, this view has been corroborated by a former senior official from the U.S. Department of Defense who was intimately involved in discussions with his Chinese counterparts and who shared his impression that "as part of the new great power relationship, China wants its influence in Southeast Asia recognized and accepted."[92] This view appears particularly acute in Hanoi, where a perspective holds that China could use leverage over North Korea as a means to obtain American agreement to dial down pressure on Chinese activities in the South China Sea and the Mekong region.[93]

Given these possibilities and concerns, and the residual fears of a recrudescence to its Cold War status as an arena for great power rivalry, the ability of regional states to fashion meaningful agreement on a feasible collective position on the issue is as urgent as it is challenging. ASEAN is torn between the desire to retain some measure of regional autonomy and the dry reality that even in the event of a successful collective mustering of will it might be unlikely that the organization can push back a China intent to press its claims increasingly on the back of military muscle. On balance, the ASEAN response has been tepid but also in keeping with the character of the organization and the nature of its diplomacy. The reality is that the "ASEAN Way" of conflict management has always relied on the exercise of restraint among member states in conflict with each other more so than the efficacy of regional mechanisms of dispute mitigation and settlement. The long-standing territorial dispute between the Philippines and Malaysia over Sabah is instructive, as was the management of the controlled outbreak of armed conflict between Thailand and Cambodia over the Preah Vihear Temple and its compound. In both instances, further escalation was averted when the parties in conflict exercised restraint on their own accord. Therein lies the rub: there is at present little evidence that China, an ASEAN "outsider," intends to exercise any restraint in its "salami slicing" in the South China Sea, while it is unclear the lengths to which the United States is prepared to go to ensure Chinese ambitions do not ultimately upend regional order.

CHAPTER SEVEN

Piecemeal Progress

AS THE PREVIOUS CHAPTER DETAILED, how the South China Sea imbroglio has evolved in recent years has cast a harsh light on the Pivot in terms of how it has drawn out the sharp edge of President Obama's much talked about regional engagement strategy. Whether by design or circumstance, this has obscured the fact that the Pivot is supposed to be an engagement policy involving a trifecta of tools. There is no doubt the United States has made its presence felt in the region militarily, much to the chagrin of China. After all, arguably nothing registers more definitively than the presence of the seventh fleet in the South China Sea, and this has been supplemented with the signing of an Enhanced Defense Cooperation Agreement with the Philippines in 2014 (ratified by the Philippine Supreme Court in January 2016) and the total lifting of the ban on the sale of lethal weapons to Vietnam in May 2016. But there are significant economic and diplomatic facets to the Pivot that warrant closer analytical scrutiny. Foremost, these have been illustrated in American leadership—despite not being the originator of the idea—of the Trans-Pacific Partnership Agreement initiative as well as diplomatic engagement with regional states that previous Washington administrations had kept at a distance. Of analytical salience, too, is the attendant issue of domestic factors that have featured in ways that have to some extent diluted these facets of the Pivot and in the process have thrown some doubt on its prospects, both in terms of intent and sustainability.

Since the Marshall Plan, economics has always been a crucial, if sometimes underappreciated, element of American grand strategy, both in terms of the U.S. economy's ability to sustain policies of security and diplomatic engagement worldwide, as well as its ability to lead and shape global trade and development in the postwar era.[1] In many respects, it has been American economic strength alongside military preponderance that underpinned the creation of the liberal international order that exists today. It should also be evident from previous chapters that although imperfect in its application, trade and investments in both multilateral and, more important, bilateral forms have constituted an important aspect of engagement with Southeast Asia through the Clinton and Bush administrations toward the ends of advancing the strategic objective of American primacy and leadership in the region. The Obama administration's engagement strategy—specifically, its economic premise—should be considered in this light.

Yet from the very onset of the Obama presidency, the economic "prong" was in danger of being compromised not only by China's own economic advances into the region—which set Chinese and American economic engagement strategies on a competitive path—but, arguably more consequentially, by the economic crisis that beset the United States toward the end of the decade. The ailments that bedeviled the American economy, and the litany of domestic ramifications they spawned, had the effect of driving the United States to necessary distraction and raising doubts over whether it could afford to make good on promises to accord greater attention to the region.

PIVOTING IN TIMES OF ECONOMIC CRISIS

One of the challenges confronting the Obama administration's efforts to ensure that the Pivot was not merely form but substance was the fact that the policy was announced at the height of a deepening fiscal crisis and escalating political polarization. When the subprime crisis, already brewing for some years, reached its climax in the period 2007–08, the U.S. economy was launched on a downward spiral to a structural crisis that was arguably the worst since the Great Depression of the 1930s. The plunge in real estate prices triggered widespread market depreciation of securities tied to the real estate industry. Financial institutions were brought to the brink of collapse—some actually folded eventually—and were rescued only by government bailouts that gradually restored a semblance of normalcy (albeit at the cost of an increase in popular resentment). A severely crippled domestic economy was conspiring to undermine American prestige and status globally.

For a time, it appeared that American forward deployment would be the prime victim of necessary fiscal discipline born of economic distress. Given the size of the Pentagon budget, it inevitably became part of the national debt tussle between the executive and legislative branches of the government. The initial result was $450 billion worth of reductions as part of the Budget Control Act in August 2011. But with the automatic sequestration clause, the damage increased to $917 billion when Congress failed to arrive at a solution by March 1, 2013.[2] The implications of these cuts for America's power projection and regional presence were undeniable. Even before the second round of cuts, Dan Blumenthal had assessed that "these cuts will affect our posture in Asia profoundly. We need more ships, more aircraft, more missile defenses."[3] In the same light, others had suggested that "the idea that these cuts can occur without affecting America's forward deployments in the Pacific is simply not credible."[4] One senior American military official (a four-star general) also speculated at the time that the Department of Defense was pondering the possibility of reducing the naval fleet by two aircraft carriers and two support carriers, which would have invariably affected the composition—let alone projection capabilities—of carrier groups.[5] Indeed, a stark picture of the devastating effect of sequestration was painted by former secretary of defense Leon Panetta during remarks made at Georgetown University in February 2013: "We're going to have to shrink our global naval operations with a reduction of as much as one-third in our western Pacific operations. The whole idea about trying to rebalance [in Asia] will be impacted."[6]

In the aftermath of sequestration, Chuck Hagel, in one of his first acts as secretary of defense, announced in April 2013 a Strategic Choices and Management Review that would enable the Pentagon to adapt to its smaller budget. He also reassured the Department of Defense that he had given personal guidance on select programs to be protected from sequestration. Ultimately, however, his presumed inability (some suggested reluctance) to resolutely defend the Defense Department's interests and insulate its budget from the effects of sequestration was cited as a source of his apparent unpopularity in the Department of Defense that, in turn, might have contributed to his eventual resignation.[7] Cognizant of the unsettling signals that sequestration was sending out to American partners and allies, then deputy secretary of defense Ashton Carter was eager to calm nerves in Southeast Asia. In a speech in Jakarta in March 2013, he remarked: "Sequester was never intended to be im-

plemented and is very disruptive because it gives us very little managerial flexibility in where we take budget adjustments this year. But wher-
ever we have flexibility, we are favoring and protecting the [Asia Pacific]
rebalance. . . . The sequester mechanism is an artificial, self-inflicted
political problem, not a structural problem. The turmoil and gridlock
will end and the U.S. can get back to normal budgeting."[8]

Although the U.S. military will maintain an unrivaled position in the
Asia Pacific for the foreseeable future, financial austerity measures imposed upon the Pentagon will inevitably have adverse effects on long-term
recapitalization for, modernization of, and innovation in the U.S. arse-
nal. It may also affect decisionmaking on the acquisition of vital but
expensive precision and networked weapons systems.[9] Given both the
severity and urgency of the crisis, it is hardly surprising if government
agencies and officials, in attempting to manage its implications, were to
fumble strategic communications. In point of fact, that was exactly what
happened in March 2014, when the assistant secretary of defense for
acquisitions Katrina McFarland confessed at a conference that "right
now, the Pivot is being looked at again, because candidly it can't happen."
McFarland's statement was almost immediately withdrawn through a
spokesperson, with the revised claim that "the rebalance to Asia can and
will continue."[10] Needless to say, such confusing signals are read closely in
the region. Retired admiral Gary Roughhead's testimony in Congress on
regional responses as well as the preparedness of the United States to fulfil
its commitments against a background of austerity offers some insight to
that effect:

> The vastness of the Asia-Pacific region, where we enjoy absolute
> air and maritime superiority, is going to require a new look at in-
> creased investments in unmanned systems. We have learned a lot
> in Iraq and Afghanistan with regard to unmanned systems. But I
> will tell you that the Pacific is very different. It is not as benign. It
> will be more challenging. And, accordingly, I believe that as we
> look at our future—and we really are in the lead in this rapidly
> developing area—we should look at how we do it, what our priori-
> ties are, what our processes are, and we have to have a greater
> sense of urgency as we move forward with unmanned [systems].
>
> I will tell you that, having recently come back from the region—
> and I have been there six times in the last, about 14 months—our
> defense budgets are watched in Asia more closely than they are

watched on the American street. People are questioning whether or not we are serious about it. And the actions are going to speak louder than any words going forward.

I would also say that, while we tend to focus on procurement and technology, near-term readiness and the near-term readiness budget is extraordinarily important. One can undergo short, rare disruptions to the near-term readiness budget. But I would submit that we are beyond that point now. I really do believe that the actions that have had to be taken are beginning to erode, not just the short-term readiness, but also will take its toll on long-term readiness and it will be more costly and longer to dig out than had we stayed in a more disciplined regime.[11]

From the perspective of U.S. defense posture in the region, the domestic debates surrounding sequestration, and the U.S. economy more broadly, sent mixed signals to a Southeast Asia worried that an American policy of engagement might lose its financial moorings. To some extent, what was striking about national discussions on sequestration was how marginal questions of American foreign policy and grand strategy were to the discussion as debates over the state and future of the American economy descended into polarized attacks ad hominem on the president. Together with debates over healthcare reform policy, this set in motion a swift downturn of relations between the presidency and the GOP (along with other conservatives) as habitual criticism of the president deteriorated into withering scorn. Needless to say, foreign policy— from Iran to Libya to China to Cuba—was not spared. In fairness, even the president's chosen lieutenants—Hillary Clinton, Leon Panetta, Robert Gates, Chuck Hagel—were undercutting him to varying degrees soon after they relinquished their respective offices, if their published memoirs are anything to go by.

In the event, the Pivot, and surely with it future iterations of engagement of Southeast Asia, has to some extent become collateral damage to such criticism. In essence, the economic crisis was instructive of how policies that would have a crucial impact not only on American standing elsewhere in the world but also how regional states, including potential adversaries, viewed U.S. credibility were held hostage to budgetary paralysis in an increasingly visceral and polarized domestic political atmosphere.

THE ART OF THE (NON)DEAL

The TPPA was touted as the economic centerpiece of the Obama administration's rebalance to Asia. Although not an agreement pertaining to or involving the entire Southeast Asian region per se, the TPPA nevertheless included four Southeast Asian states: Singapore, Brunei, Malaysia, and Vietnam. Several others also expressed interest in joining the TPPA at a future date, most notably, Indonesia. More to the point, however, the TPPA was viewed by many in the region as a litmus test of American long-term holistic commitment to the region. Foremost among the proponents of this view was Singapore, and it was put across by its foreign minister, K. Shanmugam, on the occasion of a visit to Washington, which happened to take place during heated congressional debates over the virtues (and liabilities) of the TPPA:

> Strategically, what is your engagement with Asia, what is your leverage of engagement with the fastest-growing region in the world? The only game in town is the TPP. . . . For some years now, American administrations from the president downwards have been coming out to Asia and have been saying how important it [the TPPA] is as part of the American engagement of Asia Pacific. . . . And it is really the litmus test of American ability to deliver on what it has promised, what the president has said is the most important thing America is doing in the Asia Pacific.[12]

That the foreign minister hastened the point concerning the urgency of the TPPA was indicative; it spoke to the need of an expression of American intent to play an active part in the region above and beyond the establishment or perpetuation of a military presence.

Additionally, American economic engagement was also a necessary response to emergent economic regionalism sans American participation. Proposed at the ASEAN Summit in 2011, the Regional Comprehensive Economic Partnership (RCEP) is an ASEAN-inspired regional economic integration initiative that brings together the economies of ASEAN and six dialogue partners—China, Japan, South Korea, Australia, New Zealand, and India. The ambitious initiative aims to create the largest trading bloc in the world. At its inception during the November 2012 East Asia Summit, RCEP was envisaged to reconcile the East Asian

Free Trade Agreement (EAFTA), which brought together ASEAN, China, Japan, and South Korea, and the Comprehensive Economic Partnership in East Asia (CEPEA), which also included Australia, New Zealand, and India, as well as to harmonize the raft of free trade agreements (FTAs) that ASEAN had with each of the non-ASEAN countries.

Significantly, RCEP could potentially serve as a compromise between the EAFTA, supported by China, and CEPEA, supported by Japan, both of which were progressing at a glacial pace. What distinguished RCEP from the TPPA was its basic premise of open regionalism, whereas the latter was far more ambitious in how it envisaged and legislated norms in investments, intellectual property rights, and trade. More to the point, given that RCEP includes all ten ASEAN member states, it is seen to be an important expression of ASEAN-led regionalism, even if the initiative has its fair share of skeptics who cast suspicious eyes at China's presumptive leadership (in RCEP). This contrasted with the TPPA, which by excluding six Southeast Asian states had introduced an element of discrimination and division in its model of economic regionalism. All this assumes, of course, that the RCEP will be signed, which at present has not happened.

The imperative of the TPPA gained further urgency after China declared its intention to form an Asian Infrastructure Investment Bank (AIIB) in 2013, an initiative that, at the point of its announcement, leavened China's otherwise disconcerting words and deeds with regards the South China Sea. The AIIB, with earmarked initial capital of up to $100 billion—of which China prodigiously committed to contributing half as the bank's major shareholder—is envisaged to meet the urgent need for infrastructure investment in the region. The immediate, unvarnished response of the United States leadership to the AIIB was instructive of its concern for its position of regional primacy. Fearing the possibility that the World Bank, where American leverage was considerable, could be undermined by the AIIB, senior officials from within the inner circles of the White House were quick to express misgivings immediately after the announcement that the bank would be formed. The principal reservation articulated in public was expressed as misgivings toward the matter of institutional governance and transparency. An attendant concern was for how the AIIB could potentially be a vehicle for Beijing to facilitate a further tilt of regional economic influence in its direction. It was, arguably, this apprehension that prompted Washington's negative reactions to expressions of interest on the part of its allies in Australia and the

United Kingdom to join the AIIB. Although this somewhat emotive response on the part of some White House officials may have only been a momentary lapse of reason, it nevertheless caused consternation in the region. Even if the message from the White House was not meant specifically for allies in Southeast and East Asia, the fact that it was seen as an attempt by the United States to lean on security allies and partners to reject Chinese overtures—to choose, as it were—created considerable discomfort, all the more so because the AIIB was viewed on balance to be a positive contribution to regional development rather than a reason for alarm. Somewhat reminiscent of what transpired in the mid-1970s after the United States took itself out of the regional strategic equation by virtue of its withdrawal from Saigon in 1973, which led Southeast Asian states to immediately strengthen relations with Beijing, Washington's instinctive infelicitous response to the AIIB initiative not only diminished its standing in regional economic affairs, it did nothing to dampen regional enthusiasm for the initiative. Indeed, the point was argued, not least by some American officials themselves, that U.S. interests regarding governance and transparency, all legitimate issues of concern, would be better served if Washington had in fact joined the bank.

Although the manner of the initial American response left something to be desired, the underlying logic was not entirely misplaced. Technicalities of the AIIB aside, not unlike the TPPA, it did also possess a strategic logic. China attended to regional reticence toward its growing presence and claims in the South China Sea with major initiatives such as the AIIB and the One Belt, One Road project. Whether or not they are genuinely driven by Chinese goodwill or benevolence, as its political leaders constantly proclaim, these initiatives also speak to Chinese ambitions to redefine the nature of the regional economic order in a way that revolves around Beijing as the policy nerve center and key trading nodes such as Chongqing and Kunming. Indeed, it is in this respect that the TPPA was viewed as a critical element to the American Pivot not only because of its economic but, equally pertinent, its strategic logic. In the same vein, the cool reception it received during the U.S. presidential election campaign and the eventual withdrawal of the United States from the agreement by President Donald Trump does not bode well for the future of American efforts to contribute to the shaping of the regional economic architecture, especially given the fact that Washington is now devoid of any realistic alternative vehicle through which it can exercise economic leadership and influence in the region.

Returning to the TPPA, much of the initial U.S. domestic debate over the agreement revolved around the apparent lack of transparency with regards to its contents right up to its release in November 2015. Concomitantly, the TPPA came under criticism from a wide spectrum of political interests. Needless to say, Obama administration trade officials rejected the allegations of lack of transparency. The U.S. trade representative (USTR) Michael Froman pointed out that the trade agenda under President Obama was, in fact, one of the most transparent in U.S. history. According to Froman, the Office of the USTR opened up feedback channels to an unprecedented level of public input and congressional oversight—organizing discussions with small-business owners, nongovernmental organizations, and labor unions, and holding more than 1,400 congressional briefings on the TPPA. Another factor in the equation was the passage of the critical Trade Promotion Authority (TPA), which when granted in effect secures the agreement of Congress to refrain from demanding amendments and further concessions after trade treaties such as the TPPA are signed, but on condition that the president observes certain statutory obligations in negotiating and signing the said trade treaties.[13] On this, USTR Froman wrote further in *Foreign Affairs*:

> Congress' involvement could be further enhanced and institutionalized by the passage of trade promotion authority, which would allow Congress to guide trade policy by laying out the United States' negotiating objectives, defining how the executive branch must consult with Congress about trade agreements, and detailing the legislative procedures that will guide Congress' consideration of trade agreements. At the same time, by ensuring that Congress will consider trade agreements as they have been negotiated by the executive branch, trade promotion authority would give U.S. trading partners the necessary confidence to put their best and final offers on the table. Trade promotion authority has a long, bipartisan history—stretching back to President Franklin Roosevelt and the U.S. Congress during the New Deal era—of ensuring congressional oversight while also strengthening the United States' hand at the international bargaining table.[14]

Froman's account of the scope of congressional responses permitted under the TPA, however, may have been exaggerated. The TPA allows for trade agreements to be considered under expedited legislative procedures: limited debate, no amendments, and an up-or-down vote. While Congress would be able to influence negotiation objectives and consultative and notification procedures, it will still be locked out of the actual process. In any event, securing renewal of the TPA—at the time critical for efforts to eventually fast-track the TPPA itself—proved an onerous process. As late as February 2015, the key authors of the TPA—Senator Orrin Hatch (R-Utah), Senator Ron Wyden (D-Ore.), and Rep. Paul Ryan (R-Wisc.)—were struggling to deal with the objections of Democrats who feared fast-track bills like the TPA would deprive them of the ability to influence the terms of the TPPA before it arrived at Congress for a final vote.

Conversely, introducing provisions that would make fast-tracking more acceptable to Democrats—for example, by inserting mechanisms that made it easier to defeat trade agreements—ran the risk of alienating Republicans and the business community, not to mention the risk of placing the passage of the TPPA itself in jeopardy.[15] At issue was the matter of jobs and special interest groups, many of which had lobbied extensively to block both the TPA and the TPPA.[16] At the same time, Republican support was also measured because of reluctance to further empower a president that the party had been attacking almost since he came to power for behaving as an "imperial president." Yet in spite of such considerable obstacles, the TPA managed to pass in the House of Representatives (219–211) and the Senate (60–37) in June 2015. The slim margins, which were secured only with the quid pro quo of an accompanying workers' assistance package, known as the Trade Adjustment Authority Bill, nevertheless paved the way for the administration's subsequent signing of the TPPA by trade negotiators in October 2015 and by the respective cabinet ministers in February 2016. The two-year path for ratification, however, was always expected to be paved with a good measure of domestic obstacles. Presidential candidates jostling to succeed Barack Obama, including those from his own party, such as former secretary of state and erstwhile TPPA proponent Hillary Clinton, almost all raised objections against the agreement in its current form. In any case, the fate of American membership in the TPPA was eventually sealed, at least in the short term, when President Donald Trump, who gave no quarter to the TPPA during his campaign, reserved his first executive order for the withdrawal of the United States from the agreement.

Indeed, the manner in which the TPPA was jettisoned by the Trump administration is instructive of the role that domestic politics plays in shaping American strategy and policy towards Southeast Asia. To that effect, the point needs also to be made that it was not only in the United States that domestic challenges threatened to undermine the TPPA and, by extension, progress in American economic engagement in the region. While smooth ratification of the agreement was secured in Singapore and Brunei, the picture was decidedly different in Malaysia, where considerable pressure mounted against ratification. The Malaysian case proved particularly trying. Given how the Malaysian economy had in recent decades been built on the foundations of affirmative action for the ethnic Malay majority, it was hardly a surprise when indigenous cultural and business groups intensely lobbied the government of Prime Minister Najib Tun Razak for fear that the removal of taxes on commodities and businesses, required by the TPPA, would translate to smoother entry of foreign companies into Malaysia. The TPPA also ran athwart Malaysian affirmative action on matters such as the Investor–State Dispute Settlement mechanism, which could compromise official acquisitions if the latter were to be performed in accordance with the state-sanctioned policy of preferential treatment of ethnic Malay-owned small and medium enterprises.[17] This fear was rendered more acute by the perception—misplaced yet emotive—that the TPPA was driven by the United States and hence was nothing less than a veiled expression of Western colonialism, a theme that tends to elicit exaggerated responses from a broad spectrum of the Malaysian population, but particularly from rural ethnic Malay communities, which also happened to be the bedrock of support for Najib's diminishing legitimacy.

Not surprisingly, opposition politicians and detractors were quick to denounce the TPPA for its lack of transparency and for threatening the welfare of small and medium businesses. Campaigners demonstrated when U.S. trade representatives visited Malaysia in late 2013, compelling both Prime Minister Najib and his second finance minister, Ahmad Husni, to convey these home-grown anxieties toward the TPPA to their American counterparts. To blunt the attacks emanating from various sources across Malaysian society, the Malaysian Ministry of Trade publicly declared that Malaysia was not obliged, and would not go out of its way, to conclude the TPPA in accordance with timelines set by Washington. So polarizing was the debate within Malaysia that even members of the ruling coalition and allies of the prime minister publicly expressed opposition to the TPPA. For instance, in response to the attendant intellectual property regulations in the TPPA, which would permit U.S.-based pharmaceutical firms to reinforce long-standing control over medication and drugs by preventing the manufacture of common medications (thereby potentially raising the cost of medicines), the Malaysian minister for health Liow Tiong Lai voiced his opposition: "We are against the patent extension. According to the agreement, if a medicine is launched in the U.S., and then three years later it is launched in Malaysia, the patent would start from when it is launched here and not when it was launched earlier in the U.S. This is not fair."[18]

To be sure, many of the themes that emerged in Malaysian narratives of opposition to the TPPA conformed to patterns elsewhere. Having said that, the Malaysian case was also particular in the sense that this opposition was in part also occasioned by growing disenfranchisement and frustration toward the incumbent government following a raft of allegations of corruption and malfeasance against the prime minister himself. Indeed, considering this dissensus, it was impressive that the Najib administration managed to negotiate the preservation of its affirmative action policy while also obtaining a minimum five-year grace period for the reform of its state-owned enterprises and exemption for its sovereign wealth fund that manages government-linked companies, Khazanah Nasional, from exposure to the Investor–State Dispute Settlement mechanism for a period of two years. Though these concessions were basically little more than short-term measures, they were enough to render the TPPA more palatable, thereby facilitating its passage in the Malaysian Parliament by a 127–84 vote. Yet even though the TPPA was successfully pushed through in Malaysia, politicians aligned with the incumbent party also expressed anxiety over the possibility that the TPPA might yet fail ratification in the American Congress, in which case, as one politician put it, the fact that the Malaysian leadership had "expended significant political currency" to push the deal through would redound on them, and they could well find themselves "with a lot to answer for."

OLD ENEMIES, NEW FRIENDS

Travails of the TPPA notwithstanding, some of the most significant advances in U.S.–Southeast Asia relations during the Obama administration were to be found in two sets of bilateral relationships that had hitherto been almost nonexistent, or else defined by great distrust. Indeed, in an extensive interview with President Obama published in *The Atlantic*, Vietnam and Myanmar (Burma) were identified as two opportunities "to draw Asian nations into the U.S. orbit," which Obama seized with aplomb.[19]

Vietnam

Thus far, this book has established the point that U.S. relations with several Southeast Asian states have gained greater purchase as a result of regional concern for Chinese assertiveness. As chapter 5 has already suggested, in considering the palpable upturn in U.S.–Vietnam relations, the China factor indubitably looms large.

Vietnam and China are imbricated in an exceedingly complex relationship involving not just historical baggage and ideological alignment but also deep distrust—this, despite the existence of multiple contact points including state to state, party to party, province to province, and mass organization to mass organization. It is increasingly evident that Vietnamese leaders have become acutely aware of how geopolitical trends have gradually overwhelmed the ideological affinity that exists between Beijing and Hanoi. As a Vietnamese scholar plainly pointed out, "While Vietnam will always be sensitive to the relationship with China, ideology can change but geography cannot."[20] This is not to say, however, that there is no strategic imperative to Sino–Vietnamese relations. High-ranking exchanges between Chinese and Vietnamese officials to discuss security-related matters have long been a regular fixture on the calendar of bilateral relations. This has persisted despite strains on bilateral relations caused by the South China Sea disputes and by mutual suspicions that continue to linger. Significantly, while such regularized interactions between American and Vietnamese officials are increasing, they are still embryonic in comparison to Sino–Vietnamese exchanges. Conversely, it is also noteworthy that the China factor has had the unintended effect of making strange bedfellows of the United States and Vietnam. Even though just how consequential a role the factor of China plays in determining the decision of Vietnamese leaders to draw closer to the United States may be difficult to ascertain in its entirety, few would disagree that it is a contributing factor.

Vietnamese policy toward China has to some degree been governed by domestic political and bureaucratic contention between two broad camps, even though neither is necessarily clearly defined whether in terms of composition or agenda. There is a sense that a pro-China lobby exists in the Vietnamese leadership, comprising party conservatives initially aligned with former general secretaries Le Kha Phieu and Nong Duc Manh, former president Truong Tan Sang, and, to a lesser extent, Nguyen Phu Truong, the current party secretary, that seeks to prioritize engagement and deepening of bilateral links with China even as they nurse long-standing suspicions of the United States. Though not to be mistaken for genuflection in the direction of Beijing, it was still this conservative view that informed Vietnam's concessions on Sino–Vietnamese border issues with the 1999 and 2000 Tonkin Gulf agreements.[21] For Vietnam, improvement in ties with the United States, though necessary and prudent, cannot be pursued at the expense of long-standing connections with China. Cognizant of a need not to strain relations with China, an aide to Le provided a glimpse into the logic behind Vietnam's presumed deference toward China: "We live adjacent to a big country; we cannot afford to maintain tension with them because they are next door to us."[22]

It can be argued that this view has held even in times of bilateral crisis insofar as pro-China sentiments are concerned. In the wake of a standoff in mid-2014 between Chinese and Vietnamese vessels triggered by the former's deployment of the *Hai Yang Shi You 981* oil rig in the latter's EEZ, Defense Minister Phung Quang Thanh dismissed the altercation as a dispute between "brothers," while Foreign Minister Pham Binh Minh was instructed—allegedly at the behest of the Politburo—to postpone a trip to the United States during the time of the standoff.[23] The head of the Communist Party's Department of Propaganda and Education, Dinh The Huynh, apparently also instructed state media not to cast a negative light on China in its reporting on the incident. Be that as it may, the point should nevertheless be registered that measured against the attendant complex historical baggage that defines the Sino–Vietnamese relationship, the incident also predictably prompted a deepening of Vietnamese suspicions of their larger neighbor. As a Vietnamese diplomat explained, "while this [the oil rig issue] is not a big deal for China, for Vietnam it was a turning point since the normalization of ties in September 1990."[24]

If conservative sentiments toward China have for the most part been cautiously conciliatory, there is another camp within the Vietnamese establishment that harbors apprehensions toward Beijing's intent, especially on South China Sea matters, and whose policy positions have been shaped by these apprehensions. To large extents, those wary of Chinese motives can be described as "internationalists" by dint of the fact that they are also proponents of economic reform via a broader international engagement strategy in order to balance against overreliance on China. This strategy encompasses strengthening relations with the United States, Japan, and Western Europe. This internationalist camp is strongly associated with former prime minister Nguyen Tan Dung, who drew his support from key leaders hailing from southern Vietnam. The internationalists advocate the view that the country's economic future rests on deeper integration with ASEAN and cautious but necessary pursuit of closer relations with the West. A prodigy of party stalwart Vo Van Kiet, Nguyen Tan Dung broke from past tradition, where newly appointed prime ministers made China their first official introductory stop, when he visited Japan and declared Vietnam's intention to develop a strategic partnership with Japan.[25] Internationalists and economic reformers gained an upper hand in decisionmaking following the Tenth Party Congress (2006–11), when they managed to secure a significant presence in the Politburo. Subsequently, the steady growth of the economy strengthened the credentials of the reformists and emboldened them on issues of foreign policy. The ascent of the internationalists and economic reformers, however, was thrown into doubt after a leadership reshuffle initiated at the January 2016 party congress saw Nguyen Tan Dung replaced as prime minister by the conservative candidate Nguyen Xuan Phuc. However, it was widely believed that Nguyen Tan Dung's consequent inability to secure another senior position in the party— there were rumblings that he harbored ambitions for the position of party secretary—had less to do with foreign policy positions than it did with internal party dynamics. Events since the leadership reshuffle appear to reinforce this view. In April 2016, Vietnam seized a Chinese vessel in the Gulf of Tonkin in a rare move, demonstrating that though conservative in mien, the new leadership was not about to give any quarter to Beijing.[26]

While the military has traditionally enjoyed good ties with China, increased tension and actual confrontations have led more and more of the senior military leadership to gravitate away from the influence of Beijing. Such a shift was already in evidence in 2009 when the Vietnamese military took issue with Chinese bauxite mining in the central highlands of Vietnam, claiming that this activity constituted a security concern because it afforded China economic leverage that placed Vietnamese interest at risk. Concomitantly, war heroes Vo Nguyen Giap and Nguyen Trong Vinh went so far as to write to the Politburo urging it to reconsider authorization that would inadvertently proffer China the opportunity to establish a permanent presence in the region.[27]

The point has already been made that under the Obama administration the American position on the South China Sea had started to take on a different hue. This came to be expressed in vocal and active American responses to Chinese activities in the area and also the deepening of American defense cooperation and support for regional states embroiled in the dispute. Yet although it was hardly a surprise that U.S. relations with treaty ally the Philippines had strengthened in response to developments in the South China Sea, the manner in which the issue hastened progress in defense cooperation with Vietnam has captured much attention.

In 2011, the United States moved to forge a deeper strategic relationship with Vietnam by way of a Memorandum of Understanding to improve defense relations and a pledge to provide $18 million to assist in the purchase of patrol vessels. This was followed by an agreement to establish a "comprehensive partnership" in 2013 and a decision to partially lift a long-standing ban on the transfer of lethal weapons to Vietnam in October 2014.[28] These developments set the stage for a landmark visit by General Secretary Nguyen Phu Truong to the United States in July 2015, where a Joint Vision Statement was signed. Describing the significance of this visit, a Vietnamese scholar offered the following vignette: "Vietnam sees this visit as significant because he is the first communist party leader to have visited the U.S. and to have received official treatment. General Secretary Nguyen later declared the country's embassy in the United States to be of utmost importance and stated the country's agreement to join the TPP, a sign of Vietnam's pivot to the United States. Previously, Vietnamese leaders would have found such actions sensitive."[29] The fact that as party secretary Nguyen was granted a meeting with President Obama, a special dispensation that went against protocol, spoke further to the value that the United States placed on this relationship.

In May 2016, President Obama took advantage of his attendance at the G-7 Summit meeting in Tokyo to make a visit to Hanoi, where he announced that the United States would finally lift its long-standing lethal arms embargo on Vietnam. The significance of this policy shift, at least at the outset, lay not in the anticipation that the floodgates would now open for Hanoi to purchase American military platforms to any significant quantity. At any rate, such purchases would still be subject to the approval of a Congress intent on close scrutiny of Vietnam's checkered human rights record. Rather, the significance lay in the symbolism that attended Obama's Hanoi visit. This symbolism is evident on at least two counts. First, even as negotiations were successfully concluded on the sidelines of the visit for American universities to open branches and facilities in Vietnam and for the entrance of the Peace Corps, an institution long viewed with suspicion in conservative Vietnamese political circles, into Vietnam for educational purposes, President Obama also took pains to reassure his hosts that the United States had no intention to impose a form of government on Vietnam. The symbolic value of this reassurance cannot be overemphasized given the legacy of the previous Clinton and Bush administrations.[30] Second, and of equal import, it was a clear signal of the growing alignment of strategic outlooks between the United States and Vietnam and the increasing attention that Hanoi was commanding in American thinking on Southeast Asia policy.

Relations with China, in contrast, soured when Beijing registered vehement protest at how Vietnam exercised its prerogative as ASEAN chair in 2010 to have the issue of the South China Sea tabled on the agenda of the regional organization's multiple major political meetings that year, including the ARF meeting that witnessed the outburst by the Chinese foreign minister Yang Jiechi. In May 2014, the episode involving China's dispatch of the *Hai Yang Shi You 981* oil rig into waters in the Paracels deemed by Hanoi to be within its EEZ stirred up anti-Chinese feeling in Vietnam, which bubbled over into nationalist demonstrations and disturbances in the streets, culminating in the mobilization of Vietnamese vessels that sailed out to the vicinity of the rig—some of which were subsequently rammed, and one sunk, by Chinese ships—amid widespread international and regional expressions of concern. Impelled by the alarming deterioration of relations, China invited General Secretary Nguyen to visit Beijing in April 2015, whereupon he was received with a twenty-one-gun salute, the highest level of protocol that can be awarded. The meeting further facilitated the creation of two working groups in infrastructure development and the initiation of several projects of mutual benefit, including the inclusion of the port of Hai Phong in China's massive Maritime Silk Road initiative.[31] Yet the point has been stressed previously that for China, economic cooperation does not negate its resolve in pressing its claims over the South China Sea. If anything, economic inducements appear part of the broader strategy to reinforce its claims in the way of neutralizing opposition. This was made abundantly clear on the eve of General Secretary Nguyen's visit to Washington in July 2015, when the *Hai Yang Shi You* oil rig was deployed yet again into waters claimed by Vietnam.

The realization of the Vietnamese leadership that they need perforce to manage relations with China bears repeating. Despite the upsurge in high-level visits between Vietnamese and U.S. leaders in recent years, these meetings still lag qualitatively and quantitatively behind the exchanges between party and state officials from Vietnam and China. At the same time, statistics bear out Vietnam's susceptibility to Chinese economic influence. China is Vietnam's biggest economic partner, with trade between the two countries amounting to $50.21 billion in 2013.[32] In comparison, U.S.–Vietnam trade for the same period was $30 billion. Vietnamese leaders are mindful of the potential economic ramifications of conflict with their largest business and trading partner. As a further indicator of the costs involved for Vietnam in the event of a downturn in relations with China, at the height of the oil rig crisis in 2014 Vietnamese sources estimated that the placement of the offshore drilling rig in Vietnam's EEZ cost the Vietnamese economy something on the order of $1.5 billion or 0.7 percent of its gross domestic product in the form of deleterious effects on the tourism, agriculture, and seafood export industries.[33] In addition to this, Vietnam's manufacturing industry has become increasingly dependent on Chinese materials. Imported goods from China to Vietnam—which accounts for a large trade gap with China—include crucial material for export-specific manufacturing industries, such as machinery and equipment, steel, chemicals, and fabrics (Vietnam obtains almost 50 percent of raw yarn and fabrics for its textile industry from China). Indeed, a Vietnamese official conceded that Vietnam's move to join the TPPA was in part motivated by a desire not to be overreliant economically on China.[34] Because of the compelling logic of growing economic dependence on China, Vietnamese leaders, including those in the reformist camp, take care to approach bilateral incidents with China with a measure of diplomatic sangfroid, oftentimes prioritizing quiet backroom diplomacy over public provocations even in the wake of the evident upsurge in nationalistic sentiments against the larger neighbor. This calibrated approach is further undergirded by an awareness that any swift or significant upturn in relations with the United States would not only be seen to undermine Vietnam's own position of nonalignment captured in its "three Nos," namely, "no military alliances, no allowance for any country to set up military bases on Vietnamese territory, and no reliance on any countries for help in combating other countries"; it would also antagonize China.[35] On this point, Vietnamese analysts have been quick to cite the analogy of Ukraine, which to their mind serves as a warning about how a larger neighbor might respond to a strategic tilt toward the United States.[36]

Perched between the United States and China, there is an additional logic to the calibrated diplomacy toward China that is acknowledged by Vietnamese policymakers. Even as mistrust of the U.S. position of "peaceful evolution" toward Vietnam gradually diminished over time, leaders in Hanoi have harbored misgivings for the possibility of Sino–U.S. collusion "as a result of the U.S.'s feeble reactions to China's actions in the South China Sea," which might lead to American "abandonment" of Vietnam as Washington did to South Vietnam in 1973, however unlikely this might seem given current circumstances.[37] In essence, Vietnamese leaders remain mindful of the lessons of history, where Vietnam has often found itself trapped and manipulated by great power politics when it was subject first to American invasion and subsequently to Chinese pressure in the lead up to the 1973 Paris Peace Accords (when China pressed Vietnam to take a more conciliatory position toward the United States). These strategic concerns are reflected in the prevailing principles of Vietnamese foreign policy in relation to major powers: "vua hop tac, vua dau tranh" ("fight against supremacy and exclusionary politics"). Yet the reality is that striking the necessary balance between major powers today will be increasingly difficult given the rise in popular resentment toward China on the one hand, which has periodically come to be expressed in public protests that the party and state struggle to manage, and the deepening economic interdependence with it on the other. At this point, it should also be stressed that this concern for a Sino–U.S. condominium on the South China Sea, one that elides or deliberately excludes inputs from regional states, that Hanoi has articulated is shared by other Southeast Asian states as well. This is especially so given how many regional states accept the uncomfortable truth of the limitations of their own efforts at regional order management.

If the strengthening of bilateral relations has been driven by strategic imperative, a persistent impediment to the further deepening of U.S.–Vietnam ties remains the issue of human rights, which has elicited a predictably strong reaction from the U.S. Congress as well as civil society groups and has obliged U.S. leaders to take care not to alienate these views as they sought to advance relations. The disapproval of human rights standards in Vietnam on the part of previous U.S. administrations had been an obvious stumbling block in bilateral relations. In the past, the American position on human rights and democracy had frequently threatened to derail piecemeal progress in bilateral relations, including during discussions over the bilateral trade agreement and cooperation on the emotive matters of POWs and MIAs, prompting then Vietnamese foreign minister Nguyen Manh Cam to warn his counterpart, Warren Christopher, "Vietnam agrees to enhance ongoing cooperation on the POW/MIA issue, but not to the attachment of human rights."[38]

By the same token, even during the Obama administration, Congress and lobby groups threatened to impose costs on Vietnam, and by extension bilateral relations, over the matter of human rights. In August 2013, the U.S. Congress passed the Vietnam Human Rights Act, which

> would condition non-humanitarian assistance to the government of Vietnam on a number of human rights benchmarks including the release of political and religious prisoners, respect for freedom of religion and the rights of ethnic minorities, and an end to Vietnamese government complicity in human trafficking. Other provisions of the bill authorize assistance to Vietnamese human rights and democracy advocates, measures to overcome the Vietnamese government's jamming of Radio Free Asia, and extension of refugee resettlement programs for applicants who were detained or otherwise denied access to these programs.[39]

The bill was applauded by civil society groups, such as Boat People SOS, which had lobbied animatedly for more stringent requirements that entailed liberalizing the political system and improvements in human rights conditions before the United States proceeded to upgrade aspects of the bilateral relationship with Vietnam. Of further significance was the fact that the House Foreign Affairs Committee had also sought to cast doubt on Vietnamese membership in the TPPA on grounds of Vietnam's human rights record. This point was emphasized by Chris Smith and Zoe Lofgren:

Among the potential partners in the Trans-Pacific Partnership, Vietnam is the only country that bans independent labor unions and religious groups. It's the only country considered one of the world's worst violators of internet freedom. It harbors severe child labor and forced labor violators, and regularly jails and tortures dissidents who speak out for human rights, political inclusion or the right to simply practice their religion. These reasons alone should give members of Congress pause before waiving their power to amend and critically analyze trade pacts like the TPP through regular order.[40]

Robust domestic pushback of this nature prevailed upon the Obama administration to link not only the TPPA but also the imperative of greater security cooperation to the matter of human rights. On the occasion of a visit to Hanoi in August 2015, John Kerry provided insight into this thinking when he stressed that "progress on human rights and the rule of law will provide the foundation for deeper and more sustainable strategy and strategic partnership between the United States and Vietnam."[41] This echoed the position staked earlier in the *National Security Strategy* of 2006, which declared that "greater economic freedom is ultimately inseparable from political liberty."[42] Elsewhere in his speech, Kerry repeated the point: "The United States recognizes that only the Vietnamese people can determine their political system. . . . But there are basic principles we will always defend: No one should be punished for speaking their mind so long as they are peaceful; and if trading goods flow freely between us, so should information and ideas."[43]

The Obama administration's decision to lift a long-standing embargo on lethal arms sales to Vietnam was also the subject of bipartisan criticism in Congress. Responding to the decision to lift the embargo, Republican senator John Cornyn, speaking on the Senate floor, maintained that

It's important to remember, even as President Obama is traveling to Vietnam, that Vietnam is a brutal communist regime that continues to disregard basic human rights. . . . Our two countries will never achieve the kind of close relationship that I know many in Vietnam and many in the United States aspire to until Vietnam releases all political prisoners, demonstrates basic respect for human rights and embraces self-government ideals that we, again, take for granted here in America.[44]

Reinforcing this view, Democrat representative Loretta Sanchez asked rhetorically: "What incentive is left for the Vietnamese government to meaningfully enact human rights reforms and respect the civil rights of the Vietnamese people?"[45]

At the same time, it should be acknowledged that unlike the Clinton administration, for whom the human rights and democracy agenda oftentimes found expression in the form of actual prescriptive policies, the Democratic administration of Barack Obama treated human rights and democracy as broad principles to inform, not dictate, the conduct of foreign policy. As Deputy National Security Advisor Ben Rhodes explained, "the U.S. role has not been to dictate political development, but support universal human rights and civil society, and support democratic transition."[46] Consequently, the Obama administration threaded cautiously in response to a host of regional issues, such as the military coup in Thailand and the repeat incarceration of former Malaysian deputy prime minister and current opposition icon Anwar Ibrahim. In the case of the coup in Thailand, while senior U.S. officials such as Danny Russel and Ambassador Glyn Davies called for the resumption of democracy and restraint in the exercise of repressive Lèse Majesté, designed to protect the monarchy from criticism, for the most part bilateral exchanges have continued.

Domestic obstacles to the deepening of bilateral relations also weigh in on the Vietnamese side of the scale. As a Vietnamese scholar suggested, "There remains domestic disagreements and power struggles within Vietnam that hinder it from seizing opportunities to enhance ties with the U.S."[47] Residual concern for U.S. subversion of the Communist Party's ideological struggle remains a common theme in party discourse, even if it has begun to quiet down. Indeed, belaboring the factor of democracy and human rights has had the paradoxical effect of ensuring the persistent relevance of conservative voices in Vietnam, who continue to enjoy an audience when they sound the bells of caution toward American engagement for fear that it might pave the way for intervention in domestic affairs. During domestic debates on the TPPA, a major point of contention arose over the extent to which the state and party could, and would, compromise on human rights issues in order to facilitate progress on the agreement.[48] On other occasions, the party central committee has issued directives calling for "stepping up the fight against the scheme of peaceful evolution in the fields of culture and ideology."[49] Similar directives have emanated from the party's Department of Propaganda and

Education, advocating caution toward American initiatives in the realms of education and volunteerism. The reticence of conservative forces toward the United States has accounted at least in part for a continued reliance, if not preference, for arms deals with Russia, premised on strong bilateral defense relations that date back to the Soviet era.[50]

Myanmar

An even more dramatic shift in America's Southeast Asia policy can be found in its response to political developments in Myanmar. The election of a nominally civilian government in 2011 in the hitherto isolated Southeast Asian country ruled tightly by military fiat prompted a reconsidering of U.S. policy. This reconsideration was registered in a slew of high-level visits to Myanmar, gradual lifting of sanctions, and open engagement of the Myanmar leadership. These initiatives marked considerable progress from where bilateral ties stood at the end of the Cold War.

Prior to the May 1990 election in the country, Myanmar officials had sought to ascertain views from regional states and major powers regarding the possibility of the country joining ASEAN. The initial response was reportedly somewhat encouraging, as the regime, then known as the State Law and Order Restoration Council (SLORC), was perceived as a more reasonable, ergo acceptable, representative of Myanmar as compared with its earlier, more isolationist iteration, the Burma Socialist Program Party. It was on that score that membership of ASEAN was viewed positively by junta leaders as a means through which the country could come out of seclusion and ease its way into the international community, albeit with the buffer of ASEAN membership governed by the principle of noninterference. This view, however, was quickly overtaken by events. The house arrest of democracy icon Aung San Suu Kyi and the military junta's rejection of the 1990 election results dampened enthusiasm and hastened a reassessment as the country's trajectory took another all-too-familiar turn toward isolationism, which in turn led it to become further ostracized by the United States and the European Union.

The attendant return of a more hardline junta rule had a predictable deleterious effect on relations with the United States. As David Steinberg surmised, "as it became evident that the SLORC had no intention of allowing a nonmilitary government to be formed and as human rights and democracy became more central to the foreign policy of a variety of states, especially the United States, U.S. attitudes toward Myanmar's joining ASEAN became vigorously negative."[51] Under the circumstances, relations with Myanmar deteriorated considerably in the period from 1990 to 2011, which witnessed U.S. assistance, already languishing at a low level, reduced further while sanctions against the military junta intensified as Washington pursued a policy to actively ostracize the country. Notwithstanding the reality that the effect of sanctions against Myanmar were probably felt more acutely by the general populace than by members of the junta, for whom China and to a lesser extent India and Thailand (and the rest of Southeast Asia) were becoming significant sources of trade and foreign exchange, American administrations continued to maintain the controversial stance that sanctions provided the best means through which pressure could be exerted on the military.

Until recent years, successive U.S. administrations had taken to describing the junta-run country with a host of epithets: international "pariah," "rogue" state, and "outpost of tyranny." American policy toward Myanmar in the initial two decades after the end of the Cold War was shaped primarily by aversion toward the military junta's extensive abuse of human rights and repression of political opponents, the most famous of whom, by far, was Aung San Suu Kyi, daughter of the nationalist hero Aung San. Indeed, during this period, the congressional record is replete with specific references to the personal plight of the Nobel Peace Prize–winning cause célèbre of the Myanmar political opposition whenever the matter of the renewal of sanctions (which for the large part of these two decades was a routine exercise) on the country was discussed. On the long shadow that Aung San Suu Kyi cast over U.S.–Myanmar relations Steinberg has poignantly observed: "It is not hyperbole to suggest that, in effect, she made U.S. policy toward that country."[52] During the Clinton administration, Secretary of State Madeleine Albright was known to have developed a close personal relationship with the opposition leader, while Congressman James Leach reportedly opined at the March 2004 congressional subcommittee hearings for the continuation of sanctions against Myanmar that "because Aung San Suu Kyi wanted sanctions continued, then the United States would continue sanctions."[53]

Myanmar was in fact already subjected to sanctions from 1988 following the military junta's violent crackdown on popular pro-democracy protests. In 1990, the junta annulled results of a general election that was resoundingly won by the opposition National League for Democracy (NLD). In response, in Western eyes the isolation of Myanmar became a matter of external validation and enforcement with the implementation of a robust and detailed sanctions regime by the United States and European Union.[54] Sanctions would gather pace over the years, both in terms of breadth of coverage and depth of deprivation. It was also at this time that the prerogative of American policy on Myanmar effectively shifted from the State Department to Congress, where numerous staffers at all levels "spent their entire careers carefully scrutinizing the wording of sanctions regimes on Myanmar."[55] Yet there were also occasions when sanctions were pursued by the executive branch not so much for sanctions' sake alone but in order to wrest the initiative away from Congress. This was occasionally the case during the Clinton administration, when the decision to impose sanctions on Myanmar in May 1997 was in fact taken to forestall bipartisan congressional efforts to introduce even harsher sanctions given Congress's assessment at the time that limited diplomatic engagement was insufficient to effect change in Myanmar. As Leon Hader explained, "The Clinton administration's lack of a coherent diplomatic strategy and the strong political ties between the Democratic administration, labor unions and human rights lobbies, explain the administration's reluctance to mount a strong political opposition against the proliferation of unilateral economic sanctions on Capitol Hill."[56]

Over time, the United States developed a formidable sanctions regime on Myanmar, containing very precise language to govern restrictions on a variety of areas ranging from broad sanctions to more targeted ones that addressed functional issues. It should be further mentioned that by the late 1990s, the fledgling Internet helped to amplify the voice and effectiveness of the anti-SLORC movement in the United States. These cyber activists were advancing their cause on two fronts: boycotting companies such as Pepsi and Unocal that were investing in Myanmar and lobbying for even more economic sanctions at the city, state, and federal levels. Specifically, "proponents of measures against the SLORC used the Internet to gather and transmit up-to-date information about conditions within Burma and the policies toward that country of various governments around the world. This helped make their arguments particularly effective, and ensured there was no disconnect between them and the pro-democracy movement inside Burma."[57]

The American disposition toward Myanmar worsened during the Bush administration, when first human rights and then democracy promotion (which many saw as a euphemism for "regime change") became definitive foreign policy catch phrases, respectively. Toward those ends, an even more extensive sanctions regime was put in place in 2003. The Burma Freedom and Democracy Act was signed by George W. Bush on July 28, 2003, and contained wide-ranging restrictions on interactions with the military junta in response to the continued incarceration of political prisoners including Aung San Suu Kyi. Pressure on the American government to retain sanctions on the Myanmar junta came not only from within Congress but also from a wide array of civil society groups, including groups and ethnic-minority organizations based in Myanmar.[58] Yet sanctions did not yield the results that the United States and its European partners had hoped. Although the Myanmar population undoubtedly suffered under the weight of sanctions as well as the depredations of the junta, as suggested earlier the economy was able to lurch along through economic and trading relations established with other regional states not given to the pursuit of values-based foreign policies. In point of fact, sanctions also carried not-insignificant diplomatic costs to the United States; not only did it impose tremendous debilitating costs on the welfare of the population of Myanmar with little effect on the junta, it also foreclosed an alternative channel through which to influence the junta's behavior—a collective, orchestrated effort at engagement in tandem with ASEAN.[59]

Unlike its predecessors, the Obama administration sought to introduce some nuance to Myanmar policy. In a departure from the preceding heavy policy focus on democratization and political change, President Obama indicated his readiness to establish contact with hitherto marginalized governments without exhorting the need for them to undergo reform in order to meet American expectations. In keeping with this outlook, for the Obama administration Myanmar policy would be pursued through a finessed combination of both engagement and sanctions. In other words, sanctions would remain in place while incremental steps were made in a cautious engagement strategy. This gradual shift in Myanmar policy was articulated by the president in Tokyo in November 2009:

Despite years of good intentions, neither sanctions by the United States nor engagement by others succeeded in improving the lives of the Burmese people. So we are now *communicating directly* with the leadership to make it clear that existing sanctions will remain until there are concrete steps toward democratic reform. We support a Burma that is unified, peaceful, prosperous, and democratic. And as Burma moves in that direction, a better relationship with the United States is possible.[60]

The proverbial olive branch extended by the Obama administration was doubtless welcomed by the military junta. In quid pro quo response, the junta freed more than 100 political prisoners and permitted American representatives to meet with Aung San Suu Kyi, although the generals remained reluctant to work with her.[61] Eventually, the United States would seize upon political changes in Myanmar to further recalibrate policy even as it nudged Myanmar toward greater openness.

Following the junta's calamitous handling of Cyclone Nargis in May 2008, a gradual shift in the Myanmar leadership's thinking on its isolationist policies was becoming evident. With the hardline junta leader Than Shwe fading into the background and preoccupied with his idiosyncratic project of the relocation of the capital from Yangon to the new palatial premises at Naypidaw, the country held general elections in 2010. The following year saw the retirement of the two remaining stalwarts of the 1988 coup d'état, Than Shwe and Maung Aye, and a new quasi-civilian government assume power, albeit with strong military influence. Economic reforms aimed at encouraging foreign investment, including the drafting of new foreign investment and labor laws, were initiated by the new government. The SPDC, the latest institutional iteration of the junta, handed over power at the end of March 2011 to a new elected government led by retired general and former prime minister Thein Sein. Prior to that, Aung San Suu Kyi was released from her house arrest in November 2010, allowed to contest a parliamentary by-election in April 2011, and eventually won a seat in the legislature. The new legislature also embarked on a languorous but welcome process of constitutional reform, the most controversial aspect of which pertained to clause 59f, which bars Myanmar citizens with family members who carry foreign citizenships from running for the presidency. In the event, the clause remained unamended after constitutional review. Indeed, Aung San Suu Kyi's ineligibility to contest for the presidency on grounds that her sons are British citizens, even after her NLD party won a landmark electoral victory to form the government in 2016, remains a residual sore point for relations between the Myanmar junta and the United States.

Nonetheless, in recognition of these reforms, the Obama administration reciprocated by relaxing some sanctions, allowing U.S. exports and investments to trickle into Myanmar.[62] Recognition was accorded through the restoration of an ambassador, and in June 2012 Derek Mitchell became the first U.S. ambassador to Myanmar since September 1990. Prior to that, Hillary Clinton became the first U.S. secretary of state to set foot on Myanmar soil since 1955, when she visited at the end of November 2011. In keeping with the quid pro quo pattern of bilateral relations that had taken shape following the change in U.S. approach to Myanmar, after Clinton's stopover the Myanmar government formulated legislation permitting nonviolent demonstrations. On December 2, 2011, Naypyidaw established a truce with the Shan State Army, a major ethnic faction that hitherto had been engaged in armed rebellion against the state. In January 2012, 651 political prisoners were offered presidential pardons and released from prison.

So significant were the measures taken by the new nominally civilian government, two senior U.S. congressmen traditionally associated with hardline positions on Myanmar, Senators Mitch McConnell and John McCain, were persuaded to visit the country in 2012.[63] Further to that, an invitation was extended to Myanmar to observe the annual Cobra Gold exercises. The progress in bilateral relations culminated in a visit to Myanmar by Barack Obama in November 2012, the first ever by a sitting American president. During the milestone but whirlwind six-hour visit, Obama met with both President Thein Sein and opposition leader Aung San Suu Kyi, whom he had welcomed in Washington earlier in September that year. Also noteworthy was the fact that the meeting of the two presidents took place in Yangon, the cultural capital of Myanmar, rather than the insipid new capital of Naypyidaw.[64] President Obama's visit also involved a meeting with students and civil society activists at Yangon University, where he extolled the virtues of democracy while praising the developments that were taking place under the leadership of both Thein Sein and Aung San Suu Kyi. The progress of democracy notwithstanding, it was also clear that not unlike developments that shaped the upturn in relations with Vietnam, for both the United States and Myanmar a larger strategic purpose obtained. Here again, it related, for the most part, to China.

Despite the long-standing ties that exist between the junta and China, a growing unease had gathered in certain segments of the Myanmar leadership that Naypyidaw was hazarding too much by gravitating too far toward China. For its part, the United States, and ASEAN for that matter, had also been concerned about the implications of Myanmar's growing proximity to and reliance on China, whether it was by choice or circumstance. In the event, this consternation precipitated efforts to explore strategic alternatives on Myanmar's part. The immediate and most obvious and accessible path was to deepen relations with ASEAN, and this was indeed pursued with little controversy. The improvement of ties with the United States also began to appear a realistic possibility—if not an inevitability—given the growing mood even in conservative military circles that Chinese influence had to be balanced. It should be noted that China, too, was alert to the implications of such a drift away from Beijing toward Washington. To that effect, a Chinese source surmised that closer relations with the United States would afford Myanmar "strategic maneuvering room" and reduce reliance on China.[65]

This is not to say, however, that trust was established overnight. Explaining American policy toward Myanmar post-2011, U.S. ambassador Derek Mitchell clarified that "Ours is an action-for-action policy. We are realistic, it is not a full embrace."[66] Indeed, on the occasion of his second visit to Myanmar in November 2014, Obama was visibly less enthused compared with 2012 and cautioned that the gradual progress then under way toward further democratization was "by no means complete or irreversible."[67] His remarks were prompted by an apparent back-sliding of the reform process, including intractable resistance to constitutional reform, which might have allowed Aung San Suu Kyi to run for the presidency, periodic clampdown on the fledgling independent media, the government's inability (or reluctance) to quell violence against the minority Rohingya community, and reported attempts by military members of the National Defense and Security Council, empowered to replace the regime in times of crisis, to expand its scope of powers. Over time, and following the inauguration of a democratically elected civilian government, the United States has begun to reassess this "action-for-action" policy in favor of more proactive initiatives.[68] Moreover, until the assumption of power by the NLD in April 2016, the lifting of American sanctions has been taking place only incrementally, and at a much slower pace than was the case with the European Union. Although U.S. businesses have started returning to Myanmar, sanctions remained in place that specifically targeted the military junta (more than 100 corporate entities remain on the U.S. blacklist), with the existence of robust legislation to stop American companies from collaborating on projects linked to the regime. The National Emergencies Act, which prohibits U.S. individuals and businesses from financing or transacting with persons associated with the Myanmar military suppression of the democracy movement after 1985, remained in place until May 2014.[69] Meanwhile, even Aung San Suu Kyi herself was reported to have expressed the view upon her party's assumption of power that Myanmar was still "not yet ready" for a full lifting of sanctions.[70]

It is worth emphasizing at this point that prior to the formation of the NLD government, the Obama administration's policy of engagement toward Myanmar remained subject to a chorus of opposition from Congress, which, notwithstanding the political reforms enacted under President Thein Sein, gave no quarter to the civilian–military leadership that ruled between 2011 and 2016. During this period, Congress consistently voted to renew an import ban on Myanmar that was first introduced in 2003. The ban is significant given that U.S. imports of Myanmar products in 2002, the last full year before the ban was introduced, stood at $356.4 million—a not inconsequential source of foreign exchange for the country. After the ban, the figure fell to almost zero. By way of illustration of typical congressional pressure on Myanmar policy, the cautionary remarks of Ed Royce, chairman of the House Foreign Relations Committee, on the eve of John Kerry's visit to Myanmar in 2014 were instructive:

> It is time that we take off the rose-colored glasses and see the situation in Burma for what it is. We cannot continue to lavish more incentives on the government of Burma in hopes that it will do the right thing. We must immediately cease military-to-military cooperation with Burma until the systematic persecution of Rohingya Muslims and other minorities has ended there. Too often the administration, like the administrations that preceded this administration, is more interested in not ruffling diplomatic feathers than carrying out the difficult, but necessary task of pressing for human rights. But human rights do not have to take a back seat to strategic considerations. The administration must recognize that its rebalance to Asia will be unsustainable without improvements in this area.[71]

This followed a move several months earlier which saw more than forty members of Congress dispatch a letter to President Obama demanding that he pressure his Myanmar counterpart to ensure the continued progress of democratic reforms in Myanmar. The trigger, in this instance, was concern for mounting violence against the Rohingya in Rakhine state and the government's evident reluctance to take stronger measures to curb attacks on this Muslim minority, as well as impediments to domestic political discussions about religious freedoms and interfaith relations more generally.

In the same vein, congressional concern was frequently expressed over the pace of normalization of U.S.–Myanmar military ties. Republican congressman Steve Chabot, chairman of the Foreign Affairs Subcommittee on Asia and the Pacific, along with Democrat Joseph Crowley sponsored an April 2, 2014, bill in the House of Representatives aiming to set new standards for U.S. collaboration with the Myanmar military. The bill stemmed from worries that having commenced partial collaboration with the Tatmadaw (the armed forces of Myanmar), the Obama administration was advancing too rapidly without demanding further reform from the Myanmar leadership. In particular, the bill was designed to strengthen regulation and restriction of expenditure for aid to Myanmar. The Chabot–Crowley proposal set the following conditions for financial support: the termination of military ties to North Korea, opening up the process of constitutional amendment (presumably in the name of transparency and accountability), the halting of the military's commercial activities, and an end to ethnic conflicts.[72] It should be pointed out, however, that the robust manner in which the United States continues to scrutinize aid and investments into Myanmar has afforded other states, most notably China, strategic leverage over Naypyidaw, especially in the wake of Myanmar's opening to the global economy. In 2015, Myanmar drew $8 billion worth of direct foreign investments, with the usual suspects China, Singapore, Thailand, Hong Kong, and Japan commanding the lion's share. By comparison, U.S. investments stood at a paltry $248 million.[73]

There is a familiar and important sidebar to this discussion. The position of the U.S. government on Myanmar is not homogenous, especially in terms of the details and implementation of policy. For example, the State Department had watered down the 1997 congressional motion for sanctions, which restricted new investments but did not apply it retroactively. Within the State Department too, there have been periodic differences on Myanmar policy, albeit more in terms of the degree and extent of sanctions than bigger strategic issues, and any major shift in policy would, as is the case with many other similar issues, require concurrence from both Congress and the sitting administration.[74] The same can be said for Myanmar, perhaps more so given the likely divergence on certain policy issues between the military and the civilian government. Still immensely influential despite the April 1, 2016, inauguration of the first civilian government in the country since 1962, the Tatmadaw has long nursed acute sensitivity toward anything it construed to resemble, or provide opportunity for, foreign intervention. The narrative of how the military "rescued" the country from Western colonial forces continues to generate currency and underpins its legitimacy as an institution. It is through this lens that it cautiously approaches the issue of relations with the United States and keeps its distance, even with the realization of the equally urgent imperative of keeping Chinese influence at bay.

A further issue of variance that weighs on U.S.–Myanmar relations pertains to the intractable conflict between the state and ethnic minorities in Myanmar. A defining feature to politics in Myanmar has been the existence of prolonged strife between a wide range of ethnic groups and between these groups and the central state. These intrastate conflicts can be traced back to the end of World War II and failed attempts to implement the Panglong Agreement, which was devised in 1947 to resolve interethnic tension between the Burmese-dominated nascent postcolonial state and a wide array of ethnic minority groups agitating for autonomy and independence. In the wake of the failure of the Panglong Agreement, ethnic groups mobilized to form a wide range of insurgent and separatist movements that took up arms against the state in various border regions. Needless to say, these insurgencies, some of which remain active today, have imperiled stability and security of state and society in Myanmar and have all but accounted for the long shadow that the military has cast over society. These conflicts have also caused the displacement of large numbers of ethnic minorities in Myanmar's border regions, and this has played no small part in contributing to the international pressure Myanmar has come under on the matter of human rights.

Given the thaw in U.S.–Myanmar relations in recent years, ethnic minority groups have seized the opportunity to lobby the Obama administration to bring pressure to bear on the previous government of Thein Sein toward the ends of a nationwide cease-fire agreement. These organizations include the Karen Environmental and Social Action Network, the Shan Human Rights Foundation, the Kachin Peace Network, and the United Nationalities Federation Council. Some have even called for the United States to be actively involved in peace negotiations, a suggestion that gained little traction with the Myanmar government wary of motives involved and the danger that this might provide a pretext for intervention. In July 2014, thirteen ethnic groups from Shan State wrote to the U.S. consulate based in Chiang Mai, Thailand, cautioning against engaging the junta. Khun Htun Oo, a popular Shan leader, exclaimed, "What if ethnicities are attacked with U.S.-provided technologies? That's the question. We don't even know what will happen in 2015. We don't know whether the election will be free and fair. Now, proportional representation is being debated and we don't know how things will develop."[75] Similar misgivings were expressed by leaders of other ethnic minority groups, some who have maintained that cease-fires between the state and armed ethnic groups have not had the intended effect. Their point was that the Myanmar military has used the lull of cease-fires to reinforce its military presence in border regions.[76]

It has been violence between the Buddhist majority and the Muslim minority in Rakhine State—known to the world as Rohingya, a term that is, however, rejected by both the junta and the NLD government—that has proven a particularly prickly issue for relations between the United States and Myanmar. In 2012, riots broke out in Rakhine in May, June, and October between ethnic Rakhine Buddhists and Rohingya Muslims. The initial cause was the rape and murder of a Rakhine woman in May that year by a group of men alleged by locals to be Rohingya Muslims. In response, a mob of ethnic Rakhine attacked a bus, killing ten Muslims and set off cascading violence between the two communities. The government of Myanmar responded to the violence by deploying troops and imposing curfews. In June 2012, a state of emergency was declared in Rakhine State. The violence resulted in more than 100 deaths, the displacement of more than 200,000 people (mostly Rohingya) triggering a refugee crisis in Southeast Asia, and the destruction of thousands of homes. In the course of violence, the Myanmar military has been accused by human rights groups both from inside Myanmar and abroad of targeting Rohingya Muslims through mass arrests and arbitrary attacks that were passed off as security operations.

Prior to his visit in November 2014, President Obama admonished the Myanmar government for its lackluster response to the violence and called for its leadership to condemn attacks against Rohingya and to grant them the same liberties as other citizens of the country. In addition, the United States has contributed up to $7.3 million in humanitarian assistance for Rakhine minorities, including Rohingya Muslims, since June 2012. In an unequivocal demonstration of immediate American interest in the issue, Ambassador Mitchell personally made several trips to Rakhine State since the outbreak of violence in May 2012. Back home, the Obama administration came under domestic pressure to compel the Myanmar leadership to resolve the Rohingya issue. This has included demands that President Obama move beyond expressing concern to demanding action to avert further violence. Meanwhile, entities such as the bipartisan U.S. Commission on International Religious Freedom has called for the resumption of sanctions against Myanmar in order to enforce accountability for the harassment of religious minorities.

The case of the Rohingya minority speaks not only to U.S. views of the Tatmadaw and the military junta that ruled Myanmar until recently but also to relations with the new civilian government. To be sure, with the election of the NLD into power by dint of a landslide election victory in 2015, political reform in Myanmar has taken on new meaning for the inchoate democracy. Against the large shadow cast by Aung San Suu Kyi, the advent of a truly civilian, democratically elected government following the transfer of power in March 2016 has occasioned hopes of a sea change in Myanmar, not least in the U.S. Congress and among American policymakers who have staked an interest in the cause of democratization in that country. Yet it remains unclear if American expectations, whether grounded or otherwise, will be met under the new civilian leadership. It is here that the Rohingya issue is instructive. Indeed, a potential point of contention has already arisen in respect to the criticism of Aung San Suu Kyi for her deafening silence on the issue of violence against the Rohingya. Even when she eventually released statements, they were unremarkable and failed to inspire the imagination as congressional officials and much of the Western media had hoped given their faith in her clout as a long-standing international human rights icon. This view was expressed by a senior congressional staffer who in a typical reaction highlighted that while the citation accorded Aung San Suu Kyi for her Nobel Peace Prize award "mentioned her struggle for democracy and human rights, she has checked the first box, but she hasn't checked the second."[77] Further representing this view are the following remarks published in the *International New York Times*:

In the end, the reason why Ms. Aung San Suu Kyi doesn't want the Americans to say "Rohingya" doesn't really matter. What matters is that a woman whose name has been synonymous with human rights for a generation, a woman who showed unflinching courage in the face of despotism, has continued an utterly unacceptable policy of the military rulers she succeeded. Ms. Aung San Suu Kyi would be wise to reconsider her stance. Her halo has been a central factor in Myanmar's reacceptance into the world community after decades of ostracism, but already there are calls by human rights groups in the United States for President Obama to renew sanctions against the country.[78]

To say nothing of Aung San Suu Kyi's personal views on the issue, which she has been reluctant to share publicly, such remarks betray both a misreading of the prevailing political realities in the country, which is in turn leading to unrealistic expectations. The point here is certainly not to whitewash the violence or to absolve Aung San Suu Kyi and her NLD administration of the responsibility to the Rohingya. Yet it is equally important to point out the fact that in exerting excessive international pressure on the incumbent government in Myanmar, foreign actors, including the United States, must be mindful of the reality that having finally come to assume power, Aung San Suu Kyi will be especially careful not to convey any hint of an impression that under her leadership Myanmar will bend to American or European pressure.

What Congress needs to comprehend on this issue are the risks that the existence of issue-specific blinkers pose to the larger goal of furthering U.S.–Myanmar relations, especially under the democratically elected NLD government. The reality is that although there are understandably few common denominators between Aung San Suu Kyi and her NLD government and the military junta that preceded them, the one issue where their respective positions hew closely to each other is on the matter of the Rohingya, specifically on whether and how to address the issue of recognition of the identity and status of the Rohingya. A Myanmar foreign ministry official, Kyaw Zay Ya, left no doubt of the NLD government's stand on the issue: "We won't use the term Rohingya because Rohingya are not recognized as among the 135 official ethnic groups. . . . Our position is that using the controversial term does not support the national reconciliation process."[79] Further, in the euphoria of the NLD victory in the 2015 elections, it has probably escaped attention that a not-insignificant segment of Aung San Suu Kyi's support base in the party in fact share anti-Rohingya, if not anti-Muslim, sentiments. It is striking, too, with regards to this issue, that not a single Muslim was appointed to the NLD cabinet. From this, it is reasonable to conclude that although it may be a combustible issue in the international arena that will continue to negatively affect the reputation of Myanmar and of Aung San Suu Kyi, the resolution of the plight of the Rohingya is clearly not a domestic issue of priority.

There are, however, intriguing alternative prospects that attend to the larger question of how ethnic minority groups position themselves between the Myanmar government and the United States. The Obama administration's move to improve relations with the military junta and downplay political injustices and humanitarian distress in Myanmar's borderlands could risk pushing these minority groups closer to China. This was implied in a statement by a Kachin Independence Army officer, who offered the following perspective: "We are really careful about inviting U.S. observers to peace talks because the Chinese are not happy about Americans meddling in their backyard. As the U.S. is only interested in Naypyidaw, we should invest in good relations with China now."[80] There is precedent for the view that China could sway relations between some ethnic minority rebel groups and the Myanmar state. Chinese arms dealers are apparently already providing furtive military support in the form of portable air defense systems, armored vehicles, machine guns, rocket launchers, and missile-equipped helicopters to the United Wa State Army, and this has served as a reminder of China's ability to interfere and influence domestic affairs in Myanmar.[81] In the case of the Rohingya, it might only be a matter of time before transnational religious extremist groups seize on the issue to include the plight of Muslims in Rakhine State into their narratives of violence.

THE PHILIPPINES AND THE ENHANCED DEFENSE COOPERATION AGREEMENT: OLD WINE, NEW BOTTLES

Mindful of its location on the maritime border between China and Southeast Asia, and its asymmetrical relationship with Beijing, with which it also has ongoing territorial disputes in the Spratly Islands, the Philippines has sought to strengthen long-standing, albeit periodically troubled, defense ties with the United States. Concomitantly, under the former president, Benigno Aquino III, Manila was arguably the most ardent supporter of the Pivot. This was most clearly expressed in the passage of the Enhanced Defense Cooperation Agreement (EDCA) with the United States.

In April 2014, just hours ahead of President Obama's trip to Manila as part of a round of visits in Asia, the United States and Philippines managed to finalize agreement on EDCA. In brief, EDCA would allow for a rotational deployment of American troops in the Philippines and for the United States to use facilities in five Philippine military bases, possibly more in the future. The Philippines Supreme Court ruled on January 12, 2016, that EDCA was constitutional, thereby removing the requirement of ratification by the Philippines Senate and, presumably, putting an end to heated domestic debate over concessions made under its rubric and the manner through which it would be bestowed legal identity. Describing the significance of EDCA, Foreign Secretary Albert Del Rosario explained that its approval "opens new opportunities to further deepen" the U.S.–Philippines alliance and that "one factor behind this is the conscious effort of our leaders to invest in our enduring engagement, and another factor is the emergence of regional challenges that have underscored the need for concerted effort to protect our common values."[82]

As alluded to above, the ruling was significant given the baggage, discussed in chapter 3, that accompanies any discussion of U.S. military presence on Philippine soil. In the event, the wave of nationalism and anti-Americanism that underscored the decision not to renew American leases on Philippine military bases in the early 1990s has abated somewhat since then as China's "increasingly assertive behavior in the South China Sea"—to use the administration's language—has driven the government in Manila to set aside this baggage and rethink its strategic calculus. This reassessment has been expressly evident not only in the policy establishment but also in the general population more broadly. A survey conducted by the independent pollster Social Weather Stations and commissioned by the Philippine Department of Foreign Affairs in February 2014 showed that an overwhelming 81 percent of Filipinos surveyed supported President Aquino's decision to seek legal clarity on China's claims in the South China Sea by way of an international Arbitral Tribunal. Eighty percent of those surveyed also believed that Manila should request the assistance of other countries to balance China's growing military muscle in the disputed sea.[83]

Despite a palpable tilt toward the United States, there are still those in the Philippines who oppose U.S. bases and EDCA, or at least remain suspicious of the arrangement. Primary domestic concerns slowing the ruling process include wariness of undue American control over Philippine foreign policy, the anticipated rise of the sex trade around bases with American troops present (for which there has been precedence), and a raft of criminal charges leveled against U.S. troops stationed in the Philippines in the past, all of which were issues that previously bedeviled U.S.–Philippine defense cooperation and accounted for the groundswell of opposition to the renewal of U.S. leases to Philippine bases at the end of the Cold War.[84] Notwithstanding its ratification via the judicial process, political actors and civil society groups have persisted in their opposition to EDCA, on grounds ranging from allegations that the process through which the agreement was arrived was unconstitutional since it elided the need for Senate concurrence, to the anticipated upsurge of violence against women.[85] All said, this reticence speaks to how U.S.–Philippine relations, though among the closest and most established between Washington and a Southeast Asian state, remain fraught with historical baggage. As one U.S. Defense Department official shared, half in jest, as he recalled a trip accompanying former secretary of state Hillary Clinton to Manila: "I don't think Hillary Clinton had so many things thrown at her motorcade anywhere else in the world!"

Indeed, whether in Vietnam, Myanmar, or even the Philippines, the strategic imperative has had to compete with voices predisposed to suspicion of American intent that continue to present all manner of obstacles for deeper engagement with the United States. On this score, the election of Rodrigo Duterte in May 2016 may well complicate relations with the United States, at least with regards to the South China Sea. Prospects for Chinese investments in infrastructure suggest that under President Duterte, the Philippines can be expected to draw closer to China. In fact, Duterte has already unapologetically revealed that his campaign ads were paid for by an "anonymous Chinese donor."[86] Indeed, while the United States and other regional states have called for China to respect international law, Duterte has told Beijing that he was prepared to set aside Manila's South China Sea claims if Beijing also desists and helps to build infrastructure.[87] Indeed, the indicators thus far are that the Duterte administration appears intent on pursuing foreign policy that will be different, if not in substance certainly in form, from that pursued by his predecessor. This could herald intriguing portents for the region and, by virtue of the fact that the Philippines and the South China Sea have become the focal point of the strategic dimension of U.S. presence in the region, for American engagement in Southeast Asia.

CHAPTER EIGHT

The United States in Southeast Asia

Prospect and Retrospect

SINCE THE ADVENT of the postwar era, the United States has always been an external actor of considerable consequence and influence in Southeast Asian affairs. Although an external power, it is looked upon as a leader, an offshore balancer, a guarantor of regional security and stability, and a source of investments that drive economic growth and innovation in Southeast Asia. Turning to the other side of the coin, by dint of its geographic location astride major sea lanes and at the intersection of interactions among major regional powers (China, Japan, and India), its economic potential, the presence of maturing democracies, and its favorable demographics, Southeast Asia should merit strategic and policy consideration in Washington.

Yet, from the episodic and inconsistent manner through which U.S. policies toward the region have been formulated and implemented since the end of the Cold War, how Washington has reacted to regional developments that may not have been factored in its initial strategic calculus and, indeed, from the nature of domestic discussions regarding American commitments in the region, it is not immediately evident (beyond the labors of the small community of East Asia and Southeast Asia hands in government and the think tank community) that the value of deepening engagement with Southeast Asia registers to any considerable extent in U.S. discussions of its role in the world or that American interests in Southeast Asia resonate with sufficient traction in the United States the way interests elsewhere in the world do (that is, Europe pre-Trump and the Middle East). Needless to say, this presents a complex challenge for a

Southeast Asia anxious for certainty and assurances against the back-drop of shifting geopolitical circumstances and distribution of power and influence, complex domestic and regional political terrains that impinge on foreign policy decisionmaking, and the limitations of regional autonomy in the management of the regional security order that also manifests in conflicted ambivalence about the United States.

At issue for the American foreign policy establishment has been the challenge of conceptualizing how Southeast Asia fits in its vision of the U.S. role in the Asia Pacific. Attendant to this, from the perspective of the region, rather than a durable commitment, U.S. policy toward Southeast Asia has often been considered episodic, extemporaneous, improvised, and reactive, devoid of strategic context and logic. For long periods, Southeast Asia was viewed as a second-, perhaps even third-tier concern for the United States. Following its military withdrawal from Vietnam, American attention shifted to Europe and the Middle East. With the end of the Cold War, Eastern Europe and the Balkans were deemed issues (and arenas) of a greater magnitude of importance commanding American global attention. With the advent of the post–September 11 era, it was the Middle East and Central Asia that preoccupied Washington. Even when Asia gained prominence, compared with Northeast Asia, Southeast Asian countries were by far the poor cousins by measure of American attention received. Indeed, because of this, regional states have harbored persistent anxieties that American policy in Southeast Asia can easily be given to disinterest and distraction, notwithstanding the protestations of American politicians and officialdom. At issue, as this book has contemplated, are a set of attendant concerns that speak to the absence from the vantage of Southeast Asia of a clear guiding strategic imperative behind Washington's policies toward the region after the mid-1970s or, at the same time perhaps, the existence of some form of strategic imperative that nevertheless does not sit all too comfortably with regional states at times; uncertainty about the place of the region in America's grand strategic outlook, which in turn gives rise to inconsistent signaling and policy implementation; and the absence of domestic political consensus in the United States, and Southeast Asia as well, regarding the value and importance of efforts to deepen U.S.–Southeast Asia relations. To this can be added the accented point that Southeast Asian anxieties have also been rendered more acute by the limitations confronting indigenous efforts at regional order management, which by definition has led many regional states to look to the United States to play a major role albeit without necessarily being in concert about what that role is and how it should be received. This in turn speaks to the existence of different and divergent strategic outlooks among Southeast Asian states.

The ambiguities surrounding American engagement are thrown into sharper relief by the manner in which the course of U.S. relations with Southeast Asia reflects uneven progress of American engagement with the region since the end of the Cold War, where it has waxed and waned depending on the priorities of U.S. administrations as well as strategies (or lack thereof) that have shaped their conduct of foreign and security policy. The immediate post–Cold War era witnessed the inception of a season of triumphalism as America vanquished its Cold War adversary, the Soviet Union, with a combination of American power and principle. Notwithstanding domestic talk of a retrenchment in America's global presence and the existence of mounting economic constraints on U.S. projection of power, this period ushered in what some had termed the "unipolar moment," where the United States stood on the world stage as the sole superpower.

Significantly, the preponderance of power enjoyed by the United States during this time existed alongside a sense of purpose that came to be expressed in a distinct focus on humanitarian approaches to world affairs. During the presidency of Bill Clinton, this found expression in how American power was harnessed in pursuit of lofty declaratory goals regarding human rights and democratization, from which derived strategy that caused consternation to Southeast Asian states, most of which by virtue of their own political cultures, systems, and histories were not given to supporting this agenda upon which American policy was predicated. Consequently, Southeast Asian states struggled with the contradictions of desiring the United States to demonstrate a robust security and economic presence in the region against the backdrop of an emerging new global order with all its uncertainties, on the one hand, and deep apprehension at how Washington's penchant for a robust pursuit of a values-based foreign policy was impinging on bilateral relations with key regional partners, on the other. The result of this was persistent irritants of varying degrees deriving not only from differences of opinion but in some instances from actual U.S. policies, such as in the case of military-to-military ties with Indonesia and Thailand.

This trajectory of U.S. foreign policy took a sharp turn after September 11, 2001, when tragic terrorist attacks on the American homeland prompted a fundamental reprioritization of U.S. interests and foreign policy goals, not to mention the strategies devised to attain them. Although the imperative of human rights and democratization still held, they were recast as pivotal elements for American security on the premise that radicalism and terrorism spawned from decidedly undemocratic societies that engaged in persistent violations of human rights. Corresponding with the neoconservative worldview of the George W. Bush administration, the Global War on Terror saw the promotion of democracy pursued in earnest through the Bush doctrine. For Southeast Asian states, the Bush administration's attention and approach to Southeast Asia was met with a mix of appreciation and apprehension not dissimilar to previous reactions to the terms of engagement under the Clinton administration.

Of course, given the escalation of the terrorist threat in Southeast Asia during this time, the fact that the United States was prepared not only to support but, more important, invest heavily in regional counterterrorism efforts was doubtless welcomed. Perhaps the best example of the dividends derived from this can be found in Indonesia, where, with U.S. support, the counterterrorism capabilities of the Indonesian security establishment improved significantly. Yet at the same time, regional states, particularly those with sizable Muslim populations, were compelled to distance themselves to varying degrees from the United States. This had less to do with what the United States was doing in the region than elsewhere, especially in Afghanistan and Iraq. Seized with the view that the United States was waging war on their religion under the mendacious pretense of a fight against terrorism guided by the controversial principles of the Bush doctrine, Muslim populations exerted considerable pressure on their leaders, many of whom were in turn prepared to yield for reasons of opportunism and in the interest of their own political legitimacy. This pressure was expressed in strong anti-American sentiments that sharply exacerbated tensions between Southeast Asian countries with significant Muslim constituents and the United States during this time. Much in the same vein, the Bush administration's articulation of its doctrine of unilateralism and pre-emption was met with widespread opposition across Southeast Asian civil society, further constraining open support of American policies by Southeast Asian governments, not least by allies and security partners. Singapore prime minister Lee Hsien Loong alluded to this in an interview with the *Wall Street Journal*, where he tellingly noted that "no one in Asia is rooting for an American retreat," and that if a "secret poll" was taken, "every nation would vote for broader American engagement no matter what they might say in public."[1] What is revealing is not so much the speculative result of such a poll, which would likely prove correct, but the fact that for a representative result, the poll would need to be "secret" at all.

For most of Asia, the trajectory of American engagement took an important and welcome turn with the advent of the Obama administration. In her important November 2011 article in *Foreign Policy* magazine, then secretary of state Hillary Clinton heralded the coming of a "Pacific Century." This was hardly hyperbole. The Asia Pacific was recognized as not only home to nearly half of the world's population and eight of the world's ten largest armies but also the engine of the global economy. In 2014, the region accounted for some 40 percent of world gross domestic product (GDP) and nearly two-thirds of global GDP growth. Secretary Clinton's widely read article, which she deliberately titled "America's Pacific Century," and President Obama's speech before the Australian Parliament in Canberra that same month together introduced the administration's Pivot policy. The Pivot, later rechristened the "rebalance," was articulated as a comprehensive strategy containing a trifecta of elements encompassing distinct diplomatic, economic, and military prongs, which were collectively aimed at reorienting U.S. grand strategy toward this increasingly vital part of the world.

For present purposes, what was significant about the Pivot was that it was not only about Northeast Asia. Considerable effort—including by President Obama personally—was invested in enhancing engagement with Southeast Asia. By the end of his presidency, President Obama had visited nine of the ten Southeast Asian countries.[2] It was during the Obama administration that the United States joined the East Asia Summit after its landmark signing of the ASEAN Treaty of Amity and Cooperation, an act many hitherto thought unlikely. In June 2010, the United States established a permanent mission to ASEAN in Jakarta, and in 2016, President Obama hosted ASEAN leaders at Sunnylands in an unprecedented U.S.–ASEAN Summit outside of the region. It had been some time since Southeast Asia enjoyed such extensive attention from Washington, D.C. More important, this attention constituted a holistic engagement, rather than being focused on any particular issue, which tended to be the case during previous U.S. administrations. All of this raised the possibility that American engagement in Southeast Asia might have finally turned the page and entered an era of greater commitment and clarity.

Yet at the end of the Obama administration's tenure, there remains little consensus on the impact and effectiveness of the Pivot. The debate over the success of the Pivot can hardly be resolved here and indeed is likely to preoccupy scholars and analysts of America's Asia policy for some years to come. For current purposes, the point to stress is that these domestic discussions and debates have been followed closely by the political leaderships and foreign policy establishments of Southeast Asian states. That the veracity of the Pivot has been questioned and doubted in certain segments of the American intelligentsia and policy establishment is sufficient to sow further doubts about the viability and endurance of its various elements. To that end, the fact that Southeast Asia and ASEAN hardly featured at all during Donald Trump's presidential election campaign or after chimes with the exigencies of regional anxiety.

U.S. POLICY CONDITIONS AND CONSTRAINTS

Kevin Fogg, a historian of Southeast Asia, shared the following rumination of the region's place in the study of global history:

> Southeast Asia is so tricky as a region to study that even the current name for this region was fundamentally a neologism forged in the wake of the Second World War, to replace other names that inherently overlooked the region. Traditionally the peninsula was called "Indochina," despite being neither India, nor China. The archipelago carries the indigenous Malay name of "Nusantara," meaning the "Archipelago In Between," explicitly seeing this as on the way to somewhere. Even the great public intellectual and father of the modern Indonesian language Sutan Takdir Alisjahbana suggested calling mainland Southeast Asia "Bumantara," or "Land In Between"—a name that felicitously never stuck. The idea of Southeast Asia as a place in between, or on the way to somewhere, but not as a destination in and of itself is in fact grimly reflective how global historians have treated it lo these many years.[3]

These are not mere abstract, theoretical ruminations, for they have considerable policy salience. Indeed, similar sentiments could arguably be expressed in relation to the place of Southeast Asia in American calculations of their interests and strategy.

Since the end of the Cold War there has been much debate over U.S. grand strategy in the consequent "new world order." Writing within a few years of the advent of the post–Cold War era, Barry Posen and Andrew Ross had suggested that U.S. grand strategy during this period encompassed four competing visions: neoisolationism, selective engagement, cooperative security, and primacy.[4] What is perhaps most significant about this typology is its reflection of the incoherence that characterized U.S. grand strategy or, perhaps more appropriately, the *categorization of* U.S. grand strategy, during this period. Although there is broad consensus that the American grand strategic objective should be about the preservation of liberal hegemony, that is to say preservation of America's status as the preponderant power and the use of this power to further American purpose in terms of its values and leadership, how this is to be operationalized in terms of grand strategy is where the rubber meets the road. Indeed, while the election of Donald Trump to the office of president may cast some doubt on these objectives in the short term, they are likely to still remain the defining questions for American strategists and foreign policymakers for some time to come.

Yet to be fair, because of the diversity of policy challenges that are confronting the United States, ranging from new regional economic agendas and the emergence of potentially revisionist powers to the proliferation of nonstate actors seeking to reshape global affairs, it is even more difficult to establish a coherent set of guiding principles—a grand strategy—or even clarity of strategic thought and purpose akin to containment during the Cold War years. In addition, notwithstanding American military might, the United States is arguably more vulnerable today compared with the Cold War given the nature of threats that it now faces. Finally, it has to deal with the weight of expectation. Here, the cautious words of Jessica Matthews warrant our attention:

> Being a lone superpower is harder, and harder for others to accept, than being one of two. Mistakes and overreaching that would have been forgiven in a mortal conflict are not forgiven now. The triumphalism that followed the American victory in the cold war was short-lived in its acute form, but it lingers in outsized expectations

on the part of both Americans and non-Americans of what the
U.S. can do and should do.[5]

It is this context of ongoing debate about American grand strategy in the
post–Cold War era that hastens Southeast Asian anxieties about where
the region stands in American strategic thinking, all the more so with
the election of Donald Trump to high office.

This strategic complexity is perhaps most evident in Southeast Asia
today, where the geostrategic and security environment, not to mention
power stratification, is changing considerably. Since the end of the Second World War, it had been an article of faith that an American-led order
would undergird security, prosperity, and stability in the region. But
American leadership in the region is now being tested, as is the regional
order it has underpinned. The region is witnessing at close quarters the
rise of China, which, unlike the Soviet Union in a bygone era, is not only
emerging as a strategic power of consequence but very much an economic
and political one as well. On this score, one need only be cognizant of the
growing consumerist middle class in China, which affords it strategic
leverage—by dint of offering global multinationals a huge market—that
the Soviet Union never had at its disposal. China's military power is increasing, even as Beijing looks askance at what it perceives to be American
attempts to contain it and curb its rise. Its economic growth is generating
an irresistible gravitational pull on regional states. In the political sphere,
the winds are also shifting. China is increasingly a point of reference for
conversations on regional order, and it is axiomatic that its rise will
transform this order in one way or another. Meanwhile, the election of
Donald Trump has also given pause. Thus far, divining the elements of a
coherent Trump administration grand strategy remains an arduous task,
not least given the internal discord between the White House and the
cabinet. Nevertheless, there are some discomfiting aspects that are evident if the new president's worldview (and tweets) is taken into consideration: protectionism and hostility towards free trade, scaling back on
support of traditional allies, bellicosity towards China, and, thus far, absolute disregard for ASEAN and Southeast Asia except for the possibility
of a more aggressive posture on the South China Sea. To give edge to all
of this, the security environment in Southeast Asia is also changing. It is
today a more complex environment, where new and resurgent security
challenges coexist with deep economic interdependence. Indeed, it is such

strategic and security complexity attendant in the region that forms the backdrop to regional uncertainties about where Southeast Asia sits in Washington's list of priorities and the extent to which the United States is capable of an engagement strategy that is broad enough not to be beholden to issue-specific imperatives and robust enough to be insulated from the dangers of distraction.

At a structural level, the case can be made that although Southeast Asia is an important region to the United States for a host of reasons already elaborated in the book—trade, freedom of navigation, presence of allies, and so forth—it still occupies an uncertain place in terms of strategic priorities for the United States. This is particularly so when one looks beyond officials from the Departments of State and Defense specifically tasked with formulating, articulating, and defending Southeast Asia policy to consider the views of a larger swathe of the political leadership and decisionmaking community in the executive and legislative branches of government. The vacillation of American policy postures toward the region since the end of the Cold War, which in all likelihood will be even more so under the Trump presidency, suggests an element of ambiguity in strategic thinking when it comes to Southeast Asia. This, in turn, arguably implicates a lack of a strong strategic foundation to United States policy toward Southeast Asia. This uncertainty is animated by a further three factors: geographic distance, the absence of any core American interests directly associated with the region, and, for the time being at least, the absence of a clear and present threat.

This ambivalence cuts both ways, for the same can be said of Southeast Asia, where there is no consensus on the existence of a compelling strategic imperative to fully endorse American leadership or even a shared strategic outlook on what this leadership should look like. Indeed, it is the lack of a coherent view on American engagement that renders anxieties toward it all the more acute. At this juncture, it is important to register that a large part of this regional dissensus derives not only from the encounters that Southeast Asian states have had with the United States in the past, but also from how these states view the role that China is playing, and is expected to play, in regional affairs as well. Although China's assertiveness in the maritime domain has been a matter of some concern for regional states, Beijing has at the same time also established itself as an indispensable actor situated at the heart of regional economic dynamism. The point should also be stressed that, increasingly, China's economic centrality has translated to leadership, for instance, through initiatives such as the Asian Infrastructure Investment Bank, One Belt, One Road, and even within regional economic institutions such as ASEAN Plus Three and Regional Comprehensive Economic Partnership. Simply put, Southeast Asian leaders would not want to publicly rebuke China for fear this would provoke backlash, but they do seek a continued U.S. security presence to mitigate against Chinese dominance, albeit not in a way that conveys to Beijing the mistaken impression that a posture (if not policy) of containment is imminent, if not already in practice.

There is a corollary to the absence of clear and consistent interests and strategies in how the United States engages Southeast Asia. Notwithstanding gradual attentiveness to ASEAN and its various functional multilateral efforts, for a long time the preferred mechanism for Southeast Asia policy has been bilateral. The reason for the U.S. preference for bilateralism was summarized in the following manner a decade ago but is still relevant now:

> Bilateralism will thus prevail as the dominant ordering mechanism in the Asia-Pacific region for some time to come. The rapidly changing nature of interests and threats in the region have ironically worked to make a more compelling force for galvanizing regional security collaboration than those organizations such as ASEAN espousing norms or rationales that for now can only remain ideals rather than generate sufficient consensus to convert them into action.[6]

Yet having said that, U.S. efforts to further regional engagement at the bilateral level have periodically been imperiled by anti-Americanism across several Southeast Asian states. Mindful of issues of sovereignty and not wanting to be seen as complicit in the extension of U.S. interests into the region, especially in the eyes of domestic audiences, regional states ranging from old allies to new friends have tread cautiously in terms of alignment with the American strategic outlook and interests. While in most cases leaders and officials—both American and Southeast Asian—have managed to eventually smoothen the passage of crucial bilateral initiatives, for instance, the Enhanced Defense Cooperation Agreement in the case of the Philippines, the lifting of the arms embargo on Vietnam, and counterterrorism cooperation with Malaysia and Indonesia, it remains the case that popular anti-American sentiments that have grown increasingly vocal compared with the era of the Cold War will be a persistent impediment that, though insufficient to scuttle initiatives, can nevertheless impair the decisionmaking process and stall efforts to bring policy formulations to fruition.

The absence of clarity of strategy and the anxieties that attend it have often been compounded by the matter of policy follow-through and implementation. Even if inchoate elements of a U.S. strategy toward Southeast Asia can be discerned, implementation and execution has been inconsistent. The dithering over the conduct of FONOPS in 2015, detailed in chapter 6, even as China willy-nilly changed facts in the seas, and the final fate of American involvement in the TPPA, serve as two clear examples that implicate poor implementation and execution. Here again, domestic obstacles loom large. To be sure, this book has not attempted to divine the day-to-day workings of foreign policy decisionmaking complexities in the United States. This would take the study too far afield, and in any case, the topic has already been the subject of voluminous study in the existing literature. The point to stress here is how domestic circumstances and the vicissitudes of politics in the United States have contrived to imperil efforts at enhancing engagement by holding policies hostage. A foremost concern in this regard is the economic adversity that confronts the United States. This has not only amplified an already polarized political scene; it has also imposed, and will continue to impose, considerable constraints on the wherewithal available to invest in the reinforcing of the American presence in the region. Specifically, fiscal austerity measures in the form of budget sequestration are anticipated to take a long-term toll on American power projection capabilities. While some Department of Defense officials have sought to reassure the region that budget cutbacks will not compromise the ability of the United States to sustain, if not augment, its presence in the region, others have been more reticent. Indeed, a former naval commander and current senior aide to a ranking Republican senator summed up the reality of the situation with the following remark: "at the end of the day, we still do not know the full impact that sequestration will have on U.S. defense postures."[7]

A concluding word should be said about how Southeast Asian anxieties regarding American commitment to the region ultimately also inflect toward themselves, specifically, their own limitations as far as the matter of self-assumed indigenous responsibilities to manage regional order are concerned. The harsh reality is that as the institutional expression of collective regional aspirations, ASEAN is beset by challenges that raise questions about its unity and coherence. It warrants repeating that one must be careful not to assume a unity of outlook and purpose in Southeast Asia embodied in the narrative of the ASEAN community when, in reality, ASEAN is given to divergent, and at times competing, interests and strategic outlooks, exacerbated by both material changes in the balance of power as a consequence of economic interdependence as well as residual mutual suspicion and mistrust between member states. Apropos of this, the sharing of similar concerns with regards to security challenges confronting the region do not preclude misalignment—or rather disalignment—in the perspectives of regional states as to the best means of response. The South China Sea is particularly illustrative in how it threatens to unravel the singular fiction of ASEAN unity. Optimism for a conclusive Code of Conduct is in short supply, shorter still for the prospect of eventual resolution of the South China Sea disputes. Not only is this because China has given short shrift to the positions of Southeast Asian claimant states that have taken a firmer line on the issue—Vietnam, Singapore, and pre-Duterte Philippines, to be precise—it is also a function of ASEAN's inability to forge a coherent and consistent position on the South China Sea. It is not difficult to infer from this that ASEAN unity, at least on the specific issue of the South China Sea, remains a chimera.

The elusiveness of unity exposes a contradiction at the core of the ASEAN project of Centrality: Centrality is proclaimed from a position of weakness, not strength, that in turn relies on external parties to recognize it and accord it a place at the heart of the regional security architecture. It is on this score that the role of the United States, and its explicit support of ASEAN Centrality, comes to assume greater import. Yet even so, it should be evident that no singular perspective exists that adequately describes how Southeast Asia views the United States or the role the states of the region are prepared to ascribe to it. There should be no doubt that all Southeast Asian states desire for the United States to remain engaged in the region and to deepen that engagement. This was expressly evident from the reception that the Pivot received in all the regional capitals. It is less clear, however, as preceding chapters have labored to show, whether regional states share the same view regarding just what sort of role they envisage for the United States in Southeast Asia.

FINAL THOUGHTS

Something of ambivalence can be discerned in U.S. engagement in Southeast Asia over the course of the two and a half decades since the end of the Cold War, and it has been a cause of anxiety in the region. This ambivalence, it should also be added, derives not so much from the absence of the United States from the region but rather from the episodic and piecemeal nature of American attention to and involvement in regional affairs and lingering doubts over the sustainability of this interest.

There should be no doubt that Southeast Asia should be a region of considerable relevance for U.S. interests. Free and open access to the sea lanes of Southeast Asia, primarily the Malacca Straits and the South China Sea, are issues of abiding concern to the United States and have long been pivotal to American interests. So, too, is the imperative of economic engagement with one of the world's fastest growing economic regions. It is also in Southeast Asia that one finds long-standing friends and allies of the United States: Thailand has always proudly claimed to be America's oldest ally in Asia by virtue of the Treaty of Amity and Commerce, signed in 1833; the Philippines was a former colony and is currently a treaty ally; and Thailand and the Philippines, collectively with Singapore, Malaysia, and Indonesia, under the leadership of Suharto, constituted the founding members of ASEAN, who were staunch supporters of the U.S. war effort in Vietnam.[8]

Yet this relevance has not inspired a consistent, sustained strategy of engagement from Washington. Over the three presidencies and twenty-four years covered in this book, it is evident that American policy toward Southeast Asia has been episodic and fluctuates frequently, informed and dictated by different agendas and priorities of respective administrations. These fluctuations have created the impression that the United States is a reactive power that responds only to crisis rather than a proactively engaged actor in regional affairs. The tendency toward reactive and crisis-driven policies sits uncomfortably with the leadership role the United States often assumes (or desires to assume) and has sent confusing signals to the region that betray ambivalence in the United States' engagement. Indeed, in several extreme cases, American "leadership" has even proven to be more of an impediment than a source of support (for example, the Asian Financial Crisis and Washington's initial reaction to the Asian Infrastructure Investment Bank). Needless to say, these confusing signals have been a source of some consternation for American friends, partners, and allies in Southeast Asia and have lent to heightened anxiety over the question of the focus and sustainability of American commitment to deepen engagement with the region.

As the Obama administration drew to a close, the United States could claim several political and diplomatic victories in its engagement with Southeast Asia. These were not inconsequential. Foremost was the uptick in bilateral relations with Vietnam and Myanmar, the renewed commitment of the United States to regional diplomacy through ASEAN, and enhanced strategic involvement in the South China Sea. Yet as this book has shown, uncertainties linger across Southeast Asia regarding the sustainability of this commitment at the dawn of a new administration. These uncertainties have grown stronger and more urgent with the election victory of Donald Trump.

Whether as individual states or collectively as ASEAN, Southeast Asia sets great store by state sovereignty and regional autonomy. It wants to be dominated neither by China nor by the United States. Rather, it seeks to accommodate all major powers in the region toward the ends of stability and prosperity. For Southeast Asia, a constant and consistent American engagement is crucial to the achievement of these ends. It is for this reason that the American presence in and commitment to Southeast Asia on the military, economic, and diplomatic register is greatly valued; and conversely, signs of ambivalence on the part of Washington toward any of these roles are the cause of great anxiety across the region.

CHAPTER NINE

Policy Considerations
and Recommendations

THE PRECEDING CHAPTERS CONTEMPLATED U.S.–Southeast Asia relations since the end of the Cold War by focusing on the advances made
and obstacles met in relation to American strategic priorities, domestic
constraints, and the aspirations and shortcomings of Southeast Asian
regionalism, which have sharpened regional anxieties toward the role of
the United States in, and commitment to, the region. As I have surmised,
notwithstanding the robust strategic, economic, and diplomatic push of
the Obama administration's Pivot strategy, some of these anxieties still
exist and are likely to intensify as we move further into the Trump
administration.

Bearing all this in mind, what follows are general observations of the
policy challenges germane to American efforts to further engagement of
Southeast Asia after the Obama administration and a discussion on policy implications and choices for the United States toward this end. These
are further granularized into recommendations about how the United
States can build on the accomplishments of the Obama presidency to
advance its engagement of Southeast Asia and in the process provide re-
assurances, ameliorate lingering concerns, and ensure an American
stake in the region. To be sure, from what we can see with the new administration, some of the recommendations may well be asking too
much. Nevertheless, the American strategic thinking and foreign policy
establishment writ large should still bear these in mind, for American
interests and U.S.–Southeast Asia relations will survive the Trump
presidency.

CONTINUE THE PURSUIT OF ENHANCED
ENGAGEMENT WITH THE REGION

The withdrawal of the United States from Vietnam in 1973 foreshadowed a season of neglect in the Southeast Asia component of Washington's Asia strategy. Although the advent of the post–Cold War era has witnessed the United States return some measure of attention to the region, Southeast Asia policy has often appeared ad hoc and reactive for want of clear thinking over where the region fit in broader U.S. strategy. This was evident, as previous chapters have illustrated, in the U.S. position on the South China Sea or on regional economic cooperation, at least prior to the advent of the Obama administration.

Things changed to some degree with the announcement of the Pivot policy under the Obama administration, which went some distance to address the perception that Southeast Asia is frequently overlooked by the United States even in the context of Asia policy. Regardless of its discomfiting nomenclature and inevitable shortcomings, the fact is that with the Pivot, the Obama administration broadly set U.S.–Southeast Asia relations on the right path. It is incumbent on future administrations to continue on this path and, where possible, to inject even more clarity, coherence, and purpose. This should be done not for reasons of altruism but because it is squarely in the American interest to do so. It is imperative that this effort be guided by a coherent strategy that draws on and integrates all the tools of engagement available to the United States.

The United States must be consistent, persistent, and visible in the region. It cannot show up only when there is a crisis or allow itself to be distant in the absence of one. One step to consider in this regard is the regularization, if not institutionalization, of the U.S.–ASEAN Summit that was initiated at Sunnylands in 2016. Although widely recognized as a personal initiative of President Obama, the elevation of such a meeting into a regular event would go some distance in reassuring Southeast Asian states of sustained American interest in and commitment to the region. Likewise, senior cabinet officials should maintain the frequency of visits made by their predecessors to Southeast Asia, bearing in mind that "merely turning up" at regional meetings is in and of itself an invaluable gesture in the nature of regional diplomatic culture.

In further enhancing engagement with Southeast Asia, it is imperative that Washington keeps the larger strategic picture in view. An

American long-term strategy of engagement in Southeast Asia must be predicated on the prevention of the dominance of any single external power in the region, including the United States itself. Unlike the 1970s, when ASEAN states harbored misplaced aspirations that they could keep external powers at bay by way of a Zone of Peace, Freedom, and Neutrality, the present era sees Southeast Asia welcome the involvement of external powers in regional affairs as stakeholders with an interest in stability and prosperity. On this score, it is necessary that the United States maintain a credible military and economic presence in the region, along with strong support structures that can serve to augment this presence.

DOWNPLAY IDEOLOGICAL ELEMENTS OF ENGAGEMENT STRATEGY

In devising a strategy for engagement of Southeast Asia, the United States must take care not to miss the forest for the trees. In the past, U.S. strategic engagement with Southeast Asia was always constrained by elements of a values-based foreign policy that Washington espoused.

While engrained in the American psyche, the propensity to link human rights and democracy with U.S. foreign policy creates inevitable hurdles in Washington's policy toward Asia, particularly as it relates to America's security engagement with countries in the region. Moreover, the persistent U.S. uneasiness with engaging with illiberal regimes in Southeast Asia (although it doesn't seem to matter as much in other regions such as the Middle East) has the ability to hamper a unified and regionwide military posture in the region. This was very evident in relations with Indonesia, Southeast Asia's largest country and recognized as the most important member of ASEAN, in the first decade of the post–Cold War era. Because of human rights violations that took place during the *Reformasi* era of the late 1990s and various crises involving East Timor, Washington faced intense pressure from Congress and influential lobby groups, and as a consequence, progress in strengthening bilateral relations with the largest country in Southeast Asia slowed down markedly. By the same token, Washington's single-minded pursuit of its Global War on Terror during the Bush administration allowed China to steal a march on the United States in the region through its "charm offensive" pursued under the leadership of Hu Jintao and implemented by Wen Jiabao. A similar risk appears to be unfolding in Myanmar policy, where congressional frustration and disillusionment with the new government's approach to the Rohingya issue places at risk the prospects for deeper and more holistic engagement. To that effect, it is worth asking an inconvenient but valid question: whether decades of sanctions in fact achieved their intended objectives at all in Myanmar. To that end, it is worth registering the point that while former secretary of state Hillary Clinton is known to have claimed credit for "opening up" Myanmar, the view from within the region as to what accounted for political change in the country is decidedly different.

DEAL WITH CHINA WITHOUT MAKING
THE REGION CHOOSE

The crafting of a coherent U.S. strategy toward Southeast Asia must take into account the reality that the regional distribution of power is changing in considerable and, for all intents and purposes, irreversible ways. China has become an economic powerhouse, and although the economic growth rates of the first two decades after the end of the Cold War are probably not sustainable, the fact is that China has emerged as the preponderant economic power in mainland Southeast Asia, if not the whole of Southeast Asia. Indeed, while debate rages on in the scholarly and think tank communities about China's credentials as a global power, the reality for Southeast Asia is that China is already a regional power of considerable consequence and one that appears intent on a position of strategic primacy in its "near abroad."

The baggage of history, encapsulated most profoundly in the carefully cultivated national narrative of "a hundred years of humiliation," weighs heavily on the shoulders of present and future generations of the Chinese leadership and will continue to be mobilized to fan the embers of Chinese nationalism, which will, in turn, inevitably inform China's strategic outlook. Accurately or otherwise, this outlook sees the United States proactively trying to curb its rise. Much has been said elsewhere about whether China is content with a place in the existing international rules-based order that is viewed in Beijing as U.S.-centric or if it intends to disrupt or overturn it. No doubt that script is still unfolding. Yet arriving states seldom, if ever, are satisfied to merely partake in a prevailing order. They oftentimes wish to transform that order in a way that recognizes their power and influence, failing which they are prepared to create alternatives. This will be a strategic dilemma that will exercise the U.S. foreign policy establishment for many years to come as it seeks to balance between accommodating China's rise and maintaining American primacy.

Although the United States has repeatedly proclaimed that it welcomes China's rise, Trump's hostility towards China on the trade and commercial front notwithstanding, it needs to also address the question of how to cope—and help the region to cope—with China's slew of regional strategic initiatives, which have come to give form and substance to this rise. On balance, a congenial response, which includes active participation, would inspire confidence in American regional leadership. Toward that end, the United States should not only welcome the establishment of the Asian Infrastructure Investment Bank and announcement of the One Belt, One Road initiative by China, it should actively engage Southeast Asian partners in discussions on how best to leverage and capitalize on these opportunities. Moreover, should the United States join the AIIB, it would both allow Washington to influence issues of governance, an issue about which American policymakers have expressed concerns, and afford American industry access to bidding opportunities in the region. Ironically, even for the present administration in Washington intent on exacerbating rivalry with China, such a move would offer a means through which Chinese influence can be attenuated in a transactional, as opposed to hostile, manner. The United States should also constantly engage China in discussions on regional architecture mechanisms that can accommodate both American and Chinese interests together. Such discussions can begin by addressing shared concerns over climate change, humanitarian relief, and natural disaster management as they relate to Southeast Asia. Ongoing efforts at fostering deeper military-to-military interaction, such as China's participation in the Rim of the Pacific Exercise, should also continue.

Due consideration should be given to the discursive elements of relations with China. While it will at times be necessary for the United States to take visible and robust positions in response to Chinese actions, care should be taken not to employ confrontational language or phrases, issue public ultimatums, or cast the choices facing China in moralistic terms (some U.S. officials have taken to the unfortunate practice of pointing out that the choices confronting China are a matter of "good" and "evil"). Aside from the fact that rhetorical broadsides will more likely than not provoke China to dig in, they will also place Southeast Asian states in a delicate position. In dealing with China, the United States must bear in mind that although it enjoys a considerable measure of goodwill from Southeast Asia, for reasons of deepening economic interdependence the region also seeks to strengthen relations with Beijing and will always take care not to convey any impression that it is complicit in any perceived attempt to contain or isolate China. Hence, in pursuing its interests in the region, the United States must be careful not to make statements or assume postures that can be construed as such. In this regard, it is heartening that the Trump administration has desisted from its original intent to name (and try to shame) China as a currency manipulator on questionable grounds.[1] Nor should the United States expect Southeast Asian states to embrace American policies and initiatives if these require them to compromise on their equally imperative objective of strengthening relations with China.

The case of Singapore is instructive. China is Singapore's largest trading partner, while the United States is the largest source of foreign direct investment (FDI) in Singapore, and Singapore is China's biggest investor. Since the signing of a U.S.–Singapore free trade agreement in 2004, bilateral trade has grown by 50 percent, totaling $47 billion in 2014. U.S. FDI in Singapore amounted to nearly $180 billion in 2014.[2] Trade between Singapore and China is nearly twice that with the United States, reaching $91.4 billion in 2013. In 2014 Singapore became China's largest foreign investor, with $7.3 billion in FDI in 2013. Beyond trade ties, Singapore enjoys good diplomatic relations with both China and the United States. In 2015, President Xi Jinping lauded China's "all-round cooperative partnership" with Singapore. China also has a large overseas diaspora population living and working in Singapore. The United States and Singapore have had close diplomatic relations since the early days of the Cold War and in 2012 signed a strategic partnership, outlining their shared commitment to "freedom of navigation, and lawful, unimpeded commerce, respect for international law, and the peaceful settlement of disputes."[3] In December 2015, Singapore and the United States' defense departments inked an Enhanced Defense Cooperation Agreement, further elevating security ties. While other regional states may experience different figures and patterns in trade, security, and political relations with the United States and China, it would be a matter of degree and not kind.

DISTINGUISH INTERESTS IN AND ENGAGEMENT
OF SOUTHEAST ASIA FROM CHINA AND NORTHEAST ASIA

Because of growing bilateral strategic competition, it is becoming increasingly evident that American policy in East Asia—certainly in Southeast Asia—cannot but be viewed through a China prism. In a sense, this is a natural outcome of great power politics and hence is understandable. Nevertheless, it would also be useful to bracket China policy within a larger framework that takes full account of regional dynamics on their own merits, so as to avoid allowing China policy to dictate, shape, or overshadow engagement policy toward the region. Nor should the furtherance of Sino–U.S. relations be pursued in a manner that gives the region cause for alarm that a transactional G-2-type condominium is materializing toward the end of addressing regional issues without input from Southeast Asia. In other words, the United States must find at least some strategic, economic, and diplomatic bandwidth to engage Southeast Asia on its own terms. It would serve American interests to strengthen relations with Southeast Asia independent of China for it avoids creating the impression that the United States is making its regional partners choose sides amid all the complexities of the Sino–U.S. relationship.

Even before the end of the Cold War, United States policy toward Southeast Asia had been predicated for the most part on the strengthening of a collection of bilateral relationships with regional states, consonant with its hubs-and-spokes model of security architecture built around alliances. The United States should further bilateral relations with Southeast Asian states, paying particular attention to new relationships that have developed in recent years with Myanmar and Vietnam, for which there is much potential but also obstacles. In developing these relationships, the United States must be mindful of issues of sovereignty (or the importance of having the impression of sovereignty), which regional states value a great deal even as they seek to improve relations with Washington. In particular, the United States should demonstrate sensitivity to the fact that its "new friends" in the region are also states and political and economic systems that are in transition, given to the ebbs and flows that come with gradual liberalization, and hence still fragile and vulnerable to recrudescence to illiberalism. Concomitantly, while the United States should extend support to these governments to build more robust institutions and liberal norms, care should be taken not to compel social and political change at a pace faster than incumbent governments are comfortable with or, worse, by the appearance of diktat from Washington. In particular, pressure on these governments for the liberalization of the press and civil society, or of policies pertaining to minorities against the backdrop of historical baggage, should be very carefully calibrated.

Equally important will be to sustain engagement of ASEAN as an institutional expression of Southeast Asia as a region. Attendant to this, efforts should be made to continue reinforcing ASEAN's central role in the regional architecture. ASEAN is surely not without its own short-comings, some of which are quite severe. Its aspirations to assume the obligation of regional order management have rarely been matched by political will, let alone action. Yet it remains core to the regional secu-rity architecture by virtue of the neutral platform it provides, and it is in the U.S. interest to ensure that the organization continues to mature in its role in the "driver's seat" of regional security initiatives.

To be sure, U.S. administrations have tended to harbor equivocal views on ASEAN. At issue has always been the ASEAN norm of deci-sionmaking by consensus, which holds the organization structurally hostage to the lowest common denominator, and its preference for form over substance. At least in part because of these reservations, the United States has often prioritized bilateral cooperation in its Southeast Asia policy while expressing token regard for ASEAN. Yet notwithstanding Washington's continued preference for bilateral cooperation, given the importance of ASEAN unity and coherence to the pursuit of centrality, the United States can also support ASEAN's self-assumed obligations for regional order management by furthering efforts to engage ASEAN-centered multilateral platforms. To that effect, the United States can focus on several practical measures that will contribute to the strength-ening of ASEAN. First, Washington should pursue continued engage-ment of China and other regional powers through ASEAN platforms such as the ASEAN Regional Forum, the East Asia Summit, and the ASEAN Defense Ministers' Meeting Plus, and encourage other external powers to do the same. Again, the logic to this is less a matter of altru-ism as it is the fact that ASEAN remains the only neutral platform available. Second, given that differences such as territorial disputes re-main between ASEAN member states that might obstruct deeper coop-eration between them, the United States can work to persuade ASEAN states to resolve these issues among themselves as resolution of intra-ASEAN disputes can only strengthen the regional institution's resolve when dealing with external powers. Third, the United States should continue exploring the possibility of a free trade agreement with ASEAN, if not during the current administration then certainly in the longer term. This would go some distance in supporting further regional economic integration and would also offer Southeast Asian economies a viable and attractive alternative to China, into whose economic orbit the region has been inevitably gravitating. In the event that a free trade agreement with ASEAN remains unfeasible, the United States should seek out alternative avenues to deepen economic engagement with regional economies.

BE MINDFUL OF FOLLOW-THROUGH
ON COMMITMENTS AS CREDIBILITY IS AT STAKE

The Obama administration's Pivot policy heightened expectations across Southeast Asia. The challenge for the United States will be to maintain, if not enhance, the level of engagement that President Obama's focus on Southeast Asia has occasioned and to follow through on commitments so as to avoid the danger of flattering to deceive.

That American engagement with Southeast Asia has been afflicted by an element of ambivalence has in part been a consequence of inconsistent policy implementation and weak follow-through due to disagreements within the U.S. government and constraints of the decisionmaking system. This has frequently found expression in the inability of American political and decisionmaking bodies to make good on commitments expressed at the executive level. In some respects, the eventual fate of American participation in the TPPA was perhaps the most devastating demonstration of this. Identified with robust language by its proponents in the Obama administration as the economic centerpiece of the Pivot, the harsh reality for the United States has been its eventual victimization by domestic politics. During election year, American politicians are wont to focus in the main on domestic and reelection issues. Foreign policy seldom features as a priority in this regard. As a consequence, foreign policy initiatives get lost in the cacophony of the campaigning season, casting doubt on the ability and bandwidth of political leaders to follow through on commitments. With regard to the imperative of ratification of the TPPA, the risks and costs were already vividly described by the foreign minister of Singapore on the occasion of a visit to Washington, D.C.:

If having marched everybody up the hill, you march down now, it would have been better if we never started on this journey. So getting it passed is absolutely crucial. Unfortunately, at least in our interactions and in the reports I've read so far, it's not a done deal. It's not a given. In the last two days I've been talking to a variety of congressmen, senators and leaders. Frankly, my sense of it is that at an intellectual level everyone knows that it makes sense. It ought to be done. No one seriously argues with me against it at an intellectual level. Yet I know as a politician this is one of those things that people hope it gets done but without their fingerprints on it. Without having to pay a political price for it.[4]

In short, the fate of American commitment to the TPPA serves as a timely reminder of how vital it is that the executive branch, Congress, and interest groups reach consensus on how to move U.S. engagement policy in the region forward in a coherent and strategic manner.

Being able to coordinate implementation, speak with one voice, and project unity is critical to the credibility of American engagement. By this token, another challenge that has confronted U.S. policy in Southeast Asia has been the lack of policy coordination across various government departments, which impedes effective policy implementation. This was evident, for instance, when the Defense Department and National Security Council provided conflicting explanations of freedom of navigation exercises in the South China Sea or when Secretary Ashton Carter, on orders from the White House, refused to confirm before the Senate Armed Forces Committee under questions by Senator John McCain that such an operation even took place.[5]

No doubt, the challenges of implementation speak to the nature of the political system in the United States that frames decisionmaking. At a fundamental level, the democratic form of governance has placed certain constraints on the ability of the U.S. president to carry out a seamless rebalance policy, where President Obama had to wrestle with a system that imposes checks and balances on the White House. In addition to that, during Obama's tenure the legislative branch was often at variance with the executive branch, with Congress frequently attempting to curtail the president's authority. The result was a competing array of initiatives running parallel and sometimes at odds with one another, all with varying degrees of emphasis and volume. Efforts have to be taken to avoid excessive polarization of domestic politics, and ad hominem attacks should not be allowed to imperil foreign policy. Unfortunately, on present evidence it appears that the Trump administration is likely to be bedeviled by similar exigencies with White House and cabinet senior officials all too frequently speaking past each other despite having been in office for only a brief period of time (at the point of writing).

ENGAGE AMERICANS ON SOUTHEAST ASIA

There is a tendency among American officials, and this was especially true during the Obama administration, to stress the importance of Southeast Asia to Southeast Asians. This is doubtless welcomed as a source of reassurance, but it is also akin to preaching to the converted. Given the previous point on the need for robust follow-through, it is essential that the general American population and its political leaders be informed, instructed, and convinced of the strategic and economic value of Southeast Asia to American national interests. To that end, speeches on the importance of Southeast Asia should be delivered not only in the region but across the United States as well, with regularity and to different sectors of the population.

In particular, congressional knowledge and appreciation of Southeast Asia in consonance with American interests must be deepened beyond the constant refrain of human rights. This can begin with efforts to encourage congressional committee members to travel to Southeast Asia on a more frequent basis in order to provide continuity so as to minimize the deleterious effects of the electoral cycle. The fact that this will be difficult given the political system in which domestic fundraising for reelection appears to be the foremost priority for members of Congress only means that greater effort and coordination must be undertaken by individuals and committees already committed to the region.

U.S. government agencies should also harness the full spectrum of interest in Southeast Asia by way of facilitating regular interactions with other stakeholders from the business, nongovernmental organization, and academic community, perhaps even drawing them into the decision-making process. Such collective interactions are critical not only because they both broaden and deepen understanding and appreciation of Southeast Asia, they can also be tapped to further enhance the government's signaling, messaging, and outreach on Southeast Asian matters to a broader American audience. At the same time, coordinated interactions of this nature can also head off interdepartmental rivalries that bedevil foreign policymaking.

STAKE A CLEAR AND CONSISTENT POSITION ON THE SOUTH CHINA SEA BASED ON INTERNATIONAL LAW

Many of the policy challenges and considerations already discussed converge in the South China Sea. For better or worse, the South China Sea has become the central preoccupation in U.S.–Southeast Asia relations, especially in the second term of the Obama presidency, and will likely remain so at least in the near future. The United States must not allow the South China Sea to dictate and ultimately overwhelm its engagement with Southeast Asia the way terrorism did during the George W. Bush presidency. Having said that, it is also the issue that poses the most immediate test for the United States in terms of policy toward both China and Southeast Asia. In response to Chinese assertiveness, all maritime Southeast Asian states have moved to strengthen ties with the United States. From this, it is evident that maritime Southeast Asia sees the American military and diplomatic role as crucial to check Chinese ambitions in the South China Sea.

Beijing appears to have calculated that under President Obama, the United States would do little more than register verbal protests against Chinese actions in the South China Sea and that the United States would not risk confrontation with China over the disputes. Even so, the United States must keep up steady political pressure on China on the back of messaging and signaling that this is being done not for negative ends of containment of Beijing but for positive ones of upholding the legitimacy of international law and open access to maritime commons. Measures also need to be undertaken to signal to Beijing that Chinese adventurism in the South China Sea is undermining the prevailing order that all other states concerned have an interest in and are committed to uphold, and hence will have costs and risks. To that end, together with like-minded states, the United States has to take the lead in ensuring the continued viability of the present rules-based order in the South China Sea. This should be done through the continued pursuit of actions, such as freedom of navigation operations as well as flyovers in the event an Air Defense Identification Zone is declared over any part of the South China Sea, that call into question claims of ownership by any of the claimant states in the South China Sea disputes. It is also vital that the United States is able to stay the course even if such actions do not result in an immediate scale-back of Chinese activities. Having said that, there is a need to balance such a posture with the risk of excessive publicity, such as the case with the U.S.S. *Lassen* FONOPS in October 2015, lest it be misinterpreted as an attempt to embarrass China. After all, prior to the October 2015 FONOPS and before the two-year self-imposed moratorium, the U.S. navy had already been conducting such operations without fanfare or publicity. Regular but low-key operations that send an unequivocal message should continue.

Because of the attendant risk of such demonstrations of resolve, they are best pursued alongside intense diplomatic efforts aimed at fostering dialogue and negotiation. To that effect, the priority of the United States' South China Sea policy should not be the flexing of military muscle but to persuade all claimant states to conclude a binding Code of Conduct within an ASEAN framework and to work toward a moratorium on further expansion of claims, especially the building of installations and so-called reclamation of land on these features. The United States should also encourage claimant states to build conflict management regimes and seek resolution with each other. Given that the territorial disputes involve not only China but several Southeast Asian states as well, such efforts should also include putting pressure on Southeast Asian claimant states to resolve their own differences.

Finally, in pursuing these approaches, the United States should be mindful that the fact it has not ratified UNCLOS has denied it the moral high ground in its dealings with China on the South China Sea and compromises its claims to be upholding the spirit of international law. Indeed, Chinese officials have already latched on to this, with Rear-Admiral Guan Youfei castigating the United States on how "with such a big principle, the U.S. still neglects [it]. We cannot help wondering what kind of principle the U.S. adheres to."[6]

ENGAGE LOCAL AND DOMESTIC CONSTITUENCIES IN SOUTHEAST ASIA

Changes in political systems across Southeast Asia have influenced the undercurrents of the relations between many regional states and the United States. For example, the end of Suharto's New Order gave rise to an open democratic climate that, among other things, fueled visceral anti-Americanism during the period of the war on terror. Cognate obstacles obtained in the relationship with the Philippines, where efforts to further defense cooperation persistently met with domestic opposition from various quarters, especially after the fall of the Marcos regime, which the Philippine opposition saw as being propped up by the United States.

To mitigate the anticipated hostility from anti-U.S. sentiments, the United States needs to look beyond the government of the day and deepen its engagement of Southeast Asian societies. This includes engagement with local nongovernmental organizations and civil society groups by promoting dialogue and collaboration on issues such as poverty alleviation, education, nature conservation, healthcare, and human trafficking, with an eye to building local capacity in all these areas. In so doing, the prospects are higher that the United States can achieve the crucial twin objectives of dulling the lingering sharp negative edges of regional misgivings toward its intentions and contributing to building social stability in Southeast Asia. This will in turn have the effect of casting a more positive light on the U.S. presence and role in the region. While some initiatives of this nature are already under way, as suggested previously, they can be pursued in a more coherent and integrated fashion on the basis of collaboration between the American private and public sectors. To that effect, one specific area to focus attention on is healthcare and pharmaceuticals, where access to affordable drugs is an urgent need across the region and indeed was an issue of some contention during the TPPA negotiations, and where the United States was singled out in negative terms.

While such local engagement can be informed by the American imperative of encouraging democratization, the United States should recognize and accept that, ultimately, democratization needs be an indigenous process pursued on indigenous terms, and its outcomes may not correspond with American values and principles of democracy. In coaxing Southeast Asian states down the road of democratization, the United States must be mindful not to attempt to remake Southeast Asian societies in its own image. Much in the same vein, American political leaders should also refrain from taking credit for democratization in Southeast Asia, as some have done in the case of Myanmar, for this might have the unintended consequence of implying that democratically elected incumbent regimes rule at the pleasure of Washington.

REVITALIZE THE AMERICAN ECONOMY

Ultimately, efforts to sustain and deepen engagement with Southeast Asia turn on the wherewithal that the United States can bring to bear on the formulation and implementation of Southeast Asia policy, be they military, economic, or social. But the harsh reality in recent years is that foreign policy in the United States is running up against considerable budgetary constraints. Indeed, fiscal pressures pose the greatest risk to the American military presence in the region as sequestration will invariably precipitate cutbacks in resources needed to enhance operational readiness and for training for American forces as well as those of their allies and security partners in Southeast Asia.

The point was made in earlier chapters that the reality of legislated fiscal austerity might make it difficult for the United States to achieve security objectives of rebalancing military forces to Asia and augmenting its military presence in Southeast Asia. Simply put, having just weathered economic hardship, the United States may not have the resources or political appetite for extensive foreign policy commitments, especially in regions so far afield geographically from the homeland. Indeed, this was to some extent the narrative that undergirded Donald Trump's successful presidential campaign. Yet it is axiomatic that the United States must show that it remains an established power and is not a declining power.

The challenges confronting the region are long-term, and the ability of the United States to perform the role that the region desires, and which is also in the American interest, will ultimately depend on the strength of the American economy to sustain the physical and material expression of American commitment. The key remains domestic economic policies—not inward looking mercantilist measures that would see the United States isolated from global growth and wealth creation, but rather policies that can enhance productivity, efficiency, and competitiveness through training (and retraining) of the labor force, innovation, and sustainable federal government revenue collection. Indeed, because of a strong tradition of innovation and technological superiority, the challenge for the United States may be not so much one of competitiveness but domestic disharmony, fiscal discipline, a realistic assessment of where growth constraints and potential lie, and ultimately, economic common sense.

Turning to Southeast Asia, two issues loom large for regional efforts to contribute to the ultimate ends of regional stability and the building of a more robust security architecture.

ASEAN UNITY

There is no gainsaying that ASEAN is facing the intensification of great power rivalry in its backyard. China has challenged ASEAN Centrality by putting forward its own ideas for regional initiatives, such as the Maritime Silk Road, One Belt One Road, the AIIB, and vague talk of a new security cooperation architecture. In pursuit of its own interests, China has also demonstrated no qualms in segregating ASEAN. This was demonstrated when it leaned on the Cambodian chair of ASEAN in 2012 and with its puzzling yet alarming claim to have reached a "four point consensus" with Cambodia, Laos, and Brunei that the South China Sea dispute would not be allowed to affect relations between China and ASEAN. Within ASEAN, fears exist that some members, especially those susceptible to economic inducements, might increasingly genuflect toward China, if not by choice then most certainly by circumstance.

While individual Southeast Asian states have responded to the changing geostrategic realities with a combination of hedging, balancing, and bandwagoning, collectively they need to continue to stress the centrality of ASEAN in the regional security architecture. At the center of this is unity among member states, which is vital for ASEAN in order for it to possess a strategic logic that will be larger than the sum of its parts.

That having been said, ASEAN needs to be mindful that centrality is not to be assumed nor taken for granted but built and reinforced. This needs to be done not by paying lip service to ASEAN Centrality but by demonstrating unity and cohesion in a concrete and practical fashion. What this translates to in the economic sphere is the need for ASEAN to further deepen its integration process in order to minimize overreliance of any individual states on China. Likewise, in the strategic sphere ASEAN needs to take a consistent, united stand on regional security issues in the face of any effort by external powers to extend their strategic parameter into Southeast Asia.

ADVANCING REGIONAL SELF-HELP

Southeast Asia has historically looked to the United States to play the role of "balancer" in regional security. For reasons already discussed in great detail, this continues by and large to be the case. At the same time, it is in the context of ASEAN Centrality that Southeast Asian states also explore greater security diversification and pursue self-help strategies by way of enhanced defense and security cooperation not only with other external powers, which many regional states are already doing in earnest, but with each other as well. Likewise, having established and strengthened bilateral defense relations with individual Southeast Asian states via the hubs-and-spokes model, the United States should explore ways to facilitate security cooperation between the respective "spokes."

EPILOGUE

The rulings of the Arbitral Tribunal in response to the Philippines' 2013 submission over the maritime entitlements and status of features encompassed in China's expansive South China Sea claims were released on July 12, 2016. Taken together, the rulings were clear, crisp, comprehensive, and nothing short of a categorical rejection of Chinese claims.

Among other things, the court ruled that the historical grounds on which China's nine-dash line claim to the South China Sea was predicated were invalid because of Beijing's earlier ratification of UNCLOS. In a move that surprised many observers, the court also ventured a ruling on the status of every feature in the Spratly Islands, clarifying that none of them were islands and hence do not generate an EEZ. Significantly, it ruled that Mischief Reef, which China has occupied since 1995, and Second Thomas Shoal, where China has blockaded Philippine marines garrisoned on an old vessel that was deliberately run aground there, are located within the EEZ of the Philippines.

For the Philippines, the legal victory presents a paradoxical challenge for the new government. Even before the ruling was announced, newly elected president Rodrigo Duterte had already indicated on several occasions that he was prepared to depart from his predecessor's more hardline position on the South China Sea to engage Beijing in dialogue and possibly joint development. He even hinted that he would tone down Manila's claim in exchange for infrastructure investment. Given that the ruling decisively turns things in Manila's favor, it remains to be seen whether the populist Duterte administration will be able to sell the idea of joint development of what are effectively Philippine resources without risking a popular backlash. This will be difficult but not necessarily impossible, given that the Philippines would likely still require logistical and infrastructural support of some form or other for such development projects, support that China would be able to provide. Initial signs are that the Duterte administration intends to reopen dialogue with China and is happy to set aside the South China Sea dispute in order to focus on a broader, more comprehensive agenda for bilateral relations. Importantly, the absence of schadenfreude in the response of the Philippines (and indeed the United States as well) to China's predicament following the Arbitral Tribunal ruling demonstrates the exigent restraint necessary for the prevention of further escalation of tensions.

Since the submission of the Philippine case in 2013, China has taken the position of "no recognition, no participation, no acceptance, and no execution." Despite the ruling of the Arbitral Tribunal, Beijing continues to adhere to this position and is likely to dig in its heels given the comprehensive nature of the court's rejection of China's claims. Given how nationalist sentiments had been stoked in the buildup to the case, it is nigh impossible for Beijing to withdraw its expansive claims. Not surprisingly, in defiance of the ruling, Chinese recalcitrance continues to insist on straight baselines and EEZs in the Spratlys, and Chinese fishing and coast guard activities have returned to the vicinity. Away from the glare of the media, however, the rulings are likely to occasion intense internal discussions and debates within the Chinese leadership as to how best to proceed. Many analysts have the not-unfounded concern that hawkish perspectives will prevail in this debate, at least in the short term—fed by deep sensibilities to issues of security and sovereignty and a (misplaced) sense of injustice.

The Arbitral Tribunal ruling on the Philippine case against China has thrown ASEAN incongruence into even sharper relief. The point has already been made that China has been cultivating support within Southeast Asia, focusing on the employment of economic inducements vis-à-vis the more dependent regional states. By this token, the 2012 incident in Phnom Penh, where ASEAN failed to arrive at a consensus for a joint communiqué as a consequence of Chinese pressure on the Cambodian chair, foreshadowed the struggle that would confront ASEAN at every turn as the South China Sea issue cast a long and ominous shadow over ASEAN meetings. The absence of an ASEAN response to the Arbitral Tribunal ruling, and evident Cambodian and Laotian resolve not to allow ASEAN statements to make any allusion to the ruling or to Chinese behavior, all but reinforced further the severity of the challenge. At this point, prospects of other Southeast Asian claimant states—Vietnam in particular—parlaying the precedent set by the ruling by launching their own legal cases against Beijing appear remote, but discussions toward that end are nevertheless also taking place in Hanoi and Kuala

Lumpur. Given the sensitivity of the immediate situation and the absence of clarity that still obtains in the aftermath of the Arbitral Tribunal ruling—for instance, what Vietnam can, should, and will do about its own claims in the Spratlys in light of the ruling—it is perhaps wise for all states concerned to exercise a measure of restraint.

As this book has already demonstrated, as an Asia Pacific country, the United States has set great store by the principle of freedom of navigation and has articulated this as a national interest with regards to the South China Sea. There are, however, several challenges for the United States as it proceeds to refine its policy in the region in light of the Arbitral Tribunal ruling.

First, by virtue of the attention it has commanded in Washington, it appears that the ruling might push the South China Sea issue to become the definitive point of reference of America's Southeast Asia policy, especially now that the economic and diplomatic prongs of this policy have withered considerably. Conversely, Southeast Asian states have expressed their desire precisely that the South China Sea issue should not overshadow or dominate the regional agenda. Hence, even as regional states hope for the United States to remain present and engaged on South China Sea issues in the region, the mood is also that equal attention, if not more, should be afforded to broaden the scope of this engagement.

Second, in pushing back Chinese assertiveness in the South China Sea, the United States must be careful not to inadvertently contribute to the militarization of the region. Immediately after the ruling, there were some rumblings about the deployment of a second carrier group to the region, and the U.S.S. *John C. Stennis* and U.S.S. *Ronald Reagan* are already patrolling the Philippine Sea. On the one hand, this is presumed to enhance the deterrent effect of the American presence in the region. On the other hand, Washington should be mindful of the fact that China's South China Sea claim is also informed by a deep sense of vulnerability, especially to the military activities that the United States conducts in its vicinity. More to the point, the United States should leaven its approach on the South China Sea by emphasizing the need for a serious conversation between the United States and China over their respective understandings of the notion of militarization, particularly as it has unfolded in the South China Sea.

Third, the United States should continue to persuade claimant states to engage in further dialogue and to support all efforts at such dialogue toward the end of concluding a Code of Conduct to govern the prosecution of claims in the South China Sea.

Finally, in order to pursue its own interests while also reassuring the region, the United States ought to prioritize the strengthening of its relations with regional partners and allies. This is necessary, and to the extent that it may be done during the Trump administration, it would also be welcomed. At the same time, however, Washington should also ensure that this strengthening and deepening of relations is undergirded by an alignment of interests and shared outlooks. This cannot, and should not, be assumed.

Appendix

Congressional Bills Involving Southeast Asia (1993–2016)

Reference	Last action	Year	Presidency	Level passed	Sponsor	Cosponsors	Title (abbreviated)	Country	Issue area	Affect U.S. foreign policy?
H.Res.282	13-Nov-1997	1997	Clinton	House	Benjamin Gilman	4	Congratulating ASEAN on 30th anniversary	ASEAN	Cooperation	No
S.Res.4	4-Jan-2005	2005	G. W. Bush	Senate	William Frist	99	Sympathy for loss of life caused by tsunami on Dec. 26, 2004	ASEAN	Natural disaster	No
S.2697	8-Sep-2006	2006	G. W. Bush	Senate	Richard Lugar	7	U.S. Ambassador for ASEAN Act	ASEAN	Cooperation	Yes
S.Res.110	6-Nov-2007	2007	G. W. Bush	Senate	Richard Lugar	10	Sense of Senate regarding 30th anniversary of ASEAN–U.S. dialogue	ASEAN	Cooperation	No
S.Con.Res.56	4-Dec-2007	2007	G. W. Bush	Senate	Barbara Boxer	2	Encouraging ASEAN to ensure peaceful democratic transition in Burma	ASEAN	Elections	Yes
S.Res.640	23-Sep-2010	2010	Obama	Senate	John Kerry	1	Sense of Senate regarding U.S. engagement with ASEAN	ASEAN	Cooperation	Yes
H.Res.345	26-Mar-1996	1996	Clinton	House	Doug Bereuter	8	Concern about deterioration of human rights in Cambodia	Cambodia	Human rights	Yes
H.R.1642	25-Sep-1996	1996	Clinton	Became Law	Philip Crane	2	To extend nondiscriminatory (most favored nation) treatment to products of Cambodia	Cambodia	Trade	Yes
S.Res.285	28-Sep-1996	1996	Clinton	Senate	William Roth Jr	2	Sense of Senate that enforcement of Cambodia Genocide Justice Act, human rights, environment, narcotics trafficking, and government conduct should be objectives of United States in relations with Cambodia	Cambodia	Human rights	Yes

Bill	Date	Year	President	Chamber	Sponsor	Cosponsors	Description	Country	Topic	Passed
S.Res.69	16-Apr-1997	1997	Clinton	Senate	John McCain	10	Sense of Senate regarding terrorist grenade attack on March 30, 1997	Cambodia	Terrorism	No
H.Res.121	21-May-1997	1997	Clinton	House	Stephen Horn	4	Sense of House regarding terrorist grenade attack on March 30, 1997	Cambodia	Terrorism	No
H.Res.195	28-Jul-1997	1997	Clinton	House	Benjamin Gilman	8	Regarding crisis in Cambodia	Cambodia	Elections	Yes
H.Res.361	17-Mar-1998	1998	Clinton	House	Doug Bereuter	7	Calling for free and impartial elections in Cambodia	Cambodia	Elections	Yes
H.Res.533	10-Oct-1998	1998	Clinton	House	Dana Rohrabacher	8	Sense of House regarding culpability of Hun Sen for war crimes and genocide in Cambodia	Cambodia	Genocide	Yes
S.Res.353	25-Jan-2006	2006	G. W. Bush	Senate	William Frist	5	Concern with undermining democratic freedoms in Cambodia by Hun Sen and Government of Cambodia	Cambodia	Elections	Yes
H.Con.Res.238	27-Jan-2006	2006	G. W. Bush	House	Juanita Millender-McDonald	34	Honoring victims of Cambodia genocide	Cambodia	Genocide	No
S.Res.515	29-Apr-2008	2008	G. W. Bush	Senate	Sheldon Whitehouse	11	Commemorating life and work of Dith Pran	Cambodia	Genocide	No
H.Res.728	12-Sep-2016	2016	Obama	House	Alan Lowenthal	21	Supporting human rights, democracy, and rule of law in Cambodia	Cambodia	Human rights	Yes
H.Res.32	11-Mar-1999	1999	Clinton	House	Doug Bereuter	13	Expressing support for elections in Indonesia	Indonesia	Elections	Yes
S.Res.166	5-Aug-1999	1999	Clinton	Senate	Craig Thomas	0	Resolution relating to elections in Indonesia	Indonesia	Elections	Yes

(Continued)

(Continued)

Reference	Last action	Year	Presidency	Level passed	Sponsor	Cosponsors	Title (abbreviated)	Country	Issue area	Affect U.S. foreign policy?
S.Res.91	20-Jun-2001	2001	G. W. Bush	Senate	Bill Nelson	3	Condemning murder of U.S. citizen and failure of Indonesian judicial system	Indonesia	Law enforcement	Yes
S.Res.350	17-Oct-2002	2002	G. W. Bush	Senate	Dianne Feinstein	0	Expressing sympathy for Bali attack on October 12, 2002	Indonesia	Terrorism	No
H.Res.767	22-Sep-2004	2004	G. W. Bush	House	Dan Burton	1	Expressing sympathy for terrorist attack in Jakarta on September 9, 2004	Indonesia	Terrorism	No
S.Res.264	4-Oct-2005	2005	G. W. Bush	Senate	William Frist	4	Expressing sympathy for Bali attacks on October 1, 2005	Indonesia	Terrorism	No
H.Res.456	18-Dec-2005	2005	G. W. Bush	House	Joseph Crowley	32	Expressing support for Aceh peace process memorandum of understanding	Indonesia	Conflict	Yes
S.Res.503	9-Jun-2006	2006	G. W. Bush	Senate	Russell Feingold	4	Mourning loss of life caused by earthquake on May 27, 2006	Indonesia	Natural disaster	No
H.Res.238	17-Sep-2007	2007	G. W. Bush	House	Joseph Crowley	31	Commending democratic elections in Aceh	Indonesia	Elections	Yes
H.Res.675	29-Jul-2009	2009	Obama	House	David Price	32	Condemning terrorist bombings and condolences to Indonesia	Indonesia	Terrorism	No
H.Res.810	14-Oct-2009	2009	Obama	House	Dan Burton	28	Condolences to Indonesia after Sumatra earthquake	Indonesia	Natural disaster	No
S.Res.237	10-Jul-1998	1998	Clinton	Senate	Russell Feingold	19	Sense of Senate regarding situation in Indonesia and East Timor	Indonesia and Timor-Leste	Conflict	Yes

Bill	Date	Year	President	Chamber	Sponsor	No.	Description	Country	Category	Passed
H.Res.292	28-Sep-1999	1999	Clinton	House	Doug Bereuter	28	Sense of House on referendum in East Timor calling on Indonesia to end violence	Indonesia and Timor-Leste	Conflict	Yes
H.Res.169	16-Nov-1999	1999	Clinton	House	Bruce Vento	26	Sense of House with respect to democracy, elections, and human rights in Lao People's Democratic Republic	Laos	Human rights	Yes
S.Res.309	19-Jul-2000	2000	Clinton	Senate	Russell Feingold	6	Sense of Senate regarding conditions in Laos	Laos	Human rights	Yes
H.Con.Res.88	11-Dec-2001	2001	G. W. Bush	Both chambers	Thomas Tancredo	0	Sense of Congress to recognize contribution of Lao-Hmong in defending freedom and democracy	Laos	Human rights	No
H.Con.Res.406	18-Oct-2002	2002	G. W. Bush	House	George Radanovich	36	Honoring Lao veterans of America for contributions to United States	Laos	Conflict	No
H.Res.402	6-May-2004	2004	G. W. Bush	House	Dan Burton	48	Sense of House regarding need for freedom, democratic reforms, human rights, and religious liberty in Lao People's Democratic Republic	Laos	Human rights	Yes
S.Res.475	20-Nov-2004	2004	G. W. Bush	Senate	Norm Coleman	3	Condemning human rights abuses in Laos	Laos	Human rights	Yes
S.Res.294	21-Oct-1998	1998	Clinton	Senate	Craig Thomas	4	Expressing sense of Senate over arrest of Anwar Ibrahim	Malaysia	Human rights	Yes
S.Res.247	17-Oct-2003	2003	G. W. Bush	Senate	Frank Lautenberg	18	Calling for president to condemn anti-Semitic comments of Dr. Mahathir Mohamad	Malaysia	Racism	Yes

(Continued)

(Continued)

Reference	Last action	Year	Presidency	Level passed	Sponsor	Cosponsors	Title (abbreviated)	Country	Issue area	Affect U.S. foreign policy?
H.Res.409	30-Oct-2003	2003	G. W. Bush	House	Roy Blunt	108	Repudiating anti-Semitic comments of Dr. Mahathir Mohamad	Malaysia	Racism	Yes
H.Res.518	17-Sep-2007	2007	G. W. Bush	House	Gregory Meeks	71	Recognizing Malaysia's 50th anniversary of independence	Malaysia	Cooperation	No
S.Res.520	31-Jul-2014	2014	Obama	Senate	Christopher Murphy	3	Condemning downing of MH17	Malaysia	Terrorism	No
S.Res.112	27-May-1993	1993	Clinton	Senate	Daniel Moynihan	9	Urging sanctions to be imposed on Burmese government	Myanmar	Human rights	Yes
S.Res.234	15-Jul-1994	1994	Clinton	Senate	Daniel Moynihan	9	Sense of Senate concerning 5th year of imprisonment of Aung San Suu Kyi	Myanmar	Human rights	Yes
H.Res.471	25-Jul-1994	1994	Clinton	House	Gary Ackerman	1	Urge Burma to release Aung San Suu Kyi	Myanmar	Human rights	Yes
H.Res.274	19-Dec-1995	1995	Clinton	House	Benjamin Gilman	3	Concerning Burma and UN General Assembly	Myanmar	Human rights	Yes
S.Con.Res.113	20-Jul-2000	2000	Clinton	Senate	Daniel Moynihan	18	Sense of Congress in recognition of 10th anniversary of Burma elections	Myanmar	Elections	No
H.Con.Res.328	11-Oct-2000	2000	Clinton	House	John Edward Porter	49	Sense of Congress in recognition of 10th anniversary of Burma elections	Myanmar	Elections	No
H.Con.Res.211	23-Jan-2002	2002	G. W. Bush	House	Peter King	38	Commending Aung San Suu Kyi on 10th anniversary of receiving Nobel Peace Prize	Myanmar	Human rights	No

Bill	Date	Year	President	Status	Sponsor	No.	Title	Country	Topic	Passed
S.1215	11-Jun-2003	2003	G. W. Bush	Senate	Mitch McConnell	61	Burmese Freedom and Democracy Act 2003	Myanmar	Human rights	Yes
H.R.2330	28-Jul-2003	2003	G. W. Bush	House	Tom Lantos	51	Burmese Freedom and Democracy Act 2003	Myanmar	Human rights	Yes
H.J.Res.97	7-Jul-2004	2004	G. W. Bush	Became Law	Tom Lantos	41	Renewal of import restrictions contained in Burmese Freedom and Democracy Act	Myanmar	Trade	Yes
S.Res.431	22-Sep-2004	2004	G. W. Bush	Senate	Mitch McConnell	10	Sense of Senate that UN Security Council should respond to threat of State Peace and Development Council in Burma	Myanmar	Human rights	Yes
H.Res.768	7-Oct-2004	2004	G. W. Bush	House	Elton Gallegly	31	Calling on UN Security Council to respond to threat of State Peace and Development Council to ASEAN region	Myanmar	Human rights	Yes
S.Res.174	16-Jun-2005	2005	G. W. Bush	Senate	Mitch McConnell	5	Recognizing Aung San Suu Kyi as symbol of struggle for freedom in Burma	Myanmar	Human rights	No
H.J.Res.52	27-Jul-2005	2005	G. W. Bush	Became Law	Tom Lantos	46	Renewal of import restrictions contained in Burmese Freedom and Democracy Act	Myanmar	Trade	Yes
S.Res.484	18-May-2006	2006	G. W. Bush	Senate	Mitch McConnell	11	Sense of Senate condemning junta on campaign of terror against minorities	Myanmar	Human rights	Yes
H.J.Res.86	1-Aug-2006	2006	G. W. Bush	Became Law	Tom Lantos	21	Renewal of import restrictions contained in Burmese Freedom and Democracy Act	Myanmar	Trade	Yes
S.Res.250	22-Jun-2007	2007	G. W. Bush	Senate	Mitch McConnell	9	Sense of Senate condemning junta on detention of Aung San Suu Kyi	Myanmar	Human rights	Yes

(Continued)

(*Continued*)

Reference	Last action	Year	Presidency	Level passed	Sponsor	Cosponsors	Title (abbreviated)	Country	Issue area	Affect U.S. foreign policy?
H.J.Res.44	1-Aug-2007	2007	G. W. Bush	Became Law	Tom Lantos	29	Renewal of import restrictions contained in Burmese Freedom and Democracy Act	Myanmar	Trade	Yes
S.Res.339	1-Oct-2007	2007	G. W. Bush	Senate	John Kerry	26	Sense of Senate regarding situation in Burma	Myanmar	Human rights	No
H.Con.Res.200	3-Oct-2007	2007	G. W. Bush	House	Peter King	41	Sense of Congress regarding immediate release of Aung San Suu Kyi and human rights in Burma	Myanmar	Human rights	Yes
H.R.4286	6-May-2008	2008	G. W. Bush	Became Law	Joseph Crowley	291	To award Congressional Gold Medal to Aung San Suu Kyi	Myanmar	Human rights	Yes
H.Con.Res.317	7-May-2008	2008	G. W. Bush	House	Rush Holt	50	Concerning Burmese regime's undemocratic draft constitution and scheduled referendum	Myanmar	Elections	Yes
S.Res.554	7-May-2008	2008	G. W. Bush	Senate	John Kerry	19	Sense of Senate on humanitarian assistance to Burma after Cyclone Nargis	Myanmar	Natural disaster	Yes
H.Res.1181	13-May-2008	2008	G. W. Bush	House	Joseph Crowley	33	Condolences to Burma after Cyclone Nargis	Myanmar	Natural disaster	No
H.Res.1341	15-Jul-2008	2008	G. W. Bush	House	Howard Berman	0	Concurrence by House with Senate on H.Res.3890 (Burmese JADE Act)	Myanmar	Human rights	Yes
H.J.Res.93	29-Jul-2008	2008	G. W. Bush	Became Law	Joseph Crowley	32	Renewal of import restrictions contained in Burmese Freedom and Democracy Act	Myanmar	Trade	Yes

Bill	Date	Year	President	Status	Sponsor	Cosponsors	Title	Country	Topic	Became Law
H.R.3890	29-Jul-2008	2008	G. W. Bush	Became Law	Tom Lantos	40	Tom Lantos Block Burmese Junta's Anti-Democratic Efforts (JADE) Act of 2008	Myanmar	Human rights	Yes
H.Res.1370	30-Jul-2008	2008	G. W. Bush	House	Howard Berman	19	Calling China to end human rights abuses and support for government of Burma	Myanmar	Human rights	Yes
S.Res.160	21-May-2009	2009	Obama	Senate	Judd Gregg	11	Condemning actions of SPDC against Aung San Suu Kyi and calling for her release	Myanmar	Human rights	Yes
H.J.Res.56	28-Jul-2009	2009	Obama	Became Law	Joseph Crowley	29	Renewal of import restrictions contained in Burmese Freedom and Democracy Act	Myanmar	Trade	Yes
S.Res.480	7-May-2010	2010	Obama	Senate	Judd Gregg	6	Condemning detention of Aung San Suu Kyi	Myanmar	Human rights	Yes
H.J.Res.83	27-Jul-2010	2010	Obama	Became Law	Joseph Crowley	21	Renewal of import restrictions contained in Burmese Freedom and Democracy Act	Myanmar	Trade	Yes
H.Res.1677	18-Nov-2010	2010	Obama	House	Donald Manzullo	14	Condemning Burmese regime's undemocratic elections of November 7, 2010	Myanmar	Elections	Yes
H.J.Res.66	15-Sep-2011	2011	Obama	Both chambers	Joseph Crowley	11	Renewal of import restrictions contained in Burmese Freedom and Democracy Act	Myanmar	Trade	Yes
H.Con.Res.135	3-Aug-2012	2012	Obama	House	Joseph Crowley	0	Authorizing use of rotunda of the Capital for presentation of Congressional Gold Medal to Aung San Suu Kyi	Myanmar	Human rights	No
H.R.6431	5-Oct-2012	2012	Obama	Became Law	Edward Royce	0	U.S. flexibility to support assistance provided by international financial institutions to Burma	Myanmar	Cooperation	Yes

(Continued)

(Continued)

Reference	Last action	Year	Presidency	Level passed	Sponsor	Cosponsors	Title (abbreviated)	Country	Issue area	Affect U.S. foreign policy?
H.Res.418	7-May-2014	2014	Obama	House	James McGovern	50	Urge Burma to end persecution of Rohingya	Myanmar	Human rights	Yes
S.Res.320	16-Dec-2015	2015	Obama	Senate	John McCain	3	Congratulating Burma on commitment to peaceful elections	Myanmar	Elections	No
H.Res.404	9-Jun-1998	1998	Clinton	House	Benjamin Gilman	18	Commemorating 100 years of relations between United States and Philippines	Philippines	Cooperation	No
S.Res.235	12-Jun-1998	1998	Clinton	Senate	Daniel Akaka	28	Commemorating 100 years of relations between United States and Philippines	Philippines	Cooperation	No
S.Con.Res.91	11-Dec-2001	2001	G. W. Bush	Senate	Jesse Helms	3	Gratitude to Philippines for sympathy and support after September 11	Philippines	Terrorism	No
H.Con.Res.273	19-Dec-2001	2001	G. W. Bush	House	Dana Rohrabacher	34	Reaffirming special relationship between United States and Philippines	Philippines	Cooperation	Yes
S.Res.152	21-May-2003	2003	G. W. Bush	Senate	Richard Lugar	1	Welcoming president of Philippines and gratitude for strong cooperation	Philippines	Cooperation	No
H.Res.800	15-Oct-2009	2009	Obama	House	Jackie Speier	78	Sympathy for dealing with Tropical Storm Ketsana and Typhoon Parma	Philippines	Natural disaster	No
H.Con.Res.218	19-Dec-2009	2009	Obama	House	Howard Berman	22	Sympathy for 57 civilians killed in southern Philippines on November 23, 2009	Philippines	Terrorism	No

Bill	Date	Year	President	Chamber	Sponsor	No.	Title	Scope	Topic	Passed
S.Res.481	5-Jun-2012	2012	Obama	Senate	Richard Lugar	6	Celebrating 60th anniversary of U.S.–Philippines Mutual Defense Treaty	Philippines	Cooperation	Yes
S.Res.292	14-Nov-2013	2013	Obama	Senate	Brian Schatz	13	Support for victims of typhoon in the Philippines	Philippines	Natural disaster	No
H.R.3771	25-Mar-2014	2014	Obama	Became Law	Eric Swalwell	35	Philippines Charitable Giving Assistance Act	Philippines	Cooperation	Yes
S.1821	25-Mar-2014	2014	Obama	Senate	Hirono Mazie	3	Philippines Charitable Giving Assistance Act	Philippines	Cooperation	Yes
S.Con.Res.29	28-Jun-1993	1993	Clinton	Senate	Harlan Matthews	25	Relating to Asia Pacific Economic Cooperation (APEC)	Regional	Trade	Yes
H.Con.Res.113	13-Oct-1993	1993	Clinton	House	Jim McDermott	11	Relating to APEC	Regional	Trade	Yes
S.Res.97	22-Jun-1995	1995	Clinton	Senate	Craig Thomas	12	Sense of Senate on peace and stability in South China Sea	Regional	South China Sea	Yes
S.Con.Res.48	8-Sep-1999	1999	Clinton	Senate	Craig Thomas	3	Relating to APEC	Regional	Trade	Yes
S.Con.Res.58	11-Dec-2001	2001	G. W. Bush	Both chambers	Daniel Akaka	1	Support for 10th meeting of Asia Pacific Parliamentary Forum	Regional	Cooperation	No
H.Res.12	4-Jan-2005	2005	G. W. Bush	House	Henry Hyde	39	Sympathy for loss of life caused by tsunami on December 26, 2004	Regional	Natural disaster	No
S.Res.305	6-Oct-2009	2009	Obama	Senate	Dianne Feinstein	2	Support for victims of natural disasters in Indonesia, Cambodia, Vietnam, Philippines, and others	Regional	Natural disaster	No
S.Res.217	27-Jun-2011	2011	Obama	Senate	Jim Webb	3	Peaceful resolution of maritime territorial disputes	Regional	South China Sea	Yes

(Continued)

Reference	Last action	Year	Presidency	Level passed	Sponsor	Cosponsors	Title (abbreviated)	Country	Issue area	Affect U.S. foreign policy?
H.R.2042	3-Nov-2011	2011	Obama	House	Rick Larsen	19	APEC Business Travel Cards Act 2011	Regional	Trade	No
S.1487	12-Nov-2011	2011	Obama	Senate	Maria Cantwell	2	APEC Business Travel Cards Act 2011	Regional	Trade	No
S.Res.524	2-Aug-2012	2012	Obama	Senate	John Kerry	7	Support for Declaration of Conduct in South China Sea	Regional	South China Sea	Yes
S.Res.167	29-Jul-2013	2013	Obama	Senate	Robert Menendez	5	Support for peaceful resolution of territorial, sovereignty, and jurisdictional disputes in Asia Pacific	Regional	South China Sea	Yes
S.Res.412	10-Jul-2014	2014	Obama	Senate	Robert Menendez	7	Support for freedom of navigation and internationally lawful uses of sea in Asia Pacific	Regional	South China Sea	Yes
S.Res.462	24-Jul-2014	2014	Obama	Senate	Marco Rubio	4	Recognizing Khmer and Lao/Hmong freedom fighters of Cambodia and Laos during conflict in Southeast Asia	Regional	Vietnam War	No
H.Res.714	3-Dec-2014	2014	Obama	House	Eni Faleomavaega	6	Support for peaceful resolution of disputes in South China and East China Sea	Regional	South China Sea	Yes
S.Con.Res.42	7-May-2003	2003	G. W. Bush	Senate	Christopher Bond	4	Resolution welcoming the prime minister of Singapore	Singapore	Cooperation	No
H.Res.329	23-Jul-2003	2003	G. W. Bush	House	David Dreier	0	Providing for consideration to implement U.S.–Chile and U.S.–Singapore free trade agreements (FTAs)	Singapore	Trade	Yes

Bill	Date	Year	President	Chamber	Sponsor	Cosponsors	Title	Country	Category	Passed
S.Res.211	31-Jul-2003	2003	G. W. Bush	Senate	Jeff Sessions	11	Sense of Senate regarding Chile and Singapore FTA temporary provisions	Singapore	Trade	Yes
H.R.2739	3-Sep-2003	2003	G. W. Bush	Became Law	Tom DeLay	1	U.S.–Singapore FTA Implementation Act	Singapore	Trade	Yes
S.Res.344	3-May-2004	2004	G. W. Bush	Senate	Christopher Bond	1	Resolution welcoming the prime minister of Singapore	Singapore	Cooperation	No
S.Res.196	12-Jul-2005	2005	G. W. Bush	Senate	Christopher Bond	1	Resolution welcoming the prime minister of Singapore	Singapore	Cooperation	No
S.Res.515	14-Jul-2016	2016	Obama	Senate	Benjamin Cardin	2	Resolution welcoming the prime minister of Singapore	Singapore	Cooperation	No
H.Res.374	23-Jul-2016	2016	Obama	House	Denny Heck	29	Reaffirming Singapore's strategic partnership with United States	Singapore	Cooperation	Yes
S.Res.174	11-Mar-1998	1998	Clinton	Senate	William Roth Jr	4	Sense of Senate that Thailand is a key partner of United States	Thailand	Cooperation	Yes
S.Con.Res.150	10-Aug-2002	2002	G. W. Bush	Senate	Christopher Bond	0	Welcoming Queen Sirikit to United States	Thailand	Cooperation	No
H.Con.Res.492	17-Oct-2002	2002	G. W. Bush	House	Dana Rohrabacher	4	Welcoming Queen Sirikit to United States	Thailand	Cooperation	No
H.Con.Res.409	22-Jun-2006	2006	G. W. Bush	Both chambers	James Leach	29	60th anniversary of ascension of King Bhumibol Adulyadej	Thailand	Cooperation	No
S.Con.Res.66	11-Mar-2008	2008	G. W. Bush	Senate	Jim Webb	7	175th anniversary of special relationship between United States and Thailand	Thailand	Cooperation	No
H.Con.Res.290	12-Mar-2008	2008	G. W. Bush	House	Donald Manzullo	30	175th anniversary of special relationship between United States and Thailand	Thailand	Cooperation	No

(Continued)

(Continued)

Reference	Last action	Year	Presidency	Level passed	Sponsor	Cosponsors	Title (abbreviated)	Country	Issue area	Affect U.S. foreign policy?
S.Res.538	24-May-2010	2010	Obama	Senate	Jim Webb	3	Support of United States for alliance with Thailand	Thailand	Cooperation	Yes
H.Res.1321	1-Jul-2010	2010	Obama	House	Eni Faleomavaega	29	Support of United States for alliance with Thailand	Thailand	Cooperation	Yes
S.Res.469	28-Sep-2010	2010	Obama	Senate	Richard Lugar	3	60th anniversary of Fulbright program in Thailand	Thailand	Cooperation	No
S.Res.343	5-Dec-2011	2011	Obama	Senate	John Kerry	3	84th birthday of King Bhumibol Adulyadej	Thailand	Cooperation	No
S.Res.77	9-Apr-2013	2013	Obama	Senate	Robert Menendez	3	Sense of Congress commemorating 180th anniversary of diplomatic relations between United States and Thailand	Thailand	Cooperation	No
H.Con.Res.405	22-May-2002	2002	G. W. Bush	House	Christopher Smith	19	Commemorating independence of East Timor and commending president for promptly establishing diplomatic relations	Timor-Leste	Cooperation	Yes
S.Con.Res.109	4-Jun-2002	2002	G. W. Bush	Senate	Lincoln Chafee	2	Commemorating independence of East Timor	Timor-Leste	Cooperation	No
S.J.Res.168	25-May-1994	1994	Clinton	Became Law	Charles Robb	18	Designating May 11, 1994, as Vietnam Human Rights Day	Vietnam	Human rights	Yes
H.Con.Res.216	8-Oct-1994	1994	Clinton	House	Benjamin Gilman	10	Sense of Congress regarding human rights in Vietnam	Vietnam	Human rights	Yes
H.Con.Res.278	8-Oct-1994	1994	Clinton	House	Gary Ackerman	1	Sense of Congress regarding U.S. policy to Vietnam	Vietnam	Human rights	Yes

Bill	Date	Year	President	Chamber	Sponsor	No.	Description	Country	Category	Passed
S.Res.174	19-Sep-1995	1995	Clinton	Senate	Rod Grams	3	Sense of Senate that secretary of state should aggressively pursue release of political prisoners in Vietnam	Vietnam	Human rights	Yes
H.Res.231	13-Nov-1997	1997	Clinton	House	Dana Rohrabacher	7	Urge president to make clear American commitment to democracy and religious and economic freedom for Vietnam	Vietnam	Human rights	Yes
H.Res.360	12-Feb-1998	1998	Clinton	House	Newt Gingrich	13	Recognizing courage of Vietnam vets and calling for full accounting of MIAs	Vietnam	Conflict	No
S.Res.177	12-Feb-1998	1998	Clinton	Senate	Paul Coverdell	5	Recognizing courage of Vietnam vets and calling for full accounting of MIAs	Vietnam	Conflict	No
S.Res.196	17-Mar-1998	1998	Clinton	Senate	Trent Lott	99	Recognizing John McCain and calling for full accounting of MIAs in Vietnam	Vietnam	Conflict	No
H.Con.Res.295	4-May-2000	2000	Clinton	House	Dana Rohrabacher	6	Continuing human rights violations and oppression in Vietnam	Vietnam	Human rights	Yes
H.Con.Res.322	11-Jul-2000	2000	Clinton	House	Tom Davis	21	Sense of Congress regarding Vietnamese Americans who seek to improve conditions in Vietnam	Vietnam	Cooperation	Yes
H.R.2833	14-Sep-2001	2001	G. W. Bush	House	Christopher Smith	13	Vietnam Human Rights Act	Vietnam	Human rights	Yes
S.Res.167	3-Oct-2001	2001	G. W. Bush	Senate	John McCain	6	Recognizing Douglas Peterson for service to United States as ambassador to Vietnam	Vietnam	Cooperation	No

(Continued)

Reference	Last action	Year	Presidency	Level passed	Sponsor	Cosponsors	Title (abbreviated)	Country	Issue area	Affect U.S. foreign policy?
H.J.Res.51	16-Oct-2001	2001	G. W. Bush	Became Law	Richard Armey	2	Extension of nondiscriminatory treatment to products from Vietnam	Vietnam	Trade	Yes
H.Res.62	28-Feb-2003	2003	G. W. Bush	House	Tom DeLay	80	Recognizing courage of Vietnam vets and calling for full accounting of MIAs	Vietnam	Conflict	No
H.Res.427	19-Nov-2003	2003	G. W. Bush	House	Loretta Sanchez	22	Sense of the House on courageous leadership of United Buddhist Church of Vietnam	Vietnam	Human rights	No
H.Res.613	11-May-2004	2004	G. W. Bush	House	Tom Davis	7	Recognizing Vietnam Human Rights Day	Vietnam	Human rights	Yes
H.Con.Res.378	13-May-2004	2004	G. W. Bush	House	Christopher Smith	106	Calling on Vietnam to release Father Thaddeus Nguyen Van Ly	Vietnam	Human rights	Yes
H.R.1587	23-Jul-2004	2004	G. W. Bush	House	Christopher Smith	35	Vietnam Human Rights Act 2004	Vietnam	Human rights	Yes
H.Con.Res.320	6-Apr-2006	2006	G. W. Bush	House	Christopher Smith	34	Calling Vietnam to release Dr. Pham Hong Son, political prisoners, and prisoners of conscience	Vietnam	Human rights	Yes
H.Res.415	19-Sep-2006	2006	G. W. Bush	House	Loretta Sanchez	26	Sense of House that Vietnam do more to resolve claims for confiscated property	Vietnam	Human rights	Yes
H.Res.243	2-May-2007	2007	G. W. Bush	House	Christopher Smith	29	Calling Vietnam to release political prisoners and prisoners of conscience	Vietnam	Human rights	Yes

Bill	Date	Year	President	Chamber	Sponsor	No.	Title	Country	Topic	Became law
H.R.3096	19-Sep-2007	2007	G. W. Bush	House	Christopher Smith	12	Vietnam Human Rights Act 2007	Vietnam	Human rights	Yes
H.Res.986	22-May-2008	2008	G. W. Bush	House	John Boehner	57	Recognizing courage of Vietnam vets and calling for full accounting of MIAs	Vietnam	Vietnam War	No
H.Res.672	21-Oct-2009	2009	Obama	House	Loretta Sanchez	21	Calling on Vietnam to release imprisoned bloggers	Vietnam	Human rights	Yes
H.Res.20	17-Dec-2010	2010	Obama	House	Edward Royce	27	Calling on State Department to list Vietnam as "Country of Particular Concern" over religious freedom	Vietnam	Human rights	Yes
H.Res.484	11-Sep-2012	2012	Obama	House	Loretta Sanchez	29	Calling Vietnam to respect basic human rights and cease abusing national security provisions	Vietnam	Human rights	Yes
H.R.1410	12-Sep-2012	2012	Obama	House	Christopher Smith	15	Vietnam Human Rights Act 2012	Vietnam	Human rights	Yes
H.R.1897	9-Sep-2013	2013	Obama	House	Christopher Smith	16	Vietnam Human Rights Act 2013	Vietnam	Human rights	Yes
S.J.Res.36	1-Aug-2014	2014	Obama	Senate	Robert Menendez	2	Approval for nuclear cooperation between United States and Vietnam	Vietnam	Cooperation	Yes
H.R.2140	20-May-2015	2015	Obama	Became Law	Christopher Smith	18	Vietnam Human Rights Act 2015	Vietnam	Human rights	Yes
S.2632	3-Mar-2016	2016	Obama	Became Law	Bill Cassidy	1	Vietnam Human Rights Act 2016	Vietnam	Human rights	Yes

Figure A-1. Congressional Bills Relating to Southeast Asia (1993–2016)

Number of bills

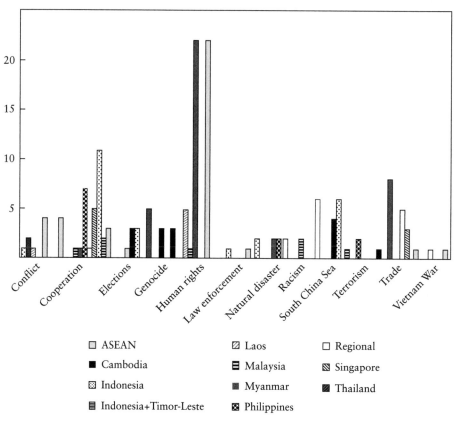

ASEAN   Laos   Regional
Cambodia   Malaysia   Singapore
Indonesia   Myanmar   Thailand
Indonesia+Timor-Leste   Philippines

Source: Author.

Notes

PREFACE

1. Saul Bernard Cohen, *Geopolitics: The Geography of International Relations*, 3d ed. (London: Rowman & Littlefield, 2015), p. 48.

2. See Joseph Chinyong Liow and Ang Cheng Guan, "The Fall of Saigon: Southeast Asian Perspectives," *Brookings South East Asia View*, no. 2, April 2015.

CHAPTER 1

1. Interview with a former official from the Department of Defense, Washington, D.C., February 9, 2015.

2. In fact, it can be argued that in spite of the ZOPFAN declaration, as early as the Third Indochina War—when Vietnam invaded Cambodia—ASEAN states were already looking for external powers to play a major role in the resolution of the conflict. See Ang Cheng Guan, *Singapore, ASEAN, and the Cambodian Conflict, 1978–1991* (National University of Singapore Press, 2015).

3. Natasha Hamilton-Hart, *Hard Interests, Soft Illusions: Southeast Asia and American Power* (Cornell University Press, 2012), p. 88.

4. Graham Allison and Robert Blackwill, "Interview: Lee Kuan Yew on the Future of U.S.–China Relations," *The Atlantic*, March 5, 2013.

5. Truong Tan Sang, "Remarks at Working Lunch with John Kerry," Washington, D.C., July 24, 2013.

6. Jared Diamond, *Guns, Germs, and Steel: The Fates of Human Societies* (New York: W. W. Norton, 1997); David Landes, *The Wealth and Poverty of Nations: Why Some Are So Rich and Some So Poor* (New York: W. W. Norton, 1998).

7. Colin S. Gray, "Geography and Grand Strategy," *Comparative Strategy* 10, no. 4, 1991, p. 311.

8. The costliest signal is a readiness to engage in a military conflict in the region as it did with the Vietnam War.

9. Indeed, one could argue that this explains at least in part why Southeast Asian states care so much about seemingly trivial matters like who the American administration sends to regional meetings and summits.

10. Interview with a serving member of Congress, Washington, D.C., December 10, 2015.

11. Brantly Womack, "Southeast Asia and American Strategic Options," in *Obligations of Empire*, edited by James Hentz (University of Kentucky Press, 2004), pp. 175–95.

12. For instance, for security planners Southeast Asia became an integral part of the new concept of the "East Asian littoral," which essentially comprises the first island chain. Meanwhile, economics and trade officials ramped up exploration of free trade agreements with various Southeast Asian states during this period.

13. The U.S. presidential election of November 8, 2016, was won by a candidate—Donald Trump—who campaigned on a platform that, among other things, rejected the TPPA. Upon his inauguration on January 20, 2017, one of Donald Trump's first acts as president of the United States was to sign an executive order withdrawing the United States from the TPPA.

14. Robert C. Horn, "Southeast Asian Perspectives of U.S. Foreign Policy," *Asian Survey* 25, no. 6, June 1985.

CHAPTER 2

1. Consider the three chapters on Southeast Asian cases in *The New U.S. Strategy towards Asia*, edited by William T. Tow and Douglas Stuart (London: Routledge, 2015).

2. This view was expressed to the author in the course of discussions with Thai and Indonesian officials.

3. The tone and discourse of such views are summarized in Alice Ba, "Systemic Neglect? A Reconsideration of U.S.–Southeast Asia Policy," *Contemporary Southeast Asia* 31, no. 3, 2009, pp. 370–71.

4. Abdullah Badawi, "Creating a Better Understanding of ASEAN–United States Relations," speech delivered at the Asia Society, New York, September 15, 2005.

5. "Finding Our Way: Debating American Grand Strategy," Center for a New American Security, 2008 (http://www.cnas.org/files/documents/publications /FlournoyBrimley_Finding%20Our%20Way_June08.pdf).

6. See Barry R. Posen, *Restraint: A New Foundation for U.S. Grand Strategy* (Cornell University Press, 2014).

7. See Stephen G. Brooks and William C. Wohlforth, *World out of Balance: International Relations and the Challenge of American Primacy* (Princeton

University Press, 2008); John J. Mearsheimer, *The Tragedy of Great Power Politics* (New York: W. W. Norton, 2014). Mearsheimer echoes Hans J. Morgenthau, *In Defense of the National Interest: A Critical Examination of American Foreign Policy* (New York: Alfred A. Knopf, 1951).

8. The White House, *National Security Strategy 1996*, February 1996.

9. The White House, *National Security Strategy 2002*, September 2002.

10. The White House, *National Security Strategy 2010*, May 2010.

11. Barack Obama, "State of the Union Address," January 26, 2013.

12. National Intelligence Council, "Global Trends 2030: Alternative Worlds," December 2012, p. x.

13. Ibid, p. xii.

14. House of Representatives, Subcommittee on East Asia and the Pacific, Committee on International Relations, *Southeast Asia after 9/11: Regional Trends and U.S. Interests.* 107th Cong., 1st sess., December 12, 2001.

15. Steve Yetiv, *The Absence of Grand Strategy: The United States in the Persian Gulf* (Johns Hopkins University Press, 2008).

16. David Baldwin, *Economic Statecraft* (Princeton University Press, 1985), p. 8.

17. See Dov Zakheim, *A Vulcan's Tale: How the Bush Administration Mismanaged the Reconstruction of Afghanistan* (Brookings, 2011).

18. A fine study that illuminates this challenge for American foreign policy is Hal Brands, *What Good Is Grand Strategy? Power and Purpose in American Statecraft from Harry S. Truman to George W. Bush* (Cornell University Press, 2015).

19. Robert Kagan, *The World America Made* (New York: Vintage Books, 2013), pp. 14–15.

20. Consider, for instance, Joseph M. Grieco, "Realism and Regionalism: American Power and German and Japanese Institutional Strategies during and after the Cold War," in *Unipolar Politics: Realism and Regional Strategies after the Cold War,* edited by Ethan Kapstein and Michael Mastanduno (Columbia University Press, 1999), pp. 107–31; Peter J. Katzenstein, *A World of Regions: Asia and Europe in the American Imperium* (Cornell University Press, 2005); Mark Beeson, "American Hegemony and Regionalism: The Rise of East Asia and the End of the Asia-Pacific," *Geopolitics* 11, no. 4, 2006, pp. 541–60; Michael Mastanduno, "The United States: Regional Strategies and Global Commitments," in *Security Politics in the Asia Pacific: A Regional–Global Nexus?* edited by William Tow (Cambridge University Press, 2009), pp. 67–84.

21. The subsequent economic data were obtained from *ASEAN Matters for America; America Matters for ASEAN* (Honolulu: East-West Center, 2014) (http://www.asiamattersforamerica.org/sites/all/themes/eastwestcenter/pdfs/Asean_Matters_for_America_brochure2.pdf).

22. Whereas TIFA was an American initiative, it is important to remember that the TPPA was not. It originated as an ongoing discussion between Brunei, Chile, New Zealand, and Singapore under the auspices of the Trans-Pacific Strategic Economic Partnership Agreement (TPSEP). The United States joined

the discussion in 2008, and the agreement itself soon morphed into what is now known as the TPPA.

23. There is, nonetheless, an important caveat to register: although the figures of U.S. FDI (foreign direct investment) in Singapore dwarf those of other Southeast Asian states, it should be recognized that Singapore is frequently used as a base from which U.S. companies invest in the rest of the region. Consequently, such investments, although originating from U.S. corporations, may be recorded as Singaporean investments rather than U.S. investments into other regional economies. Although there is no way to parse the investment data, even allowing for this anomaly it is highly likely that U.S. investments in Singapore that stay in Singapore still outweigh those going to other states in the region.

24. A Congressman who was otherwise very sympathetic toward the need for deeper American interest in and engagement with Southeast Asia also shared the political constraints he faces, with an estimated 30 percent of jobs in his constituency that could potentially be lost to Asia as a result of the TPPA. Interview, Washington, D.C., December 10, 2015.

25. Of course, the freedom of commercial shipping is also understandably a matter of interest to other regional powers as well, including China, strategic competitor of the United States in the region.

26. The American defense policy establishment remains exercised by this question of how far to the brink they are prepared to go to push back, at the behest of regional allies, Chinese assertiveness in the South China Sea.

27. The point should be made that the alliance with Thailand, often referred to as the oldest alliance of the United States by virtue of the 1833 Treaty of Amity and Cooperation, is today far more form than substance, to the extent that even some younger Thai military officers are unaware of the alliance relationship.

28. Craig Whitlock, "U.S. Seeks Return to SE Asian Bases," *Washington Post*, June 22, 2012.

29. Remarks made at the press briefing on Asia–Pacific U.S. Military Review, Washington, D.C., January 27, 2012.

30. National Intelligence Council, "Global Trends 2030: Alternative Worlds," December 2012, p. ix.

31. Donald Rumsfeld, "The Price of Inaction Can Be Truly Catastrophic," *Asahi Shimbun*, September 10, 2002.

32. The White House, *National Security Strategy 2002*, p. 13.

33. Interview with a serving official from the Department of Defense, Washington, D.C., February 5, 2016.

34. The seminal statement to this effect was made by Kenneth Waltz, *Theory of International Politics* (New York: McGraw-Hill, 1979).

35. At the same time, it is important to recognize that there is also a body of literature that argues for domestic politics to be considered a key determinant of strategy and foreign policy. See, for instance, Jack Snyder, *Myths of Empire: Domestic Politics and International Ambition* (Cornell University Press, 1991);

Bruce Bueno de Mesquita and David Lalman, *War and Reason: Domestic and International Imperatives* (Yale University Press, 1994); Helen Milner and Robert Keohane, eds., *Internationalization and Domestic Politics* (Cambridge University Press, 1996).

36. So, too, it can be argued, does the impetus of isolationism, although its ideological influence on American foreign policy has arguably waned over the years. See Henry R. Nau, *At Home Abroad: Identity and Power in American Foreign Policy* (Cornell University Press, 2002).

37. The terms "values-based diplomacy" and "moral foreign policy" were used by Assistant Secretary of State for East Asian and Pacific Affairs Daniel Russel, in a talk in Singapore on January 22, 2016.

38. See Morton H. Halperin, Priscilla A. Clapp, and Arnold Kanter, *Bureaucratic Politics and Foreign Policy*, 2d ed. (Brookings, 2006).

39. Joel S. Migdal, *State in Society: Studying How States and Societies Transform Each Other and Constitute One Another* (Cambridge University Press, 2001), pp. 15–16.

40. Barack Obama, White House Press Conference, October 2, 2015.

41. Interview included in the documentary *Last Days in Vietnam*. Directed by Rory Kennedy; released January 17, 2014.

42. James Hookway, Natasha Brereton-Fukui, and Peter Nicholas, "Obama Absence Gives China Opening," *Asian Wall Street Journal*, October 4, 2013.

43. Jane Perlez, "Cancellation of Trip by Obama Plays to Doubts of Asia Allies," *New York Times*, October 4, 2013.

44. Graham Allison and Robert Blackwill, "Interview: Lee Kuan Yew on the Future of U.S.–China Relations," *The Atlantic*, March 5, 2013.

45. As Stewart Patrick observed, despite its purported advocacy for an "assertive multilateralism," the Clinton administration "demonstrated a growing willingness to act alone and to opt out of multilateral initiatives." See Stewart Patrick, "America's Retreat from Multilateral Engagement," *Current History* 99, December 2000, pp. 430–39.

46. See Samuel P. Huntington, "The Lonely Superpower," *Foreign Affairs* 78, no. 2, March/April 1999, p. 42. As Indian author Arundhati Roy has put it, "American foreign policy has created a huge, simmering reservoir of resentment." Quoted in Stephen M. Walt, *Taming American Power: The Global Response to American Primacy* (New York: W. W. Norton, 2005), p. 68.

47. Interview with a former senior official from the Department of Defense, Washington, D.C., February 9, 2016.

48. For more on the limited role of Congress in foreign policy, see Marie T. Henehan, *Foreign Policy and Congress: An International Relations Perspective* (University of Michigan Press, 2000). The précis states: "Henehan argues that the only way to understand the way congressional behavior varies over time is by looking at the rise and resolution of critical issues in foreign policy, which in turn have their origin in the international system. When a critical foreign policy issue arises, congressional activity and attempts to influence foreign policy

increase. Once the debate is resolved and one side wins, a consensus emerges and Congress settles into a more passive role."

49. Indeed, it was partly to respond to such criticisms that the ASEAN Charter, which bestows upon ASEAN a legal identity as an international organization, was instituted.

50. ASEAN's narrative of centrality is predicated on the role the organization played in the final decade of the Cold War to muster international support in order to block the puppet regime of Heng Samrin, installed with Hanoi's backing after Vietnam's invasion of Cambodia in 1978, from taking the Kampuchean seat at the United Nations.

51. Hillary Clinton, speech delivered at Honolulu, Hawaii, on October 28, 2010 (www.cfr.org/asia-and-pacific/clintons-speech-americas-engagement-asia -pacific-october-2010/p23280).

52. Mark Beeson, "ASEAN Plus Three and the Rise of Reactionary Regionalism," *Contemporary Southeast Asia* 25, no. 2, August 2003, p. 251.

53. Bilahari Kausikan, "ASEAN Centrality and Regional Security," paper delivered at the Conference on Regional Integration in the Indo-Pacific: Prospects and Challenges, New Delhi, November 24–25, 2014.

54. See Alice Ba, "ASEAN Centrality Imperiled? ASEAN Institutionalism and the Challenges of Major Power Institutionalization," in *ASEAN and the Institutionalization of East Asia*, edited by Ralf Emmers (New York: Routledge, 2011), p. 122.

55. Shaune Narine, *Explaining ASEAN: Regionalism in Southeast Asia* (London: Lynne Rienner Publishers, 2002), p. 189.

56. Interview with a senior Cambodian official, Phnom Penh, January 25, 2017. From 1972 to 1974, the United States financed $274 million worth of purchases of cotton, rice, and wheat flour during the anticommunist administration of Prime Minister Lon Nol, freeing up the immediate financial burden for the government in order to allow it to focus on ill-fated efforts to prevent the Khmer Rouge from taking over the country. With interest, the accumulated debt is now more than $400 million and remains a source of friction for the two countries.

CHAPTER 3

1. Stephen M. Walt, "Two Cheers for Clinton's Foreign Policy," *Foreign Affairs* 79, no. 2, March/April 2000, p. 63.

2. James M. McCormick, "Clinton and Foreign Policy: Some Legacies for a New Century," in *The Postmodern Presidency: Bill Clinton's Legacy in U.S. Politics*, edited by Steven E. Schier (University of Pittsburgh Press, 2009), p. 61.

3. Anthony G. McGrew and Chris Brook, *Asia-Pacific in the New World Order* (London: Routledge, 1998), p. 172.

4. Michael Cox, Timothy J. Lynch, and Nicholas Bouchet, *U.S. Foreign Policy and Democracy Promotion: From Theodore Roosevelt to Barack Obama* (London: Routledge, 2013), p. 159.

5. Ibid., p. 164.

6. Bob Catley, "Hegemonic America: The Benign Superpower?" *Contemporary Southeast Asia* 18, no. 4, 1997, p. 394.

7. Interview with a former senior Defense Department official, Washington, D.C., February 12, 2016.

8. Byung-joon Ahn, "The United States in Asia: Defining a New Role," in *The New Asia-Pacific Order*, edited by Chan Heng Chee (Singapore: Institute of Southeast Asian Studies, 1997), p. 147.

9. Goh Chok Tong, "ASEAN–U.S. Relations: Challenges," speech delivered at the Asia Society, New York, September 7, 2000.

10. Lewis M. Stern, "Diverging Roads: 21st Century U.S.–Thai Defense Relations," *Strategic Forum*, no. 241, June 2009, p. 3.

11. Ibid., p. 2.

12. Chalidaporn Songsamphan, "Thailand: Slow Government, Sluggish Democratization," in *Southeast Asian Affairs 1995,* edited by Daljit Singh and Liak Teng Kiat (Singapore: Institute of Southeast Asian Studies, 1995), p. 340.

13. Stern, "Diverging Roads," p. 2.

14. Donald Weatherbee, "Southeast Asia at Mid-Decade: Independence through Interdependence," in *Southeast Asian Affairs 1995*, edited by Singh and Liak, p. 16.

15. Earlier in March, U.S. ambassador David Lamberston had suggested that the Thai military had not cut off ties with the Khmer Rouge. This triggered a strong protest in response by the Thai government, which was in turn sensationalized in the local press. A few months later, former U.S. ambassador Morton Abramowitz wrote that Khmer Rouge successes owed something to Thai support and urged the United States and its allies to pressure Thailand regarding the matter. This led to another outcry and suggestions that Abramowitz be barred from entering the country. See Songsamphan, "Thailand: Slow Government, Sluggish Democratization," p. 340.

16. Ahn, "The United States in Asia," p. 150.

17. Marvin Kalb and Deborah Kalb, *Haunting Legacy: Vietnam and the American Presidency from Ford to Obama* (Brookings, 2011), p. 152.

18. Ibid., p. 153.

19. Weatherbee, "Southeast Asia at Mid-Decade," p. 16.

20. John Garver, "China's Push through the South China Sea: The Interaction of Bureaucratic and National Interests," *China Quarterly*, no. 132, 1992.

21. Although the government of South Vietnam had requested assistance from the U.S. seventh fleet, the latter was instructed not to intervene, in line with American withdrawal from the region after the signing of the Paris Peace Agreements in January 1973. See Ngo Minh Tri and Koh Swee Lean Collin, "Lessons from the Battle of the Paracel Islands," *The Diplomat*, January 23, 2014 (http://thediplomat.com/2014/01/lessons-from-the-battle-of-the-paracel-islands/).

22. Taylor M. Fravel, "The U.S. and China in Regional Security—Session IV: What Issues and Whose Core Interests?" Discussion Paper (Berlin: Konrad-

Adenauer-Stiftung and Stiftung Wissenschaft und Politik, 2012), p. 4. Fravel quotes from Daily Press Briefing, U.S. Department of State, May 10, 1995 (http://dosfan.lib.uic.edu/ERC/briefing/daily_briefings/1995/9505/950510db .html).

23. Charles H. Stevenson, "U.S. Foreign Policy in Southeast Asia: Implications for Current Regional Issues," *Contemporary Southeast Asia* 14, no. 2, 1992, p. 103.

24. See Evelyn Goh, "Great Powers and Hierarchical Order in Southeast Asia: Analyzing Regional Security Strategies," *International Security* 32, no. 3, 2007.

25. Sheldon Simon, "U.S. Strategy and Southeast Asian Security: Issues of Compatibility," *Contemporary Southeast Asia* 14, no. 4, 1993, p. 303.

26. Ibid., p. 307.

27. Ralph A. Cossa, "Evolving U.S. Views on Asia's Future Institutional Architecture," in *Asia's New Multilateralism: Cooperation, Competition, and the Search for Community*, edited by Michael J. Green and Bates Gill (Columbia University Press, 2009), p. 36.

28. See Susumu Awanohara, "Group Therapy," *Far Eastern Economic Review*, April 15, 1993; Evelyn Goh, "The ASEAN Regional Forum in United States East Asian Strategy," *Pacific Review* 17, no. 1, 2004.

29. Jorn Dorsch, "The U.S. and Southeast Asia," in *Contemporary Southeast Asia*, edited by Mark Beeson (London: Palgrave Macmillan, 2008), p. 224.

30. Goh, "The ASEAN Regional Forum in United States East Asian Strategy," p. 53.

31. Ted Galen Carpenter, "Washington's Smothering Strategy: American Interests in East Asia," *World Policy Journal*, Winter 1997/1998, p. 23.

32. T. J. Pempel, "The 'Unbundling' of East Asia," *Global Asia* 3, no. 4, Winter 2008, 78.

33. Mahathir had earlier proposed the establishment of an East Asia Economic Caucus that excluded the United States and viewed Clinton's initiative as competition and a direct affront.

34. Donald E. Weatherbee, *Historical Dictionary of United States-Southeast Asia Relations* (Lanham, Md.: Scarecrow Press, 2008), p. 94.

35. Susan L. Shirk, "The Northeast Asia Cooperation Dialogue: An Experiment in Track II Multilateral Diplomacy," in *Security Cooperation in Northeast Asia: Architecture and Beyond*, edited by T. J. Pempel and Chung-Min Lee (London: Routledge, 2012), p. 208.

36. Bruce Cumings, "The History and Practice of Unilateralism in East Asia," in *East Asian Multilateralism: Prospects for Regional Stability*, edited by Francis Fukuyama (Johns Hopkins University Press, 2008), p. 49.

37. William T. Tow, "Great Powers and Multilateralism: The Politics of Security Architectures in Southeast Asia," in *ASEAN and the Institutionalisation of East Asia*, edited by Ralf Emmers (London: Routledge, 2011), p. 158.

38. Marshall Ingwerson, "U.S., Philippines to Debate Future of Military Bases," *Christian Science Monitor*, May 14, 1990.

39. These comments, reportedly articulated by Francis Underhill while he served as counselor in Manila, were repeated by Senator Jovito Salonga during a congressional debate on the bases. See the *Philippine Star*, September 22, 1991.

40. Lee Poh Ping, "Southeast Asia in 1990: A Year of Challenges," in *Southeast Asian Affairs 1991*, edited by Sharon Siddique and Ng Chee Yuen (Singapore: Institute of Southeast Asian Studies, 1991), p. 15.

41. William E. Berry Jr., *U.S. Bases in the Philippines: The Evolution of a Special Relationship* (Boulder, Colo.: Westview Press, 1989), p. 36.

42. Ibid., p. 82.

43. Senator Millard Tydings was of the view that an American military presence in the Philippines was not intended to subjugate the local population to U.S. hegemony but rather to make sure that a younger generation would not need to experience the horrors of war. In contrast, U.S. secretary of war Henry Stimson argued that the bases were necessary simply because the Philippines would otherwise be unable to defend itself against external aggression. Ibid., p. 13.

44. See *Journal of Senate Hearings*, September 14 and 16, 1991, p. 440, cited in Belinda B. Ella, "Is the U.S.–Philippine Alliance Doomed?" M.Sc. Dissertation, Nanyang Technological University, 2000, p. 22.

45. Charles P. Wallace, "Manila Senate Rejects U.S. Pact," *Los Angeles Times*, September 16, 1991.

46. *Journal of Senate Hearings*, September 14 and 16, 1991, p. 487, cited in Ella, "Is the U.S.–Philippine Alliance Doomed?" p. 24.

47. The twelve senators who voted for Resolution No. 1259 to oppose the treaty were Joseph Estrada, Wigberto Tanada, Teofisto Guingona, Victor Ziga, Ernesto Maceda, Jovito Salonga, Agapito Aquino, Juan Ponce Enrile, Sotero Laurel, Orlando Mercado, Aquilino Pimentel Jr., and Rene Saguisag.

48. "Philippines Ends Bases Agreement," Associated Press, May 15, 1990.

49. Philip Senon, "Philippines Senate Votes to Reject U.S. Base Renewal," *New York Times*, September 16, 1991.

50. Richard Halloran and John Schidlovsky, "Dear President Clinton: Voices from Asia and the Pacific," *Asia-Pacific Issues* 6, 1993, pp. 1–15.

51. Jusuf Wanandi, *Asia Pacific after the Cold War*. Jakarta: Centre for Strategic and International Studies, 1996, pp. 172, 189.

52. Roland G. Simbulan, "Why the Senate Should Reject the VFA," briefing paper submitted to the Philippine Senate on the Visiting Forces Agreement, February 11, 1999; "Another Death Linked to Toxic Wastes: Clark Special Economic Zone," *Philippine Daily Inquirer*, April 4, 2000; "Support the Troops: U.S. Military Should End Its Role in Asian Sex Trade," *San Francisco Chronicle*, June 2, 1999.

53. *Journal of Senate Hearings*, May 26–27, 1999, p. 446, cited in Ella, "Is the U.S.–Philippine Alliance Doomed?" p. 33.

54. Larry Niksch, "Indonesia: U.S. Relations with the Indonesian Military," *CRS Report for Congress*, August 10, 1998 (http://congressionalresearch. com/98-677/document.php?study=INDONESIA+U.S.+RELATIONS+WITH+ THE+INDONESIAN+MILITARY).

55. John B. Haseman and Eduardo Lachica, "Toward a Stronger U.S.–Indonesia Security Relationship," August 2005, p. 27 (http://usindo.org/wp-content /uploads/2010/08/Security_Relations.pdf); Walter Lohman, "U.S.–Indonesia Relations: Build for Endurance, Not Speed" (www.heritage.org/research/reports /2010/03/us-indonesia-relations-build-for-endurance-not-speed).

56. Haseman and Lachica, "Toward a Stronger U.S.–Indonesia Security Relationship," p. 28.

57. Ibid., p. 33.

58. Harold Crouch, "Indonesia: An Uncertain Outlook," in *Southeast Asian Affairs 1994*, edited by Daljit Singh (Singapore: Institute of Southeast Asian Studies, 1994), p. 138.

59. Angel Rabasa and John Haseman, *The Military and Democracy in Indonesia: Challenges, Politics, and Power* (Washington, D.C.: RAND, 2002), p. 114 (www.rand.org/content/dam/rand/pubs/monograph_reports/2002 /MR1599.pdf).

60. Crouch, "Indonesia: An Uncertain Outlook," p. 138.

61. Ibid., p. 39.

62. Rabasa and Haseman, *The Military and Democracy in Indonesia*, p. 114.

63. "Background on East Timor and U.S. Policy," *East Timor Action Network* (http://etan.org/timor/BkgMnu.htm).

64. Niksch, "Indonesia."

65. "Background on East Timor and U.S. Policy."

66. John Bresnan, "Indonesia and U.S. Policy," Discussion Paper No. 4, Discussion Paper Series APEC Study Center, Columbia University, June 1997, p. 15 (www8.gsb.columbia.edu/apec/sites/apec/files/files/discussion/bresnan .pdf).

67. "Background on East Timor and U.S. Policy."

68. International Crisis Group, "Indonesian–U.S. Military Ties," July 17, 2001 (www.crisisgroup.org/~/media/files/asia/south-east-asia/indonesia/indone sian%20us%20military%20ties.ashx).

69. Haseman and Lachica, "Toward a Stronger U.S.–Indonesia Security Relationship," p. 33.

70. Rizal Sukma, "Indonesia: A Year of Politics and Sadness," in *Southeast Asian Affairs 1998*, edited by John Funston and Derek da Cunha (Singapore: Institute of Southeast Asian Studies, 1998), p. 119.

71. Crouch, "Indonesia: An Uncertain Outlook," p. 139.

72. John Bresnan, "Indonesia and U.S. Policy," p. 15.

73. Rabasa and Haseman, *The Military and Democracy in Indonesia*, p. 114.

74. Bresnan, "Indonesia and U.S. Policy," p. 15.

75. "Background on East Timor and U.S. Policy," *East Timor Action Network*, May 2000 (http://etan.org/timor/BkgMnu.htm).

76. Ibid.

77. The Indonesian government and military, however, did demonstrate a commitment to prevent incursions by militia groups from West Timor into East Timor, with such incidents largely curtailed (with help from the robust responses by UN peacekeeping forces as well, it should be added). However, given the situation of political upheaval, frequent leadership changes, and internal security concerns, military reform was often overlooked amid more pressing concerns.

78. See International Crisis Group, "Indonesian–U.S. Military Ties," *ICG INDONESIA Briefing*, July 17, 2001.

79. Bui Thanh Son, "Vietnam–U.S. Relations and Vietnam's Foreign Policy in the 1990s," in *Vietnamese Foreign Policy in Transition*, edited by Carlyle A. Thayer and Ramses Amer (Singapore: Institute of Southeast Asian Studies, 1999), p. 210.

80. "The President of Socialist Republic of Vietnam Received U.S. Defense Secretary William Cohen," text of report by Vietnamese radio, March 14, 2000, in Summary of World Broadcasts.

81. Bui Thanh Son, "Vietnam–U.S. Relations and Vietnam's Foreign Policy in the 1990s," p. 210. The American view has been further described as such: "The normalization of Vietnam is the best way to facilitate the social change in Vietnam. Over the long term, they hope political and economic change cannot be separated. The marketplace will make 'peaceful evolution' in Vietnam inevitable." See Frederick Z. Brown, "The United States and Southeast Asia Enter a New Era," *Current History* 94, no. 596, 1995, p. 402.

82. Samantha Marshall, "U.S.–Vietnam Trade Pact Still in Limbo— Politburo Hard-Liners Fret That Economic Openness May Foment Instability," *Wall Street Journal*, October 7, 1999.

83. The point should be noted, however, that the criticism of Nguyen Tan Dung derived as much from personal and factional differences with the president, Truong Tan Sang, as it did from the economic logic of mismanagement.

84. Shiumei Lin and Alexander Koff, "U.S.–Vietnam Bilateral Trade Agreement Road Map 1," *United States–Vietnam Trade Council Forum*, October 2, 2000, p. 3 (http://www.usvtc.org/trade/bta/roadmap1.pdf); "U.S.–Vietnam Bilateral Trade Agreement Commitments Road Map Phase III," *United States–Vietnam Trade Council Forum*, March 27, 2001, p. 25 (http://www.usvtc.org/trade/bta/roadmap3.htm).

85. Carlyle A. Thayer, "Vietnam: The Politics of Immobilism Revisited," in *Southeast Asian Affairs 2000*, edited by Daljit Singh (Singapore: Institute of Southeast Asian Studies, 2001), p. 318.

86. Stein Tonnesson, "Vietnam's Objective in the South China Sea: National or Regional Security?" *Contemporary Southeast Asia* 22, no. 2, 2000, p. 199.

87. This summary of the Asian financial crisis is taken from Joseph Chinyong Liow, *Dictionary of the Modern Politics of Southeast Asia,* 4th ed. (London: Routledge, 2015), pp. 90–91.

88. "Japan and the United States in the Asian Financial Crisis Management," p. 174 (https://www.press.umich.edu/pdf/0472112112-ch8.pdf).

89. Richard P. Cronin, "Asian Financial Crisis: An Analysis of U.S. Foreign Policy Interests and Options," *CRS Report for Congress,* January 28, 1998 (http://fas.org/man/crs/crs-asia.htm).

90. Larry Niksch, "Indonesia: U.S. Relations with the Indonesian Military," *CRS Report for Congress,* August 10, 1998 (http://congressionalresearch.com /98-677/document.php?study=INDONESIA+U.S.+RELATIONS+WITH+THE +INDONESIAN+MILITARY).

91. It should be noted that the United States continued to commit $70 million in food and emergency assistance despite the IMF freeze in its funding.

92. Tom Shorrock, "IMF and U.S. Response to the Asian Financial Crisis," *Foreign Policy in Focus* 3, no. 8, 1998 (https://www.globalpolicy.org/compo nent/content/article/209/42877.html).

93. International Crisis Group, "Indonesian–U.S. Military Ties," *Indonesia Briefing,* July 17, 2001 (http://www.crisisgroup.org/~/media/files/asia/south -east-asia/indonesia/indonesian%20us%20military%20ties.ashx).

94. Rabasa and Haseman, *The Military and Democracy in Indonesia,* p. 115; Haseman and Lachica, "Toward a Stronger U.S.–Indonesia Security Relationship," p. 29.

95. Haseman and Lachica, "Toward a Stronger U.S.–Indonesia Security Relationship," p. 34.

96. See International Crisis Group, "Indonesian–U.S. Military Ties."

97. Haseman and Lachica, "Toward a Stronger U.S.–Indonesia Security Relationship," pp. 29–30.

98. Frida Berrigan, "Indonesia at the Crossroads: U.S. Weapons Sales and Military Training," Arms Trade Resource Center, *World Policy Institute,* October 2001 (http://www.worldpolicy.org/projects/arms/reports/indo101001.htm).

99. Stern, "Diverging Roads," pp. 3–4. This could have been retaliation for Thailand's reluctance to support the U.S. request for a flotilla to be stationed in the Gulf of Thailand, as discussed earlier in this chapter.

100. Donald K. Emmerson, "U.S. Policy Themes in Southeast Asia in the 1990s," in *Southeast Asia in the New World Order: The Political Economy of a Dynamic Region,* edited by David Wurfel and Bruce Burton (New York: St. Martin's Press, 1996), p. 123.

101. Interview with a former senior diplomat who served in Washington, D.C., Singapore, October 18, 2015.

CHAPTER 4

1. See GOP Debate, Larry King Show, February 15, 2000.

2. Department of Defense, "Quadrennial Defense Review Report," September 30, 2001, p. 4.

3. Francis T. Miko, "Removing Terrorist Sanctuaries: The 9/11 Commission Recommendation and U.S. Policy," Congressional Research Service, Library of Congress, February 11, 2006, p. 16.

4. "Congress Approves Resolution Authorizing Force," CNN, September 15, 2001 (http://www.cnn.com20OllUS/09/15/congress.terrorism/).

5. Address at the Joint Session of Congress, September 20, 2001 (http://edition.cnn.com/2001/US/09/20/gen.bush.transcript/).

6. "Text of Bush's Speech at West Point," *New York Times*, June 1, 2002.

7. The White House, *National Security Strategy 2006*, March 2006, p. 12.

8. The White House, *National Security Strategy 2002*, September 2002, p. 26.

9. David Capie, "Between a Hegemon and a Hard Place: The 'War on Terror' and Southeast Asian–U.S. Relations," *Pacific Review* 17, no. 2, 2004, p. 242.

10. John Gershman, "Is Southeast Asia the Second Front?" *Foreign Affairs*, July/August 2002, pp. 60–74.

11. William J. Fallon, Testimony before the Committee of the Armed Services, U.S. Senate, March 7, 2006.

12. Barry Wain, "Unfriendly Fire," *Far Eastern Economic Review*, September 12, 2002.

13. JI was formally founded by two Darul Islam activists, Abdullah Sungkar and Abu Bakar Ba'asyir, while they were taking refuge in Malaysia from the Suharto government in 1993. Other prominent JI leaders include Riduan Isamuddin (better known as Hambali), an Indonesian, and two Malaysians, Nordin Mohamed Top and Azhari Hussein. Many JI members also come from the network of the Pondok Ngruki, an Islamic boarding school started by Ba'asyir and Sungkar in 1972. Some observers have argued that the school's curriculum promotes an extreme interpretation of Islam, which promotes violence. The group's violent turn occurred in 1998 during the communal conflicts in Maluku and Poso, when JI leaders deemed it an obligation for Muslims to engage in jihad to defend Islam in Indonesia against the perceived threat of Christian proselytization.

14. Bruce Vaughn, Emma Chanlett-Avery, Mark E. Manyin, and Larry A. Niksch, "Terrorism in Southeast Asia," Congressional Research Service, September 2008, executive summary.

15. Remarks at the National Singapore University in Singapore, November 16, 2006.

16. Cited in Renato Cruz de Castro, "The Revitalized U.S.–Philippine Security Relations: A Ghost from the Cold War or an Alliance for the 21st Century?" *Asian Survey* 43, no. 6, 2003, pp. 982–83.

17. Preeti Bhattacharji, "Terrorism Havens: Philippines," Council on Foreign Relations, June 1, 2009 (www.cfr.org/philippines/terrorism-havens-philippines/p9365).

18. "The Philippine Connection," *Wall Street Journal*, September 28, 2001.

19. Castro, "The Revitalized U.S.–Philippine Security Relations," p. 981.

20. Larry Niksch, "Abu Sayyaf: Target of Philippine–U.S. Anti-Terrorism Cooperation," CRS Report for Congress, January 24, 2007 (http://www.law .umaryland.edu/marshall/crsreports/crsdocuments/RL31265_01242007.pdf).

21. Peter Symonds, "Why Has South East Asia Become the Second Front in Bush's 'War on Terrorism'?" World Socialist Web Site, April 26, 2002 (www .wsws.org/en/articles/2002/04/asia-a26.html).

22. "The Philippines and Terrorism," Anti-Defamation League, April 2004 (http://archive.adl.org/terror/tu/tu_0404_philippines.html#.U6EwGpSSzP0).

23. The kidnapping of a Philippine civilian in Iraq led to the withdrawal of Philippine forces in July 2004, much to the chagrin of the United States.

24. Bhattacharji, "Terrorism Havens."

25. John Hendren and Richard C. Paddock, "U.S. Military Plan Shelved in Philippines," *Los Angeles Times*, March 1, 2003.

26. Bruce Vaughan and others, "Terrorism in Southeast Asia," Congressional Research Service, October 16, 2009 (www.fas.org/sgp/crs/terror/RL34194 .pdf).

27. Rommel C. Banlaoi, "Counter Terrorism Measures in Southeast Asia: How Effective Are They?" Yuchengco Center, De La Salle University—Manila, 2009 (www.academia.edu/1833307/Counter_Terrorism_Measures_in_Southeast _Asia_How_Effective_Are_They_by_Rommel_Banlaoi).

28. David Capie, "Between a Hegemon and a Hard Place: The 'War on Terror' and Southeast Asian–U.S. Relations," *Pacific Review* 17, no. 2, 2004, p. 228.

29. Office of the Press Secretary, "U.S. and Indonesia Pledge Cooperation," White House, September 19, 2005 (http://whitehouse.gov/news/releases/2001 /09/20010919-5.html).

30. Vaughan and others, "Terrorism in Southeast Asia."

31. U.S. Congress, "H.R.3057—Foreign Operations, Export Financing, and Related Programs Appropriations Act, 2006," 109th Cong. (2005–2006), November 14, 2005 (www.congress.gov/bill/109th-congress/house-bill/3057).

32. "Kopassus Not in U.S.–RI pact," *Jakarta Post*, June 16, 2010.

33. John Pomfret, "U.S. Floats Plan to Lift Ban on Training Indonesia's Kopassus Unit," *Washington Post*, March 3, 2010.

34. Emma Chanlett-Avery, Ben Dolven, and Wil Mackey, "Thailand: Background and U.S. Relations," Congressional Research Service, July 29, 2015 (http://www.fas.org/sgp/crs/row/RL32593.pdf).

35. Sheldon W. Simon, "U.S.–Southeast Asia Relations: A WMD Discovery in Malaysia and Counter-Terrorism Concerns in the Rest of Southeast Asia" (http://csis.org/files/media/csis/pubs/0401qus_seasia.pdf).

36. Eric Biel, Neil Hicks, and Michael McClintock, eds., "Losing Ground: Human Rights Defenders and Counterterrorism in Thailand," Human Rights Defenders and Counterterrorism Series No. 4 Human Rights First, 2005 (http:// www.humanrightsfirst.org/wp-content/uploads/pdf/06713-hrd-thailand-rep -web.pdf).

37. Banlaoi, "Counter Terrorism Measures in Southeast Asia."

38. Vaughan and others, "Terrorism in Southeast Asia."

39. Biel, Hicks, and McClintock, "Losing Ground."

40. Interview with a retired intelligence official, Kuala Lumpur, September 8, 2003.

41. Vaughan and others, "Terrorism in Southeast Asia."

42. "Bush Says It Is Time for Action," CNN, November 6, 2001 (http://edition.cnn.com/2001/US/11/06/ret.bush.coalition/index.html).

43. Evelyn Goh, "Hegemonic Constraints: The Implications of September 11 for American Power," *Australian Journal of International Affairs* 57, no. 1, 2003, pp. 77–97.

44. S. Jayakumar, "Remarks on the Strategic Situation in the Region by Minister for Foreign Affairs, Prof. S. Jayakumar," Singapore, May 16, 2002 (www.mfa.gov.sg/content/mfa/media_centre/press_room/tr/2002/200205/transcript_20020516_04.html).

45. Richard K. Betts, "The Soft Underbelly of American Primacy: Tactical Advantages of Terror," *Political Science Quarterly* 117, no. 1, 2002, p. 26.

46. Pew Research Center, "U.S. Image up Slightly but Still Negative," Pew Global Attitudes Project, June 23, 2005 (www.pewglobal.org/files/2005/06/Pew-Global-Report1-6-23-05-final-with-Morocco-note-and-topline.pdf). There were no records for Malaysia.

47. "Assault on American Politics: Indonesians Demonstrate against U.S.," *Financial Times*, September 29, 2001.

48. "U.S. Is Creating New Terror, Not Ending It," *Antara*, October 8, 2001.

49. Daniel Benjamin, *America and the World in an Age of Terror: A New Landscape in International Relations* (Washington, D.C.: Center for Strategic and International Studies, 2005), p. 82.

50. Anthony Davis, "Thailand Faces up to Southern Extremist Threat," *Jane's Intelligence Review*, October 1, 2003.

51. "Strategi KSAL Kent Sondakh Untuk Pertahanan Kedaulatan Negara" (Indonesian Navy Chief Kent Sondakh's Strategy for the Defense of National Waters), *Tempo*, December 9, 2004 (https://nasional.tempo.co/read/news/2004/12/09/05552542/strategi-ksal-kent-sondakh-untuk-pertahanan-kedaulatan-negara).

52. Benjamin Cole, "Introduction," in *Conflict, Terrorism, and the Media in Asia*, edited by Cole, p. 30.

53. "Malaysian Islamic Leader Vows Support for Afghanistan," *Dow Jones International News*, September 24, 2001.

54. In the case of Malaysia, it is quite clear that the Internal Security Act had also been manipulated by the incumbent regime for political purposes during this period. See Joseph Chinyong Liow, "The Mahathir Administration's War against Islamic Militancy: Operational and Ideological Challenges," *Australian Journal of International Affairs* 58, no. 2, 2004.

55. It is important to note the unfamiliarity of Southeast Asians with the nature and style of government in the United States, specifically the scope and division of powers between the executive, the legislature, and the judiciary.

56. David Bourchier, "The United States, Bush, and Indonesia: Bitter Memories, New Eggshells," in *Bush and Asia: America's Evolving Relations with East Asia,* edited by Mark Beeson (London: Routledge, 2006), p. 170.

57. However, many scholars have pointed out that the Muslim electorate in Indonesia have, in fact, shied away from political Islam. One of the best treatments of this subject can be found in Robin Bush, *Nahdlatul Ulama and the Struggle for Power within Islam and Politics in Indonesia* (Singapore: Institute of Southeast Asian Studies, 2009).

58. David Capie, "Between a Hegemon and a Hard Place: The 'War on Terror' and Southeast Asian–U.S. Relations," *Pacific Review* 17, no. 2, 2004, p. 228.

59. See Joseph Chinyong Liow, *Piety and Politics: Islamism in Contemporary Malaysia* (Oxford University Press, 2009).

60. Remarks Following Discussions with Prime Minister Lee Hsien Loong of Singapore, May 4, 2007.

61. Ibid.

CHAPTER 5

1. From President Bush's 2005 inaugural speech (http://www.npr.org/tem plates/story/story.php?storyId=4460172).

2. William Kristol and Robert Kagan, "Toward a Neo-Reaganite Foreign Policy," *Foreign Affairs* 75, no. 4, 1996, pp. 18–32.

3. National Security Council, *U.S. National Strategy for Countering Terrorism* (Washington, D.C.: National Security Council, September 2006).

4. Barbara Ann J. Rieffer with Kristan Mercer, "U.S. Democracy Promotion: The Clinton and Bush Administrations," *Global Society* 19, no. 4, 2005.

5. U.S. Department of State, *The United States and Southeast Asia: Developments, Trends, and Policy Choices.* Statement before the House International Relations Committee, Subcommittee on Asia and the Pacific, Washington, D.C., September 21, 2005.

6. Ibid.

7. Samuel P. Huntington, *The Third Wave: Democratization in the Late Twentieth Century* (University of Oklahoma Press, 1992).

8. Amitav Acharya, "Democratization and the Prospects for Participatory Regionalism in Southeast Asia," *Third World Quarterly* 24, no. 2, 2003, pp. 375–90; Pierre P. Lizee, "Civil Society and Regional Security: Tensions and Potentials in Post-Crisis Southeast Asia," *Contemporary Southeast Asia* 22, 2000. A more dated discussion is that by Clark D. Neher, *Democracy and Development in Southeast Asia: The Winds of Change* (Boulder, Colo.: Westview Press, 1996).

9. Anti-Americanism has earned sufficient attention by international relations scholars to justify an entire volume on the topic. See Peter J. Katzenstein and Robert O. Keohane, eds., *Anti-Americanism in World Politics* (Cornell University Press, 2006).

10. Stephen M. Walt, *Taming American Power: The Global Response to U.S. Primacy* (New York: W. W. Norton, 2005), p. 125.

11. On the link between democratization, belligerent nationalism, and war, see Edward Mansfield and Jack Snyder, "Democratization and War," *Foreign Affairs* 74, May/June 1995, pp. 79–97; Edward D. Mansfield and Jack Snyder, "Democratic Transitions, Institutional Strength, and War," *International Organization* 56, no. 2, 2002, pp. 297–337. In much the same vein, a report on China released by the Australian Strategic Policy Institute noted: "An authoritarian China has been highly predictable. A more open and democratic China could produce new uncertainties about both domestic policy and international relations." Quoted in Jonathan Eyal, "Democratic China May Pose More, Not Less, Danger," *Straits Times*, March 4, 2006.

12. On the distinction between democratic transition and consolidation, see, for example, Andreas Schedler, "What Is Democratic Consolidation?" *Journal of Democracy* 9, no. 2, April 1998, pp. 91–107.

13. "Filipinos Protest U.S. Refusal on Marines," *Washington Times*, January 17, 2006.

14. Jose T. Almonte, "Enhancing State Capacity and Legitimacy in the Counter-Terror War," in *After Bali: The Threat of Terrorism in Southeast Asia*, edited by Kumar Ramakrishna and See Seng Tan (London: World Scientific, 2003), pp. 221–40.

15. Sheldon W. Simon, "U.S. Policy and Terrorism in Southeast Asia," in *Fighting Terrorism on the Southeast Asian Front*, Asia Program Special Report No. 112 (Washington, D.C.: Woodrow Wilson International Center for Scholars, June 2003), p. 16.

16. See Joseph Chinyong Liow, "The Security Situation in Southern Thailand: Towards an Understanding of Domestic and International Dimensions," *Studies in Conflict and Terrorism* 27, no. 6, 2004.

17. David Wright-Neville, "Prospects Dim: Counter-Terrorism Cooperation in Southeast Asia," in *Fighting Terrorism on the Southeast Asian Front*, p. 6.

18. James A. Kelly, "U.S. Trade and Commercial Policy toward Southeast Asia," testimony before the House International Relations Committee, June 25, 2003 (http://2001-2009.state.gov/p/eap/rls/rm/2003/21942.htm).

19. United States White House, "National Security Strategy of the United States of America," September 2002, p. 17 (www.state.gov/documents/organization/63562.pdf).

20. Jon M. Huntsman Jr., "U.S.–Asia Trade after September 11," November 29, 2001 (http://avalon.law.yale.edu/sept11/huntsman_001.asp).

21. Greg Mastel, "The Rise of the Free Trade Agreement," *Challenge* 47, no. 3, 2004, p. 48.

22. Seiji F. Naya and Michael G. Plummer, *The Economics of the Enterprise for ASEAN Initiative* (Singapore: Institute of Southeast Asian Studies, 2005), p. 423.

23. Ibid., p. 423.

24. Kristin Paulson, "U.S.–Singapore FTA: An American Perspective," in *U.S.–Singapore FTA: Implications and Prospects*, edited by Tommy Koh, Vikram Khanna, Kristin Paulson, and Jose Tongzon (Singapore: Institute of Southeast Asian Studies, 2003), p. 9.

25. "Free Trade Agreement: U.S. and Malaysia," Office of the United States Trade Representative, March 8, 2006 (www.sice.oas.org/TPD/USA_MYS /Studies/USTRBenefits_e.pdf).

26. "Rundingan FTA dengan AS ditangguh," *Utusan Malaysia*, January 13, 2009.

27. "The U.S.–Malaysia Free Trade Agreement," *Penang Economic Monthly* 8, no. 5, 2006.

28. "Trade Pact with U.S. Depends on Thailand," *Bangkok Post*, March 10, 2010.

29. James Gannon, "Engaging in Asia: The Evolving U.S. Approach to Regional Community Building," in *A Pacific Nation: Perspectives on the U.S. Role in an East Asia Community*, edited by Mark Borthwick and Tadashi Yamamoto (New York: Japan Center for International Exchange, 2011), p. 30.

30. Amy Searight, "The United States and Asian Economic Regionalism: On the Outside Looking In?" in Borthwick and Yamamoto, *A Pacific Nation*, p. 67.

31. Ibid.

32. Ibid., pp. 67–68.

33. The Massachusetts legislature famously passed the Massachusetts Burma Law in 1996.

34. See, for instance, "Kachin Organizations and Civil Society Groups Urge the United States Government to Renew the Burmese Freedom and Democracy Act," *Burma Partnership*, July 11, 2013 (www.burmapartnership.org/2013/07 /kachin-organizations-and-civil-society-groups-urge-the-united-states -government-to-renew-the-burmese-freedom-and-democracy-act/).

35. Leon T. Hadar, "Burma: U.S. Foreign Policy as Morality Play," *Journal of International Affairs* 54, no. 2, 2001, p. 411.

36. "United States Relations with the Association of Southeast Asian Nations (ASEAN)," November 16, 2009, p. 13 (http://fpc.state.gov/documents /organization/133919.pdf).

37. "Bush to Take Security Agenda to APEC Meeting," *USA Today*, November 19, 2004.

38. Diane K. Mauzy and Brian L. Job, "U.S. Policy in Southeast Asia: Limited Re-engagement after Years of Benign Neglect," *Asian Survey* 47, no. 4, 2007, p. 637.

39. Elizabeth Economy and Adam Segal, "President Bush Faces a Skeptical Asia," *International Herald Tribune*, October 16, 2003.

40. Mauzy and Job, "U.S. Policy in Southeast Asia," p. 632.

41. In article 2e of chapter 1 of the TAC, signatories agree to "renunciation of the threat or use of force."

42. James Kynge, "Exports and Weak Dollar Lift China Trade Surplus," *Financial Times*, January 10–11, 2004.

43. Malcolm Moore, "China and Southeast Asia Create Huge Free Trade Zone," *The Telegraph*, December 30, 2009.

44. Huong Le Thu, "The Mekong: An Emerging Security Frontier in China–Vietnam Relations," *CogitAsia*, April 24, 2016 (http://cogitasia.com/the-mekong-an-emerging-security-frontier-in-china-vietnam-relations/).

45. Thitinan Pongsudhirak, "China's Alarming 'Water Diplomacy' on the Mekong," *Nikkei Asian Review*, March 21, 2016.

46. Wen Jiabao, "Join Hands to Create a Better Future for ASEAN–China Relations," speech delivered at the China–ASEAN Summit, Nanning, October 30, 2006.

47. Catharin Dalpino, "China's Emergence in Asia and Implications for U.S. Relations with Southeast Asia," Hearing on the Emergence of China throughout Asia: Security and Economic Consequences for the U.S., United States Senate Foreign Relations Committee, June 7, 2005 (www.globalsecurity.org/military/library/congress/2005_hr/050607-dalpino.pdf).

48. Ibid.

49. James A. Kelly, "U.S. Trade and Commercial Policy toward Southeast Asia," testimony before the House International Relations Committee, Washington, D.C., June 25, 2003.

50. Elizabeth Economy, "China's Rise in Southeast Asia: Implications for the United States," *Journal of Contemporary China* 44, no. 4, 2005, p. 413.

51. Eric Teo, "Strategic Dimension of ASEAN–China Economic Relations," in *ASEAN–China Economic Relations*, edited by Saw Swee Hock (Singapore: Institute of Southeast Asian Studies, 2007), p. 318.

52. Speech by Mr. Goh Chok Tong, prime minister of Singapore, at the Research Institute of Economy, Trade, and Industry, Tokyo, March 28, 2003.

53. Economy, "China's Rise in Southeast Asia," p. 414.

54. Ian Storey, "China–Indonesia: Military-Security Ties Fail to Gain Momentum," *China Brief* 9, no. 4, February 20, 2009, p. 7.

55. Ibid., pp. 7–8.

56. Barry Wain, "China and ASEAN: Taking Charge," *Far Eastern Economic Review*, November 14, 2002, p. 26.

57. Alastair Iain Johnston, "Is China a Status Quo Power?" *International Security* 27, no. 4, 2003, pp. 5–56.

58. Interview with a Vietnamese foreign ministry official, Singapore, January 19, 2016.

59. Alexander L. Vuving, "Strategy and Evolution in Vietnam's China Policy: A Changing Mixture of Pathways," *Asian Survey* 46, no. 5, 2006, pp. 817–21.

60. Le Hong Hiep, "The Vietnam–U.S.–China Triangle: New Dynamics and Implications," *ISEAS Perspective*, no. 45, August 25, 2015, p. 5.

61. "Sino–Vietnamese Relations Take a Further Dive," *Straits Times*, January 23, 2007.

62. David Koh, "Hanoi's Catch-22 Situation," *Straits Times*, January 23, 2008.

63. Shawn W. Crispin, "Chinese Shadow over Vietnamese Repression," *Asia Times*, September 12, 2009 (www.atimes.com/atimes/China/KI12Ad04.html).

64. "Joint Statement between the United States of America and the Socialist Republic of Vietnam," June 24, 2008 (http://vietnamembassy-usa.org/news /story.php?d=20080627045153).

65. Greg Torode, "Vietnam Protests over Chinese 'Invasion Plans,'" *South China Morning Post*, September 5, 2008; Jonathan Adams, "Vietnam Protests Hawkish Chinese Web Postings," *Christian Science Monitor*, September 10, 2008.

66. "Patrol Ships Trawl for Disorder in Beibu Gulf," *China Daily*, May 28, 2009.

67. Peter J. Brown, "Calculated Ambiguity in the South China Sea," *Asia Times*, December 8, 2009 (www.atimes.com/atimes/Southeast_Asia/KL08Ae01 .html).

CHAPTER 6

1. Tom Donilon, "The United States and the Asia-Pacific in 2013," remarks made at the Asia Society, New York, March 11, 2013 (www.whitehouse.gov/the -press-office/2013/03/11/remarks-tom-donilon-national-security-advisor -president-united-states-an).

2. Cited in Susan Rice, remarks at the Brookings Institution, Washington, D.C., September 22, 2014 (www.brookings.edu/~/media/events/2014/09/22 -rice_shanmugam/20140922-singapore-rice-transcript.pdf).

3. Robert M. Gates, "America's Security Role in the Asia-Pacific," 8th International Institute for Strategic Studies Asia Security Summit—The Shangri-La Dialogue, May 30, 2009 (www.iiss.org/conferences/the-shangri-la-dialogue /shangri-la-dialogue-2009/plenary-session-speeches-2009/first-plenary-session /dr-robert-gates/).

4. Australian Broadcasting Corporation, "Face to Face with Obama," 7:30 Report, April 14, 2010 (www.abc.net.au/7.30/content/2010/s2872726.htm).

5. East Asia Forum, "Campbell Testimony on the Rudd Proposal," June 14, 2009 (www.eastasiaforum.org/wp-content/uploads/2009/06/Campbell-Testi mony-on-the-Rudd-Proposal.pdf?1db5e0).

6. Barack Obama, "The Future of U.S. Leadership in the Asia Pacific Region," speech delivered in Tokyo, Japan, November 14, 2009 (www.whitehouse .gov/videos/2009/November/111409_TokyoJP.mp4).

7. Deputy National Security Advisor Ben Rhodes pointed out during a public talk at the Center for American Progress, Washington, D.C., on February 11, 2016, that sometime in the middle of 2015 President Obama had instructed his Asia advisors that he wished to start an institutionalized meeting with his Southeast Asian counterparts.

8. Jeremy Au Yong, "Asia 'Pivot' Left out of Obama Foreign Policy Speech," *Straits Times*, May 28, 2014.

9. Hillary Clinton, "On America's Pacific Century," speech delivered at the East-West Center, Honolulu, Hawaii, November 10, 2011.

10. Obama, "The Future of U.S. Leadership in the Asia Pacific Region."

11. Interview with a senior State Department official, Washington, D.C., November 24, 2014.

12. "A Conversation with Pham Binh Minh," Council on Foreign Relations, September 27, 2011 (www.cfr.org/vietnam/conversation-pham-binh-minh /p26046).

13. "How Emerging Powers Will Reshape Global Politics," *Strategic Review*, September 26, 2012 (www.sr-indonesia.com/events/view/how-emerging -powers-will-reshape-global-politics).

14. Statement of President Aquino during the press conference with U.S. President Obama, April 28, 2014 (http://www.gov.ph/2014/04/28/statement-of -president-aquino-during-the-press-conference-with-u-s-president-obama-april -28-2014/).

15. Joint Press Statement between President Barack Obama and Prime Minister Yingluck Shinawatra, November 18, 2012 (http://www.mfa.go.th/main/en /media-center/14/29599-Joint-Press-Statement-between-President-Barack-Oba .html).

16. This view was expressed in the course of discussions during a ministerial-level delegation visit, Washington, D.C., April 23, 2015.

17. Rebalancing to the Asia-Pacific Region and Implications for U.S. National Security: Committee on Armed Services, House of Representatives, 113th Cong., 1st sess., hearing held July 24, 2013. United States Congress. House. Committee on Armed Services, 2014, p. 4 (http://docs.house.gov /meetings/AS/AS00/20130724/101183/HMTG-113-AS00-Wstate-AuslinM -20130724.pdf).

18. Interview with an Indonesian foreign ministry official, Jakarta, February 24, 2016.

19. Interview with an Indonesian foreign ministry official, Washington, D.C., April 12, 2016. The view is widely held in Indonesia that the United States had supported first the Dutch, who were reluctant to relinquish colonial control over the province of West Papua (Irian Jaya), and later the emergence of West Papuan independence movements in the early 1960s.

20. Interview with a member of a Cambodian think tank, Phnom Penh, January 26, 2017.

21. Vijavat Isarabakdi, "U.S.-Thailand Strategic Partnership," lecture delivered at the Fletcher School, Tufts University, Nedford, M.A., November 21, 2014.

22. Ibid.

23. Ian Storey, "China–Vietnam's Year of Friendship Turns Fractious," *Straits Times*, May 26, 2009.

24. This view was expressed to me by a Chinese general during a bilateral meeting at the National Defense University, Beijing, October 30, 2009.

25. On other occasions, other iterations of the map have shown ten- and eleven-dash lines.

26. The map is ambiguous and controversial because it is not yet clear what China's claims within the parameters of the nine-dash lines actually are.

27. In hindsight, given the likelihood that land reclamation projects of the scale that China had embarked on in recent years require several years of planning, it is quite possible that the decision was made during this period to build artificial islands in the South China Sea to further China's claim and afford it the ability to assert a permanent military presence in the region.

28. Because of the two-year hiatus on FONOPS instituted by the White House, the otherwise routine operation by the U.S.S. *Lassen* became one of massive international interest. It is on that score that it can be argued the operation itself was poorly planned. News of the operation leaked to Reuters before the operation took place. Coincidentally, Defense Secretary Ashton Carter was scheduled to give a testimony to the Senate Armed Service Committee where he was evasive (apparently, at the instruction of the White House) in response to Senator Dan Sullivan's question on the FONOPS, prompting committee chair Senator John McCain to demand a written explanation. Interview with a Senate Armed Services Committee staffer, Washington, D.C., March 24, 2016.

29. Interview with a senior PACOM official, Singapore, March 15, 2015.

30. Christopher P. Cavas, "Navy Chiefs Talk, New Details on Destroyer's Passage," *Defense News*, October 31, 2015 (www.defensenews.com/story /defense/2015/10/31/navy-china-richardson-wu-destroyer-lassen-south-china -sea-innocent-passage/74881704/).

31. Bonnie S. Glaser and Peter A. Dutton, "The U.S. Navy's Freedom of Navigation Operation around Subi Reef: Deciphering U.S. Signalling," *National Interest*, November 6, 2015 (http://nationalinterest.org/feature/the-us -navy's-freedom-navigation-operation-around-subi-reef-14272).

32. "U.S. Naval Passage that Angered Beijing Pleases Some in China-Wary Vietnam," *Vietnam Tribune*, October 29, 2015 (www.vietnamtribune.com /index.php/sid/238052655).

33. Ibid.

34. Aya Lowe, "Philippines' Aquino Welcomes U.S. Warship's Deployment in Disputed Area," *Channelnews Asia*, October 27, 2015 (www.channelnewsasia .com/news/asiapacific/philippines-aquino/2221382.html).

35. "Indonesia Calls on U.S.–China to 'Restrain Themselves,' Lashes U.S. 'Power Projection' after Spratly Sailby," *South China Morning Post*, October 28, 2015.

36. Remarks made at the Brookings Institution, Washington, D.C., October 27, 2015.

37. "Beijing Holds Defence Forum as South China Sea Festers," *Channelnews Asia*, October 16, 2015 (http://www.channelnewsasia.com/news/asia pacific/beijing-holds-defence/2198174.html).

38. Evan Laksmana, "Here's Why Jakarta Doesn't Push Back when China Barges into Indonesian Waters," *Washington Post*, April 28, 2016.

39. "Indonesia: Natuna Incident Not Related to South China Sea Dispute," *Jakarta Globe*, March 21, 2016.

40. Interview with a senior Indonesian Foreign Ministry official, Jakarta, February 22, 2016.

41. Cited in David Han, "Why Malaysia's South China Sea Policy Seems Confused," *Straits Times*, May 5, 2016.

42. Ibid.

43. Ayomi Amindoni, "Govt to Formulate Official Stance on South China Sea Dispute," *Jakarta Post*, June 13, 2016.

44. Melissa Sim, "U.S., China Cross Swords over S. China Sea," *Straits Times*, February 25, 2016.

45. R. D. Hill, Norman G. Owen, and Elfed Vaughan Roberts, *Fishing in Troubled Waters: Proceedings of an Academic Conference on Territorial Claims in the South China Sea* (Hong Kong: Centre of Asian Studies, 1991), p. 49.

46. It should be noted that all the claimant states include some element of "history" in their respective claims, especially with regard to what was inherited from previous colonial administrations. Nevertheless, in the case of China and Taiwan, the historical basis has served as the primary impetus.

47. Mohan Malik, "Historical Fiction: China's South China Sea Claims," *World Affairs*, May/June 2013 (www.worldaffairsjournal.org/article/historical -fiction-china%E2%80%99s-south-china-sea-claims). See also Termsak Chalermpalanupap, "Known Knowns, Known Unknowns, Unknown Unknowns, and Unknown Knowns in the South China Sea Disputes," *Kyoto Review of Southeast Asia*, no. 15, March 2014 (http://kyotoreview.org/issue-15/known -knowns-known-unknowns-unknown-unknowns-and-unknown-knowns-in -the-south-china-sea-disputes/) and Bill Hayton, *South China Sea: The Struggle for Power in Asia* (Yale University Press, 2014).

48. Robert Beckman and Clive Schofield, "Mapping Way out of South China Sea Rows," *Straits Times*, April 20, 2014.

49. Scot Marciel, "Maritime Issues and Sovereignty Disputes in East Asia," U.S. Department of State, July 15, 2009 (https://www.gpo.gov/fdsys/pkg /CHRG-111shrg53022/pdf/CHRG-111shrg53022.pdf).

50. Ibid.

51. Ibid.

52. Gordon G. Chang, "Hillary Clinton Changes America's China Policy," *Forbes*, July 28, 2010. This was confirmed in an interview in Washington, D.C., with a National Security Council official on September 25, 2014.

53. Interview with a former senior State Department official, Washington, D.C., February 12, 2016. The official also shared that her Southeast Asian counterparts had recommended that the issue not be raised "too provocatively."

54. Mark Landler, "Offering to Aid Talks, U.S. Challenges China on Disputed Islands," *New York Times*, July 23, 2010.

55. This point was made by senior administration officials at a talk at the Center for New American Security, Washington, D.C., on April 26, 2016.

56. "Chinese FM Refutes Fallacies on the South China Sea Issue," *China Daily*, July 25, 2010.

57. Floyd Whaley, "Clinton Reaffirms Military Ties with the Philippines," *New York Times*, November 16, 2011. Emphasis added.

58. Interview with a senior diplomat, Manila, October 12, 2013.

59. Taylor M. Fravel, *The U.S. and China in Regional Security—Session IV: What Issues and Whose Core Interests?* (Berlin: Konrad-Adenauer-Stiftung and Stiftung Wissenschaft und Politik, 2012), p. 5.

60. "U.S. to China: We Will Protect Philippines," *Philippine Inquirer*, April 10, 2014.

61. Correspondingly, would the United States be prepared to intervene in the event of an attack on Philippine "armed Forces, public vessels or aircraft in the Pacific," according to article V of the treaty? The text of the treaty can be found at http://www.chanrobles.com/mutualdefensetreaty.htm#.WLSRDRSNzww.

62. Interview with a senior Department of Defense official, Singapore, July 6, 2015.

63. See Dennis Blair and John Huntsman, "Commentary: A Strategy for the South China Sea," *Defense News*, July 13, 2015 (www.defensenews.com/story /defense/commentary/2015/07/13/commentary-strategy-south-china-sea/300 84573/).

64. As a retired four-star general, a self-professed Democrat, observed: "when Bush needed to act for the nation's interests, he acted decisively. When Obama needs to act, he calls in a bunch of lawyers while the Russians and the Chinese act." Interview, Washington, D.C., May 4, 2016.

65. See Edward Schwark, "China versus America: The 'Freedom of Navigation' Debate," *National Interest*, August 21, 2014 (http://nationalinterest.org /blog/the-buzz/china-vs-america-the-freedom-navigation-debate-11116).

66. It is important to establish that paradigm shifts dictated by changing political, economic, and strategic circumstance are not foreign to ASEAN. Consider the reasons for the institution of ASEAN summitry in 1976 or the formulation of the ASEAN Charter in 2007.

67. David Scott, "Conflict Irresolution in the South China Sea," *Asian Survey* 52, no. 6, November/December 2012, p. 1019.

68. Ibid, p. 1027.

69. Amitav Acharya, *Constructing a Security Community in Southeast Asia: ASEAN and the Problem of Regional Order* (New York: Routledge, 2014), p. 122.

70. Nayan Chanda, "Divide and Rule: Beijing Scores Points on South China Sea," *Far Eastern Economic Review*, August 11, 1994, p. 18.

71. Joseph Chinyong Liow, "Malaysia–China Relations in the 1990s: The Maturing of a Partnership," *Asian Survey* 40, no. 4, 2000.

72. Donald Weatherbee, "Southeast Asia and ASEAN: Running in Place," *Southeast Asian Affairs* 1, no. 3, 2012, p. 10.

73. "ASEAN Fails to Reach South China Sea Accord; Indonesia Slams Members, While U.S. and China Downplay Friction," *International Business Times*, July 13, 2012.

74. Selected Impromptu Comments by Samdech Techno Hun Sen at the Graduation and Diploma Presenting Ceremony of the National University of Management, Phnom Penh, February 5, 2016 (www.pressocm.gov.kh/site/detail /8759.html#.VsHoIlK1nwz).

75. Interview with a former senior State Department official, Washington, D.C., February 10, 2016.

76. For a detailed discussion on these submissions, see Robert C. Beckman and Tara Davenport, "CLCS Submissions and Claims in the South China Sea," paper presented at the Second International Workshop on the South China Sea: Cooperation for Regional Security and Development, Ho Chi Minh City, Vietnam, November 10–12, 2010, pp. 18–24 (http://cil.nus.edu.sg/wp/wp -content/uploads/2009/09/Beckman-Davenport-CLCS-HCMC-10-12Nov2010 -1.pdf).

77. Letter to the Secretary General of the United Nations, Doc. No. 240/ HC-2009, New York, August 18, 2009, supra note 3 (www.un.org/Depts/los /clcs_new/submissions_files/vnm37_09/vnm_re_phl_2009re_vnm.pdf).

78. Nguyen Hong Thao and Ramses Amer, "Coastal States in the South China Sea and Submissions on the Outer Limits of the Continental Shelf," *Ocean Development & International Law* 42, no. 3, 2011, pp. 254–55.

79. Ibid., pp. 256–57.

80. Interview with an ASEAN senior official, Bali, April 22, 2014.

81. Aileen San Pablo-Baviera, "The South China Sea Disputes: Is the Aquino Way the 'ASEAN Way'?" *RSIS Commentaries*, January 5, 2012.

82. "Full Text: DFA Chief Del Rosario's Speech at UN Tribunal," Inquirer, July 8, 2015 (http://globalnation.inquirer.net/125726/full-text-dfa-sec-albert -del-rosarios-speech-at-un-tribunal).

83. James Hardy, "Analysis: ASEAN Finds Voice over South China Sea," *IHS Jane's 360*, August 14, 2014.

84. Chairman's Statement of the 26th ASEAN Summit, Kuala Lumpur and Langkawi, April 27, 2015.

85. Chairman's Statement of the 27th ASEAN Summit, Kuala Lumpur, November 21, 2015.

86. Tang Siew Mun, "China's Dangerous Divide and Conquer Game in ASEAN," *Today*, April 29, 2016.

87. Interview with a Southeast Asian ambassador to ASEAN, Jakarta, June 20, 2016.

88. Matthew Lee, "South China Sea Dispute: Clinton to Urge ASEAN Unity," *Huffington Post*, March 11, 2012 (www.huffingtonpost.com/2012/09 /03/south-china-sea-dispute-clinton_n_1852692.html).

89. Vignesh Ram, "ASEAN Reboots on South China Sea." *Asia Times*, April 30, 2013 (www.atimes.com/atimes/Southeast_Asia/SEA-01-300413 .html).

90. Humphrey Hawksley, "With Tensions Rising, Asia Should Not Delay Settling South China Sea Disputes," *Yale Global*, February 9, 2016 (http://yaleglobal.yale.edu/content/us-china-tension-rising-asia-should-not-delay-settling-south-china-sea-disputes).

91. Zbigniew Brzezinski, "The Group of Two that Could Change the World," *Financial Times*, January 13, 2009.

92. Interview with a former Department of Defense official, Washington, D.C., February 9, 2016.

93. Interview with a Vietnamese official, Washington, D.C., February 11, 2016.

CHAPTER 7

1. See Robert D. Blackwell and Jennifer M. Harris, *War by Other Means: Geoeconomics and Statecraft* (Cambridge, Mass.: Belknap Press, 2016).

2. Michael Evans, "American Defence Policy and the Challenge of Austerity," *Journal of Southeast Asian Economies* 30, no. 2, 2013, pp. 164–78.

3. Daniel Blumenthal, "Against the East Asia Pivot," *Foreign Policy*, November 18, 2011 (http://foreignpolicy.com/2011/11/18/against-the-east-asia-pivot/).

4. Dean Cheng and Bruce Klingner, "Defense Budget Cuts Will Devastate America's Commitment to the Asia-Pacific," *Backgrounder #2629 on National Security and Defense*, Heritage Foundation, December 6, 2011 (www.heritage.org/research/reports/2011/12/defense-budget-cuts-will-devastate-americas-commitment-to-the-asia-pacific).

5. Interview, Singapore, July 31, 3013.

6. Remarks by Secretary Leon E. Panetta at Georgetown University, Washington, D.C., February 6, 2013. See www.defense.gov/transcripts/transcript.aspx?transcriptid=5189.

7. Interview with a senior official, Department of Defense, September 27, 2015.

8. Cited in Michael Evans, "American Defence Policy and the Challenge of Austerity," *Journal of Southeast Asian Economies* 30, no. 2, 2013, pp. 164–78.

9. Ibid.

10. Stephanie Gaskell, "The Pivot to Asia Hits Rough Waters," *Government Executive* 43, no. 6, 2014, pp. 40–41.

11. Rebalancing to the Asia-Pacific Region and Implications for U.S. National Security: Committee on Armed Services, House of Representatives, 113th Cong., 1st sess., hearing held July 24, 2013 (https://www.gpo.gov/fdsys/pkg/CHRG-113hhrg82464/pdf/CHRG-113hhrg82464.pdf).

12. "K. Shanmugam Tells Singapore Caucus in the U.S. that TPP Is about Credibility, Not Economics," *Straits Times*, June 17, 2015.

13. The TPA was granted under the 2002 Trade Act. Upon expiry in 2007, it was updated by the 2007 Bipartisan Trade Deal. In 2013, and again in early 2015, President Obama issued calls for the TPA to be reinstated.

14. Michael Froman, "The Strategic Logic of Trade," *Foreign Affairs* 93, no. 6, 2014, pp. 111–18.

15. William Maudlin, "Lawmakers Grapple with 'Fast Track' Trade Bill," *Wall Street Journal*, February 24, 2015.

16. An investigative report by the *Washington Post* revealed that Obama's trade agenda had been hijacked by special interest groups. Out of 566 advisory group members that, unlike Congress members and their staff, are permitted to look and comment on U.S. trade proposals, 480 of them represent industry or trade association groups. See Christopher Ingraham and Howard Schneider, "Industry Voices Dominate the Trade Advisory System," *Washington Post*, February 27, 2015.

17. Discussion with a Malaysian politician, November 5, 2015.

18. Nile Bowie, "Malaysia Risks Takeover," *Asia Times*, September 13, 2012 (www.atimes.com/atimes/Southeast_Asia/NI13Ae01.html).

19. See Jeffrey Goldberg, "The Obama Doctrine," *The Atlantic*, April 2016.

20. Interview with a Vietnamese scholar, Singapore, December 14, 2015.

21. Le Kha Phieu came under heavy criticism from the reformists for excessive concessions to the Chinese. See Carl Thayer, "Vietnamese Perspectives of the China Threat," in *The China Threat: Perceptions, Myths and Reality*, edited by Herbert Yee and Ian Storey (New York: RoutledgeCurzon, 2002), pp. 280–81.

22. Alexander Vuving, "Strategy and Evolution in Vietnam's China Policy," *Asian Survey* 46, no. 6, November/December 2006, p. 808.

23. Duy Hoang, "Rights before Weapons for Vietnam," *Asia Times*, August 20, 2014 (www.atimes.com/atimes/Southeast_Asia/SEA-01-200814.html).

24. Interview with a Vietnamese official, Singapore, January 19, 2016.

25. Vo Van Kiet had allegedly articulated the view that Vietnam was "living in a region surrounded by a dragon and the continued backwardness of the country is the biggest security threat to the nation." See Allen E. Goodman, "Vietnam at 1994: With Peace at Hand," *Asian Survey* 31, no. 1, 1995, p. 98.

26. "Vietnam Seizes Chinese Ship in South China Sea in Rare Move," *Straits Times*, April 4, 2016.

27. "Vietnamese War Hero Fires Salvo over Mining Plan," *Agence France-Presse*, May 7, 2009.

28. "A Deepening Partnership with Vietnam," *New York Times*, October 24, 2014. The Obama administration has since clarified that the transfer of lethal weapons will initially materialize only at a modest level and directly related to enhancing Vietnam's maritime capability to defend itself. See "U.S. Eases Arms Embargo against Vietnam for Maritime Security," *Reuters*, October 2, 2014 (www.reuters.com/article/2014/10/02/us-usa-vietnam-arms -idUSKCN0HR29V20141002).

29. Interview with a Vietnamese official, Singapore, December 14, 2015.

30. David Koh, "Will There Be a Vietnamese Pivot to the U.S.?" *Straits Times*, June 6, 2016.

31. Le Hong Hiep, "The Vietnam–U.S.–China Triangle: New Dynamics and Implications," *ISEAS Perspective*, no. 45, August 25, 2015, p. 4.

32. "China Remains Vietnam's Biggest Trade Partner in 2013," *China Daily*, January 29, 2014.

33. "Chinese Oil Rig Cost Vietnam 0.7% of GDP," *Dantri International News*, July 30, 2014 (www.dtinews.vn/en/news/018/35830/chinese-oil-rig-cost -vietnam-0-7--of-gdp.html).

34. Interview, Singapore, January 19, 2016.

35. Vu Truong Minh and Nguyen Thanh Trung, "A U.S.–Vietnam Alliance or (Still) a U.S.–China–Vietnam Triangle?" *International Policy Digest,* March 10, 2014 (http://internationalpolicydigest.org/2014/10/03/u-s-vietnam-alliance -or-u-s-china-vietnam-traingle/).

36. Ibid.

37. Interview with a Vietnamese scholar, Singapore, December 14, 2015.

38. Nguyen Huu Quyet, "Vietnam's ASEAN Strategic Objectives since the 1986 Doi Moi Reform," PhD diss., National Graduate Institute for Policy Studies, 2013, p. 75.

39. "Vietnam Human Rights Press Passed," *Asian American News,* August 11, 2013 (http://aapress.com/ethnicity/vietnamese/vietnam-human-rights -act-passed/).

40. The full statement by the two Republican congressmen is accessible at http://thehill.com/opinion/op-ed/242022-human-rights-abuses-in-vietnam -make-tpp-unacceptable.

41. Michael Gordon, "Kerry Tells Vietnam that U.S. Ties Will Deepen if Human Rights Are Protected," *New York Times*, August 7, 2015.

42. *The National Security Strategy* (Washington, D.C.: White House, 2006), p. 25 (https://georgewbush-whitehouse.archives.gov/nsc/nss/2006/).

43. Gordon, "Kerry Tells Vietnam that U.S. Ties Will Deepen."

44. "As Obama Lifts Vietnam Arms Embargo, Human Rights Groups Lament Lost Leverage," *Washington Times*, May 23, 2016.

45. Ibid.

46. Remarks made at a seminar at the Center for New American Security, Washington, D.C., February 11, 2016.

47. Interview, Singapore, December 14, 2015.

48. Vu and Nguyen, "A U.S.–Vietnam Alliance?"

49. Le, "The Vietnam–U.S.–China Triangle," p. 5.

50. Vietnam purchased six Kilo class submarines and up to twenty Sukhoi Su-30 bombers from Russia in 2010.

51. David I. Steinberg, *Burma: The State of Myanmar* (George Washington University Press, 2001), p. 237.

52. David I. Steinberg, "Myanmar and the United States, Closing and Opening Doors: An Idiosyncratic Analysis," *Social Research* 82, no. 2, 2015, p. 432.

53. David I. Steinberg, *Turmoil in Burma: Contested Legitimacies in Myanmar* (Norwalk, Conn.: Eastbridge, 2006), pp. 191–92.

54. Explaining this "gap" of two years before the United States began taking harsh measures against the military regime, Renaud Egreteau and Larry Jagan argued that although the United States had grave concerns following the 1988 crackdown, the utility of bilateral cooperation with the military regime to monitor the drug trafficking situation in the Golden Triangle prevented greater U.S. pressure. See Renaud Egreteau and Larry Jagan, *Soldiers and Diplomacy in Burma: Understanding the Foreign Relations of the Burmese Praetorian State* (National University of Singapore Press, 2013), pp. 206–07.

55. Interview with a former senior Defense Department official, Washington, D.C., February 12, 2016.

56. Leon T. Hadar, "Burma: U.S. Foreign Policy as Morality Play," *Journal of International Affairs* 54, no. 2, 2001, p. 411.

57. Tiffany Danitz and Warren P. Strobel, "The Internet's Impact on Activism: The Case of Burma," *Studies in Conflict and Terrorism* 22, no. 3, 1999, p. 262.

58. See, for instance, "Kachin Organizations and Civil Society Groups Urge the United States Government to Renew the Burmese Freedom and Democracy Act," Burma Partnership, July 11, 2013 (www.burmapartnership.org/2013/07/kachin-organizations-and-civil-society-groups-urge-the-united-states-government-to-renew-the-burmese-freedom-and-democracy-act/).

59. Hadar, "Burma."

60. Remarks by President Barack Obama at Suntory Hall, November 14, 2009 (http://www.realclearworld.com/articles/2009/11/14/president_obama_address_to_japan_97357.html).

61. Thant Myint-U, *Where China Meets India: Burma and the New Crossroads of Asia* (London: Faber and Faber Limited, 2011), p. 74.

62. Information on U.S. sanctions can be found at www.treasury.gov/resource-center/sanctions/Programs/pages/burma.aspx.

63. Nehginpao Kigpen, "U.S.–Burma Relations: Change of Politics under the Bush and Obama Administrations," *Strategic Analysis* 37, no. 2, 2013, p. 203.

64. While U.S. officials explained that President Obama's delegation was constrained by time and hence could not make the trip to Naypyidaw, the choice of Yangon was nevertheless still seen as symbolic given the fact that Naypyidaw was built by the military junta precisely to serve as the new national capital. Equally symbolic was the fact that President Thein Sein agreed to the meeting in Yangon.

65. Shi Qingren, "美国意图制衡中国在缅甸的影响力" [The United States' Objective Is to Counter Chinese Influence in Myanmar], *Zhongguo Qing Nian Bao* (China Youth Daily), January 4, 2013.

66. Comments at a public lecture hosted by the Lee Kuan Yew School of Public Policy, Singapore, March 11, 2015.

67. "Myanmar Reforms Are by No Means Complete or Irreversible: Obama," *Straits Times*, November 14, 2014.

68. See, for example, Lynn Kuok, *Promoting Peace in Myanmar: U.S. Interests and Role* (Washington, D.C.: Center for Strategic and International Studies, May 2014).

69. The U.S. Treasury maintains records on hundreds of Myanmar businesses forbidden from transacting with U.S. shareholders. The companies desiring to have their record expunged must demonstrate that they have eliminated links to the military and opened up their corporate governance. See David Tweed and Kyaw Thu, "U.S. Companies Skirting Myanmar Sanctions Fuel Record Investment," *Bloomberg*, November 17, 2014.

70. Gwen Robinson, "Washington Lifts Some Myanmar Sanctions, but Doubts Remain," *Nikkei Asian Review*, May 30–June 5, 2016, p. 32.

71. "Spotlighting Human Rights in Southeast Asia," Hearing Before the Committee on Foreign Affairs, House of Representatives, 113th Cong., 2d sess., July 9, 2014, p. 2.

72. Steve Hirsch, "Cracks Appear in U.S. Myanmar Rapprochement," *The Diplomat*, April 30, 2014.

73. Robinson, "Washington Lifts Some Myanmar Sanctions."

74. David I. Steinberg, *Myanmar: The State of Burma* (Georgetown University Press, 2001), p. 300.

75. Naing Zaw Htet, "Ethnic Minorities Question U.S.–Burma Military Ties," *The Irrawaddy*, August 21, 2014 (www.irrawaddy.org/burma/ethnic -minorities-question-us-burma-military-ties.html).

76. Interview with a leader of the Karen National Union, Jakarta, March 2015.

77. This point was made during a panel discussion on the Myanmar elections at the Brookings Institution, Washington, D.C., November 20, 2015.

78. "Aung San Suu Kyi's Complicity," *International New York Times*, May 11, 2016.

79. "Aung San Suu Kyi Asks U.S. Not to Use 'Rohingya,'" *Today*, May 7, 2016.

80. David Brenner, "Washington's Flawed Myanmar Policy," *The Diplomat*, April 27, 2014 (http://thediplomat.com/2014/04/washingtons-flawed-myanmar -policy/).

81. "Wa Army Fielding New Chinese Artillery, ATGMs," *Jane's Defence Weekly*, July 22, 2015. Aside from the military dimension, there is a further reality that confronts Myanmar. Chinese ownership of and access to capital dominates Myanmar's private sector and could well serve as yet another point of influence.

82. "What You Need to Know about EDCA," CNN Philippines, April 14, 2016 (http://cnnphilippines.com/news/2016/01/13/what-you-need-to-know-about -edca.html).

83. Ernest Z. Bower, "Enhanced Defense Cooperation Agreement: Manila's Most Credible Deterrent to China," cogitASIA, May 29, 2015 (http://cogitasia .com/enhanced-defense-cooperation-agreement-manilas-most-credible-deter rent-to-china/).

84. Although there is no substantive evidence of correlation, the resolution of the Joseph Pemberton trial in December 2015, the U.S. marine convicted for the murder of the Filipino transgender woman Jennifer Laude, may conceivably have smoothed the way for the Supreme Court ruling.

85. Patricia Lourdes Viray, "Miriam: EDCA Void without Senate Concurrence," *Philippine Star*, November 10, 2015; Ghio Ong, "Anti-EDCA Groups Eye Appeal," *Philippine Star*, January 13, 2016.

86. Mike Frialde, "Duterte Says Unknown Donor Paid for His Pre-Campaign Ads," *Philippine Star*, March 11, 2016. It is not known if the anonymous Chinese donor was a Chinese Filipino or a citizen of the People's Republic of China.

87. Germelina Lacorte, "Duterte Tells China: Build Us a Railway and Let's Set Aside Differences for a While," *Philippine Inquirer*, February 29, 2016.

CHAPTER 8

1. William McGurn, "Lee Hsien Loong's American Exceptionalism," *Wall Street Journal*, March 31, 2016 (www.wsj.com/articles/lee-hsien-loongs-american-exceptionalism-1459464855).

2. If it was not for a canceled trip in 2013 because of the federal government shutdown, Obama would have visited Brunei as well.

3. Kevin Fogg, "Global History vs Area Studies," December 7, 2015 (www.kevinwfogg.net/blog/4570569437).

4. Barry R. Posen and Andrew L. Ross, "Competing Visions for U.S. Grand Strategy," *International Security* 21, no. 3, 1996/97, pp. 52–53.

5. Jessica T. Matthews, "What Foreign Policy for the U.S.?" *New York Review of Books*, September 24, 2015.

6. William Tow, "U.S. Bilateral Security Alliances in the Asia Pacific: Moving beyond Hub and Spokes," University of Queensland, September 29, 2003 (www.utas.edu.au/government/APSA/Wtow.html).

7. This view was expressed to me in Singapore, June 3, 2016.

8. In the case of Thailand and the Philippines, troops were even committed to support the war effort.

CHAPTER 9

1. Questionable in the sense that despite two cycles of devaluation in 2015, the Chinese currency is in fact overvalued.

2. Murray Hiebert, "President Obama Needs to Visit Singapore Next Year," Center for Strategic and International Studies, November 12, 2015 (www.csis.org/analysis/president-obama-needs-visit-singapore-next-year).

3. U.S. Department of State, "Joint Statement of the United States-Singapore Strategic Partners Dialogue," January 18, 2012 (https://www.mfa.gov.sg/content/mfa/overseasmission/washington/newsroom/press_statements/2012/201201/press_201201.html).

4. Vivian Balakrishnan, remarks at the Center for Strategic and International Studies, Washington, D.C., June 9, 2016.

5. See Helen Cooper and Jane Perlez, "White House Moves to Reassure Allies with South China Sea Patrol, but Quietly," *New York Times*, October 27, 2015.

6. Goh Sui Noi, "U.S. 'Neglects International Norms that It Champions,'" *Straits Times*, June 5, 2016.

Index

Surnames starting with "al-" are alphabetized by the subsequent word.

Asia, 10; in South China Sea disputes, 176, 248
Laskar Jihad, 103, 104
Lassen, U.S.S., 155–56, 245
Le Ke Lam, 156
Le Kha Phieu, 75, 193
Leach, James, 203
Leahy Amendment of 1999, 80, 95
Lee Hsien Loong, 109, 222–23
Lee Kuan Yew, 5–6, 37, 66, 132–33
Liow Tiong Lai, 191
Lofgren, Zoe, 199–200
Lon Nol, 150
Lord, Winston, 52, 57, 61
Lower Mekong Initiative, 128
Luhut Pandjaitan, 157

Macapagal-Arroyo, Gloria, 91, 92, 93, 113
Maceda, Ernesto, 67
Mahathir Mohamad, 52, 60, 78, 98, 99, 102
Malacca Straits: in international trade, 2, 231; U.S. deployments in, 103–04
Malaysia: anti-American sentiment in, 38, 104; Chinese involvement in domestic affairs of, 130–31; condemnation of U.S. operations in Afghanistan and Iraq, 104–05; counterterrorism efforts in, 97–99, 108, 228; defense relationship with U.S., 29, 108; democratization processes in, 113; diplomatic visits to, 145; economic engagement with, 116, 118–19; financial crisis in, 75, 76, 77, 78; as founding member of ASEAN, 231; human rights issues in, 52; military access arrangements with U.S., 83; Muslim communities in, 2, 11, 88, 102, 107; in South China Sea disputes, 54, 151–53, 158, 169–73; and TPPA, 185, 190–91
Malaysia–Philippines–Indonesia (MAPHILINDO) confederation, 65
Manifest destiny, 20
Manila Declaration (2011), 166
Manila Pact (1954), 96
Marciel, Scott, 163
Marcos, Ferdinand, 38, 65
Maritime Security Initiative, 144
Maritime Silk Road initiative, 196, 248
Market-based democracies, 49

Marshall Plan, 180–81
Marx, Karl, 46
Massaoui, Zacarias, 97–98
Matthews, Jessica, 225–26
Maung Aye, 206
Mayaguez, SS, 50
McCain, John, 73, 207, 242
McClellan, Scott, 122
McCloskey, Peter, 36
McConnell, Mitch, 207
McFarland, Katrina, 183
Megawati Sukarnoputri, 93–94, 102–03
Mekong subregion, 126–28
Mercado, Orlando, 66
Middle East: coherence of strategic policies toward, 27; dictatorships in, 49; political violence in, 1; religio-cultural narratives in, 2; strategic value to U.S., 9; terrorist threats in, 33, 109. *See also specific countries*
Al-Midhar, Khalid, 98
Migdal, Joel, 35
Military exercises: Balikatan, 91, 92, 144; Cobra Gold, 50, 81, 144, 207; Rim of the Pacific, 237. *See also* Defense relationships
Mischief Reef, Chinese occupation of, 55, 67, 82–83, 165, 249
Mitchell, Derek, 207, 208, 213
Mohammad, Khalid Shaikh, 97
Monroe Doctrine (1823), 7
Moro Islamic Liberation Front (MILF), 88, 89, 90, 92
Moro National Liberation Front (MNLF), 90
Most favored nation trading status, 73, 74
Muslim communities: anti-American sentiment in, 11, 38, 39, 114, 222; and counterterrorism efforts, 98; Global War on Terror as perceived by, 101–5, 222; politicization of, 106–07; radicalization within, 95, 103, 107; religio-cultural narratives involving, 2; Rohingya people, 39, 208, 209, 210, 212–15; terrorist threats from, 33, 88–89
Mutual Defense Treaty (1951), 64, 67, 91, 166
Myanmar: anti-American sentiment in, 39; democratization processes in, 2, 206–07, 208, 213, 246; diplomatic visits to, 145, 202, 207, 213; engagement with, 28,

Simon, Sheldon, 113

Singapore: Chinese involvement in domestic affairs of, 131; counterterrorism efforts in, 11, 99–100; defense relationship with U.S., 29–30, 99, 238; economic engagement with, 28, 116, 117–18, 238; and foreign direct investments, 210, 238; as founding member of ASEAN, 231; human rights issues in, 52; military access arrangements with U.S., 66, 83, 99; Muslim communities in, 101–2; perceptions of U.S. role in Southeast Asia, 44; strategic partnership with U.S., 99, 238; terrorist threats in, 123; and TPPA, 185, 190

Siregar, Arifin, 71

SLORC (State Law and Order Restoration Council), 202, 204

Smith, Bob, 73

Smith, Chris, 199–200

Sondakh, Bernard Kent, 103–04

South China Sea disputes, 151–79; Arbitral Tribunal rulings on, 162, 173, 177, 216, 249–51; ASEAN on, 55, 152, 160, 173–79; Clinton administration on, 55–56; Code of Conduct for, 160, 165, 173–75, 230, 245, 252; debate over U.S. involvement in, 8, 154–55; four-point consensus agreement on, 176, 248; and freedom of navigation, 29, 54–56, 147, 157–59, 167, 251; international significance of, 2, 54, 163, 231; intra-ASEAN conflicts in, 168–75; James Shoal conflict in, 152–53, 154; land reclamation projects in, 154, 162, 174–75; legal considerations in, 160–63; Natuna Islands in, 157–58; naval operations related to, 29, 155–57, 245; negotiations on, 133–35, 176; "nine-dash line" map in, 152, 157, 160, 162, 164, 249; Obama administration on, 13, 22, 56, 155, 167, 195; Palmas Island in, 173; Paracel Islands in, 54–55, 134, 138, 154–55, 159, 196; Pivot strategy on, 163–64, 180; Pratas Islands in, 54; Second Thomas Shoal in, 153; territorial conflicts in, 53–55, 138–40, 151–52; U.S. position on, 163–68, 244–45, 251–52. *See also* Spratly Islands

Southeast Asia: Chinese charm offensive toward, 32, 124, 130–35, 151, 154,

235; coherence of strategic policies toward, 27; Cold War in, 1–2, 4, 5; congressional bills relating to (1993–2016), 39, 254–70; debates regarding U.S. interests in, 27–33; diplomatic visits to, 145; diversity of, 9–10, 16; economic growth of, 1, 2, 76; geostrategic influences over, 4–5, 124, 130; Greater Mekong Subregion of, 126–28; interstate peace in, 1–2; perceptions of U.S. role in, 6–7, 10–11, 15–16, 38, 44, 66, 219–21; as "Second Front" in Global War on Terror, 11–12, 87, 90–100; security challenges for, 5, 226–27; in study of global history, 224; terrorist threats in, 33, 87–90, 222. *See also* Association of Southeast Asian Nations (ASEAN); Muslim communities; Regional order management; U.S.-Southeast Asia relations; *specific countries*

Southeast Asia Treaty Organization (SEATO), 56–57

South Korea: alliance relationship with U.S., 3, 29, 31, 56; and EAFTA, 186; financial crisis in, 75; in Pivot strategy, 143; and RCEP, 185

Soviet Union: collapse of, 4, 23, 46; in Cuban missile crisis, 7; occupation of Afghanistan by, 88–89. *See also* Cold War

Spratly Islands: Arbitral Tribunal rulings on features in, 249; detainment of Vietnamese fishing boats near, 138; exclusive economic zones in, 160, 161, 250; historical claims to, 159; intra-ASEAN conflicts over, 169–70, 172; land reclamation projects in, 154, 174; Mischief Reef, 55, 67, 82–83, 165, 249; territorial disputes regarding, 54

Statecraft, 25–26

State Law and Order Restoration Council (SLORC), 202, 204

State terrorism, 98

Steinberg, David, 202–03

Storey, Ian, 133

Subprime crisis (2007–08), 22, 181

Sudrajat, Edi, 71

Sufaat, Yazid, 98

Suharto: criticisms of, 49; democratization and downfall of, 111; New Order regime of, 67, 68, 245;

reforms implemented by, 79; resignation of, 71, 78, 80; response to antigovernment protests, 69

Summers, Lawrence, 79

Sunnylands Summit, 41, 145

Super Ferry 14 bombing (2004), 90

TAC. *See* Treaty of Amity and Cooperation of 1976

Taiwan, Chinese challenges to governmental legitimacy of, 54, 135

Tariffs, 74, 126

Terrorism: Bush on, 33; democratization as remedy for, 100, 111; foreign policy influenced by threat of, 33; Rumsfeld on, 32; in Southeast Asia, 33, 87–90, 222; state terrorism, 98; transnational character of, 88. *See also* Counterterrorism; Global War on Terror; *specific incidents*

Thailand: alliance relationship with U.S., 29, 50–51, 56, 231; anti-American sentiment in, 113; arms sales to, 82, 96; coherence of strategic policies toward, 27; counterterrorism efforts in, 96–97; defense relationship with U.S., 50–51, 96; democratization processes in, 2, 111, 113; economic engagement with, 116, 118, 119; ethnic separatist movements in, 101; financial crisis in, 75, 76–77, 78; foreign direct investments by, 210; as founding member of ASEAN, 231; in Greater Mekong Subregion, 126–27; military access arrangements with U.S., 83; military coups in, 50, 96, 118, 119, 148, 201; perceptions of U.S. role in Southeast Asia, 44; on Pivot strategy, 148; Preah Vihear Temple conflict with Cambodia, 179; social unrest in, 1, 50

Thaksin Shinnawatra, 96, 113, 119

Thalib, Ja'afar Umar, 104

Than Shwe, 206

Thein Sein, 206, 207, 209, 211

Third Wave of Democratization, 111

TIFA. *See* Trade and Investment Framework Agreement

TNI. *See* Indonesian National Armed Forces

TPA (Trade Promotion Authority), 188–89

TPPA. *See* Trans-Pacific Partnership Agreement

Trade: ASEAN imports and exports with U.S. vs. China, 125; bilateral trade agreements, 74–75, 116, 118, 137; Bush administration policies on, 116–20, 121–22; congressional role in policymaking on, 119, 120, 188–89; domestic influences on, 37; free trade agreements, 116–20, 121, 125–26, 186, 241; import bans on, 209; initiatives for promotion of, 12, 28; liberalization initiatives, 59, 60, 115–16, 121–22, 126; most favored nation trading status, 73, 74; social costs of, 119; and tariffs, 74, 126; waterways important for, 2, 29; World Trade Organization, 116, 120, 137

Trade Adjustment Authority Bill of 2015, 189

Trade and Investment Framework Agreement (TIFA), 28, 116, 120

Trade Promotion Authority (TPA), 188–89

Tran Cong Truc, 156

Trans-Pacific Partnership Agreement (TPPA), 185–91; domestic challenges to, 190–91, 201, 241–42; human rights and, 199–200; Investor–State Dispute Settlement mechanism in, 190, 191; motivations for joining, 197; negotiations regarding, 118–19, 188–89, 246; Obama administration on, 12, 144, 185; opposition to, 37, 188, 189–91; and Pivot strategy, 180, 187; RCEP vs., 186; Trump administration withdrawal from, 28, 187, 189

Treaties. *See specific name of treaty*

Treaty of Amity and Cooperation of 1976 (TAC), 12, 41, 123–24, 129, 145, 223

Trump, Donald: campaign narratives of, 247; on China, 237, 238; competing initiatives in administration of, 243; grand strategy influenced by, 225, 226; and Southeast Asia, 224, 227, 232, 233, 252; TPPA withdrawal by, 28, 187, 189

Truong Tan Sang, 6, 193

United Malays National Organization, 107

United Nations Commission on the Limits of the Continental Shelf (CLCS), 151–52, 171–73